SUEÑOS
WORLD SPANISH 1
NEW EDITION

Mike González
Luz Kettle
María Elena Placencia

Sueños World Spanish 1 includes:
- a 288-page coursebook
- 4 x 75-minute audio CDs or cassettes
- an 80-page activity book
- a video pack (5 hours of video and video guide)
- free online activities at www.bbc.co.uk/languages

Television producer: Terry Doyle
Radio producer: Mick Webb
Audio producer: Colette Thomson for Footstep Productions Ltd
Audio producer for new edition: John Green, TEFL tapes

A 20-part TV series from all around the Spanish-speaking world is shown on the BBC Two Learning Zone. To get TV schedule information, access free online activities and much more, go to the BBCi Languages website at www.bbc.co.uk/languages.

The TV transcripts and complete tutor's guide can be ordered on 08705 210 292 or bbclanguages@twoten.press.net.

Developed by BBC Languages
Edited by Sarah Boas
Second edition edited by Cheryl Lanyon
Consultant: Derek Utley
Glossary compiled by Valerie Elliston
Project management and typesetting by Gene Ferber for Book Creation Services Ltd., London
Illustrations and artwork by Carey Bennett, Andy Brown, Beatriz Custodio, Antonia Enthoven, Joy Fitzsimmons, Elly King, Martin Mulloy, Peter Mulvey, Sylvie Rabbe
Cover artwork by Sue Climpson
New edition cover design by Harwood Lawrence Philippson

© BBC Worldwide Ltd 2003

ISBN 0 563 47246 4

Published by BBC Languages,
BBC Worldwide Ltd
New edition 2003
Reprinted 2003 (twice)

Printed and bound in Great Britain by Butler & Tanner Ltd, Frome, Somerset
Cover printed by Belmont Press Ltd, Northampton

Contents

Introduction iv
Course menu viii

Unit 0   ¡Bienvenido al español! 1
Unit 1   Primeras impresiones 5
Unit 2   ¿Quién es quién? 15
Unit 3   Mi ciudad y mi barrio 25
Unit 4   ¿Dónde está? 37
Unit 5   En el mercado 49
Puesta a punto 1 59

Unit 6   Así se nos va el día 61
Unit 7   Ésta es su casa 71
Unit 8   En cuerpo y alma 83
Unit 9   Hoy es fiesta 93
Unit 10   De viaje 105
Puesta a punto 2 115

Unit 11   Nos quedamos para el festival ... 117
Unit 12   Estuve en Acapulco 127
Unit 13   Cuando era joven 137
Unit 14   Las estaciones y el tiempo 147
Unit 15   Pasó hace mucho tiempo 159
Puesta a punto 3 169

Unit 16   ¡A comer! 171
Unit 17   Sueños y deseos 181
Unit 18   De compras 191
Unit 19   ¿Has visto la última película? ... 203
Unit 20   Te llamaré mañana 213
Puesta a punto 4 224

Reference section

Answers 226
Grammar 233
Cassette/CD transcripts 242
Word Groups 254
Spanish-English glossary 260

[iii]

Introduction

SPANISH ACROSS THE WORLD

We have called this book *'World Spanish'*. From the beaches of northern Spain to the semi desert of southern Patagonia, people speak Spanish. Accents vary, of course, and the words that refer to local realities – birds and animals, food, weather, trees and plants – vary enormously from place to place. But the shape and structure of the language is essentially the same everywhere and many of the words and expressions are common to all. So despite their very different environments the Spaniard and the Patagonian, the Chilean and the Spanish-speaking citizen of the United States can speak directly to one another. That is why we can say that Spanish is a world language.

LEARNING SPANISH – OUR APPROACH

We wrote this course with two things in mind. First, that you may well have little or no experience of Spanish, or indeed of any other foreign language either. Secondly, that while you will want to learn how to function in a Spanish-speaking world – ask your way, find things out, order food and drink and so on – learning the language will also give you access to the whole culture and history of that world in all its enormous diversity.

The approach of the course is both communicative (you want to learn through practising the language in real and recognisable situations) and cultural (you want to understand and enjoy aspects of the Spanish-speaking world that give the language life and meaning). The coursebook sets out to provide you with the means to express yourself in a particular context and to ensure that you learn not just phrases or expressions but also patterns of language that you can use and combine in other contexts and situations. Each unit also has a theme that links its several parts (as well as the TV and audio material). The **Temas** section in each unit explores aspects of the culture of the Spanish-speaking world (be it Spain, Latin America, or the Spanish of the United States). We look, for example, at the influence of Arab Spain, the origins of the tango, the history of the Conquest of Latin America and the state of health in the contemporary Spanish-speaking world. And we include poetry and songs by writers from many countries and periods; you will find that even as a beginner you can read and enjoy them.

WHAT'S IN THE BOOK?

Sueños World Spanish has been written with the independent learner in mind, as well as those who will be using it in the classroom. The book consists of twenty units, each containing a language-learning section divided into three parts (**Así se habla**), a cultural section (**Temas**), and a review and revision section (**Veamos de nuevo**), at the end of which is a checklist for you to check your progress. (The section **'How to use this book'** shows you how each section breaks down into parts and how you can work with each unit.) After every five units there is a section of revision exercises (**Puesta a punto**), so that you can practise again what you have learned. This is particularly useful if you are learning on your own. At the end of the book are the Reference sections that you can consult while you are working your way through *Sueños*: Answer Key, Grammar Summary, English-Spanish Word Groups, Spanish-English Glossary, together with transcripts of the recordings that accompany the course. This new edition has been revised and updated to include the euro and other important changes.

OTHER MATERIAL

Sueños World Spanish is accompanied by a range of additional learning materials:

Cassettes and CDs: the series of cassettes or CDs that go with the book include voices and dialogues recorded around the whole of the Spanish-speaking world – the real Spanish – that you will use for listening and speaking exercises.

Television programmes: the book title refers to a series of twenty television programmes, in each of which an individual or group explains a dream or ambition and how they set about achieving it. The settings include Andalucía (where a photographer dreams of setting up a photo-library) and Mexico City (where two women are opening a restaurant). Each programme combines interviews and comments in Spanish by the main characters – and some language-teaching elements which are developed in the corresponding unit of the book. The programmes are regularly repeated on the Learning Zone on BBC Two.

Activity Book: this follows each unit closely and provides additional activities and practice around the key points addressed in the text book.

Online: free online activities that complement the units of the book are available at www.bbc.co.uk/languages

Video: The 20 television programmes are available for purchase on two VHS cassettes.

TAKING THE PLUNGE: HINTS ON LEARNING

1. Making connections: when you come across a new word or phrase, does it remind you of something in your own language? You could guess that the word *Francia*, for

Introduction

example, means France. But words are not always what they seem and it is important to look at the context as well in guessing the meaning. Understanding the context will often allow you to anticipate what's coming and listen out for it.

2. Looking it up: used properly, a good dictionary is a useful tool, not only to look up words you don't understand but also to try to find new and different words and expressions you might want to use. But again, you always need to be aware of the context, as one word may have several meanings.

3. Remembering words: it's a good idea, when you first learn a word, to try to associate it with an object, a person, a feeling or a situation; it will make it far easier to remember. Similarly, it's easier to learn words in groups – *padre* (father) with *madre* (mother), etc. Try making your own lists of words, grouping together words with similar meanings, or opposites, for example. (We have tried to work on the same principle in providing Word Groups for the topic of each unit. These are at the back of the book.)

4. Learning to hear: you can use the recorded material in different ways. Try listening without reading at first and see how much you understand. Then read the text if it is printed in the unit (or check the transcript at the back of the book) and listen again to see how much more you can pick up next time. The dialogues provide an opportunity to practise speaking as well as listening. You could listen and then repeat the words on the recording, taking care about pronunciation, stress and intonation. Does the voice go up and down in the course of a phrase? Does that tell you something about its meaning (is it a question, for example)? You could stop the recording and play one of the parts, trying to guess what the speakers might say. You can also listen to it when you don't have the book with you and repeat out loud what people are saying.

5. Seeing patterns: languages consist of words combined into patterns and structures – that is their grammar. In the book, the dialogues and activities are chosen to illustrate different patterns, and show them in use – they are then translated (**Así se dice**). But they are not just phrases for you to learn – they are models that you can fill with many different words and phrases. The **Gramática** section at the end of each unit sets them out again, with explanations. But it is very worthwhile to see if you can detect those structures yourself by looking at the examples. Once you have worked out the rules, try writing out some patterns yourself e.g. try writing out a new verb in all its persons.

BEYOND THE BOOK

Beyond using the book, learning a language is always more successful – and more enjoyable – if it is also a means to entering another world, another way of life, another culture. Look out for films in Spanish on TV or in your local cinema, or try reading Spanish-language newspapers or magazines. If you have cable television you can almost certainly tune in to Spanish-language TV channels. You'll be surprised and pleased at how much you can understand even at a very early stage – after all, many of the things that concern their audience will be the same things that concern you, too.

Browse Spanish language websites and explore the other resources available at www.bbc.co.uk/languages. Eat out in Spanish or Latin American restaurants – it's all part of learning a language. It is important to hear yourself speak, so say things out loud (the neighbours won't mind!) and try recording your Spanish accent and see how close it comes to the native speech.

Sueños is carefully structured so that each exercise you do is a step forward from the one before – and you can see and measure your own progress as you travel through the book. Our hope is that it will be an interesting, instructive and enjoyable journey that will continue after unit 20 – and bring you into closer contact with a world of several hundred million people who speak world Spanish.

A NOTE TO TEACHERS

In the classroom situation, *Sueños* should be seen as the core of a range of activities. *The Tutor's Guide* offers a range of suggestions as to how to use the material available as well as a number of possible associated activities. Much of it can be directly copied and used with students in the classroom in different learning contexts. The **Temas** section in each unit offers ample material for classroom development – sources for further discussion, wider reading, exercises and class discussions. The **Veamos de nuevo** section provides grammatical explanations (which are then presented in more schematic form in the **Grammar Summary** at the back of the book) and reinforcement in the shape of practice activities as well as extension exercises based on the changing contexts and situations. It is equally suitable for individual, pair or group work. For the tutor, these can serve as practice material, but also as suggestions and pointers to further classroom and independent activities. The television transcripts and tutor's guide are also available for purchase (see p. ii).

How to use this book

1. Each Unit has three learnings sections under the heading **Así se habla**.

2. Listen to people speaking.

3. Read what they say and see how much you recognise and understand.

4. Information on aspects of life in the Spanish-speaking world.

5. Help with vocabulary and grammar in the middle column.

6. The expressions you have learned are set out here with other examples.

7. Refers to a specific exercise on this point.

8. A chance to practise what you have learned.

9. Imagine yourself in new situations. Use what you have learned to speak for yourself.

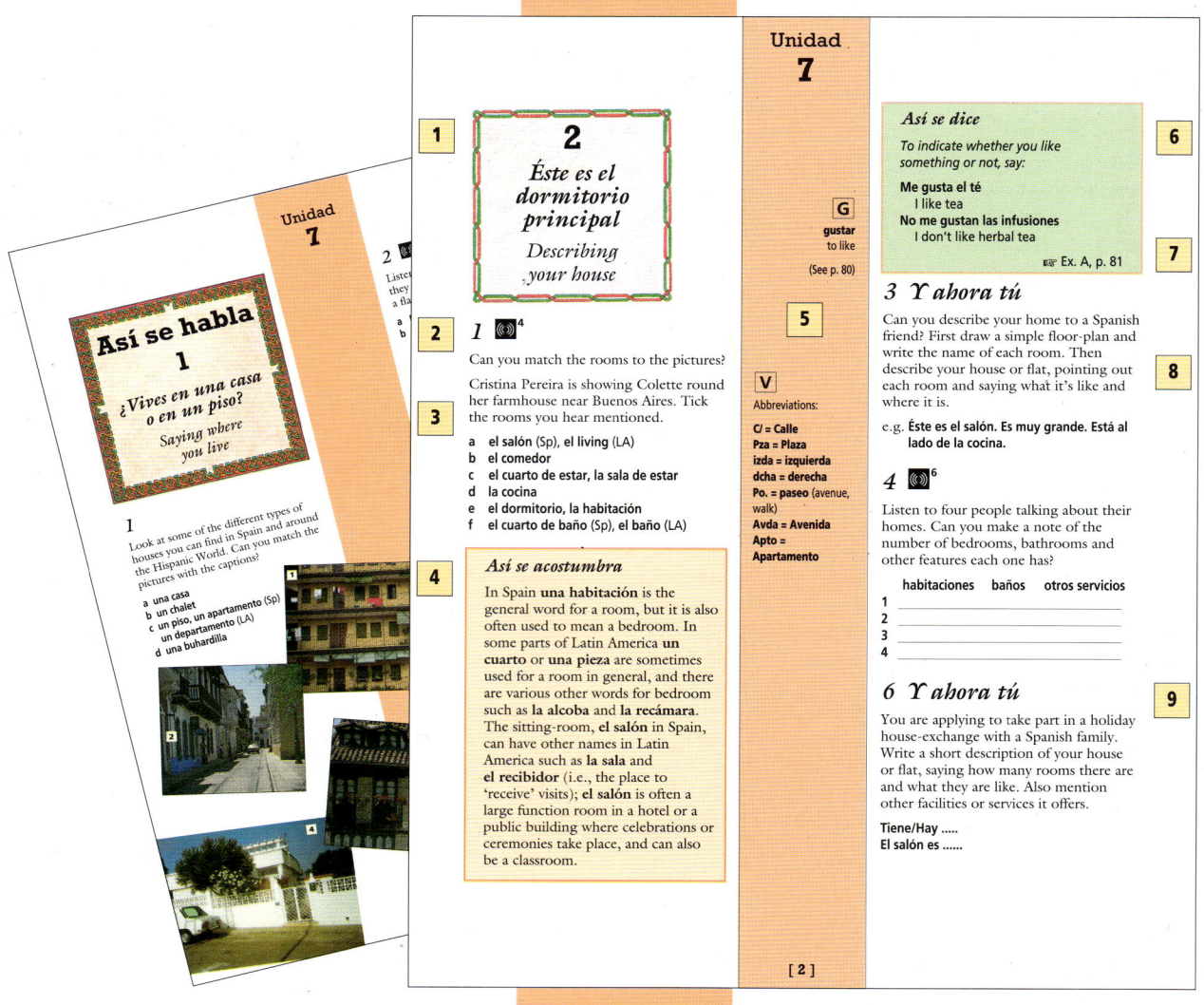

[vi]

How to use this book

10 Explores the culture of the Spanish-speaking world. The topics are related to the theme of the Unit.

11 Some poetry or prose to read and respond to.

12 Sets out clearly and simply the grammar points that arise in the Unit.

13 Gives more practice of specific grammar points.

14 Takes further what you have learned. Use the language in new (but real) situations.

15 Read and understand real Spanish in contexts related to the topic of the Unit.

16 Listen to people speaking and test your understanding.

17 Check your progress: having completed the Unit this is what you can do and say.

[vii]

Course menu

Functions	Themes	Grammar	Vocabulary
UNIT 0 *¡Bienvenido al español!* 1 Words that walk 2 Saying hello & goodbye	Meeting people & saying hello *Gracias, muy amable*		Greetings
UNIT 1 *Primeras impresiones* 1 Asking someone's name and giving yours 2 Saying where you're from and where you live 3 Saying what languages you speak	Background to the language *El español - idioma mundial*	**hablar** (to speak) **vivir** (to live) **ser** (to be) Asking questions	Countries Languages
UNIT 2 *¿Quién es quién?* 1 Saying what your nationality is 2 Saying what you do 3 Meeting the family and introducing people	TV and the media *Sueños a las cuatro de la tarde*	**el, la, los, las** Nouns and genders **tener** (to have) **mi, tu, su**	Nationalities Occupations Family Numbers
UNIT 3 *Mi ciudad y mi barrio* 1 Saying what your home town is like 2 Describing people and places 3 Saying what there is in your town	Town and city life *La ciudad de los sueños*	**un, una, unos, unas** **hay** Plurals; Adjectives	Buildings Places Descriptions
UNIT 4 *¿Dónde está?* 1 Saying where a place is 2 Asking for things. Talking about distances 3 Asking for and giving directions	The Moorish legacy The gypsies *Andalucía, ayer y hoy*	**estar** (to be) **ir** (to go) **delante, detrás** etc **a la derecha**, etc	More buildings Monuments Numbers Directions
UNIT 5 *En el mercado* 1 Shopping for groceries 2 Shopping for fruit and vegetables 3 Finding out what things cost	The language of food *El encuentro de los gustos*	**querer** (to want) **este, esta, estos, estas** **¿cuánto? ¿cuántos?**	Numbers Containers/measures Food shopping
UNIT 6 *Así se nos va el día* 1 Saying how often you do things 2 Talking about the time 3 Describing your daily routine	The routines of daily life *El ritmo de vida*	Present tense of regular verbs – all groups Reflexive verbs	Personal habits
UNIT 7 *Ésta es su casa* 1 Saying where you live 2 Describing your house 3 Offering someone a drink. Saying what you like	Houses and hospitality *Vivir y sobrevivir*	**me gusta** + objects **querer** + infinitive	Houses Rooms, furniture Drinks
UNIT 8 *En cuerpo y alma* 1 Describing people 2 Describing your symptoms 3 Getting the remedy	Health care in Spain and Latin America *La salud hace el hombre*	**ser** and **estar** **tiene que** (obligation) **me duele** (it hurts)	Parts of the body Character/personality Symptoms/illnesses
UNIT 9 *Hoy es fiesta* 1 Saying what you like doing 2 Dates and celebrations 3 Ordering drinks and snacks	Festivals and celebrations *El día de los muertos*	More on **gustar** Using **para** (who it's for)	Dates and months Events More food & drink

Course menu

UNIT 10 *De viaje*
1 Talking about travel
2 Asking about routes and times
3 Buying tickets

Getting around
Trenes, buses y aviones

Radical-changing verbs
se puede
Further uses of **para**

Means of transport

UNIT 11 *Nos quedamos para el festival*
1 Booking a hotel room
2 Checking in and out. Making complaints
3 What's on and where to buy tickets

The Golden Age of Spain
El gran teatro del mundo

Past participles
More radical-changing verbs: **e > i**

Hotels
Theatre, entertainments, events, etc

UNIT 12 *Estuve en Acapulco*
1 Saying where you went on holiday last year
2 Saying what you did
3 Saying when you did something

Holidays and leisure
Hay muchas maneras de escaparse

Preterite tense (1)

Geographical features
Holiday activities
Time expressions

UNIT 13 *Cuando era joven*
1 Saying what sports you liked
2 Saying what you used to do
3 Contrasting the present with the past

History of the gauchos
En la pampa argentina

Imperfect tense

Sports and pastimes

UNIT 14 *Las estaciones y el tiempo*
1 Talking about the weather
2 Making comparisons
3 Saying which is the longest or most expensive

Environmental matters
La tierra es frágil

hace calor, frío, etc
Present continuous tense
más/menos (comparisons)

Seasons
Weather/climate

UNIT 15 *Pasó hace mucho tiempo*
1 Telling your life story
2 Saying how long ago and how long for
3 Talking about history

Cortés and Pizarro
De Extremadura salieron

Preterite tense (2)
hace and **llevar**
conocer +personal **a**
Object pronouns: him/her

Historical terms

UNIT 16 *¡A comer!*
1 Ordering food in a restaurant
2 Saying what you eat every day
3 Describing recipes

Meals and eating habits
La comida es cultura

Advice and instructions
Exclamations

Cooking & eating
Utensils, appliances
Cooking terms

UNIT 17 *Sueños y deseos*
1 Talking about your dreams and ambitions
2 Instructions and commands
3 Saying what you like to wear

Fashion and dress
Las apariencias y las ilusiones

Instructing people: the imperative
llevar (to wear)

Careers and ambitions
Clothes

UNIT 18 *De compras*
1 Making plans and suggestions
2 Buying clothes
3 Buying souvenirs and bargaining

Crafts and industries
Manos juntas

Future: **ir a**+ infinitive
Object pronouns and their position

More clothes
Colours, materials
Patterns, style

UNIT 19 *¿Has visto la última película?*
1 Saying what you have or haven't done
2 Describing what has happened
3 Recalling childhood memories

Antonio Gaudí
La construcción del sueño

Perfect tense

Time expressions

UNIT 20 *Te llamaré mañana*
1 Talking on the phone
2 Making arrangements to go out
3 Talking about plans and intentions

Spanish in the USA
Unidos en la lengua

Future tense
Indirect object pronouns

Telephone language
Time expressions

Pronunciation

A GUIDE TO PRONUNCIATION

a	as in b**a**ck	c**a**sa	m	as in **m**other	**m**alo
e	as in **e**nd	**e**lena	n	as in **n**ever	**n**unca
i	like **ee** in r**ee**d	m**i**ra	ñ	like **ny** in ca**ny**on	ni**ñ**o
o	as in c**o**t	r**o**pa	p	as in **p**en	**p**asa
u	like **oo** in c**oo**l	l**u**cha	qu	like **k** in **k**eel	**qu**ien
b	as in **b**eg	**b**ote	r	between vowels or	pe**r**o
c	before **a, u ,o**: as in **c**ar	**c**aro		at end of word as in rule	pensa**r**
	before **e, i**:			at beginning of word rolled	**r**osa
	in Spain like **th** in **th**ick	**c**ien	rr	rolled as in cu**rr**y	co**rr**e
	in LA like **s** in **s**even	**c**ien	s	as in **s**oon	**c**osa
d	at start of word as in **d**entist:	**d**ía	t	as in **t**ent	**t**omate
	between vowels softer	a**d**iós	v	like **b** in **b**eg	**v**ista
	at end of word like **th** in **th**in	Madri**d**	w	like **v** in **v**iew	**w**ater
f	as in **f**ew	**f**alta	x	at beginning of word like **s**	**x**ilófono
g	before **a, o, u** as in **g**ot	**g**ato		before a consonant like **s**	e**x**tranjero
	before **e, i** like **ch** in lo**ch**	**g**itano		between vowels like **ks**	ta**x**i
gu	before **e, i** like **g** in **g**ot	**gu**itarra		in some words like **ch** in lo**ch**	me**x**icano
h	always silent	**h**ombre	y	as in **y**es	**y**o
j	like **ch** in lo**ch**	**j**amón	z	in Spain like **th** as in **th**ick	**z**apato
k	as in **k**ick	**k**ilo		in LA, Canaries and S. Spain like **s**	
l	as in **l**ong	**l**argo		in **s**even	
ll	in Spain as **lli** in mi**lli**on	**ll**amar			
	in LA, Canaries, S. Spain like **y** in **y**ear				
	in southern LA like **sh** in **sh**atter				

WHERE TO PUT THE STRESS

In Spanish, stress in a word is a straightforward matter.

1. With words that end in a vowel, or -**n** or -**s**: on the syllable before the end
   – za**pa**to, **ca**sas, re**co**rre, meloco**to**nes
2. With words that end with a consonant other than -**n** or -**s**: on the last syllable
   – Ma**drid**, espa**ñol**, je**rez**.
3. If it comes elsewhere it must be marked with a written accent
   – re**pú**blica, lle**gó**, qui**zás**, po**li**cía, esta**ción**, **plá**tano.

Unidad 0

¡Bienvenido al español!

Así se habla
Words that walk
Saying hello and goodbye

Temas
Gracias, muy amable

Veamos de nuevo

Unidad 0

Así se habla 1

Las palabras andantes
Words that walk

1

How many of these words do you recognize? Can you say what they mean? Look up any you don't know in the Glossary at the back of the book.

gracias   adiós   poncho
   sierra   sangría   salsa
paella   tacos   tango
   playa   carne   chocolate

Así se acostumbra

It's surprising how many words of Spanish or Latin American origin you already know, particularly in the world of food. Some of them are very close to home. Take **patata** (potato), for instance, which came from the native peoples of the Caribbean; or **chocolate** and **maíz**, which the Spanish Conquerors first ate in Aztec Mexico. 'Jerky', or jerked meat, was the **charqui** that the Inca runners took with them on long journeys in the High Andes. Green and red **chile** (chilli peppers) spiced the **salsa** (sauce) that gave its name to the dance that, like the food, was also a mixture of many ingredients. So you might already know more Spanish than you think ...

2

The following clues and their answers are jumbled up. Can you sort them out?

1	Tomorrow (and morning)	a	Madrid
2	Capital of Spain	b	Grande
3	¡----- España! (Long live!)	c	¡Olé!
4	The big river: Río	d	Mañana
5	Hoorah! (to the bull or bullfighter)	e	¡Viva!

2

Saludos y otras fórmulas
Saying hello and goodbye

1 Saying hello 1

There are several different ways of saying 'hello' in Spanish. Here are some of them. Listen to the recording, read them and then try them out loud yourself.

> Hola, ¿qué tal?
> Hola, ¿cómo estás?
> Buenos días

Así se dice

When you're greeting a friend, say:

Hola, ¿qué tal?/Hola, ¿cómo estás?
  Hello, how are you?

If it's someone you know less well you could say:

Buenos días. ¿Cómo está?
  Good morning. How are you?
Buenas tardes/Buenas noches
  Good afternoon/Good evening

Unidad 0

2

Imagine you are in the situations below. How would you say hello?

a You are going into a shop. It's 3 p.m.
b On the stairs at your college you meet a close friend.
c On your way to the office you bump into the director of your company. It's 9 a.m.
d You have just arrived at a restaurant in the evening and a waiter comes over to you.

3

Listen and read the following conversation. Are both the speakers well?

— Hola, ¿cómo estás?
— Muy bien, ¿y tú?
— Yo, fatal.

Así se dice

When someone asks how you are, you often reply with a similar question, but you might also want to say how you really are:

Muy bien ¿y tú? *or* **¿y usted?**
   I'm well. How are you?
Estupendo/Bien/Regular/Mal/Fatal
   Fine/Well/O.K./Not well/Terrible

Así se acostumbra

There are two commonly used words for 'you' – **tú** (informal) and **usted** (formal). In most areas of the Spanish-speaking world, when you are with friends or people of your own age, or when addressing younger people, you can use **tú**. (There are some Latin American countries where you say **vos** instead of **tú**.) But if you want to be polite or formal, then you use **usted**.

V
también
too, also

4

Listen to the conversations. Can you tell which are formal and which are informal, and what time of day it is, if this is inferred? The first one has been done for you.

	Formal/Informal	a.m./p.m.
1	✗	✗
2		✓
3	✓	
4		✓
5		

5 Saying goodbye

There are also several ways of saying 'goodbye' in Spanish. Listen and look at the following:

— Adiós, hasta luego
— Adiós

Así se dice

The most common expression is:

Adiós   Goodbye

In more formal situations you can say:

Adiós, buenos días/Adiós, buenas tardes
   Good morning/ Good afternooon
Adiós, buenas noches
   Good night

If you know someone better, try:

Hasta luego/(Sp)/Nos vemos (LA)
   'Bye/See you later

6 Y ahora tú

Imagine you're in a café and two people come by and stop to pass the time of day. Listen and reply to their greetings and their goodbyes.

Unidad 0

Temas

Gracias, muy amable

Veamos de nuevo

Saying please and thank you

It is always a good idea to say '**por favor**' ('please') and '**gracias**' ('thank you'). However, Spaniards think it is odd to say 'please' too often, whereas in Latin America it is best to say it wherever it fits. If you are thanking someone very much you can say '**Muchas gracias**' or in Latin America '**Mil gracias**' ('a thousand thanks') or even '**Un millón de gracias**' ('a million thanks'). You can add '**Muy amable**' ('How kind') or say '**Muy agradecido/agradecida**' ('I'm very grateful'). Politely the reply will come '**De nada**' or '**No hay de qué**' ('Don't mention it').

Saying sorry/Excusing yourself

If you don't quite understand what someone says to you, judge your speaker with care. **¿Cómo?** ('What?') might do; '**Perdón**' ('I'm sorry, I beg your pardon') might be better. '**Disculpe, no le entendí**' ('I'm sorry I didn't understand') could be best. In a queue when you want to get by someone, you could just push and say '**Perdón**', **¿Puedo pasar?** or '**Con permiso**' ('Excuse me, may I get past').

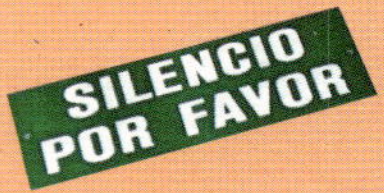

A Hello and goodbye

Say hello in the appropriate way to the following people:

1. to your brother whom you are meeting off a train
2. to an old friend of your mother's who came to your house this afternoon

Can you also say goodbye …?

3. to your boss, for whom you have been working late
4. to a friend whom you hope to see again soon

B The right expression

Which phrases would you use in the following situations?

1. You didn't understand what someone said to you.
2. A friend invites you to his house to have a meal with his family.
3. An old man whom you have helped across the road says thank you.
4. You need to get past the man in front to catch a bus that's just leaving.

Congratulations! Now move on to Unit 1!

Unidad 1

Primeras impresiones

Así se habla

Asking someone's name and giving yours

Saying where you are from and where you live

Saying what languages you speak

Temas

Español: idioma mundial

Veamos de nuevo

Unidad 1

Así se habla 1

¿Cómo te llamas?
Asking someone's name and giving yours

1

Listen to Isabel interviewing three people. Number the conversations as you hear them.

☐ – ¿Cómo te llamas?
   – Me llamo Raquel.
☐ – Hola, ¿cuál es tu nombre?
   – Mi nombre es Marco Antonio Castillo Morán.
☐ – Buenas tardes. ¿Cómo se llama?
   – Me llamo María Florencia Ferrari.

Now listen to the tape once more and repeat the dialogues.

Así se acostumbra

In Spain and Latin America people often have more than one first name, such as Marco Antonio, and they can use both their mother's and their father's surname (**apellido**). For example, the name of Gabriel García Márquez, the famous Colombian writer, consists of both his father's name, García, and his mother's, Márquez. Nowadays most married women in Spain keep their own name, but in other countries some still adopt or add their husband's name, as in Carmen Rosa Jiménez *de* Guzmán (literally, of Guzmán).

a) Carlos Silva
b) Antonia Sánchez
c) José Valbuena

Así se dice

To ask someone's name, say:

¿Cómo te llamas?
   What's your name?

You answer by saying:

Me llamo .....
   My name is .....

Another way of asking someone's name is to say:

¿Cuál es tu nombre?

to which the reply is:

Mi nombre es .....
   My name is .....

More formally you would ask:

¿Cómo se llama? *or:*
¿Cuál es su nombre?
   What's your name?

2

How would you ask the people in the photographs what their names are? How would they answer?

a .....   b .....   c .....

3 Y ahora tú

¿Cómo te llamas? or ¿Cuál es tu nombre?

4 Nombres y apellidos

Can you identify first names in the following jumbled list?

(Julio)	Hernán	Toaquiza
Sierra	Muro	Matilde
Colomina	Nieto	Isabel
José	Vega	Salazar	Ana

Unidad 1

5 🔊 ²

Listen to three people giving their names. Can you pick out their full names, all taken from the list in Ex. 4. Listen again and complete the dialogues.

– ¿..... te .....?
– ..... llamo Matilde .....

– ¿Cuál .....su .....?
– Mi .... Sierra .....

– ¿Cómo se .....?
– Yo .... José ....

6 El alfabeto español 🔊 ³

Here are the letters of the Spanish alphabet. Each letter is followed by a Spanish name. Practise saying the sounds and the names out loud.

a	b	c	d	e	f
a	be	ce	de	e	efe
<u>A</u>na	<u>B</u>egoña	<u>C</u>arlos	<u>D</u>olores	<u>E</u>lena	<u>F</u>elipe
		Ce<u>c</u>ilia			
g	h	i	j	k	l
ge	hache	i	jota	ka	ele
<u>G</u>erardo	<u>H</u>éctor	<u>I</u>nés	<u>J</u>osé	<u>K</u>ike	<u>L</u>uis
<u>G</u>uido					
m	n	ñ	o	p	q
eme	ene	eñe	o	pe	qu
<u>M</u>aría	<u>N</u>oelia	To<u>ñ</u>o	<u>Ó</u>scar	<u>P</u>epe	<u>Q</u>uico
r	s	t	u	v	w
ere	ese	te	u	uve	uve doble
<u>R</u>osa	<u>S</u>usana	<u>T</u>eresa	<u>Ú</u>rsu<u>r</u>la	<u>V</u>ioleta	<u>W</u>ilfrido
Lau<u>r</u>a					
x	y	z
equis	i griega	zeta
<u>X</u>avier	<u>Y</u>olanda	<u>Z</u>ilda
Fé<u>x</u>		

V
viuda de
literally, widow of
típico de aquí
typical of this place

7

Using the table as a guide, try saying the names of some famous people:
Carreras; Cervantes; Caballé; Guevara; Gaudí; Buñuel.
Do you know who they are?

8 🔊 ⁴

Ana interviewed Blanca Margarita in Mexico and found she had a rather unusual surname. Can you say what it is? Listen and complete the conversation.

– ¿Cómo se llama?
– Yo me llamo Blanca Margarita ..... viuda de Ferros.
– ¿Es un nombre típico de aquí?
– Es un apellido español.
– Y ¿cómo se escribe?
– _ _ _ _ _ _ _ _

> ### Así se dice
> To find out how to spell someone's name, ask:
>
> **¿Cómo se escribe tu nombre/apellido?**
> How is your name written?

9 Y ahora tú

¿Cómo se escribe tu/su nombre completo?

How would you spell your name out loud in Spanish?

Unidad 1

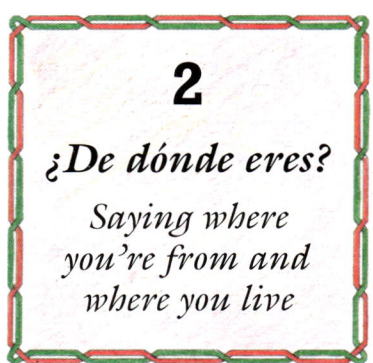

2
¿De dónde eres?
Saying where you're from and where you live

1 Países de habla hispana

Do you know which countries make up the Hispanic World? List as many as you can and then check on the map to see how well you did.

2 🔊 5

When Carlos was asked the same question, he could only remember some of them. Can you circle on the map the ones he mentions?

V
de
from
D.F. = Distrito Federal,
i.e. Mexico City

G
ser
to be
(yo) soy
(See p. 13)

G
vivir
to live
(yo) vivo
(See p. 13)

3 🔊 6

Listen to Carmen interviewing Claudia Patiño. Where is she from and where does she live now?

– ¿Cómo te llamas?
– Yo soy Claudia Patiño.
– Y ¿ de dónde eres?
– Soy de ..... y vivo en .....

Así se dice

To ask where someone comes from, say:

¿De dónde eres (tú)? (informal)
¿De dónde es (usted)? (formal)
  Where are you from?

Answer by saying:

Soy de ...
  I come from

To find out where someone lives, ask:

¿Dónde vives (tú)?
¿Dónde vive (usted)?
  Where do you live?

To say where you live you can say:

(Yo) vivo en ...
  I live in ...

4 *Y ahora tú*

¿De dónde eres? ¿Dónde vives?

5 [7]

Listen to these people saying where they come from and where they live now. Make a note of their details.

	Origen (Origin)	Lugar de residencia (Place of residence)
a **Adriana**	**México**	**Ciudad de México**
b **Silvia**		
c **Alicia C.**		
d **Carmen**		
e **Carmen R.**		

Así se dice

To find out about someone else, ask:

¿De dónde es (él/ella)?
Where is he/she from?
(Él/Ella) es de .....
He/She is from .....
¿Dónde vive (él/ella)?
Where does he/she live?
(Él/Ella) vive en .....
He/She lives in .....

6

Can you now report the details about the people in Activity 5 to a friend?

e.g. **Adriana es de México y vive en la Ciudad de México.**

7 *Otros países*

Many names of countries are similar in Spanish and English. Match the English word with its Spanish equivalent.

1 Italy	a Canadá
2 United States	b Estados Unidos
3 Canada	c Francia
4 Great Britain	d Italia
5 France	e Gran Bretaña

Unidad 1

V

Nací en ...
I was born in ...
Soy de Salamanca
I'm from Salamanca

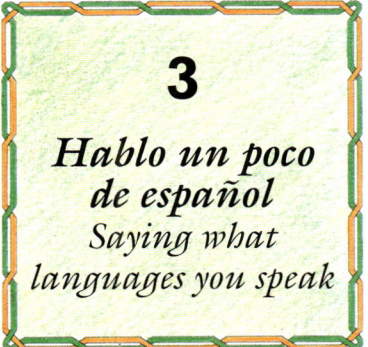

3 *Hablo un poco de español*

Saying what languages you speak

1 *Escuela de idiomas*

A group of international students is meeting for the first time. What language (**idioma** or **lengua**) does each person speak? Can you match the names with the languages and say each language out loud?

alemán **francés** **italiano** **español** **inglés**

Giovanni **José** **Kate** **Françoise** **Helmut**

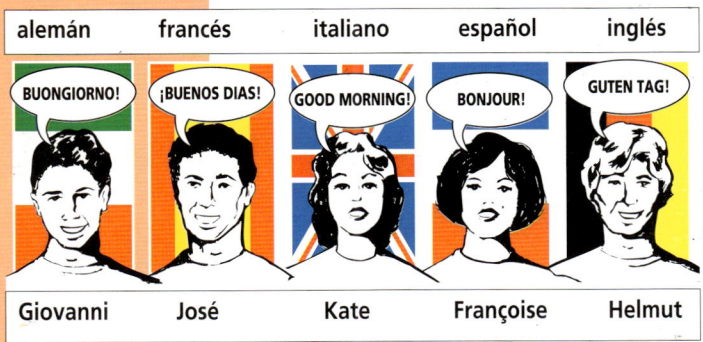

V

y
and

(For more words for languages see Word Group W 4.)

2 [8]

Listen to this student in Salamanca. Where is she from and what languages does she speak?

– ¿Cómo te llamas?
– Hola, me llamo Clara.
– ¿Y de dónde eres?
– Soy de Santander.
– ¿Y qué lenguas hablas?
– Pues hablo un poquito de inglés... un poquito de italiano.

V

un poco de
a little
un poquito de
a very little

Unidad 1

G
hablar
to speak
(See p. 12)

Así se dice

To find out what languages someone speaks, say:

¿Qué lenguas hablas (tú)? *or:*
¿Qué lenguas habla (usted)?
　What languages do you speak?

Answer by saying:

Hablo ..... y un poco de .....
　I speak ..... and a little .....

3

Look again at the people in Activity 1. How would they give their names and say what language they speak?

e.g. **Me llamo Giovanni y hablo italiano.**

4 *Y ahora tú*

¿Qué lenguas hablas?

5 🔊⁹

Listen to more students in Salamanca, and note where they come from and the languages they speak.

	Nombre	Origen	Lenguas/idiomas
a	Begoña		
b	Linda	Suecia	
c	Fátima		
d	Simona		

Así se dice

To ask about someone else, say:

¿Qué lenguas habla?
　What languages does he/she speak?

And to answer, say:

Habla .....
　He/She speaks .....

6

If you were describing these students to a friend how would you say what languages each student speaks?

e.g. **Begoña habla vasco y español.**

Así se dice

To find out if someone speaks a language, ask:

¿(Tú) hablas *inglés*?　　*or:*
¿(Usted) habla *francés*?　*or:*
¿Habla usted *francés*?
　Do you speak French?

Sí, hablo *inglés*
　Yes, I speak English
No, no hablo *francés*
　No, I don't speak French

7 *Y ahora tú*

¿Hablas francés?　¿Hablas inglés?
¿Hablas alemán?　¿Hablas italiano?

V
Estoy aprendiendo inglés
I'm learning English

[10]

Unidad 1

Temas

El español: idioma mundial

Spanish is spoken not only in Spain but across the world; in Spain, it shares the peninsula with other languages. In Latin America, it is spoken in most of the republics of the continent, sharing it with French, English, Dutch, Portuguese, and the many indigenous languages spoken by the original inhabitants of Latin America. In the United States, people have come from many places to add their voices to the chorus. Some 22 million North Americans are Spanish speakers now, and Spanish is also spoken in the former colonies of Africa and in the Philippines.

The Spanish state embraces a variety of languages and cultures; yet the Franco government (1939-76) banned the language of Cataluña (**el catalán**) and the Basque Country (**el vasco** or **el euskera**) as well as the language of Galicia (**el gallego**). Today they all enjoy the status of official languages in their regions. In Latin America, the Spanish language was brought in 1492 to a continent occupied by a whole range of native peoples. In Mexico, for example, the Aztecs (**los aztecas**) – themselves a conquering people – had spread their own language (**el nahuatl**) across a wide area. In southern Mexico and Central America the language of the Mayas (**el maya**) was widely spoken. Both survive and are spoken by millions, especially in Guatemala where half the population speak Spanish only as a second language. The same is true of Peru where the great Inca civilization (**los incas**) imposed its own court language (**el quechua**) as the language of government across its great empire. It is still spoken by millions of people today, mainly in Peru, Ecuador and parts of Bolivia. The mountain people of Bolivia speak a language that is equally ancient (**el aymará**). In Paraguay, Spanish shares the status of official language with **el guaraní**, while in southern Chile the last community to be overwhelmed by the **conquistadores** were the Araucanian indians whose language (**el mapuche**) is widely spoken but still unacknowledged by government.

All of these ancient languages have given words to the Spanish of what was called the New World – and indeed to other languages. **El tomate**, **el chocolate** and **el tabaco** were brought from the other side of the Atlantic to Europe. In Peru, Colombia and Chile people speak of a **guagua** when they mean a child (in Cuba and the Canaries it means a bus!). The African peoples brought in as slaves to work in the New World have left their mark on the language too, in words like **la marimba** (a wooden xylophone) and **el merengue** (a dance).

So Spanish is a world language in several senses; it is spoken by 300 million people in many different places, climates and landscapes, and it has absorbed elements from other cultures and languages. That richness is perhaps its most important quality.

Unidad 1

Veamos de nuevo
Gramática

Rubén Blades: 'Salsero Social'

Here is a song by Rubén Blades, the Panamanian salsa singer, who at one time was also a candidate to the Presidency of his country. His songs often speak about social issues – hunger, homelessness – as well as the situation in Latin America. He is known as the **salsa** singer with a social conscience – "**el salsero social**".

In this song "**Muévete**" (Get Going) Blades urges Latin Americans to join together in the battle for change.

See p. 252 for a translation of **Muévete**.

"No hay bala que pueda matar la verdad. Para acabar el racismo en Suráfrica – Lo cantan los niños, y mamá y papá: Para salvar el mundo de tanta maldad – Lo pide la gente de todas las esquinas... ¡Muévete Colombia, México, Argentina, Cuba, Guatemala! ¡Oye Costa Rica, Perú y Nicaragua, que hoy te necesita! Brasil y Bolivia, Chile y Paraguay. ¡Ay! ¡Canta Venezuela! ¡Canta el Uruguay, Jamaica, Trinidad, Guadalupe! ¡Vamos Salvador! ¡Ven Martinica, República Dominicana! ¡Avanza Ecuador!"

* He lists most of the countries of Latin America, but he misses out two Spanish-speaking countries. Can you say which they are?

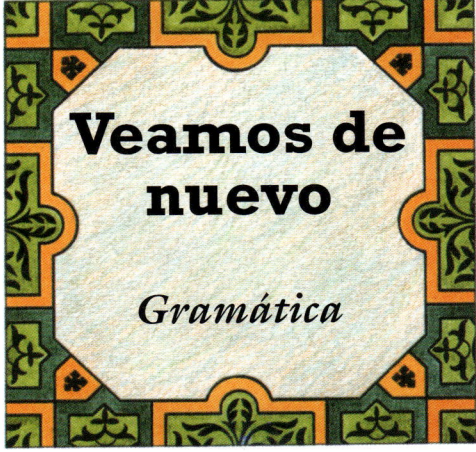

1 I speak, you speak

The endings of verbs in Spanish change according to who is the subject of the action. For example:

Singular
yo	hablo	I speak
tú	hablas	you speak (informal)
usted	habla	you speak (formal)
él, ella	habla	he, she speaks

Plural
nosotros,-as	hablamos	we speak
vosotros,-as	habláis	you speak (informal)
ustedes	hablan	you speak (formal)
ellos, ellas	hablan	they speak

The changes in the endings often make the meaning of the sentence or phrase clear without actually saying the subject of the verb. The subject pronouns (**yo**, **tú**, **él**, etc.) are not often used unless they're needed for emphasis.

Words for 'you':
There are two forms for 'you' in Spanish – a familiar one (**tú**) and a formal one (**usted**). In Spain there are also two forms for the plural – **vosotros** and **ustedes**, whereas in Latin America **ustedes** is used in both formal and informal forms of address

BLADES, LA SALSA POLÍTICA

Panamá puede tener dentro de poco el presidente más melodioso del mundo, Rubén Blades, salsero de profesión, ha decidido poner orden en su casa materna y presentarse a las elecciones presidenciales del próximo mayo.

"No vengo a llenarme los bolsillos, al contrario, estoy dejando una situación muy favorable para venir aquí", afirma el también actor, que durante años ha vivido en Estados Unidos. Los sondeos demuestran su gran popularidad, sobre todo entre los más bailones.

Unidad 1

Note: in some areas in Latin America **vos** is used instead of **tú**, and in others, both forms exist.

2 Verb groups

Hablar (*to speak*) is a regular verb, i.e. its endings follow a fixed pattern. There are three groups of regular verbs: **-ar**, **-er** and **-ir**. **Vivir** belongs to the **-ir** group:

vivo	I live
vives	you live
vive	he/she lives, you live (formal)
vivimos	we live
vivís	you live (informal)
viven	they live, you live (formal)

See Unit 6, p. 69 and Grammar G 9.1

3 I am, you are

One of the most common verbs in Spanish is **ser**, which means 'to be'. It follows a different pattern from those in the regular groups:

soy	I am
eres	you are
es	he/she is, you are (formal)
somos	we are
sois	you are (informal)
son	they are, you are (formal)

Note that the following are both correct:

Soy Juan   Yo soy Juan

4 Asking questions and saying no

Questions are always written with an inverted question mark at the beginning as well as the normal one at the end. To ask a simple question you can take the simple statement form:

Hablas español or **(Usted) habla español**

and transform it into a question by using rising intonation at the end:

¿Hablas español? ¿(Usted) habla español?

or you can put the subject pronoun **usted** after the verb:

¿Habla usted español?

Question words: Other questions start with words such as:

¿qué? (what?)   **¿cuál?** (which?)
¿dónde? (where?)   **¿cómo?** (how?/what?)

Notice the position of **de** in **¿de dónde eres?**
(For other question words, see G 5.)

Negatives: to say something is not the case you simply insert **no** immediately before the verb: **No hablo español**.

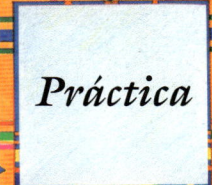

Práctica

A Get the order right!

Can you reorder these words correctly?

e.g. **Vive Madrid en María**
     María vive en Madrid

1 llamo Ricardo me
2 ¿su cuál nombre es?
3 poco un español hablo de
4 de soy Sevilla
5 ¿escribe cómo se?
6 Salamanca yo en vivo
7 nombre su Paco es

B Forming questions

Can you match the two parts of the sentences correctly to make questions?

1	¿Cómo	a	es su nombre?
2	¿De dónde	b	te llamas?
3	¿Cuál	c	idiomas habla Esteban?
4	¿Qué	d	se escribe Ion?
5	¿Cómo	e	eres?

C Making sense

Use the correct form of **ser**, **hablar** or **vivir** to complete the sentences:

e.g. María ..... en Madrid.
María vive en Madrid

1 Luis y Miguel ..... francés.
2 Juan ..... de Salamanca.
3 Yo ..... en México.
4 Yo ..... español muy bien.

D Sopa de letras

Five languages are hidden here. Can you find them? You can go up and down, forwards and even backwards!

A	L	E	M	A	N	N
A	S	S	P	K	G	F
O	X	P	N	B	A	R
C	A	A	F	P	Z	A
U	O	Ñ	A	I	L	N
B	K	O	N	I	H	C
H	E	L	N	G	L	E
O	I	N	G	L	E	S

1 Play your part!

Two students, Ian Robertson from Glasgow, and Anne Gilbert from Geneva, want to enrol on a language course for foreigners in Salamanca. Playing the part of one of them, how would you give your personal details to the language school? You would need to be able to say and spell your name, say where you are from (city and country) and what language(s) you speak.

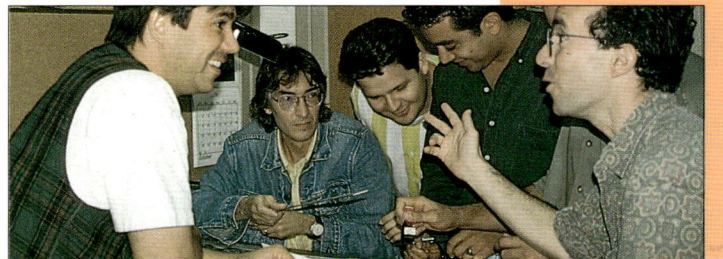

Unidad 1

Un paso más

2 Gente de hoy

Here are some brief notes about two very well-known people. After reading them, can you fill in the grid with the appropriate information?

A Don Juan Carlos de Borbón y Borbón es el Rey de España. Es español pero nació en Roma en 1938. Ahora vive con su esposa, Doña Sofía, en el Palacio de la Zarzuela cerca de Madrid. Habla muchos idiomas: francés, portugués, inglés y español.

B Gloria Estefán es una cantante popular. Su esposo se llama Emilio Estefán. Es de Cuba, pero ahora vive en Miami, Florida. Su primer grupo se llamó Miami Sound Machine. Habla inglés, español y un poco de portugués.

	Name	Surname	From	Home	Languages
A					
B					

3 A new friend 10

While travelling around the Basque Country you make a new friend, Ion. A Spanish friend in Madrid wants to know as much about him as possible. So you decide to ask Ion some questions. What questions would you ask?

Now listen to what Ion says about himself and write down the relevant information for your friend.

4 Checklist

Can you do the following? Say it and write it down.

a Ask someone's name
b Say what your name is
c Ask where someone is from
d Say where you are from
e Say what languages you speak
f Ask someone where he/she lives
g Say where you live at present

Unidad 2

¿Quién es quién?

Así se habla
Saying what your nationality is

Saying what you do

Meeting the family and introducing people

Temas
Sueños a las cuatro de la tarde

Veamos de nuevo

Unidad 2

Así se habla 1

Soy argentina

Saying what your nationality is

Isabel Allende, Chile

Antonio Banderas, España

Montserrat Caballé, Cataluña

Suecia
(Sweden)
sueco, sueca

País vasco
(Basque country)
vasco, vasca

1

Here are some nationalities. Can you guess which countries or regions they refer to? (See W 1 for other countries and nationalities.)

argentino   inglés   francés
chileno   (norte)americano español
italiano   mexicano   catalán

2

Listen to Isabel talking to three people. Can you complete the conversations?

a – ¿De qué nacionalidad eres?
  – Pues, soy ..... .
b – ¿De qué nacionalidad eres?
  – ..... .
c – ¿De qué nacionalidad es usted?
  – Soy .....

Así se dice

To ask someone's nationality, say:

¿De qué nacionalidad eres (tú)?
¿De qué nacionalidad es (usted)?
  What nationality are you?

And to answer, say:

Soy boliviano/boliviana
  I am Bolivian *(man)/(woman)*

3

Words for nationality are usually formed from the country they refer to. Can you fill in the missing words?

1 Argentina   argentino   argentina
2 México   mexicano   _____
3 España   _____   española
4 Francia   francés   _____
5 Inglaterra   _____   inglesa
6 Costa Rica   costarricense costarricense
7 Canadá   canadiense   _____

4

Imagine you were interviewing the people in these photos. How would you ask them their nationality, and how would they reply?

5 *Y ahora tú*

¿De dónde eres? ¿De qué nacionalidad eres?

6

Listen to five different people telling you their names and where they are from. Can you match names and nationalities?

a Simona   i   Swedish
b Linda   ii North American
c Stephen   iii Argentinian
d Martin   iv Italian
e Begoña   v   Basque

Así se dice

To ask where someone else is from and what nationality they are, say:

¿De dónde es María?
  Where is Maria from?
¿De qué nacionalidad es María?
  What nationality is Maria?
Es boliviana
  She is Bolivian

Unidad 2

7

Where are these people from? What nationalities could they be? Look up any you don't know.

(A) Pierre (B) Giovanna (C) Stephen (D) Clare (E) Costas

Can you name three friends from other countries and say what their names and nationalities are?

2

Soy estudiante

Saying what you do

1

Can you match the people in the pictures to these occupations?

a pintora	b cocinera	c carpintero	d médico
e secretaria	f estudiante	g actor	h profesor

V
español para extranjeros
Spanish for foreigners

2

Words for professions usually, but not always, have a masculine and feminine form. Look at the chart and fill in the missing words.

1 cocinero	cocinera
2 secretario	_____
3 profesor	profesora
4 _____	pintora
5 estudiante	estudiante
6 recepcionista	_____

3 ³

You will hear several people describe what they do. Can you match their names to the jobs in Activity 1?

1 Marco Antonio Castillo Morán
2 Cristina Pereira
3 Felipe Briceño
4 Marisa
5 Mónica Patiño
6 Andrés Macís

4 ⁴

Listen to four people being asked what their jobs are. What are the two ways of asking? How does each person say what he or she does?

a – ¿A qué te dedicas?
    – Soy actor.
b – ¿Cómo te llamas?
    – Mi nombre es Hernán Sierra Nieto.
    – Y ¿a qué te dedicas?
    – Soy arquitecto.
c – Me llamo Clara.
    – ¿A qué te dedicas?
    – Soy profesora de español para extranjeros.
d – ¿Qué haces?
    – Soy enfermero.

Unidad 2

Así se dice

To ask what people do for a living, say:

¿A qué te dedicas (tú)?
¿A qué se dedica (usted)?
¿Qué haces (tú)?
¿Qué hace (usted)?
   What do you do (for a living)?

And to answer, say:

Soy profesor/profesora
   I am a teacher

5 Y ahora tú

¿A qué te dedicas? ¿Qué haces?

(For a list of other jobs and professions see the list in W 2.)

Así se dice

To describe what someone does, say:

¿A qué se dedica?
¿Qué hace?
   What does he/she do?

And to answer, say:

Es estudiante
   He/She is a student

6

Look again at Activity 3. How would you describe to someone else what these people do?

e.g. **¿A qué se dedica Cristina? Es pintora.**

7

Can you say what two or three of your friends do?

e.g. **Marisa es actriz.**

G

trabajar
to work

estudiar
to study

(Regular -ar verbs. See p. 12)

V

enfermería
nursing
administración de empresas
management
cuidando niños
looking after children

Así se dice

If you work you might be asked:

¿En qué trabajas?
   What work do you do?

You might want to say what kind of work you do:

Trabajo de recepcionista
   I work as a receptionist

or where you work:

Trabajo en una óptica
   I work in an optician's

If you are a student you might be asked:

¿Qué estudias?
   What are you studying?

to which you might reply:

Estudio diseño
   I'm studying design

8 5

Listen to three young women talking about combining a job with studying for a career. On the chart below you will find the information has got mixed up. Can you say what each one does and studies?

		Job	Career Study
a	Sandra	de recepcionista	administración
b	Yaseña	cuidando niños	enfermería
c	Alicia	en una óptica	diseño

e.g. **Sandra trabaja ..... y estudia .....**

Unidad 2

9

The people in these illustrations are obviously out of their normal environment. Can you describe what's going on?

e.g. **Juanita es enfermera pero trabaja de profesora.**

a ....
b ....
c ....

3
Éste es mi hermano
Meeting the family and introducing people

1

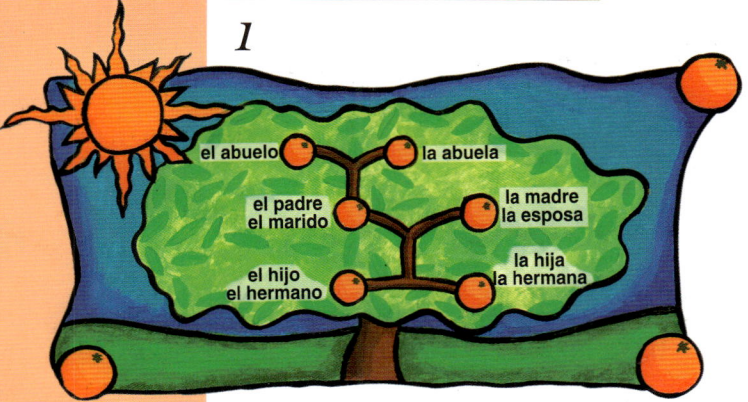

Look at the family tree and see if you can figure out the Spanish names for:

a mother   b brother   c father   d sister

2

Mafalda is a famous character in a Latin American strip cartoon. Here she is pointing out her father and mother. How would she point out her brother Guille?

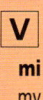
mi
my

Así se dice

To identify someone, say:

Éste es ... (man)
Ésta es ... (woman)   This is

3 Y ahora tú

Imagine you have a family photo and are pointing out members of your family to a friend. Can you say their relationship to you and give them Spanish names?

e.g. **Éste es mi hermano Juan.**

4

To whom does Begoña introduce Maria?

Begoña: **Hola, Carmen. María, te presento a Carmen.**
María: **Hola, mucho gusto.**
Carmen: **Hola, ¿qué tal?**

Begoña: **Hola, Ion. María, éste es Ion. Ion, María.**
Ion: **Mucho gusto.**

> ### Así se dice
>
> *To introduce someone, say:*
>
> **Éste es ...../Ésta es .....** *(informal)*
> **Te presento a .....**
> **Le presento a .....** *(formal)*
>   Can I introduce you to .....
>
> *To answer or acknowledge this, say:*
>
> **Mucho gusto**
>   Pleased to meet you *or:*
> **Encantado** *(man)*/**Encantada** *(woman)*
>
> *Between friends you might just say:*
>
> **Hola, ¿qué tal?**

5

Listen to these introductions. Can you distinguish formal (F) from informal (I)?

a ....   b ......   c ....   d ......

6 Y ahora tú

Now try your hand at introducing a new friend to a member of your family.

e.g. **Miguel, te presento a mi hermano Juan.**

Unidad 2

7 Los números

Here are the numbers 1–20. Say them aloud and then check your pronunciation on the tape.

1	uno	6	seis	11	once	16	dieciséis
2	dos	7	siete	12	doce	17	diecisiete
3	tres	8	ocho	13	trece	18	dieciocho
4	cuatro	9	nueve	14	catorce	19	diecinueve
5	cinco	10	diez	15	quince	20	veinte

> ### Así se dice
>
> *To ask about someone's family, say:*
>
> **¿Tiene/Tienes hermanos...?**
>   Do you have any brothers and sisters?
> **..... hijos/familia?**
>   ..... children/a family?
>
> *To answer you could say:*
>
> **Sí, tengo un hermano**
>   Yes, I have a brother
> **No, soy hijo único/hija única**
>   No, I'm an only child
>
> *To talk about age, say:*
>
> **¿Cuántos años tiene/tienes?**
>   How old are you?
> **Tengo diecinueve años**
>   I'm nineteen (years old)

G
tener
to have
(See p. 23)

V
solo/a
alone
¿cuántos años tienen?
how old are they?
el uno ... el otro, la otra
one ... the other
tiene doce años
he is twelve years old

8

Listen to Esperanza describing her family. Can you pick out how many children she has and say how old they are?

9 Y ahora tú

Do you have any brothers and sisters or children? Say what you have and if possible give their ages. (More numbers are given in Unit 4, p. 40)

Unidad 2

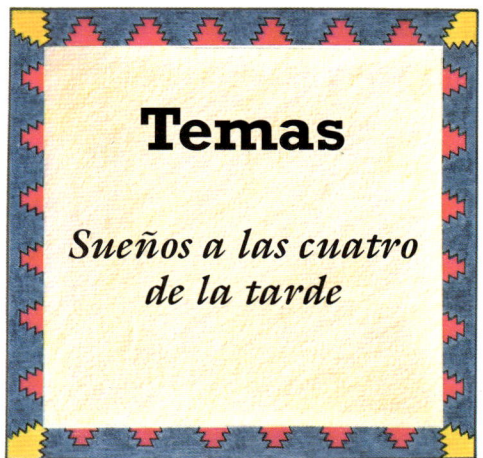

Temas

Sueños a las cuatro de la tarde

Telenovelas

The television soap opera is as big an industry in the Hispanic world as it is in Britain and the U.S. In Spain it is the Venezuelan soaps (called **culebrones**, meaning literally long snakes) like *Alejandra* that have the most devoted audiences. But the first to win the attention of the whole Spanish-speaking world was *Simplemente María* written by the Spanish romantic novelist Corín Tellado. In Latin America it was always broadcast at four in the afternoon (**a las cuatro de la tarde**) – and millions made sure they were home to watch it.

The story was familiar enough – Cinderella (**la Cenicienta**) and a rags to riches tale. María is a beautiful dark-skinned peasant girl (**una campesina**), independent and wild in her ways. When the younger son (**el hijo menor**) of the wealthy house where she is employed as a servant (**una criada**) tries to seduce her she fights him off. Eventually, however, she succumbs and is expelled from the house when the mother (**la madre**) finds out. The younger son, knowing her to be pregnant (**embarazada**), lets her take the responsibility at first. But his conscience bothers him and he brings her back to the household. When Maria is finally tamed and taught proper behaviour (**el decoro**), and when her bold independence is lost, she is allowed to remain and live in the house with her wealthy employers – after all, she has become one of them.

Later **telenovelas** have followed similar themes – though *Cuna de Lobos* (*Nest of wolves*), which has an audience of 40 million, shows a different kind of woman. Its heroine is a witch (**una bruja**) who refuses to be tamed. How times change!

Before television, soaps were popular on radio, where they were called **radionovelas**. The best known of them all, *El derecho de nacer* (*The right to be born*), was broadcast in Cuba from 1948 onwards. It was said that the cocks stopped crowing and the fleas stopped biting whenever it was on!

Watching TV watching you

País	Personas por radio	Personas por TV
Venezuela	2.4	7
Brasil	2.5	4.1
Colombia	7.3	5.9
México	5.2	8.9
Argentina	1.5	4.5
España	3.4	2.6
Gran Bretaña	0.9	2.2
Estados Unidos	0.5	1.3

Unidad 2

This chart shows the number of radio and TV sets in different countries. It also says something about the role of the media in different countries, especially the developing ones.

What conclusions do you draw from it?

In Mexico, TV reaches 70% of the population through 126 TV stations, 118 of them commercial and 8 public channels. Over half of them are affiliated to Televisa, which also has four stations in the United States. Televisa also exports 20,000 programmes to other countries – many of them soap operas – as well as producing films and merchandise.

Soap in other dishes
Fotonovelas

Apart from **telenovelas** and **radionovelas**, there are other ways of following serials. The very popular **fotonovelas** put words into the mouths of actors pictured in serial photographs.

Historietas

Comic strips (**historietas**) are also enormously popular, and a vehicle for popular characters like the resourceful eagle **Condorito** or the wily peasants of Rius' famous strips about *Los agachados* (*The oppressed*), or his **Supermachos** who poked some well-intentioned fun at Mexican male chauvinism.

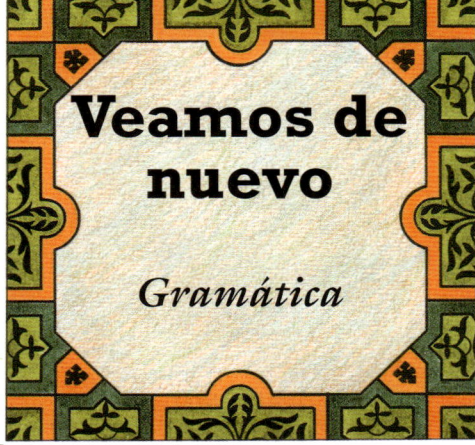

V
no entiendo
I don't understand
¡qué mala suerte!
that's bad luck

Veamos de nuevo

Gramática

1 Words for people and things

In Spanish words for people and things (nouns) are either masculine or feminine, and the word for 'the' is **el** or **la** depending on the gender of the noun it accompanies. Many masculine nouns end in **-o** and feminine nouns in **-a**:

masculine   **el** hij**o** (*the son*)
feminine   **la** famili**a** (*the family*)

With names for people it is easy to see why one word should be masculine and another feminine:

    el funcionario   (male civil servant)
    la funcionaria   (female civil servant)

but with names for objects there often seems no reason why one word should be masculine and another feminine.

As well as **-o** and **-a** there are other patterns of endings some of which we have seen in this unit. Words ending in **-or** are usually masculine and the feminine form is normally **-ora**:

    el profesor   **la profesora**

Nouns ending in **-ante** and **-ista** can be either masculine or feminine:

    el estudiante   **la estudiante**
    el dentista   **la dentista**

Unidad 2

2 Words describing nationalities

The endings of words used to describe people and things (adjectives) change according to the gender of the noun they accompany. Many end in **-o** and **-a**:

   peruano   peruana

Adjectives of nationality ending in **-s**, **-n**, or **-l** form their feminine by adding **-a**:

   inglés   inglesa
   alemán   alemana
   español   española

Some words for nationality have the same masculine and feminine form:

   costarricense; nicaraguense

3 I have, you have

Tener (to have) is a common irregular verb of the **-er** group. Here it is used to say what family you have and to give your age:

tengo una hermana   (I have a sister)
tiene veinte años   (she is twenty)

Here is its form in the present tense:

tengo	I have	**tenemos**	we have
tienes	you have (informal)	**tenéis**	you have (informal)
tiene	he/she has, you have (formal)	**tienen**	they have, you have (formal)

4 My, your, his

In this unit you have met several examples of these words (possessive adjectives):

mi mis	my	**mi madre**	(my mother)
		mis hermanas	(my sisters)
tu tus	your	**tu hijo**	(your son)
su sus	his/her/its, your (formal)	**su hermana**	(his/her/ your sister)

Note: 'my', 'your' and 'his' have the same form whether they accompany a feminine or a masculine noun. With a plural noun you add **-s**: **tus hijos** (your children). For a complete list see G 3.3.

Práctica

A To be or to have

Complete the sentences below using the correct form of **tener** or **ser**.

e.g. Yo ..... estudiante y ..... 19 años.
     Yo soy estudiante y tengo 19 años.

1 María ..... profesora.
2 Tú no ..... de Sevilla.
3 Usted ..... médico.
4 Yo ..... español.
5 Tú ..... 17 años.
6 Alicia ..... tres hijos.

B ¿De dónde son?

Can you say where these people are from and what languages they speak?

e.g. **(Juana/Sevilla) Juana es de Sevilla.**
      Es española y habla español.

1 Pierre/Lyon
2 Patricia/Buenos Aires
3 Jill/Nueva York
4 Isabella/Roma
5 Antonio/Barcelona

C Let me introduce you

Using **éste** or **ésta**, introduce your friends to members of your family.

e.g. **(Carlos: tu padre) Carlos, éste es mi padre.**

1 Betty: tu abuela.
2 Ana: tu madre.
3 Claudia: tu hermana, Federica.
4 Guillermo: tu hijo.

D What was the question?

Here are some answers. Can you write the appropriate questions?

e.g. **Tengo 15 años. ¿Cuántos años tienes?**

1 Alicia tiene cinco años.
2 Es de Edimburgo.
3 Soy escocesa.
4 Soy arquitecto.
5 Tiene dos hermanas.

Unidad 2

E What's my line?

The first letters of the answers below when put together give the name of a profession. What is it?

1 ¿De ..... eres?
2 Un habitante de ..... es ecuatoriano.
3 François ..... es español, es francés.
4 ..... no eres cubano.
5 Fergus vive en Dublín, es ..... .
6 Mi nombre es Gloria, ... nicaragüense.
7 Vivo en Salamanca y ..... de ingeniero.
8 La madre de mi madre es mi ..... .
¿Qué soy? .....

1 Applying for a job

You have been sent an application form for a job in Spain. Can you fill it in?

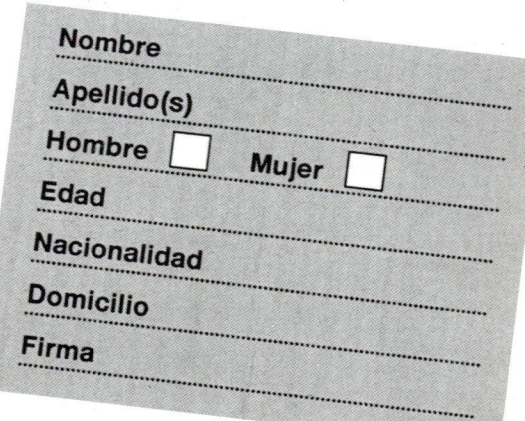

2 🔊 10

The hotel where you are staying is holding an international conference. While waiting at the reception for your friend you overhear several conversations. Fill in the grid with the details you hear.

Nombre	¿De dónde es?	¿Dónde vive?	Profesión
José	España	Madrid	Estudiante

está casada
she is married

Un paso más

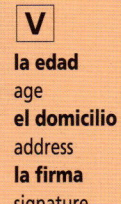
la edad
age
el domicilio
address
la firma
signature

3 Gente de hoy

The following clip appeared in a local Mexican newspaper.

Claudia Patiño es diseñadora. Tiene 38 años. Está casada con Alberto Miguel y vive en la Ciudad de México. Tiene dos hijos: Carla, su hija, estudia para chef en México. Ernesto, el hijo, estudia medicina. Su hermana, Mónica, es cocinera. Las dos tienen el restaurante La Taberna del León. Su madre trabaja en la decoración del restaurante. Mónica tiene 40 años, un marido y cuatro hijos.

A. Are the following facts true (**verdadero**) or false (**falso**)?

a Claudia is married.
b Claudia has four children.
c Carla is a designer.
d Monica's mother works as a cook.
e Alberto Miguel has two children.

B Write the story as if Claudia were talking about herself:

e.g. **Me llamo Claudia, soy .....**

4 Checklist

Can you do the following?

a Find out someone's nationality and give your own
b Ask where someone is from and say where you are from
c Ask about someone's job
d Say what you do for a living
e Introduce someone to your mother
f Ask and say what family you have
g Ask someone's age and give your own

Unidad 3

Mi ciudad y mi barrio

Así se habla
Saying what your home town is like

Describing people and places

Saying what there is in your town

Temas
La ciudad de los sueños

Veamos de nuevo

Unidad 3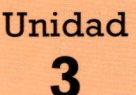

Así se habla 1

¿Cómo es?

Saying what your home town is like

1 🔊¹

Can you match the following Spanish words with their English equivalents?

1 pequeño   a modern
2 moderno   b quiet
3 antiguo   c big
4 tranquilo   d old
5 grande   e pretty
6 bonito   f small

2

Here are some pictures of districts (**barrios**) or towns (**ciudades** or **pueblos**) in the Hispanic world.

Which words in the list above best describe each picture?

3 🔊²

Listen to Carmen asking a woman about the district she lives in. What does she think of it?

– ¿Dónde vive? ¿En qué barrio?
– Santo Domingo.
– ¿Cómo es su barrio?
– Mi barrio es muy ....., muy ....., y muy alegre.

V
¿en qué barrio?
in what district?
muy
very
alegre
cheerful

Así se acostumbra

Life in many cities and towns in the Hispanic world revolves around **el barrio** (**la colonia** in Mexico) – a district in a town. It is not necessarily an official district – more an area where people know each other and meet for social events. Everyday life gives **el barrio** a certain vibrancy and people like to identify themselves with it; they call it **mi barrio**.

Así se dice

To find out what a district is like and to answer, say:

¿Cómo es tu/su barrio?
   What is your district like?
Es muy bonito y alegre
   It's very pretty and cheerful

Unidad 3

4 🔊³

Listen to three people describing their **barrio**. Do they like it? What words does each one use?

Speaker 1:
Speaker 2:
Speaker 3:

5 *Y ahora tú*

¿Cómo es tu barrio?

See W 7 for more words to describe districts or towns.

6 🔊⁴

Three people are describing the town or city where they live. Can you pick out three words each speaker uses and write them under each picture?

artístico/a   divertido/a   antiguo/a   famoso/a
grande   turístico/a   bonito/a   cálido/a

México, D.F., capital de México
....

San Sebastián, capital de la provincia de Guipúzcoa, España
....

Almagro, provincia de Ciudad Real, España
....

V
acogedor friendly
aburrido boring

V
divertido amusing
cálido hot

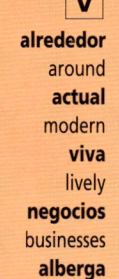

V
alrededor around
actual modern
viva lively
negocios businesses
alberga accommodates

Así se dice

To describe your town you might say:

El pueblo es antiguo y bonito
The town is old and pretty

To describe your city you might say:

La ciudad es antigua y bonita
The city is old and pretty

☞ Ex. B, C, p. 35

7

Now describe the three cities in Activity 6.

e.g. **La ciudad de México es ...**

8 *Y ahora tú*

¿De dónde eres?
¿Cómo es tu ciudad o tu pueblo?

9

This is how Juan, a businessman from Madrid, described his home town. Read and answer the following questions:

a How big is it and what is its population?
b What things or events make Madrid busy and lively?
c How many universities are there in Madrid?
d Which is the old part of the city?
e How does Juan describe the 'character' of Madrid?

'Madrid es una ciudad grande que tiene unos cuatro millones de habitantes. Se divide en dos partes: la parte antigua, alrededor de la Plaza Mayor; y la parte moderna que es la zona norte, donde se han hecho todo tipo de construcciones modernas. Es una ciudad muy alegre, con muchísimos universitarios; hay tres universidades importantes. También es una ciudad que alberga muchos negocios, mucha hostelería y mucho mundo del turismo. Muchos congresos se celebran en Madrid, es una ciudad pues actual, viva y dinámica'.

Unidad 3

2
¿Qué hay en tu barrio?
Describing people and places

la Catedral

el Ayuntamiento

1

La Plaza Mayor

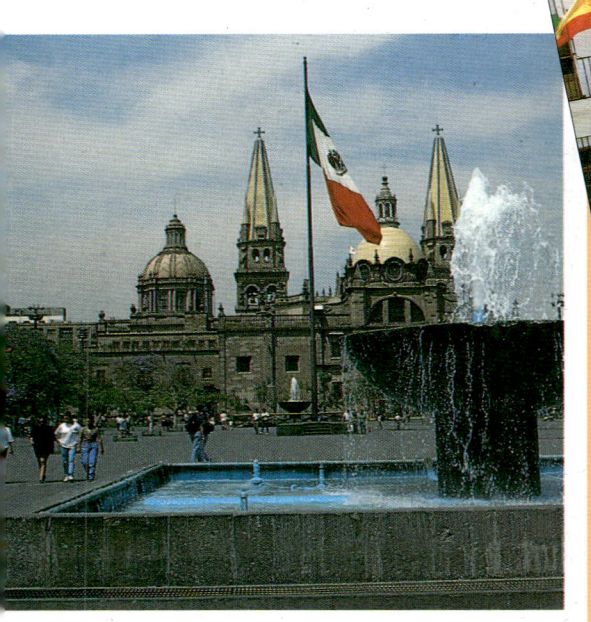

Here are some buildings, places and shops found in many Spanish and Latin American towns and cities. Can you identify them? Many are similar to English ones and you may be able to guess what they are. Look up any you don't know.

el museo	el parque	el bar
el supermercado	el restaurante	el teatro
la iglesia	la farmacia	el cine

V
el juzgado
court-house

V
una sola
just one
calle
street
tienda de comestibles
food shop
tienda de ropa
clothes shop

Así se acostumbra

In Spain **el estanco** is a shop where you can buy tobacco products, some stationery and stamps. You can also get stamps at **la oficina de Correos** (post office), which in some areas is referred to simply as **Correos** or **el Correo** (LA). Other countries have shops that are very much their own too. In Mexico, for example, **la tlapalería** is a hardware store, while in Chile you might go to **el boliche** for groceries.

2 🔊⁵

Maria, who lives in the Basque country, mentions all the main buildings in her small town. How many of them can you recognize? Some come from Activity 1.

3 🔊⁶

Listen to Maria describing her town in more detail. Is it big or small? What are its main buildings? Now read the text and check if you are correct.

– Es un pueblo muy pequeño, tiene una sola calle, y en esa calle pues hay dos iglesias, una de ellas muy antigua, hay siete bares, cinco restaurantes, dos tiendas de comestibles, un estanco, un supermercado, una tienda de ropa ...

Unidad 3

Así se dice

To indicate what buildings there are, say:

Hay ...   There is/There are ...

un supermercado, una escuela, un bar
  a supermarket, a school, a bar
dos supermercados, escuelas, bares
  two supermarkets, schools, bars
algunos museos, algunas tiendas
  some museums, some shops
muchos restaurantes, muchas farmacias
  many restaurants, many chemists

Or to say what the town has, use:

Tiene ...   It has ...

varios parques, varias galerías
  several parks, several art galleries

If you want to say what isn't there:

No hay ...   There is no/are no ...

No hay un teatro
  There isn't a theatre
No hay parques
  There aren't any parks

4

The **Barrio de San Telmo** is one of the old districts of Buenos Aires, where merchants and cattle-men had their town houses in the nineteenth century. Use this brochure and its key to find out the main places of interest (**lugares de interés**) and make a note of how many of each category there are:

a iglesia   d escuela
b plaza   e galería
c restaurante   f museo

Now tell a friend what there is to see in this part of the city:

e.g. **En San Telmo hay dos iglesias.**

G

Hay
(See p. 35)

V

la parroquia
parish
la casa
house
la tanguería
tango bar

5 *Y ahora tú*

¿Qué hay en tu barrio o en tu ciudad?

Imagine you are describing your district to someone. What are its attractions? And what is missing from your point of view?

e.g. **Hay varios bares, pero no hay un parque.**

Buenos Aires
BARRIO DE SAN TELMO

SAN TELMO
1. Plaza Dorrego 2. Iglesia de Nuestra Señora de Belén - Parroquia de San Pedro González Telmo 3. Escuela Guillermo Rawson 4. Museo Penitenciario 5. Museo de Arte Moderno
6. Galería Pasaje de la Defensa 7. Galería El Solar de French 8. Casa de Estebán de Luca
9. Restaurante La Tasca de San Fermín
10. Galería del Viejo Hotel
11. Casa de Castagnino
12. Iglesia Dinamarquesa
13. Pasaje Glufra
14. Yuchán
15. Conventillo
16. Pasaje de San Lorenzo

Unidad 3

3
¿Hay un hotel por aquí?
Saying what there is in your town

1 🔊 7

Isabel has just arrived in Taxco, a small town south of Mexico City, famous for its silversmiths (**las platerías**). She is looking for a hotel (**un hotel**). Look at the street map of Taxco and see where they are. Now listen and read her conversation with a passer-by.

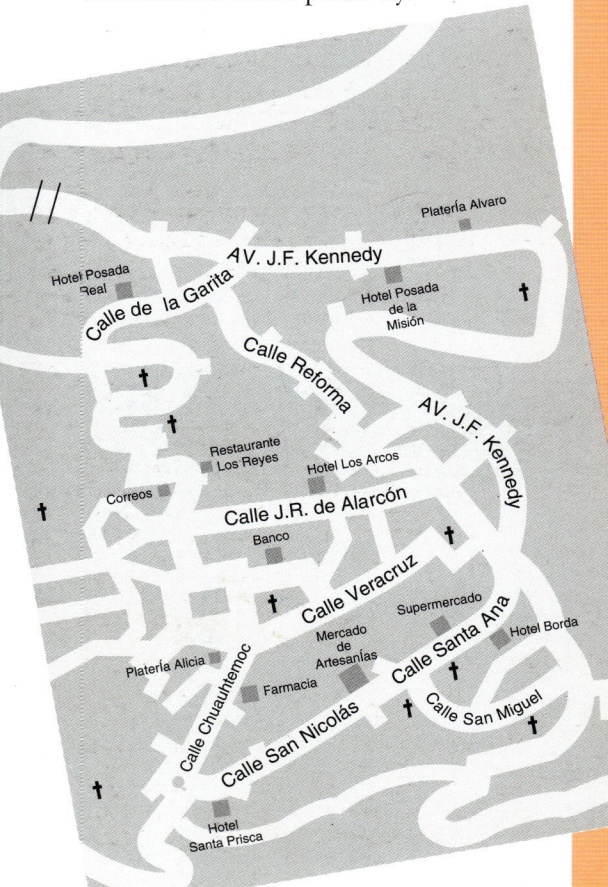

a How does she ask for what she wants?
b Where are the two hotels mentioned?

– **Perdone, ¿hay un hotel por aquí?**
– **Sí, hay uno en la calle ..... y hay otro en la avenida ..... .**
– **Gracias.**
– **De nada.**

V
por aquí
near here

Así se dice

To get someone's attention, say:

Perdone ... *or:* **Disculpe ...**
Excuse me ...

To ask if there is a particular place nearby, say:

¿Hay una farmacia por aquí?
Is there a chemist's around here?
¿Hay un hotel cerca? (de aqui)
Is there a hotel near here?

If you want to be more polite, say:

¿Me puede decir si hay un hotel por aquí?
Can you tell me if there is a hotel around here?

To answer you can say:

Sí, hay uno en la calle .....
Yes, there is one in ..... street
y hay otro en la avenida .....
and there is another one in ..... avenue
Sí, hay muchos/muchas
Yes, there are many
No, no hay
No, there aren't any
Lo siento pero no soy de aquí
I'm sorry, but I'm not from here

Unidad 3

2

Imagine you are in Taxco and need to buy a few things. Here is your shopping list:

> 4 SELLOS
> 2 RECUERDOS DE PLATA
> COMESTIBLES
> MEDICINA
> CHEQUES DE VIAJERO

Where would you go to buy the things you need? (The first one has been done for you.)

e.g. **En Correos.**

3

How would you ask someone where the places you have just mentioned are? Practise different ways of asking.

e.g. **¿Hay una oficina de Correos por aquí?**

4 [8]

Some tourists ask you about various places. You listen to their questions. Using the map in Activity 1, can you tell them where these places are?

V

un sello
stamp
un recuerdo
souvenir
un cheque de viajero
traveller's cheque

El Albaicín, Granada

Temas

La ciudad de los sueños

The cities of the Spanish-speaking world have very different histories – and very different faces.

1492: Granada

In 1492, the city of Granada was captured after a long siege. It was the last stronghold of the Moors, who had dominated Spain for the previous seven centuries. They left behind them, however, the elegant cities of Andalucía – Granada, Sevilla and Córdoba – each with their glorious palaces (**los alcázares**), their city walls (**las murallas**) and their running fountains (**las fuentes**).

Unidad 3

1760: Buenos Aires

On the banks of the River Plate (**el río de la Plata**) the small outpost of Buenos Aires began to grow. The cattle of the grass plains of southern Argentina (**las pampas**) attracted European traders. Within 50 years it became the major commercial port for the whole of southern America. By the 1880s, it was attracting immigrants from all over Europe who came in search of a new life, work, and sometimes land. These immigrants gave Buenos Aires its own, very special music, the tango (**el tango**).

1888: Barcelona

The capital of Cataluña already had a rich cultural history before it experienced a new expansion towards the end of the nineteenth century. From the 1870s, its industry began to develop and its trade with the rest of Europe grew. It developed faster than the other cities of Spain. Its planned area of urban growth – called **el Eixample** in Catalan, **el Ensanche** in Spanish – is elegant, ordered and beautiful. It gives a sense of the confident and innovative milieu which allowed a creative genius like Antonio Gaudí to work freely. His unique and eccentric buildings, like the still unfinished **Sagrada Familia** cathedral or the **Casa Milá** apartment block, were built in an art nouveau style. It is no accident that some of the most important names in the Modern movement emerged from this burgeoning European city; for Miró, Dali and Picasso all began their careers here.

Casa Milá, Barcelona

1521–2000: México D.F.

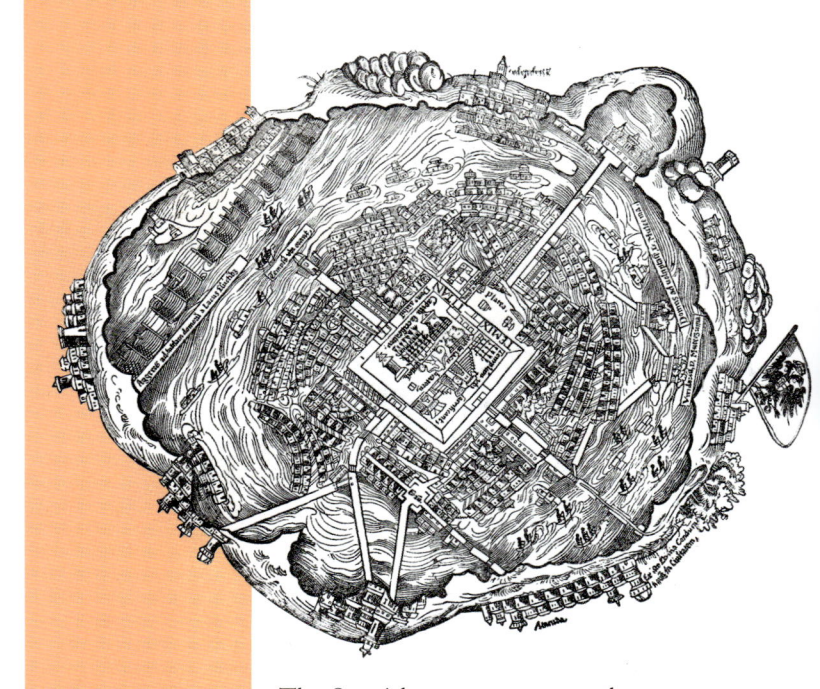

The Spanish conquerors stood open-mouthed when they first they saw the great capital city of the Aztecs of México, Tenochtitlán. One soldier described it as "like the marvellous cities of the novels of chivalry". When the Conquest ended in 1521, the Spaniards destroyed the native city and built in its place what was to become the Spanish capital of the New World – Mexico City (**la Ciudad de México**). The city grew outwards around the old colonial core; in the 1880s it grew again, and those few who enjoyed the new prosperity built fine mansions in the new city districts (**las colonias**) and frequented the European-style shops and cafés in the city centre. In the 1950s and 1960s the city exploded again, as thousands came to the capital to look for work and built their shanty towns (**ciudades perdidas**) on the outskirts. By 1994 it was the world's largest city and one of its most polluted. Its population exceeded 20 million, many of whom are without adequate jobs or housing.

Unidad 3

"Mi Buenos Aires querido"

Carlos Gardel (1891–1935) was the most famous of all the tango singers. He sang about jilted lovers, about his mother, and about the past.

**Mi Buenos Aires querido
cuando yo te vuelva a ver
no habrá más penas ni olvido.**

**Hoy que la suerte quiere que te vuelva a ver
ciudad porteña de mi único querer,
oigo la queja de un bandoneón
dentro de mi pecho pide rienda el corazón.**

**Mi Buenos Aires
Tierra querida,
donde mi vida terminará.
Bajo tu amparo no hay desengaño...**

Here is a translation:

My beloved Buenos Aires,
when I see you again
there will be no more sorrow or forgetfulness.

Today when fortune has decided I should see you again
port city my only love
I hear the wail of a bandoneón
and in my chest my heart calls out for rest.

My Buenos Aires
Beloved country
where my life will end.
Under your protection there is no disappointment...

* *Can you write down the phrases he uses for "my beloved Buenos Aires", "port city", "beloved country", "disappointment"?*

The Mexican American poet, Francisco X. Alarcón, writes of his **barrio**, **La Misión**, in San Francisco.

buenos días	good morning
colores	colours
vida mía	my life
buenas tardes	good evening
risas	laughter
pan de olor	the smell of bread
cómo están	how they are
gente	people
mitotera	having a good time
puertas tristes	sad doorways
música	music
de ventanas	from windows
caras jóvenes	young faces
riqueza	riches
de los más pobres	of the poorest people
un día	one day
yo puedo dejar	I may leave
el barrio	the barrio
pero éste	but it
nunca saldrá	will never leave
de mí.	me

* *How would you sum up the feelings for the barrio that it represents?*

"Calle Melancolía"

Joaquín Sabina, one of Spain's most famous singer-songwriters, wrote a song about his home town, the city of Madrid. It is perhaps more realistic about the contradictions of life in a modern city – and less blind to its problems. Yet it is still deeply affectionate.

El campo está verde debe ser primavera
The countryside is green it must be spring
Cruza por mi mirada un tren interminable
An endless train crosses my gaze
El barrio donde habito no es ninguna pradera
The district where I live is certainly no spring meadow

Unidad 3

Desolado paisaje de antenas y de cables
A desolate landscape of aerials and cables
Vivo en el número siete, calle Melancolía
I live at number seven, Melancholy Street
Quiero mudarme hace años al barrio de la alegría
For years I've wanted to live in the district of joy
Pero siempre que lo intento ha salido el tranvía
But every time I try to leave the tram's already gone.

* What phrases in the song give a sense of sadness? And what phrases point to the contrast with the places he dreams of?

Veamos de nuevo
Gramática

1 Plurals

The plural forms of the definite articles **el** and **la** are **los** for masculine words, and **las** for feminine.

The plural of nouns ending in a vowel is formed by adding **-s** to the singular form:

| el museo | *los* museos |
| la iglesia | *las* iglesias |

However, nouns ending in a consonant form their plural by adding **-es** to the singular form:

| la catedral | *las* catedrales |

2 'a', 'an', 'some', etc.

In Spanish indefinite articles agree with the noun they accompany or refer to, both in gender and number:

masculine
| un | museo | a museum |
| unos | museos | (some) museums |

feminine
| una | escuela | a school |
| unas | escuelas | (some) schools |

Note the following:

algunos bares	algunas tiendas
varios parques	varias iglesias
muchos museos	muchas escuelas

Unidad 3

3 Hay ¿Hay?

Hay means both 'there is' and 'there are':

Hay un hotel
    There is a hotel
Hay tres farmacias
    There are three chemists'

and is also used for the question form:

¿Hay un hotel?
    Is there a hotel?

4 Adjectives

As you saw with nationalities in Unit 2, adjectives usually agree in gender and number with the noun they describe. They normally follow the noun.

Adjectives ending in **-o**, **-a** have masculine, feminine, singular and plural forms:

un barrio tranquilo
una ciudad tranquila
unos barrios tranquilos
unas ciudades tranquilas

Adjectives ending in **-e** change their form only in the plural:

un barrio alegre   **una ciudad alegre**
unos barrios alegres **unas ciudades alegres**

Adjectives ending in a consonant sometimes but not always change their ending:

un pueblo acogedor   **calle acogedora**
un pueblo hostil   **una calle hostil**

Práctica

A What's in town?

Can you insert the correct indefinite articles?

En Segovia hay ___ castillo, ___ hospital, ___ biblioteca, ___ cine, ___ restaurantes, ___ hoteles, y ___ oficina de Correos.

B Does it fit the description?

Can you match the two parts of the following sentences correctly?

1	Salamanca es una ciudad	a	barrios alegres
2	Quito tiene muchas	b	museos interesantes
3	Onís es un pueblo	c	iglesias antiguas
4	Mi pueblo tiene muchos	d	muy bonita
5	En Buenos Aires hay varios	e	muy pequeño

C Al contrario

Your friend seems to have the wrong idea about your town, so you put him right. Can you find the right adjective in each case? Choose from the following:

alegre, bonito, limpio, tranquilo, acogedor, divertido.

e.g. **¿Es un pueblo ruidoso?**
        No, es muy tranquilo

1 ¿El barrio es hostil?
2 ¿Las calles son sucias?
3 ¿La iglesia es fea?
4 ¿La vida nocturna es aburrida?
5 ¿La gente es triste?

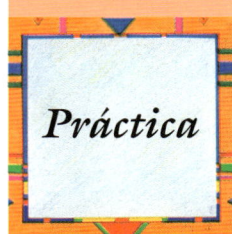

Unidad 3

Un paso más

1 San Sebastián 🔊 9

You overhear Begoña talking about San Sebastián, where she lives. Can you now give a friend some information about it? He wants to know the following:

a What kind of a city it is.
b What San Sebastián is famous for in particular.
c What buildings in the city immediately spring to mind.

2 Holiday in Valencia

You are planning to meet up in Valencia with a friend from Mexico, with whom you have corresponded but not yet met. The Oficina de Turismo there has sent you various brochures about the city. Here is part of one of them:

VALENCIA – LA TIERRA DE LAS FLORES

Valencia se conoce internacionalmente por la paella. La ciudad es histórica y antigua con muchos ejemplos romanos, árabes y góticos. Hay muchos monumentos y edificios famosos como por ejemplo la Catedral. La Basílica de la Virgen de los Desamparados es bastante antigua y muy bonita. Hay muchas iglesias como las de San Esteban y San Juan del Hospital, y varios museos como el Museo paleontológico o el Museo marítimo. También hay muchos palacios: el Palacio del Mercader y el Palacio Episcopal, entre otros. El mercado central es bullicioso y alegre.

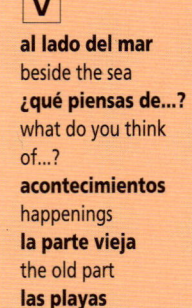

V

al lado del mar
beside the sea
¿qué piensas de...?
what do you think of...?
acontecimientos
happenings
la parte vieja
the old part
las playas
beaches
la casa de los municipales
town police

V

bullicioso
bustling

La Valencia moderna tiene el Club náutico, y el Campo de golf del Saler, uno de los más importantes de Europa. El compositor Maestro Padillo describe Valencia en tres palabras: Valencia es la tierra de las flores, de la luz y del amor.

Can you now tell your friend something about the city and answer his questions?

a ¿Por qué es famosa Valencia?
b ¿Hay monumentos y otros lugares de interés?
c ¿Qué deportes hay en Valencia?

You now need to find out what accommodation there is available. Can you ask the Oficina de Turismo if there is a hotel near the city centre?

3 Information swap

Your Mexican friend is also interested in your home town. When you write to her can you tell her something about it? You could mention what kind of place it is, and what its attractions are. If it's famous, what is it famous for?
In return, you would like to find out about Mexico City where your friend comes from. You could ask her what kind of **barrio** she lives in and whether it's quiet and peaceful or lively and noisy. You'd also like to know whether there are many historic buildings in the city.

4 Checklist:

Can you do the following?

a Ask what someone's town is like.
b Say what your district or home town is like.
c Ask whether there is a particular building in the area.
d Describe buildings and places.

Mercado central, Valencia

[36]

Unidad 4

¿Dónde está?

Así se habla
Saying where a place is
Asking for things
Talking about distances
Asking for and giving directions

Temas
Andalucía, ayer y hoy

Veamos de nuevo

Unidad 4

Así se habla 1

Está delante de la farmacia

Saying where a place is

1

You and Isabel are staying with your friend Juan in Almería, in southern Spain. Juan is showing you the area where he lives on a map. Listen to the recording and before reading the text, tick the buildings and places as you hear them mentioned.

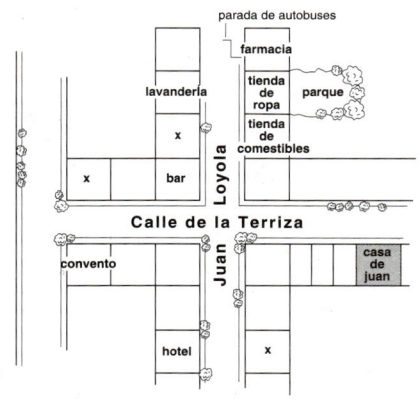

Juan:	Mi casa está aquí. La calle principal es ésta. Aquí hay varias tiendas. Hay una tienda de ropa, una tienda de comestibles y una farmacia.
Isabel:	¿Hay una lavandería?
Juan:	Sí, está aquí, enfrente de la tienda de ropa.
Isabel:	¿Y dónde está la parada de autobuses?
Juan:	Está delante de la farmacia.

2

Look at these drawings and expressions. What equivalents would you use in English?

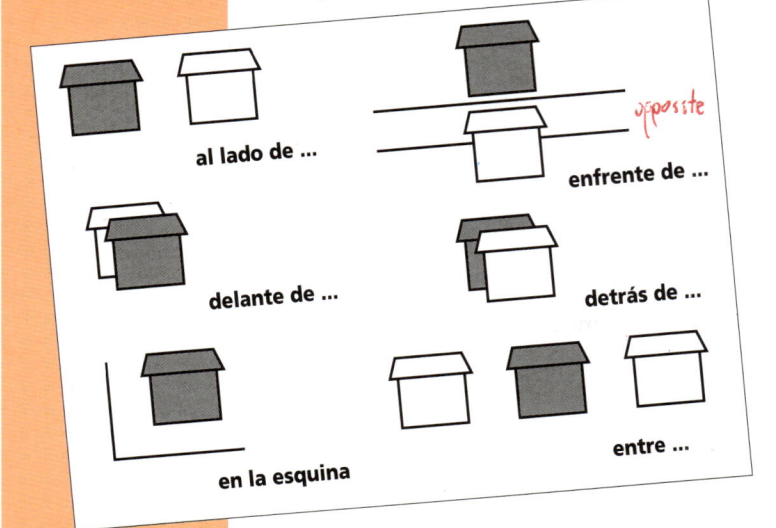

- al lado de ...
- enfrente de ... *opposite*
- delante de ...
- detrás de ...
- en la esquina
- entre ...

G
de + el = del
(See p. 46)

estar
to be
(See p. 46)

V
una lavandería
launderette

Así se dice

To ask where a place is, say:

¿Dónde está ...?
Where is ...?

And to answer, say:

Está delante de la tienda
It's in front of the shop

☞ Ex. B, p. 46

3

Look at the map in Activity 1 once more. How would you describe the location of the following buildings or places in relation to each other?

e.g. The clothes shop and the launderette
La tienda de ropa está enfrente de la lavandería.

a the grocer's and the clothes shop
b the park and the clothes shop
c the clothes shop in relation to the chemist's and the grocer's
d the hotel and the chemist's

Unidad 4

4 Y ahora tú 🔊²

You know there is also a post office, a church and a tobacconist's in Juan's neighbourhood, but you don't know exactly where.

a How would you ask?
b Now listen to the recording and mark the three places on the map in Activity 1.

5 🔊³

You are now in the town centre of Almería. You are going to hear someone asking about different places in the city. Listen and make a note of where these places are.

a **el museo arqueológico**
b **la iglesia de San Pedro**
c **el teatro Cervantes**
d **la oficina de turismo**

Así se acostumbra

In Spain, short distances are sometimes expressed in terms of the number of streets a person has to cross – **a dos calles de aquí** (two streets from here) or in terms of metres – **a doscientos metros** (two hundred metres). On the other hand, in some Latin American countries, distance is expressed in terms of blocks (**cuadras**) – **a tres cuadras de aquí** (three blocks from here). Less commonly, distance is also expressed in terms of the amount of time it will take a person to walk to a place, so you might hear, for example, **a unos veinte minutos andando** (it's a twenty-minute walk).

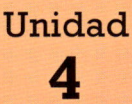

V

a dos calles de aquí
two streets from here

Almería

2
¿Tiene un folleto de Toledo?

Asking for things. Talking about distances

1

These are some of the things you can get at a tourist office:

- un mapa
- un folleto
- un plano del metro
- un horario de trenes
- un plano de Madrid

Imagine you are at a tourist office in Madrid. What would you ask for if you needed to do the following?

e.g. travel by underground
un plano del metro

a find train departure times
b find your way on foot around Madrid city centre
c find out about places in the surroundings of Madrid
d travel to Toledo by train

Unidad 4

2 🔊⁴

Listen and read these two conversations. In the first, Pilar wants a map of Madrid, in the second a brochure of Toledo. How does she ask for what she wants?

a – ¿Me puede dar un mapa de Madrid, por favor?
– Sí, mire, éste es un mapa de la ciudad de Madrid, con los medios de transporte públicos ... metro y autobuses.
– ¿Tiene monumentos este mapa?
– Sí, éste es un planito de los monumentos más característicos de la ciudad ... y aquí tiene usted una lista de los monumentos y museos en Madrid con los horarios.

b – ¿Tiene un folleto sobre Toledo?
– Sí, cómo no. Aquí tiene usted un folleto de Toledo. Dentro tiene la historia, y un pequeño planito de la ciudad de Toledo... tiene una relación de museos y monumentos.
– Ah, muy interesante. Muchísimas gracias.
– De nada.

Now read the conversations again and tick the kind of information she will find in the map and the brochure.

	mapa de Madrid	folleto de Toledo
Names of streets		
Means of transport		
Timetables		
Places of interest		
Historical info.		

Así se dice

If you want to ask for something, say:

¿Me puede dar un mapa de Madrid, por favor?
 Can I have a street map of Madrid, please?

or you could say:

¿Tiene un mapa de Madrid, por favor?
 Do you have a street map of Madrid, please?

V

cómo no
of course
un planito
a small street plan
un horario
timetable

---

3 Y ahora tú

Now say how would you ask for the items in Activity 1.

4 Los números 🔊⁵

See how numbers 20 to 99 are formed and fill in the gaps:

20 veinte	30 treinta	60 sesenta
21 veintiuno	31 treinta y uno	66 ....
22 veintidós	32 treinta y dos	70 setenta
23 veintitrés	34	77 ....
24 veinticuatro	40 cuarenta	80 ochenta
25 veinticinco	44 cuarenta y cuatro	88 ....
26 veintiséis	46	90 noventa
27 veintisiete	50 cincuenta	99 ....
28 veintiocho	55 cincuenta y cinco	
29 veintinueve	57	

5 🔊⁶

You are taking part in a raffle (**una rifa**). You are going to hear the five small prize-winning numbers announced first, followed by the big prize (**el premio mayor**). Can you write down the winning numbers? The major winner gets a trip for two (**un viaje para dos**). Can you say where the winner will be going? And what else does he/she get?

6

You were unlucky this time; someone else won **el premio mayor**. The lucky winner is now in the Tourist Office in Madrid, enquiring about interesting sights and towns near Madrid. Read the conversation and look at the photograph.

a Which is the town in the photograph?
b Where is Segovia and how far is it from Madrid?

– ¿Qué lugares de interés hay cerca de Madrid?
– Pues, está el antiguo monasterio de El Escorial; Segovia con los dos ríos, el Eresma y el Clamores, y el espectacular acueducto romano con 167 arcos; Toledo con la catedral de estilo gótico puro y pinturas de Van Dyck, El Greco y Goya ... Pues, también está el centro de esquí de Navacerrada en el invierno y, un poco más lejos, Ávila, la ciudad de las murallas...
– ¿Y dónde está Segovia?
– Está aquí, al noroeste de Madrid.
– ¿Y a qué distancia está?
– Pues está a 81 kilómetros, a más o menos dos horas en tren o autobús.

Así se dice

To indicate where a place is by compass direction, say:

Segovia está al noroeste de Madrid
  Segovia is northwest of Madrid

To ask about distance, say:

¿A qué distancia está Segovia de Madrid?
  How far is Segovia from Madrid?

To answer, say:

Está a 81 kilómetros
  It's 81 kilometres (away)
Está a dos horas en tren/autobús
  It's two hours (away) by train/bus

7 Y ahora tú

Imagine you are at the Tourist Office in Madrid and you want to know how far these places are from Madrid. How would you ask?

a El Escorial   d Alcalá de Henares
b Guadalajara   e Segovia
c Aranjuez

Unidad 4

V

el invierno
winter
las murallas
walls
más o menos
approximately

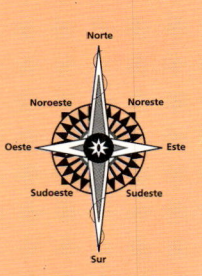

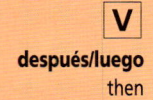

V

después/luego
then

a la derecha
a la izquierda
todo recto

---

7 The assistant in the Tourist Office gives you the information you require. Listen and note down the distances she gives and any particulars of the directions.

3
Sigues todo recto
Asking for and giving directions

1

Complete this chart of ordinal numbers:

	Masculino	**Femenino**
first	1° primero	1ª primera
second	2°	2ª segunda
third	3° tercero	3ª .....
fourth	4°	4ª cuarta
fifth	5° quinto	5ª .....

(See W 5, for more numbers)

2

Now look at these directions. Can you say what they mean in English?

a la primera calle a la derecha
b la cuarta a la izquierda
c la tercera a la derecha y luego todo recto
d tres calles y a la izquierda

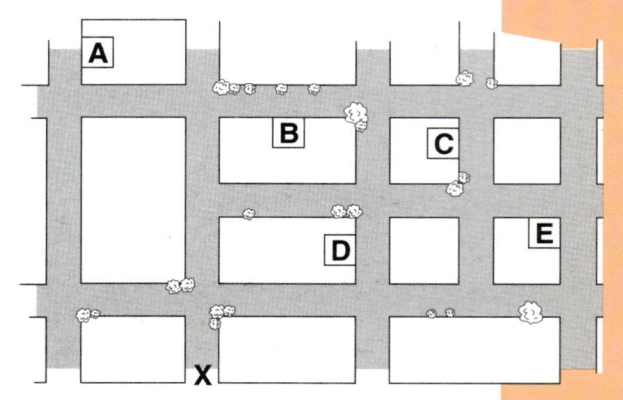

Unidad 4

3 🔊 8

Imagine you are in a Spanish town, standing where the x is marked on the map. You will hear three people asking about the cathedral, the town hall and the library. Which letter on the plan above corresponds to each of these places?

– Perdone, ¿dónde está la catedral?
– ¿Por dónde se va al ayuntamiento?
– Oiga, por favor, señor, ¿por dónde se va a la biblioteca?

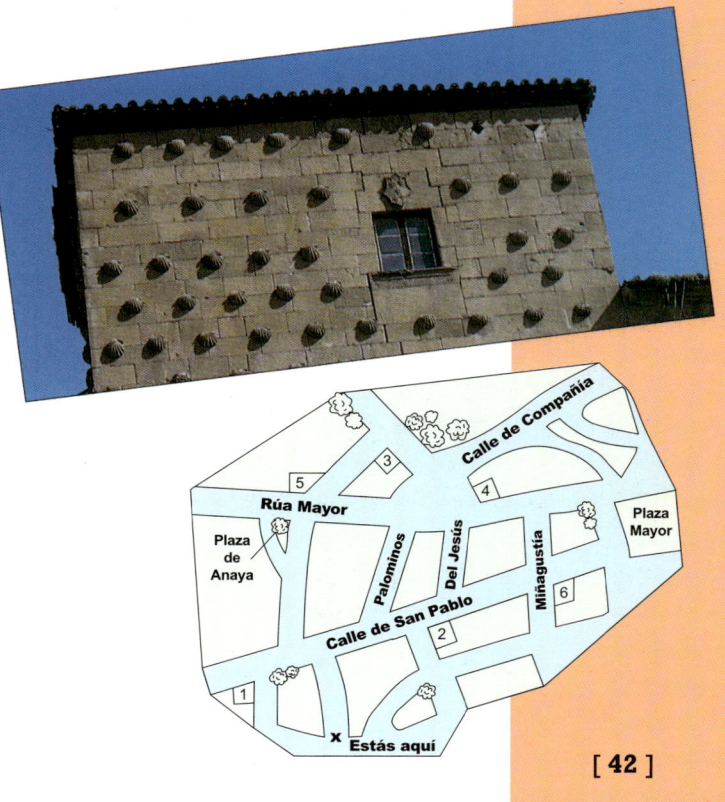

V
oiga
(literally) listen
mire
look
vamos a ver
let's see

Así se dice

To ask how to get to a place, say:

¿Dónde está el/la .....?
   Where is ....?
¿Por dónde se va al/ a la .....?
¿Cómo se va al/a la .....?
   How does one get to .....?

To answer, say:

Todo recto, Sigues todo recto
   You carry on straight on
Sigues hasta el final de la calle
   You carry on to the end of the road
A la derecha, a la izquierda
   To the right, to the left
Giras/Tuerces a la derecha
   You turn right
Tomas/Coges la primera a la izquierda
   You take the first on the left

To finish your description, say:

Y el puerto está ahí/allí
   And the port is there

To show you've understood, say:

Vale/De acuerdo/Bueno *(LA)*
   O.K./All right   ☞ Ex. C, p. 47

4 *Y ahora tú*

Using the plan of Salamanca on the left, what directions would you give to someone wanting to go to the following places? You are standing at x.

a Plaza Mayor   c Calle Miñagustín
b Plaza de Anaya   d Calle del Jesús

Unidad 4

Temas

Andalucía, ayer y hoy

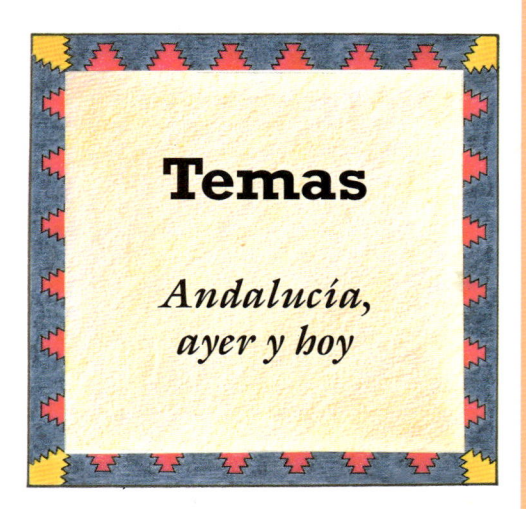

La Andalucía musulmana

For many people, Spain is Andalucía. The stern dancers moving dramatically to the music of the guitar are likely to be members of the gipsy communities first established in Andalucía. And it is the great Arabic buildings, such as the Alhambra in Granada, that are the visual image many people have of Spain. In fact, both buildings and music are a legacy of the Arab society that occupied most of the Iberian Peninsula (what we now know as Spain and Portugal) between 711 and 1492.

The first invasions, in the eighth century, took the Arab troops from North Africa into southern France, before they were driven back again. By the year 801, the new boundaries were established. They did not control Cataluña, Galicia, or the northern kingdoms of Asturias – these remained as Christian kingdoms. But the rest of the Peninsula came under Arab dominion. This was Muslim Spain (**la España musulmana**) and they called it Al-Andalus. Its capital was Córdoba, dominated by its great Mosque (**la Mezquita**).

In Córdoba, the distinctive architecture of Muslim Spain grew out of the combination of the legacy of Roman Spain (multiple arches) and the decor of the East (repeated geometrical patterns, mirror images, abstract forms). The beauty of the city's architecture was mirrored in its poetry and music which reached their richest expression under Abdel Rahman III, Caliph in tenth-century Córdoba. The elegance and symmetry of the palace walls were echoed in the wit and grace of the poetry. Even when political rivalries and power struggles led to the creation of smaller warring city-states (**Reinos de Taifas**), the poets continued to write about love, war, and the meaning of life.

By the beginning of the thirteenth century Granada was the only state left in Muslim hands. Its population of 350,000 lived from trade (with Genoa in particular) and from the production of silk (**la seda**). Thanks to some deft political manoeuvring, Granada outlived its rivals – but it fell in 1492 to the forces of Ferdinand and Isabel, Catholic monarchs of a new state – Spain – dominated by Castilla whose dialect (**el castellano**) now became its official language.

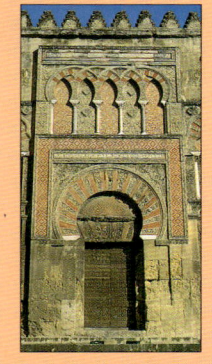

La mezquita de Córdoba

Unidad 4

Los romances fronterizos

The last battles against Granada produced a sequence of ballads called **los romances fronterizos** (frontier ballads). Their anonymous writers abandoned their earlier love poetry to describe the tragedy of war. Among the most famous is the **"Romance del rey moro que perdió Alhama"** (Ballad of the Moorish king who lost Alhama).

**Paseábase el rey moro por la ciudad de Granada
desde la puerta de Elvira hasta la de Vivarrambla
¡Ay de mí Alhama!**

(Calling together his people he tells them of the fall of Alhama)

**Allí habla un moro viejo de esta manera hablara
– ¿Para qué nos llamas rey para qué es esta llamada?
¡Ay de mí Alhama!
Habéis de saber, amigos, una nueva desdichada
que cristianos de braveza ya nos han ganado Granada.**

Federico García Lorca

V

paseábase el rey moro
the Moorish king walked around
la puerta
the city gate
¡Ay de mí Alhama!
Woe is me, Alhama!
una nueva desdichada
a distressing piece of news
ya nos han ganado Granada
they have won Granada from us.

V

el llanto
the weeping
llorar
to weep
callar
to silence
la nevada
the snowy mountains

La Andalucía gitana

Federico García Lorca died in 1936, murdered by unknown assailants for his political views and Bohemian lifestyle. He remains one of Spain's best known poets and playwrights. He devoted part of his work to rediscovering and rewriting the folk songs of his native Andalucía. He used the songs in his plays, most of which are set against an Andalucian background. The sound of the gypsy music of the region, **the cante hondo** (deep song) is famous well beyond Spain, though it is sometimes known as **flamenco**. Lorca described it as deep (**hondo**) from distant peoples (**razas lejanas**), like the sound of a baby's first cry (**el primer llanto**):

"Es hondo, verdaderamente hondo ... mucho más hondo que el corazón que lo crea y la voz que lo canta, porque es casi infinito. Viene de razas lejanas ... Viene del primer llanto y el primer beso." (*Obras completas*, Aguilar, Madrid 1962, p. 1517.)

Flamenco combines the improvised decorative singing of North Africa with the chants of the early Catholic church. It has always excited audiences across the world. At the Great Paris Exhibition of 1900 the flamenco singers at the Spanish Pavilion were the sensation of the day. But it is the singing and the dance that excite; the words are often simple.

**Empieza el llanto
de la guitarra.
Es inútil callarla.
Es imposible
callarla.
Llora monótona
como llora el agua
como llora el viento
sobre la nevada.
Es imposible
callarla.
Llora por cosas
lejanas.**

* Can you say briefly why the guitar weeps?

Unidad 4

Los gitanos de hoy

While gypsy culture is for the outside world one of Spain's main attractions, across the Iberian Peninsula gypsy communities suffer discrimination and rejection. They are often unjustly accused of being responsible for the drug trade. Gypsies (**los gitanos**) have been attacked and even murdered in the street and their homes burned down. These are some of the newspaper headlines that have recently appeared in the Spanish press:

'Quemadas en Salamanca cuatro chabolas gitanas.'
'500 vecinos de Barcelona patrullan su barrio y pegan a drogadictos.'
'Una familia de gitanos asesinada en Bilbao.'
'Los vecinos están contra los gitanos porque el 90 por ciento se dedica a la droga.'

Some Spanish school pupils were asked to give their opinion as to why gypsies were discriminated against, and whether Spain is a racist society...

¿Porqué se margina a la sociedad gitana?

Cristina Traver: **Porque tienen una cultura diferente a la nuestra y no tienen las mismas costumbres que nosotros.**
Alejandro Lorza: **Son gente diferente y pobre.**
Ruth Alonso: **Por falta de comprensión. A la gente no les interesan sus costumbres ni quieren ayudarlos a integrarse.**

V
quemadas burnt
chabola slum/shack
patrullar to patrol
pegar to beat up
los vecinos residents

¿Es España una sociedad racista?

Alejandro: **Aunque la gente no lo acepta, somos una sociedad racista.**
Susana Lareo: **Creo que la mayoría son racistas, aunque más los adultos que los jóvenes.**
Ruth Alonso: **Creo que una gran mayoría de las personas no son racistas.**
David Lopez: **No, no todos los gitanos venden droga. Los verdaderos culpables somos nosotros.**
Susana Lareo: **No todos los gitanos venden droga, hay muchos que son honrados. Los que venden droga lo hacen por necesidad.**

* *How would you sum up the views expressed by these young people on these two issues?*

Veamos de nuevo

Gramática

1 I am, you are + location

In Units 1 and 2 you met the verb **ser** (to be). Spanish also has another verb that means 'to be' – **estar**, mainly used to say where something is.

¿Dónde está el hotel?
Where is the hotel?
¿Dónde estás?
Where are you?
Estoy en Granada.
I am in Granada

Here is the present tense:

estoy	I am	estamos	we are
estás	you are	estáis	you are
está	he/she is, you are (formal)	están	they are, you are (formal)

(See G 9.5 for other uses)

2 I am going, are you going?

If you want to say where you are going you will need to use the verb **ir** (to go). It is irregular and doesn't behave like any other verb. Here is its present tense:

voy	I go	vamos	we go
vas	you go	vais	you go
va	he/she/it goes, you go (formal)	van	they go, you go (formal)

Unidad 4

G

Note: When **a** or **de** is followed by **el**, the two words contract into one:

a + el = al
al cine
de + el = del
del banco

Práctica

Note that **voy**, can mean either 'I go' or 'I am going'

Va a la escuela
He goes to school or He is going to school

3 Near and far

Words used to express where things are in relation to each other, e.g. 'near', 'far from', 'behind', 'beside', etc. are called prepositions. These can be single words like **a** (to, at), **de** (of, from) or **en** (in), or a combination of words. In this unit you have met several combinations.

El banco está *cerca de* la catedral *near (to)*
El parque está *lejos de* las tiendas *far from*
La iglesia está *detrás de* la plaza *behind*
La escuela está *delante del* parque *in front of*
El museo está *dentro de* la catedral *within*
El bar está *al lado del* teatro *beside*

A Nobody at home!

Pepe has arrived home to find the house is empty. This note from his wife, however, can explain everything! Can you complete it with the appropriate form of **estar**?

No ..... en casa. Marco y Juan ..... en el parque y María ..... en la universidad. José Luis y yo ..... en el supermercado. Si quieres comer, el queso ..... en la nevera y el pan ..... en la mesa. ¡Hasta luego!

B Make yourself useful!

People ask you where various places are in your town. Can you tell them?

e.g. **¿Dónde está la escuela?**
 (next to the church)
 Está al lado de la iglesia

1 **¿Dónde está la farmacia?** (near the cathedral)
2 **¿Dónde está el teatro?** (opposite the bank)

[46]

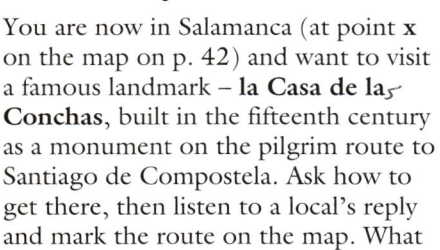

3 ¿Dónde está la oficina de turismo? (in the main square)
4 ¿Dónde está el parque? (behind the school)
5 ¿Dónde está el bar? (in front of the hotel)

C ¿Cómo se va a la catedral?

Unfortunately, nobody knows how to get there, so you have to direct them.

e.g. **La iglesia?** (First street on the right, it's there on the left)
Tomas la primera calle a la derecha. Está ahí a la izquierda.

1 ¿La catedral? (Second street on the left, in the main square)
2 ¿El banco? (Straight on. 100 metres on the right)
3 ¿La Plaza Mayor? (First street on the right, then straight ahead)
4 ¿La escuela? (In this street, 50 metres on the left)
5 ¿El hotel? (Second street on the right, opposite the library)

D Play the game, eat the cherries!

Follow the directions, collecting cherries and strawberries as you go. How many of each do you collect?

Unidad 4

Un paso más

1 2ª a la izquierda   7 2ª a la derecha
2 1ª a la derecha   8 2ª a la izquierda
3 3ª a la izquierda   9 1ª a la izquierda
4 2ª a la izquierda   10 1ª a la derecha
5 1ª a la izquierda   11 1ª a la izquierda
6 1ª a la derecha   12 todo recto al final

1 Backpacker

You are travelling around Spain and have just arrived in Salamanca. You need lodgings and want more information about the town. You go to the Tourist Office and ask for the following:

a if there is a hotel nearby.
b if the hotel is far from the city centre.
c what there is to see near the town.
d how far it is from the town.
e how one gets there.

2 Tour of Salamanca

You are now in Salamanca (at point **x** on the map on p. 42) and want to visit a famous landmark – **la Casa de las Conchas**, built in the fifteenth century as a monument on the pilgrim route to Santiago de Compostela. Ask how to get there, then listen to a local's reply and mark the route on the map. What number building is it?

Unidad 4

3 Latin American holiday

While studying in Madrid, you visit a travel agency where you happen to pick up a brochure about Lima.

Lima moderna. Lima tradicional.

Fundada en 1535, Lima, famosa por su aire señorial y su clima suave acoge a quienes la visitan. El centro de la ciudad es el Cercado, con plazas y monumentos arquitectónicos de estilo colonial. En ese sector está la plaza de Armas con el Palacio de Gobierno. Al lado del Palacio de Gobierno está la catedral, que presenta una mezcla de estilos arquitectónicos. Dentro del templo se encuentra el Museo de Arte religioso y el Palacio Arzobispal.

A una cuadra de la plaza de Armas está el convento de Santo Domingo, el primer convento de Lima, fundado en 1535. Al lado del convento está el santuario de Santa Rosa de Lima, la 'patrona de América' con el pozo de los deseos donde los devotos diariamente arrojan sus cartas para que la santa acoja sus peticiones. Lima es un centro cultural por excelencia. A cinco minutos de la plaza se encuentra la Escuela nacional de Bellas Artes. Hay otros museos importantes en Lima como el Museo de la Nación. El Museo de Oro tiene piezas importantes de las culturas antiguas del Perú.

Los dos principales barrios residenciales, Barranco y Miraflores, están bastante lejos del centro. Pero es allí donde se encuentran las tiendas y los restaurantes más populares de la ciudad.

(Adapted from *Así es el Perú*, set. 93, año 1, No. 1)

Hoping to persuade someone to go with you, you phone a Spanish friend to tell him about the city.
He wants to know:

a ¿Dónde está la catedral?
b ¿Dónde está el Palacio Arzobispal?
c ¿Hay museos y galerías?
d ¿Dónde están los bares y restaurantes?

4 Checklist

Can you do the following both in speech and writing?

a Ask for information about a place.
b Ask for directions to get to a place.
c Understand directions you are given.
d Ask about and understand distances.

V

acoge
welcomes

una mezcla
a mixture

el pozo de los deseos
wishing-well into which devout people throw letters hoping the Saint will grant their requests

Lima

Unidad 5

En el mercado

Así se habla
Shopping for groceries
Shopping for fruit and vegetables
Finding out what things cost

Temas
El encuentro de los gustos

Veamos de nuevo

Así se habla 1

¿Me da una barra de pan?

Shopping for groceries

Unidad 5

V

¿qué más?
¿algo más?
anything else
nada más
nothing else

1

You will hear the names of various items which you can buy in a food store or grocery shop. As you listen, tick the items you hear and then say them out loud.

- el vino
- el aceite
- el pan
- la leche
- el jamón
- las patatas fritas
- las sardinas
- los huevos
- el queso
- las galletas
- el arroz
- las patatas (Sp)
- las papas (LA)

2

Begoña and Miguel have gone shopping. Can you list three items each of them buys? (Don't worry about the quantities for now.)

Begoña: ....
Miguel: ....

Así se acostumbra

In Spain there are many different varieties of ham, sausages (**embutidos**) and cheese. Here are some of them:

jamón: jamón de york, jamón serrano, and the most exclusive **jamón de jabugo** – also known as **pata negra**;

embutidos: different types of **chorizo**, **salchichón** and **morcilla** (black pudding)

queso: queso manchego (originally from La Mancha), **queso de Burgos**

3

Here are three other shoppers asking for various food items. What three phrases do they use?

a – Hola, buenos días.
  – Buenos días.
  – ¿Me da una barra de pan?
  – ¿Algo más?
  – No, nada más.

b – Hola, buenos días.
  – Hola.
  – Quiero una barra de pan.
  – ¿Grande, pequeña?
  – Sí, grande.

c – Buenos días.
  – Buenos días.
  – Eh, quería jamón de york.
  – Jamón de york...

Unidad 5

Así se dice

To ask for something in a shop, say:

¿Me da...?
   Can I have ...?
Quiero... Quería... Quisiera...
   I'd like   ☞ Ex C, p. 58

Or you can simply say:

Por favor
Una barra de pan, por favor
   A loaf of bread, please

4 *Y ahora tú*

It's your turn to go shopping.
How would you ask for a) bread b) milk c) crisps d) biscuits? Try and use a different way of asking for each one.

5

Here is a list of words for quantities and containers.

Pesos y medidas
Weights and measures

cien gramos	100 grams
un kilo	1 kilo
medio kilo	half a kilo
kilo y medio	1½ kilos
un litro	a litre
una barra	a loaf
una botella	a bottle
una bolsa	a bag
un paquete	a packet
una lata	a tin
una caja	a box/case
un bote	a jar

🔊 ²

Look back at the list you made of the items which Begoña and Miguel asked for (Activity 2). This time listen for the details of each item they ask for and make a note of them.

G
querer
to want
(See p. 57)

6

Can you ask for the following items:

e.g. **una botella de vino.**

a
b
c
d

7 *Y ahora tú*

You have to make a packed lunch for four people. Make a list of what you might need, with quantities, and not forgetting that they want wine to drink. How would you ask for these items once you get to the shop?

8 *De tiendas*

The names of many food shops are based on what they sell: e.g. **la panadería** (baker's) sells **pan** (bread).
Can you match these food products to the places where you buy them?

pan	la charcutería
pasteles (pastries)	la confitería
pescado (fish)	el mercado
carne (meat)	la pastelería
verduras	la pescadería
chorizo y jamón	la panadería
confites (sweets)	la carnicería

Unidad 5

9 🔊⁴

You will hear a Spanish woman saying where she buys different types of food. Tick the products and shops you hear mentioned on the list in Activity 8.

> ### Así se dice
> To indicate where you do your shopping you can say:
>
> **Compro pan en la panadería**
> I buy bread at the baker's

10

In big towns in Spain, and around the Hispanic World, the supermarket (**el supermercado**) is nowadays where you do most of your shopping, but imagine you are living in a small town with no supermarket. Can you say where you'd buy the five products (right)?

e.g. **Compro carne en la carnicería.**

a ..... b ..... c ..... d ..... e .....

2
¿Tiene pepinos?
Shopping for fruit and vegetables

1

Match the English words for fruit and vegetables with their Spanish equivalents.

a	la pera	i	lemon
b	la coliflor	ii	pear
c	el tomate	iii	melon
d	el melón	iv	tomato
e	el limón	v	cauliflower

2 🔊⁵

Look at the pictures and read aloud the names of the fruit and vegetables on the market stall (**el puesto**). Now listen to the market seller describing what he sells. Can you tick those he mentions which are also in the picture?

Labels in picture: uva, naranja, manzana, sandía, plátano, melón, pomelo toronja, pera, tomate (Sp), melocotón (Sp) durazno (LA), patata papa, jitomate tomate (LA), cebolla, puerro, ajo, zanahoria, pepino, limón, coliflor, pimiento rojo, pimiento verde, lechuga

> ### Así se acostumbra
> In most places in the Spanish-speaking world people buy fruit, vegetables and other types of food in their local market (**el mercado**). In Mexico the market is sometimes called **el tianguis** (an Aztec word), in Argentina **la feria** (literally, 'the fair'), and sometimes in Ecuador **la plaza**. In Latin America prices are often open to negotiation, so you might need to bargain (**regatear**).

[52]

Unidad 5

3 🔊⁶

Here are three people in the market buying fruit and vegetables. What quantities of each do they buy?

a – ¿Cuántos pepinos quiere?
  – Ah, como ....
b – ¿Tiene patatas?
  – ¿Cuántas patatas quiere?
  – Me da ....
c – ¿Cuántos plátanos desea?
  – Quisiera .... , por favor.

Así se dice

If you're not sure whether something is available or not you can ask:

¿Tiene pepinos?
  Do you have any cucumbers?
¿Hay plátanos?
  Are there any bananas?

You might be asked how many you want:

¿Cuántas (manzanas) quiere?
  How many (apples) do you want?
  ☞ Ex A, p. 57

4 🔊⁷

Ana is at a market in Mexico, buying what she needs for a salad. Here is her shopping list:

2 pimientos rojos
½ kilo de tomates
1 kilo de cebollas
1 kilo de pepinos

Now listen to her conversation with the stallholder. Does she buy exactly what was on her list?
Can you make a note of what and how much of each she buys and how much she has to pay?

V
como
around

V
pimiento
pepper
verde
green
rojo
red
amarillo
yellow
una ensalada
a salad
de acuerdo
agreed
¿qué desea?
what would you like?
¿qué otra cosita le doy?
what else can I get you?

5 Y ahora tú

If you were going to the market to buy your weekly fruit and vegetables, how would you ask for them? First make a shopping list of your groceries. Then ask the shopkeeper if each is available and say how much you want.

e.g. ¿Tiene manzanas? Me da dos kilos.

Así se acostumbra

Nowadays, particularly in Spain, you buy food items by the kilo, but in some places you still buy them by the pound (**la libra**). Fruit and some vegetables can be bought by the unit as in **una piña** (one pineapple) or in some places by the dozen (**una docena de mangos**) or even in larger quantities: you might see oranges at **cinco euros tres kilos** (five euros for three kilos)

6

See how the numbers 100 to 25 000 are formed. Practise saying them aloud.

100 cien
101 ciento uno
105 ciento cinco
200 doscientos
210 doscientos diez
333 trescientos treinta y tres
460 cuatrocientos sesenta
512 quinientos doce

680 seiscientos ochenta
715 setecientos quince
809 ochocientos nueve
926 novecientos veintiséis
1 000 mil
2 000 dos mil
10 005 diez mil cinco
25 500 veinticinco mil quinientos

Now try saying the following numbers:

a 442   b 125   c 600   d 1 410   e 532   f 13 250

[53]

Unidad 5

3

¿A cómo está el jamón?
Finding out what things cost

1 🔊⁸

You will hear several people asking the price of items in the market. Listen carefully and fill in the prices.

a – Y ¿a cómo son estos tomates?
– A ..... el kilo.

b – ¿Me dice a cómo es el kilo de mangos?
– El kilo de mangos está a ..... pesos.
– ...De acuerdo, gracias.

c – ¿A cómo está la almendra ahora?
– A ..... el kilo.

Así se dice

To ask for the price of things (per kilo) you can ask:

¿A cómo *está* el kilo de manzanas?
¿A cómo *es* el kilo de manzanas?
How much *is* a kilo of apples?

¿A cómo *están* las naranjas?
¿A cómo *son* las naranjas?
How much *are* the oranges?

2

Here is your shopping list.
Before asking for each item you need to check the price per kilo, e.g.

¿A cómo está el kilo de tomates?
Quiero tres kilos.

Shopping list:
TOMATOES – 3 KILOS
POTATOES – 2 KILOS
APPLES – ½ KILO
CHEESE – 250 GRAMS
HAM – 500 GRAMS

V

estos – these
¿me dice ...? – can you tell me ...?
de acuerdo – OK
la almendra – almond
ahora – now, (*here*) today

	€/KILO
PATATA	0,75
CEBOLLA	0,75
PEPINO	1,10
TOMATE	1,49
MANGO	2,99
NARANJA	1,95
MANZANA	1,59
PERA	1,89
QUESO	
MANCHEGO	15,90
JAMÓN SERRANO	16,20

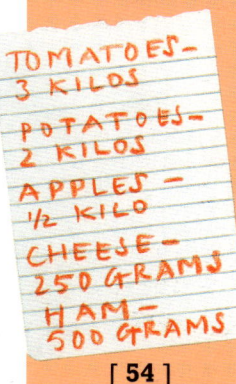

---

3 🔊⁹

Listen to five people in different countries asking how much they have to pay and tick each amount as you hear it.

a 20 ___   d 7,35 ___
b 17,50 ___   e 15.000 ___
c 12,20 ___

Así se dice

To ask for the total cost you can say:
¿Cuánto es (todo/en total)?
How much is it (altogether)?

to which the answer might be:
Son ... (mil pesos)
That's ... (1000 pesos)

And when you pay you can say:
Tenga, Tome or **Aquí tiene**
Here you are

4

Look again at Activity 2 and try asking what the total bill is. Checking the price list can you work out what the shopkeeper will reply?

Las divisas
Currencies

Here are some currencies to be found in Spanish-speaking countries:

España	el euro (€)
México, Chile, Argentina, Colombia, Uruguay	el peso
Perú	el sol oro
Ecuador	el dólar
Venezuela	el bolívar
Nicaragua	el córdoba
Honduras	la lempira
Guatemala	el quetzal

Note: **el quetzal** is taken from the name of a bird, **el bolívar** alludes to Simón Bolívar (**el libertador** – the liberator).

Temas

El encuentro de los gustos

Unidad 5

Many of our everyday fruits and vegetables came originally from Latin America; it was in Aztec Mexico, for example, that the Spanish Conquistadores first came face to face with the tomato (**el jitomate**, as the Aztecs called it, and the Spaniards shortened it to **el tomate**), and the maize or Indian corn (**el elote**, they called it, or **el maíz**) that was the most important food across the whole continent. And it was during the Conquest of Peru, then ruled by the Incas, that Spain first came across the potato (**la papa** in Latin America; **la patata** in Spain).

New kinds of fruit, too, travelled to Spain – the pineapple (**la piña** or **el ananás**) for example, the banana (**el plátano**) and the avocado (**el aguacate** or **la palta**). And a world fascinated by spices was excited by the many varieties of hot pepper (**el chile** or **el ají**) which the native people used to preserve their food. Maize, bananas, potatoes and chile are still part of a staple diet for millions – but in new forms. Maize becomes a dough (**una masa**) to make the corn pancakes called **tortillas** (**arepas** in Colombia and Venezuela); (although, in Spain **una tortilla** means something quite different – an omelette).

Drinks were different too. In Spain people drank wine, red or white (**el vino tinto** or **el vino blanco**) as well as beer (**la cerveza**) or cider (**la sidra**). The Spanish introduced these into Latin America, adding to the local brews like **la tequila** in Mexico (made from the sap of **el maguey**, the agave cactus) or **la chicha** in Peru, Bolivia and Ecuador (brewed from fermented maize). In Central America and the Caribbean the sugar the Spaniards brought from Africa also produced the universal rum (**el ron**, sometimes called **el aguardiente**). Today Chile and Argentina, for example, produce fine wines of their own and every Latin American country has its own brewery.

Over the years other peoples have added their tastes and ingredients to Latin American food. Corn pancakes are now rolled up and filled with meat to make **taco**; banana leaves are filled with dough and cooked in the ground to make **tamales**. Almonds from Spain were mixed with Mexican chocolate and chile to make **mole** sauce; and kidney beans (**los frijoles** or **los porotos**) became part of the staple diet everywhere.

Unidad 5

Recetas de cocina (Recipes)

Can you identify the main ingredients of each of the following recipes? Use the dictionary if necessary.

* *Do you know any Spanish or Latin American dishes?*

Paella valenciana
4 cucharadas de aceite
medio pollo (cuarteado)
200 gr. de judías verdes
125 gr. de mejillones
1 tomate
125 gr de gambas
12 caracoles (opcional)
5 puñados de arroz
1 litro de agua (templada)
sal
pimentón
azafrán de hebra

Frijoles de olla estilo Veracruz
4 litros de agua
Medio kilo de frijoles negros, lavados y remojados 12 horas
2 cebollas blancas
2 clavos de ajo
30 hojas de culantro
400 gr. de tocino
1½ taza queso feta
3 chiles jalapeños

The versatile tortilla

Mexican food has become enormously popular in recent years. The basis of it is the **tortilla** made of maize or wheat, wrapped around different ingredients. In fact the **tortilla** is amazingly versatile – you can eat it rolled or flat, hot or cold, fried or in a soup.

* *How many different names can you find for tortilla-based dishes?*

"Oda a la cebolla"

The great Chilean poet Pablo Neruda wrote several odes (**odas**) to his favourite foods. They include his **"Oda a la cebolla"** (Ode to the onion)

...la tierra
así te hizo,
cebolla,
clara como un planeta,
y destinada
a relucir,
constelación constante,
redonda rosa de agua
sobre
la mesa
de las pobres gentes.
....

Pablo Neruda

Neruda sees the onion as 'clear as a planet', a 'constant constellation', a 'rose of water' on the table of 'the poor people'.

* *Can you find the Spanish equivalents of these phrases?*
* *Could you describe this poem as a celebration of ordinary food?*

Unidad 5

Veamos de nuevo
Gramática

1 I want, you want ...

Quiero is part of the verb **querer** and means literally 'I want'. However, it sounds less direct in Spanish – and can be used to mean 'I'd like' when used in shopping, for example. If you want to be even more polite you can use **quería** or **quisiera** (I should like), which are also parts of the verb querer. **Querer** belongs to a group of verbs called *radical-changing* which have regular endings but change their *root*. The root of the verb is the part which remains when you remove the ending (-**ar**, -**er** or -**ir**). Thus the root of **querer** is **quer**-. Note that the root change only occurs in the singular forms and in the 3rd person plural. Here is the present tense:

qu*i*ero	I want
qu*i*eres	you want (informal)
qu*i*ere	he/she wants, you want (formal)
queremos	we want
queréis	you want (informal)
qu*i*eren	they want, you want (formal)

For more radical-changing verbs see Unit 10, p. 112 and G 9.2.

2 This, that, these and those

These words (demonstrative adjectives) change according to the gender and number of the word they refer to.

this	that
este melón	*ese* melón
esta manzana	*esa* manzana

these	those
estos plátanos	*esos* plátanos
estas patatas	*esas* patatas

3 How much/how many

If you want to ask how much to pay you say ¿**Cuánto es?** or ¿**Cuánto cuesta?** When used as an adjective, however, the ending of ¿**Cuánto?** changes according to the gender and number of the noun it refers to.

¿Cuánto	queso quiere?
¿Cuánta	carne quiere?
¿Cuántos	pimientos quiere?
¿Cuántas	barras de pan quiere?

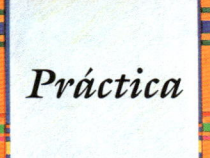

Práctica

A Ask about quantities

You want to know how much of something you get in the packet or container. How do you ask?

e.g. **¿Cuántas galletas hay en el paquete?**

1	box of eggs
2	tin of sardines
3	a case of bottles of wine
4	box of chocolates
5	bag of oranges
6	box of matches (**cerillas**)
	una caja box, **una cajita** little box

B This or that?

How do you tell the shopkeeper which particular item you want? Practise asking for the goods in Exercise A.

e.g. **Me da ese/este paquete de galletas**

Unidad 5

C What do you want?

Complete the sentences with the correct form of **querer**.

e.g. Juan no ..... pepinos.
    Juan no quiere pepinos.

1 María ..... dos kilos de patatas.
2 ¿Qué ..... usted?
3 (Yo) ..... un paquete de galletas.
4 ¿Cuántas manzanas ..... (tú)?
5 Los hijos ..... una barra grande.

1 El mercado

Read the following passage to understand the gist of it.

El mercado es uno de los elementos más importantes de la cultura hispana. Grande o pequeño, cubierto o al aire libre, es el foco de reunión en pueblos y ciudades.

Por ejemplo, el antiguo mercado de Santo Tomás en Bilbao es una feria-concurso donde se vende fruta, animales y plantas. Hay otros mercados famosos en la geografía española como el del Rastro en Madrid donde hay animales domésticos, ropa, artesanía, antigüedades y curiosidades; y el mercado de frutas y verduras de Valencia es uno de los más grandes de Europa. En México la Lagunilla es muy famoso y típico y hay de todo. En el Perú, el mercado semanal de la ciudad de Huancayo tiene mucha fama. Y en El Salvador el mercado Cuartel tiene artesanías, flores y frutas.

Which markets sell which products? Fill in the grid below.

	fruit/veg	plants	animals	antiques	handicrafts
Santo Tomás					
El Rastro					
Central					
Lagunilla					
Cuartel					

Un paso más

V
puerros leeks
una cucharada spoonful
un vaso glass
una pizca pinch

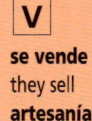

V
se vende they sell
artesanía handicrafts

---

2 At work

You work for a company called Juan Ruiz which imports exotic groceries. Your boss shows you an advert from a new supplier, and asks you to find out details of some of them:

**melocotones en coñac
anchoas en jerez
aceitunas en vino**

You phone the supplier. You need to:
a introduce yourself and say who you work for;
b ask the price of the olives and anchovies;
c say you'd like 30 jars of peaches and 24 tins of anchovies.
Try to invent one or two more exotic products and ask for them too!

3 Los menús de Arguiñano 🔊 10

On a Spanish TV cookery programme you have just seen the recipe for a vegetable soup. Unfortunately, you missed the actual quantities. So, you phone a friend who gives you the recipe in full. Can you fill them in?

..... zanahorias   ..... aceite
..... puerros   ..... agua
..... coliflor   ..... vino blanco
..... patatas   ..... sal
..... jamón serrano

4 Checklist

Can you do the following?

a Say what you want to buy.
b Ask whether a shop has a particular product.
c Ask the price of a particular item.
d Ask for a particular quantity of something.
e Ask how much it all costs.

Puesta a punto 1

1 Matchmakers

Match the answers to the appropriate questions.

a	¿Cómo te llamas?	i	Vivo en Madrid.
b	¿De dónde eres?	ii	Soy dentista.
c	¿Dónde vives?	iii	Sí, tres hermanos y dos hermanas.
d	¿Cómo es Madrid?	iv	Me llamo Berta Montes Bertrán.
e	¿A qué distancia está de León?	v	Es una ciudad moderna e interesante.
f	¿En qué barrio vives?	vi	Soy de León.
g	¿A qué te dedicas?	vii	Está a unos trescientos kilómetros.
h	¿Tienes familia?	viii	Vivo cerca del centro, en Argüelles.

2 Ser or Estar

Complete the sentences with the correct form of **ser** or **estar** as appropriate.

a Lima ..... en el Perú.
b Ion y Begoña ..... vascos.
c Málaga ..... turística y famosa.
d ¿Cuánto ..... todo?
e Las tiendas ..... enfrente del cine.
f ¿A qué distancia ..... Segovia de Madrid?
g (Yo) ..... médico.

3 ¡Qué desorden!

Put the words in the correct order.

a barrio alegre muy es Mi.
b ¿tu en ciudad hay Qué?
c ¿por un Hay aquí hotel?
d bares una tiene y restaurante un Mi pueblo muchos iglesia.
e La está lado iglesia del al Ayuntamiento.
f ¿oficina está turismo la Dónde de?

4 Clases y grupos

Classify the words under the correct headings. A few words can belong to more than one group.

español	tomate	ayuntamiento
lechuga	recepcionista	francesa
moderno	profesor	melocotón
Correos	argentino	inglés hotel
antigua	farmacia cocinera	pequeño
jamón	mexicana italiano	pintor
grande manzana	acogedor	estudiante
bar parque	iglesia artístico	vasco

Nationalities
Languages
Professions
Places
Descriptions
Food

5 La vida de Maruja

First complete the text, by choosing the correct verb for each gap and using the appropriate form. Then rewrite the text in the first person, as if Maruja were talking.

ser vivir trabajar estudiar hablar ir tener

Maruja Serrano ..... de Málaga en el sur de España. ..... con su marido en Torremolinos. Maruja ..... cincuenta y tres años. ..... en una oficina. Juan, su marido, ... jubilado. ..... sesenta y siete años. Los dos ..... inglés. Ellos ..... francés cuando ..... a Francia. ..... dos hijas y un hijo. Sus hijos ..... en las afueras de Madrid, pero ..... en el centro de la capital.

6 ¿Qué adjetivo?

Complete the sentences with the correct adjective from the list below.

inglés bonita francesas españoles cálida sevillanas tranquilo antiguo irlandesa

a María y Carlos son ..... .
b En el mercado tienen manzanas ..... y naranjas ..... .
c John es ..... , pero su mujer, Siobham, es ..... .
d Los Martínez viven en un barrio ..... y ..... .
e Trujillo es una ciudad ...... y ..... .

7 En la tienda

Complete the conversation in a grocer's shop by filling in the missing words.

Tendero: Buenos días. ¿Qué .....?
Señora: Buenos días. ¿A ..... está el queso manchego?
Tendero: Está de oferta a ..... euros el kilo.
Señora: Pues, un kilo.
Tendero: ¿ ..... más?
Señora: Sí, un pan de molde.
Tendero: Son ..... euros ¿ ..... más?
Señora: Dos ..... de patatas fritas y una ..... de aceite de oliva.
Tendero: Muy bien, ¿eso es todo?
Señora: Sí, ¿ ..... es?
Tendero: Son ..... en total.

2,95 €
1,20 €
15,90 €/Kg
1,39 €

Puesta a punto 1

8 Puesta a punto oral

Imagine you meet a few people in Spain. Can you in each case ask an appropriate question? Use the **tú** or **usted** forms of the verb as appropriate.

a Ask a young man what his name is and where he is from.
b Ask a policeman whether he speaks English.
c Ask a little girl what her name is.
d Ask a Spanish friend if he has got a map of Madrid.
e Ask the receptionist at your hotel if she has got any children, and their ages.
f Ask an elderly lady if she goes shopping in the market.
g Ask two women to describe their city.
h Ask a market trader what fruit she has got.

Unidad 6

Así se nos va el día

Así se habla
Saying how often you do things

Talking about the time

Describing your daily routine

Temas
El ritmo de vida

Veamos de nuevo

Unidad 6

Así se habla 1

Preparo la cena todas las noches

Saying how often you do things

1

Here is a list of household chores (**las tareas domésticas**). First, check their meaning in the Glossary. Which of them does Carlos do? Listen and tick the ones you hear mentioned.

a limpiar la casa
b preparar la cena
c lavar la ropa
d planchar
e fregar los platos (Sp) / lavar los platos (LA)
f sacar la basura
g barrer
h cocinar

2

You are planning your week. Can you note down in your diary when to do various household jobs?

| lunes / Monday |
| martes / Tuesday |
| miércoles / Wednesday |
| jueves / Thursday |
| viernes / Friday |
| sábado / Saturday |
| domingo / Sunday |

3

Look at the examples and say what the expressions on the left mean:

todos los días	every day
todas las mañanas	....
todas las tardes	....
todas las noches	....
todos los sábados	every Saturday
todos los domingos	....
una vez a la semana	once a week
dos veces a la semana	....
nunca	never

(See W 20 for more of these expressions)

4

Isabel talks about how often she does things in the house. Listen and fill in the gaps, using expressions from Activity 3.

Limpio la casa y barro el patio ..... preparo la cena ....., lavo la ropa ..... y ..... plancho.

G
limpiar
-ar verbs

barrer
-er verbs

(See p. 69)

Así se dice

To indicate how often you do something, say:

Preparo la cena todas las noches
  I make the dinner every night
Barro el patio todos los sábados
  I sweep the patio every Saturday

And if you never do something, say:

Nunca plancho *or* **No plancho nunca**
  I never do the ironing

To talk about what someone else does, say:

Prepara la cena
  He/She makes the dinner
Barre el patio
  He/She sweeps the patio

☞ Ex. A, B, C, p. 69

5

Look at the pictures of Mafalda's mother doing the traditional chores. How would she describe what she does? Use the verbs **lavar/secar los platos**, **cocinar**, **preparar la ensalada**.

6 *Y ahora tú*

Say how often you do **las tareas domésticas** in Activity 1.

e.g. **Limpio la casa todos los días.**

7

Which of these activities do you do regularly?

a leer el periódico
b escribir cartas
c beber vino
d comer chocolates
e hablar por teléfono

🔊 3 Isabel asks Ana and Jorge how often they do these things. Can you say who does what and how often?

Ana .....   Jorge .....

Así se dice

To find out what someone does, ask:

¿Bebes vino?
   Do you drink wine?
Sí, bebo vino (a veces)
   Yes, I drink wine (sometimes)

To say what someone else does:

Bebe vino (todas las noches)
   He/She drinks wine (every night)
☞ Ex. A, B, C, p. 69

Unidad 6

V

a veces
sometimes
de vez en cuando
from time to time

[63]

8

You are putting together a questionnaire about domestic and household activities. What questions would you ask?

e.g. **¿Limpias la casa? ¿Lees el periódico?**

9

If a friend answered this questionnaire, how would his/her answers differ from yours? What would you have in common?

e.g. **Yo limpio la casa, pero mi amigo no (limpia la casa). Mi amigo lee el periódico todos los días.**

2
¿Qué hora es?
Talking about the time

1 🔊 4

Listen to people asking and saying what time it is and tick the times as you hear them.

¿Qué hora es?

Son las dos.

Son las diez.

Es la una.

Unidad 6

Así se dice

To ask the time, say:

¿Qué hora es?

And to answer:

Es la una
   It's one o'clock
Son las dos en punto
   It's exactly two o'clock

To make clear whether it is morning, afternoon, etc., say:

Son las diez de la mañana
   It's ten o'clock in the morning
Es la una de la tarde
   It's one o'clock in the afternoon
Son las nueve de la noche
   It's nine o'clock in the evening

If you are using the 24-hour clock, say:

Son las dieciocho horas
   It's 18:00 hours (6 p.m.)

2

Read these times aloud:

a 9:00   b 12:00   c 5:00   d 23:00

3

Listen to the time given on the radio and 'set' the correct time on each clock.

Así se dice

Here are some other expressions of time:

Son las tres y cinco	It's 3:05
Son las tres y cuarto	It's 3:15
Son las tres y media	It's 3:30
Son las cuatro menos veinte	It's 3:40
Son las cuatro menos cuarto	It's 3:45

And in some parts of Latin America, you will hear instead:

Es un cuarto para las cuatro	It's 3:45
Son diez para las cuatro	It's 3:50

V
Es mediodía
It's midday
Es medianoche
It's midnight

4

Practise asking and telling the time:

a 3:10   b 2:30   c 5:15   d 10:35
e 11:50   f 1:20   g 7:45   h 8:05

5 ¿A qué hora?

Isabel is reading the entertainment section in a Spanish newspaper. She phones to make enquiries. Can you say:

a what she is enquiring about?
b what time the performance starts?

Así se dice

To ask what time an event is happening, say:

¿A qué hora es la película/el concierto?
   What time is the film/the concert?

And to answer, say:

Es a las cuatro
   It's at four o'clock

6 Y ahora tú

What questions would you ask to find out when the other events take place?

3
Me levanto a las siete de la mañana
Describing your daily routine

1 🔊 7

Listen to two people – a housewife and a soldier – Talking about their daily routine. Listen and read the conversations and find out who gets up (**se levanta**) earlier and who goes to bed (**se acuesta**) later.

– ¿A qué hora se levanta?
– A las seis y media, siete menos cuarto, una cosa así.
– ¿A qué hora se acuesta?
– A las doce.

– ¿A qué hora te levantas?
– Me levanto a las siete de la mañana.
– ¿Y a qué hora te acuestas?
– A las diez de la noche.

Así se dice

To ask at what time someone gets up and goes to bed, say:

¿A qué hora te levantas/te acuestas?
(informal)
¿A qué hora se levanta/se acuesta?
(formal)
   What time do you get up/go to bed?

To answer you can say:

(Yo) me levanto a las siete y media
   I get up at 7:30
(Yo) me acuesto a las doce
   I go to bed at 12:00

Unidad 6

V
normalmente
normally
una cosa así
something like that

G
levantarse
acostarse
etc.

(See p. 69)

---

2 Y ahora tú

¿A qué hora te levantas normalmente?
¿Y a qué hora te acuestas normalmente?
¿Y los fines de semana?

Así se dice

To ask about someone else, say:

¿A qué hora se levanta/se acuesta?
   What time does he/she get up/go to bed?
Se levanta/Se acuesta a las ...
   He/She gets up/goes to bed at ...

se acuesta   se levanta

3

Look at what Pedro and Mari-Ángeles do when they get up in the morning.

se baña   se ducha
se afeita   se maquilla

Can you say what you do?

Unidad 6

4

María is a student. The pictures represent her daily routine, but they are not in the right order. Can you order them so that they make sense of her day?

1. voy a clases
2. me acuesto
3. vuelvo a casa
4. desayuno
5. salgo de casa
6. termino clases
7. me levanto
8. ceno
9. como

a ..... b ..... c .....
d ..... e ..... f .....
g ..... h ..... i .....

🔊 8 Now listen to María talking about her routine and compare your answers. Also find out what time she does some of these things.

5

Now say what María's daily routine is. Start like this:

María se levanta ...

G
salgo/sal*ir*
to leave
vuelvo/volver
to return

G
empiezo/empez*ar*
to start
(See G 9.2)

V
sobre las ocho
at about 8 o'clock

6 *Y ahora tú*

¿Cómo es tu rutina diaria?

Describe your daily routine and say when you do things. Start: **Me levanto a las .....**

7 *El horario de trabajo*
🔊 9

Three people talk about their timetable. Who works the longest hours?

Carmen: ¿Cuál es tu horario de trabajo?
Julia: **A las siete y media salgo de casa. Llego a las ocho. A las ocho empiezo a trabajar. Termino a las tres de la tarde y, habitualmente, vuelvo en autobús a mi casa.**
Martín: **Empiezo a trabajar a las ocho. Y de las ocho, pues, hasta la una. A la una comemos, bueno de una a tres ... y de tres a cinco, pues, otra vez al trabajo.**
Teresa: **Por lo general de diez de la mañana a tres o cuatro de la tarde. Los domingos llego a eso de las nueve y media de la mañana... hasta las dos de la tarde.**

Así se dice

To indicate what time you start, say:

Empiezo a trabajar a las ocho
Empiezo el trabajo a las ocho
  I start to work/work at eight

To indicate when you finish, say:

Termino de estudiar a las seis
Termino las clases a las seis
  I finish studying/classes at six

You can also say:

Trabajo/estudio de nueve a tres
... desde las nueve hasta las tres
  I work/study from nine to three

8 *Y ahora tú*

If you work:
¿Cuál es tu horario de trabajo?
If you study:
¿Cuál es tu horario de estudios?

Unidad 6

Temas

El ritmo de vida

Un día de vida

The Spanish-speaking world has its own rhythm of life, influenced by climate and culture. In Spain the working day has always been shaped by the summer heat; the main meal of the day (**la comida** or **el almuerzo**) being eaten between 2 and 3 p.m. followed by a **siesta**. Work starts again at 4 or 5 p.m. and continues till 7.30 or 8 p.m. with supper (**la cena**) following at 9 or 9.30 p.m. Nowadays, however, this pattern is beginning to change, particularly in big cities with air-conditioned offices, where the pattern of life has become much more north European and the siesta is tending to disappear.

In Latin America there has always been variation – because there are other influences at work. Spain imposed its patterns on its colonies – but today the impact of the United States has imposed a different culture of work. Some factories and offices have a 9-to-5 or 10-to-6 working day, although a split working day still applies to most countries. In Mexico the siesta is still observed – although for those who work in the major cities and travel several hours to and from work, it is often impossible to get home in time for lunch. Weather is still a powerful influence. In the tropical heat many shops and businesses open very early in the morning and by 11 or 11.30 a.m. close for a siesta that extends into the cool of the early evening.

Unidad 6

V

atardecer
evening

Atardecer en la frontera

Petra works at General Electric's car plant at Reynosa in Mexico, near the border with the United States (**la frontera**). Her shift begins at 8.30 in the evening. Like many of her colleagues she lives in a community of plywood shacks called Colonia Roma. It has no proper drainage or services, no electricity, and for most of the year the ground is dry and hard. Petra works in one of the 2,100 assembly plants (**maquiladoras**) along the US–Mexican border. Her shift (**turno**) lasts nine and a half hours, and she earns $1.00 an hour at best.

There are half a million Mexicans working in these plants, producing everything from cars and furniture to pharmaceutical supplies. The North American Free Trade Agreement (NAFTA) signed in January 1994 opened the door to many more plants.

El hombre y los trabajos domésticos

FRECUENCIA CON QUE LOS HOMBRES REALIZAN TRABAJOS DOMÉSTICOS
(% horizontales, BASE = 1.405)

Tareas	Nunca	A veces	Casi siempre	Siempre	N/C
Hacer camas..................	40,4	43,3	6,8	9,5	0,1
Limpiar el polvo.............	56,1	35,3	3,6	4,9	0,1
Cocinar...........................	39,9	47,3	7,0	5,8	-
Lavar la ropa..................	77,0	17,2	1,8	3,9	0,1
Chapuzas........................	14,3	23,1	23,5	39,0	0,2
Fregar los platos............	44,6	41,1	7,5	6,2	0,2
Planchar.........................	86,9	9,1	1,2	2,2	0,1
Ir de compras.................	33,7	46,3	12,0	8,0	-
Cuidar los niños*............	39,7	44,1	11,6	4,1	0,5
Regar las plantas...........	43,8	36,7	9,5	9,7	0,3
Sacar la basura..............	17,2	40,9	19,1	22,7	0,1
Limpiar cristales y ventanas.....................	71,5	20,8	3,8	3,9	0,1

According to the table, which tasks do men perform most frequently around the home?

Which do they perform least often?

How would the picture look in your country?

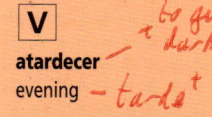

A las cinco de la tarde

Many sporting events in Spain, including bullfights, begin at 5 p.m. One of the most famous poems by the Spanish poet Federico García Lorca is an elegy, a lament for the bullfighter Ignacio Sanchez Mejías who was gored to death at five in the afternoon.

**A las cinco de la tarde
Eran las cinco en punto de la tarde.
Un niño trajo la blanca sábana
a las cinco de la tarde
Lo demás era muerte y sólo muerte
a las cinco de la tarde...
Un ataúd con ruedas es la cama
a las cinco de la tarde.
Huesos y flautas suenan en su oído
a las cinco de la tarde....
¡Ay qué terribles cinco de la tarde!**

At five in the afternoon
It was five in the afternoon exactly
A child brought the white sheet
At five in the afternoon
The rest was death and death only
at five in the afternoon.
A coffin on wheels was his bed
at five in the afternoon.
Bones and flutes echo in his ear
at five in the afternoon
How terrible this five in the afternoon!

Veamos de nuevo
Gramática

Unidad 6

	me levanto	I get up
	te levantas	you get up
	se levanta	he/she gets up, you get up (formal)
	nos levantamos	we get up
	os levantáis	you get up
	se levantan	they get up, you get up (formal)

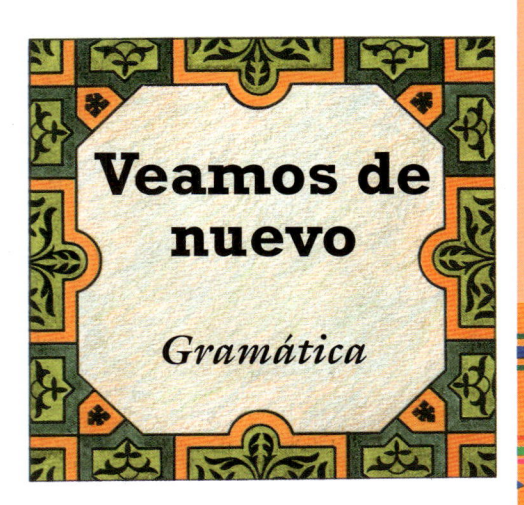

1 Present tense of regular verbs

Over the first 5 units you have seen examples of each of the three groups of Spanish verbs, **-ar**, **-er** and **-ir**, and in this unit you have met examples of all three. The following table gives you the full pattern of their endings:

	limpiar	*barrer*	*escribir*
yo	limpio	barro	escribo
tú	limpias	barres	escribes
él/ella/Vd.	limpia	barre	escribe
nosotros/-as	limpiamos	barremos	escribimos
vosotros/-as	limpiáis	barréis	escribís
ellos/ellas/Vds.	limpian	barren	escriben

Most Spanish verbs will follow one of these regular patterns, although you have already seen some that do not: for example, **estar**, **ser** and **ir**, which are described as irregular verbs. See G 18.

2 Reflexive verbs

The reflexives are a group of verbs, some of which you have met in this unit to describe personal habits. They always include a pronoun as well as the verb. In the infinitive form the reflexive pronoun is **se**. The pronoun changes with the verb endings:

Práctica

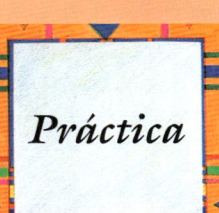

V
arreglar to tidy
todo el día all day
cansada tired

G
Other reflexive verbs include:
lavarse to wash
bañarse to take a bath
ducharse to take a shower
afeitarse to shave
maquillarse to put on make up
acostarse to go to bed

A Verb patterns

Can you conjugate these verbs using the patterns in the column opposite:

cenar; lavar; leer; vivir
e.g. **ceno, cenas, cena**, etc.

B A matter of organisation

Señora Cuchi is good at organising other people to do the jobs that need doing. Can you complete her description of the week's chores? Use the following verbs:

lavar; preparar; sacar; arreglar; pasar; limpiar; planchar; barrer

Los lunes mi marido y yo ..... la casa. Los martes mi hija mayor ..... la comida. Los miércoles mi marido ..... el patio y ..... la basura. Los jueves por la tarde yo ..... un pastel. Los viernes mi hija menor ..... y ..... toda la ropa. Los sábados mis hijos ..... sus habitaciones. Los domingos yo ..... todo el día en la cama. ¡Estoy cansada!

C What do you do?

1 A friend has asked you about some of your family's habits. Complete the answers.

a Yo ..... carne, pero Juanita ..... solamente verduras. *(comer)*
b No ..... vino. Preferimos cerveza. *(beber)*
c No, yo no ..... nunca, pero mi hermana ..... muchos libros. *(leer)*
d Mi marido y yo ..... la televisión por la noche después de cenar *(ver)*

Unidad 6

D Question time

Match the answers to the questions.

a ¿Cuándo cenáis?
b ¿A qué hora os levantáis?
c ¿Cuándo lees el periódico?
d ¿A qué hora se acuestan tus hijos?
e ¿A qué hora empiezas el trabajo?
f ¿A qué hora sales de casa?
g ¿A qué hora termina tu trabajo los sábados?

  i Uno se acuesta a las siete, el otro a las ocho.
  ii Los sábados no trabajo.
  iii Por lo general cenamos a las nueve.
  iv Nunca, no tengo tiempo para leer.
  v Salgo siempre a las ocho y cuarto.
  vi Empiezo a las ocho en punto.
  vii Nos levantamos siempre a las seis.

1 ¿Está contento con su vida?

You are interviewed in the street for a survey on the lifestyle of different people. Tick which of the three alternatives most closely applies to you, and give your reply as you do so.

a) ¿Quién limpia su casa?
   i) usted   ii) su esposo/esposa
   iii) otra persona

e.g. Yo limpio mi casa.

b) ¿Quién cocina en su casa?
   i) usted   ii) su esposo/esposa
   iii) otra persona

c) ¿Cuántas horas al día ve la televisión?
   i) una   ii) de dos a cinco
   iii) más de cinco

d) ¿Lee el periódico?
   i) nunca   ii) los domingos
   iii) cada día

e) ¿Quién hace la compra en su casa?
   i) usted   ii) su esposo/esposa
   iii) otra persona

V
cocinillas
skivvy
el cuidado de
looking after
el juez
judge
desde ... hace
since ... ago
extrañar
to miss
más ... menos
more ... less

Un paso más

Results of survey:
If all your answers are (i), you need some help at home; if all (ii), you're exploiting someone; if (iii), you must have servants!

---

2 Un día en la vida de ... 10

Many people have several jobs – **el pluriempleo**. How is this man's day organised?

3 "Soy un amo de casa"

Some men are happy to be able to enter the world of household chores and become an '**amo de casa**'. Read about Valentín, who in a recent divorce case was awarded custody of his son Alain.

Cristina Angulo, Bilbao. Valentín Arreguí, 36 años, se define así: "Soy un amo de casa y no un 'cocinillas', pero sí me gusta la cocina." Desde el nacimiento de su hijo Alain, hace cinco años, Arreguí, ex-empleado de banca, se dedica exclusivamente a las tareas domésticas y al cuidado del niño. Por esta razón, el juez le ha concedido provisionalmente la custodia del niño en este caso de divorcio. Arreguí extraña un poco la vida social de su trabajo profesional, pero en general está muy contento con su actual ocupación. Dice: "Lo que más me gusta de mi trabajo es cuidar de Alain y lo que menos me gusta es planchar."

(Adapted from *El País* – 29/10/94)

a How long has Valentín been "**un amo de casa**"?
b Where did he work before?
c Is there anything he misses from his previous work?
d What does he like best in his present occupation?
e What does he like least?
f How old is his child now?

4 Checklist

Can you do the following?

a Say what jobs you do in the house.
b Ask and say what time it is.
c Ask and say when you do things.
d Describe your daily routine.

Unidad 7

Ésta es su casa

Así se habla
Saying where you live
Describing your house
Offering someone a drink
Likes and dislikes

Temas
Vivir y sobrevivir

Veamos de nuevo

Unidad 7

Así se habla 1

¿Vives en una casa o en un piso?

Saying where you live

1

Look at some of the different types of houses you can find in Spain and around the Hispanic World. Can you match the pictures with the captions?

a una casa
b un chalet
c un piso, un apartamento (Sp)
    un departamento (LA)
d una buhardilla

2

Listen to five people talking about where they live. Decide how many people live in a flat and how many in a house.

a En un piso ....
b En una casa ....

> *Así se dice*
>
> To ask where someone lives, say:
>
> **¿Vives en una casa o en un piso?**
>   Do you live in a house or in a flat?
>
> And you can answer:
>
> **Vivo en una casa**
>   I live in a house

3 *Y ahora tú*

¿Vives en una casa o en un piso?

> *Así se acostumbra*
>
> **La casa** is the generic term for 'house', but it also means 'home'. In Spain, **un chalet** is normally a larger house on the outskirts of a town (particularly in a new development). In Spain there are two words for 'flat' – **un piso** and **un apartamento**. The **apartamento** is smaller – one or two bedrooms only – and is often more luxurious than the larger **piso**. In Latin America the word **departamento** is commonly used. **El dúplex** and **la buhardilla** are small flats. A **dúplex** normally has two levels, whereas the **buhardilla**, especially sought after by students in Madrid, is smaller and on the top floor. Many people in Spain and in large towns in Latin America live in blocks of flats. When Spaniards give their address, it can look rather complicated, as two or three numbers may be joined together.

Unidad 7

Calle Peña Auseba 24, 1°, 2ª
28130 Madrid

This reads as:
Calle Peña Auseba — street name, Peña Auseba Street
número 24 — number, number 24
primero — floor nº, first floor
segunda puerta — door nº, second door
veintitrés mil — area code, 23000
Madrid — town, Madrid

Sometimes, the address might say if the flat is on the left or the right:
Alberto Aguilera, 17, 1°, izda.
(= **puerta izquierda**/left door)
If it's a ground floor flat you might see the following:
Mirabel 32, bajo B
Addresses in other parts of the Hispanic world might be more explicit:
Almagro 1118 (street, building nº.),
Edificio Almagro (building name),
4° piso (floor no.),
Apto. 2A (flat number)
Quito
Sometimes you might even find a description rather than a precise address:
Ave. 10, 300 sur, frente al Expendio de C.N.P., edificio blanco con azul, San José (10th Avenue, 300 metres to the south, opposite Expendio de C.N.P., white and blue building).

4

Carmen jotted down some addresses of people she met at a party. This is what she wrote. Can you read them aloud?

José María Bolta
Pza de Ledesma 105
37003 Salamanca

Óscar López
Po. de Zorrilla, 70, 3°C
47007 Valladolid

Isabel Jiménez
C/ Panzano 8, bajo, izda.
50061 Zaragoza

Eulalia Velasco
Avda San Juan de la Cadena 8, 4°A.
31010 Pamplona

Marisa Vásquez
Orense, 68 5° dcha
27003 Lugo

🔊² She was in a hurry and got some of the addresses wrong. Listen and make any necessary corrections.

V
Abbreviations:

C/ = Calle
Pza. = Plaza
izda. = izquierda
dcha = derecha
Po. = paseo (avenue, walk)
Avda. = Avenida
Apto = Apartamento

5 🔊³

Ana is looking for a flat to buy in Madrid. Before you listen to her conversation with an estate agent, read the form below and see if you can find the words that mean the following:

a garage
b air conditioning
c heating
d lift/elevator
e number of bedrooms
f furnished
g area or district
h type of accommodation

Now listen to Ana's conversation with the estate agent and find out what kind of flat she wants, and complete the form as if you were the estate agent.

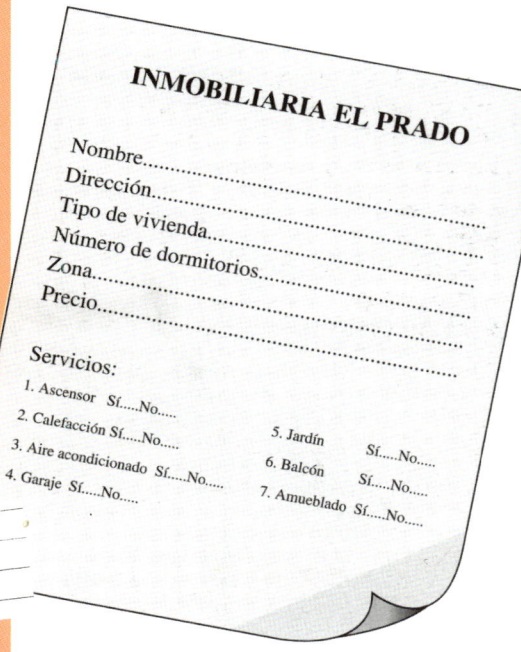

INMOBILIARIA EL PRADO

Nombre..........
Dirección..........
Tipo de vivienda..........
Número de dormitorios..........
Zona..........
Precio..........

Servicios:
1. Ascensor Sí.....No.....
2. Calefacción Sí.....No.....
3. Aire acondicionado Sí.....No.....
4. Garaje Sí.....No.....
5. Jardín Sí.....No.....
6. Balcón Sí.....No.....
7. Amueblado Sí.....No.....

6 Y ahora tú

You want to buy some property in Spain or in Latin America. Decide the type of accommodation (**tipo de vivienda**) you'd like from the list in Activity 1 and list the facilities (**servicios**) you'd like it to have from Activity 5. Now explain what you want to the estate agent.

e.g. **Quiero un apartamento con dos dormitorios .....**

Unidad 7

2 Éste es el dormitorio principal
Describing your house

1 🔊 4

Can you match the rooms to the pictures?

Cristina Pereira is showing Colette round her farmhouse near Buenos Aires. Tick the rooms you hear mentioned.

a el salón (Sp), el living (LA)
b el comedor
c el cuarto de estar, la sala de estar
d la cocina
e el dormitorio, la habitación
f el cuarto de baño (Sp), el baño (LA)

Así se acostumbra

In Spain **una habitación** is the general word for a room, but it is also often used to mean a bedroom. In some parts of Latin America **un cuarto** or **una pieza** are sometimes used for a room in general, and there are various other words for bedroom such as **la alcoba** and **la recámara**. The sitting-room, **el salón** in Spain, can have other names in Latin America such as **la sala** and **el recibidor** (i.e., the place to 'receive' visits); **el salón** is often a large function room in a hotel or a public building where celebrations or ceremonies take place, and can also be a classroom.

2 🔊 4

Listen to the conversation again and see if you can answer the following questions:

a How many bedrooms are mentioned?
b How many bathrooms?
c What does Cristina say about the following rooms?

– el comedor   ....
– el dormitorio principal   ....
– el baño   ....

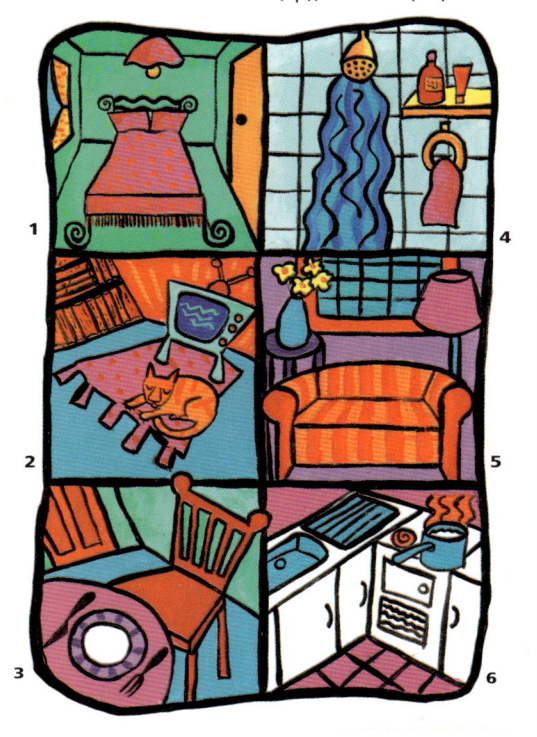

V
una chimenea fireplace
lindo/a (LA) very pretty

G
éste es ...
ésta es ...

Así se dice

To point out various rooms in your house, say:

Éste es el dormitorio. Es muy grande
    This is the bedroom. It's very big
Ésta es la cocina. Es pequeña
    This is the kitchen. It's small
Mi casa tiene dos dormitorios
    My house has two bedrooms
En mi casa hay un baño moderno
    In my house there is a modern bathroom

Unidad 7

3 Y ahora tú

Can you describe your home to a Spanish friend? First draw a simple floor-plan and write the name of each room. Then describe your house or flat, pointing out each room and saying what it's like and where it is.

e.g. **Éste es el salón. Es muy grande. Está al lado de la cocina.**

4

Listen to four people talking about their homes. Can you make a note of the number of bedrooms, bathrooms and other features each one has?

	habitaciones	baños	otros servicios
1			
2			
3			
4			

5

Here are some items of furniture:

- un sofá
- un sillón
- un estante / una estantería
- una mesa
- una cómoda
- una silla
- un escritorio
- una lámpara
- un armario
- una mesita
- una cama

Which three rooms from Activity 1 would you put these items of furniture in?

V

Here are some useful expressions:
El dormitorio ...
The bedroom
El salón ...
The sitting-room ...
... es frío ...
is cold
... es cómodo ...
is comfortable
... es abrigado ...
is warm
... es espacioso ...
is roomy

La cocina
The kitchen
... es soleada ...
is sunny
... es práctica ...
is practical

V

de una sola planta
on one floor only

V

manzanilla
camomile

---

6 Y ahora tú

You are applying to take part in a holiday house-exchange with a Spanish family. Write a short description of your house or flat, saying how many rooms there are and what they are like. Also mention other facilities or services it offers.

Tiene/Hay .....
El salón es ......

3
¿Te gustaría un café?
Offering someone a drink

1

Here is a list of drinks. Can you match the name of the drink with its picture?

a un café
b un vaso de vino, una copa de vino
c un té con limón
d una infusión de manzanilla
e un chocolate
f un zumo (Sp) un jugo (LA)
g una limonada
h una cerveza

Unidad 7

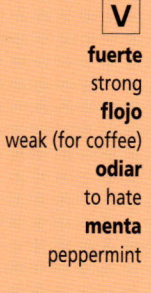

2 🔊 6

Carme is offering Olga a drink.

a What does Olga say she wants?
b Can you find phrases for 'with milk', 'with a little sugar', 'with ice'?

Carme: **¿Te gustaría tomar un café?**
Olga: **Sí.**
Carme: **¿O quieres otra cosa?**
Olga: **No, va bien un café.**
Carme: **Vale, pues ahora te traigo un café. ¿Lo quieres con leche?**
Olga: **No, sin nada ... un poco de azúcar.**
Carme: **¿Y unos ... y unos cubitos de hielo? ¿te gustaría?**
Olga: **Sí, sí. Eso sí.**
Carme: **Vale.**

Así se dice

To ask someone what they'd like to drink, say:

¿Qué te/le gustaría tomar?
... apetece tomar?
... provoca tomar? *(LA)*

To ask more than one person, say:

¿Qué os/les gustaría tomar?

More simply, you can say:

¿Qué quieres/quiere tomar?
¿Qué queréis/quieren tomar?
   What do you want to drink?

To answer you can say:

(Me gustaría) un té, gracias
(Quiero) una limonada

You can ask more specifically:

¿Le gustaría tomar un café?
¿Te apetece un té?
¿Quieres una limonada?

to which you can answer:

Sí/No, gracias.

V
otra cosa something else
vale right

V
fuerte strong
flojo weak (for coffee)
odiar to hate
menta peppermint

---

3 Y ahora tú

(i) Imagine you are in the following situations:

a A friend has just arrived. Ask him what he'd like to drink.
b Offer him an orange juice.
c Two friends are visiting. Ask them what they would like to drink.
d Offer a coffee to one of them.
e Ask the other one whether she would like a glass of wine.

(ii) At various times, friends want to know what you'd like to drink. Tell them what you'd like, bearing in mind the circumstances each time:

a It's winter and you are feeling cold.
b You've already asked for a coffee.
c You're thirsty.
d It's summer and you are feeling hot.
e You have a stomach-ache.

4 ¿Te gusta o no te gusta? 🔊 7

Juan and Rosa are talking about drinks they like or do not like. Do they like the same things?

Rosa: **Pues a mí me gustan las bebidas calientes en general – el té, el café, las infusiones ...**
Juan: **A mí me gusta el café también, pero no muy fuerte. Lo prefiero flojo. Y no me gustan las infusiones. Las odio. El té sí, pero con limón o solo y con un poco de azúcar. No me gusta el té con leche.**
Rosa: **Pues a mí tampoco, pero me gusta la infusión de manzanilla, la de menta ...**

Unidad 7

Así se dice

If you like something, say:

Me gusta el té/el vino, etc.
I like tea/wine, etc.

If you don't like something say:

No me gusta el té con leche
I don't like tea with milk

If someone says they like/dislike something and you agree, say:

A mí también/A mí tampoco
Me too/Me neither

If someone says they like something and you disagree, say:

A mí no
I don't (like it)

☞ Ex. A, p. 81

G
gustar
to like
(See p. 80)

V
más allá
beyond
las luces
lights

Temas

Vivir y sobrevivir

5

Say which drinks from Activity 1 you like or dislike.

6 *Y ahora tú* 🔊⁸

Five people tell you what they like to drink. What are these drinks? Do you agree or disagree with their tastes?

First speaker: **A mí me gusta mucho el café.**
You: **(Pues) a mí también. (Pues) a mí no.**

Más allá de las luces

The cities of Spain and Latin America are full of lights and noise and people. The crowds on their central avenues might be travelling to work or looking at the windows of bright modern shops. At the end of the day, some will go home to flats in comfortable and newly-built apartment blocks. Others, especially the immigrants, will return to a different kind of home.

When immigrants from the countryside reach a Spanish or Latin American city, its pavements are not usually paved with gold. Jobs are hard to find and it is even more difficult to find a place to live. Until the 1960s they might have squeezed into the run-down inner-city slums (called **conventillos** in Argentina or **vecindades** in Mexico), where whole families crowd into single rooms or narrow corridors behind anonymous walls. In more recent times, immigrants have built themselves makeshift shelters (called **chabolas** in Spain) on waste land on the outskirts of cities. Whole districts of them have grown up, known by a different name in each country – **callampas** (mushrooms) in Chile, **ranchos** in Venezuela, **villas miseria** in Argentina, **pueblos jóvenes** (young towns) or **barriadas** in Peru. No roads, water or electricity are provided. For those who live in these marginal

Unidad 7

districts (**barrios marginales**) life is precarious in the extreme. Few will become workers in industry (**trabajadores industriales**); most are likely to become domestic servants (**criados**) or street sellers (**ambulantes**). Even if they find stable work, there is little prospect of moving from these areas.

"La casa nueva"

Sometimes even the poorest families manage to replace their cardboard house with brick and a metal roof. Then neighbours and friends are invited in to celebrate the new house (**festejar la casa nueva**). In this song, the Chilean singer Tito Fernández, **el Temuaco**, describes one such party in a Chilean **población**.

**Hoy estamos de fiesta, tenemos nueva casa y hay que inaugurarla como Dios manda. Hay de todo ...
asado, cazuela, champaña, vino blanco y del otro; mucha gente en la casa, la casa nueva, nuestra casa. Fruto de tantos años llenos de penas blancas. ¡Hola vieja! – ¿bailamos? ... ¡quítate el delantal! Quiero verte de fiesta; ya está bueno de platos, ahora eres la reina. ¿Amigos? Amigos.
Déjame bailar contigo la alegría linda del último vals, amor, amor.
Vamos a vivir unidos en este minuto nuestra eternidad: amor, amor, amor.**

Today we're having a party, we've got a new house
and we should inaugurate it properly.
There's everything here
roast meat, stew, champagne, white wine and the other kind; lots of people in the house, our house, the fruit of so many years of little sorrows. Come on old girl, let's dance...! Take the apron off, let's see you dressed up for a party, that's enough dishes, today you're the queen. Friends, friends! Let me dance with you the joy of the last waltz, my love, my love.
We'll live out together in this moment our eternity, my love, my love, my love.

* *What names does he use to refer to his wife? Can you say, in a few lines, what the singer say about his new house?*

Unidad 7

Ésta es su casa

Ésta es su casa (this is your home) is one of the many phrases that Spaniards and Latin Americans use to offer you their hospitality. You will be invited in through a door flung wide open (**¡Pase, pase!**), invited to share in whatever they have in the house (**¿qué le ofrecemos?**) and introduced to family and friends (**te presento a mi abuela...**). Politeness and courtesy frame every conversation – particularly in public settings.

As he shows us around his large country house in Armenia, Colombia, Hernán Sierra describes the pleasure he gets from receiving guests. The idea, he says, is to make people feel at home (**como en su casa**).

A la gente en Colombia le encanta recibir, atender a la gente en sus casas. Por ejemplo, en el caso mío aquí en la finca, me encanta que venga la gente, tener traguito para repartirles comida, pasabocas, y que se sientan como en su casa...

And here is Carlos talking about his experience of Mexican hospitality towards himself and his wife:

Pues la gente se abre a nosotros, son muy cordiales, son muy cálidos, siempre te ofrecen en sus casas la comida, te ofrecen bebida, te ofrecen refrescos, te ofrecen pues todo lo que ellos puedan compartir contigo.

When you leave, there will be another round of handshakes and embraces – and reminders that you are welcome (**ya sabe, aquí tiene su casa**). It may be sometimes uncomfortable for people used to slightly more reserve to be the object of such attention – yet it is generous in its intention.

V
la finca farm
pasabocas 'nibbles'
compartir share

La historia del café

If you speak Spanish, you almost certainly drink coffee – and lots of it. But there are almost as many ways of taking it as there are people to do the drinking. You can drink it on its own (**solo**), with a little cold milk (**cortado**) or with plenty of warm milk (**con leche**), in a small or large cup, hot or cold. You can drink it cold (**frío**) or iced (**granizado**). In Mexico black coffee is called **café americano**, elsewhere in Latin America you would ask for **un tinto**. Mexican **café de olla** mixes coffee, cinammon and raw sugar (**piloncillo**) in a clay pot. Or, in the south of the continent you might drink the bitter **mate** tea from a gourd through a silver straw.

Unidad 7

Strangely, coffee had its origins in Ethiopia in the tenth century. It began to be cultivated on a large scale nearly five hundred years later, in Yemen. When it first reached Europe, it was greeted with suspicion; after all, it was a stimulant and the men stayed in the coffee houses far into the night. Later it was taken to North America, then to the Caribbean and finally to the mainland of South America. The first plant to reach Brazil was brought by an amorous military officer who had persuaded the wife of the Governor of the French colony of Cayenne to let him smuggle out a plant. Today coffee is grown almost everywhere in Latin America – in the high Colombian Andes and the volcanic soils of Brazil, as well as in Costa Rica, Peru, Venezuela, Mexico, Nicaragua. For many of these countries, it is a key export.

Coffee as a percentage of total exports:

Brazil 5.9%
Colombia 30.4%
El Salvador 58.3%
Honduras 21.3%
Nicaragua 39.9%

The Brazilian coffee harvest failed several times in the late 1980s and early 1990s. As a result coffee prices rose throughout the world, for Brazil produces 22% of the world's coffee and Colombia 15%.

Veamos de nuevo
Gramática

1 'I like it'

To say you like something you can use the verb **gustar**. **Me gusta el café** means 'I like coffee'. In the present tense there are only two forms – singular **gusta** and plural **gustan**, but the verb always appears with a pronoun that refers to the subject, i.e. the person who likes (or dislikes).

me gusta	*me* gustan	I like
te gusta	*te* gustan	you like
le gusta	*le* gustan	he, she likes,
le gusta	*le* gustan	you like (formal)
nos gusta	*nos* gustan	we like
os gusta	*os* gustan	you like
les gusta	*les* gustan	they like
les gusta	*les* gustan	you like (formal)

I like oranges: **me gustan las naranjas**
I like the book: **me gusta el libro**
he likes oranges: **le gustan las naranjas**
he likes the book: **le gusta el libro**

Other verbs that work like **gustar** include: **encantar** (to love), **apetecer** (to fancy).

2 ¿Qué quieres tomar?

Querer + infinitive is used to say what you want to do:

Quiero beber vino — I want to drink wine
Quieren vivir en Vitoria — They want to live in Vitoria

Unidad 7

3 Uses of ser and estar

As we have seen, the verbs **ser** and **estar** both mean 'to be'. Here is a summary of the uses you have seen so far:

Ser
* Nationality: **Gloria Estefán es cubana**
* Profession: **Jaime es médico**
* Description: **El salón es espacioso**
* The time: **Son las cuatro y media**

Estar
*Location: **El banco está enfrente de la farmacia**
La cocina está al lado del salón

Práctica

A ¿Qué te gusta?

You ask some friends if they like tea and coffee. How does each one reply?

	Jaime	Ana	Alberto	Pepe y Marta
té	✓✓	✓	✗	✓✓
café	✗	✓✓	✓	✓

e.g. Jaime, ¿te gusta el té?
   Sí, me gusta mucho.

Now ask the same friends if they like biscuits and cakes.

galletas	✗	✗	✓	✓✓
pasteles	✓	✗	✗	✓✓

e.g. Jaime, ¿te gustan las galletas? No, no me gustan.

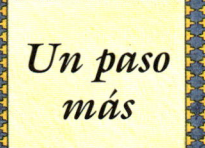

B ¿Qué quiere hacer?

Using **querer** + infinitive, fill in the gaps in the sentences below: Choose a suitable verb:

comprar – comer – tomar – trabajar – estudiar

a Ester .... un café con leche en el restaurante.
b (Yo) .... francés e inglés en la escuela.
c Isabel, Marcos y yo .... de actores en las telenovelas mejicanas.
d Los niños .... un helado en el parque.
e Los señores de Martínez .... un piso en el centro de la ciudad.

C Mi piso

Teresa is talking about her flat: fill in the gaps to complete her description.

Mi piso ..... en la calle Serrano nº 35- 3º A. ..... bastante grande. La cocina ..... amplia y soleada; ..... enfrente del cuarto de estar. Los muebles del cuarto de estar ..... modernos y prácticos. Después del hall, a la derecha, ... el dormitorio principal y a la izquierda ..... el salón. El salón ..... espacioso y alegre. El sofá ..... cómodo y original. La cama ..... en el centro del dormitorio, a cada lado ..... las mesillas de noche. El dormitorio ..... muy abrigado. Me gusta mucho mi casa.

Un paso más

1 Me encanta, me gusta y detesto

Your Spanish friend wants to know more about you. Can you tell her about your likes and dislikes? Use this diagram for ideas and make up more of your own.

e.g. **Me encantan las películas de misterio, me gusta la cocina italiana pero detesto las novelas románticas.**

Las películas
de horror
de misterio
de detectives
románticas
de ciencia-ficción

La pintura
de Dalí
de Turner
de Warhol
de Picasso
de Rembrandt

Las novelas
de aventuras
históricas
románticas
biográficas
policíacas

La cocina
vegetariana
francesa
italiana
india
española

Unidad 7

2 El Cortijo Rosario

Your friend wants to go on holiday in Spain and has picked up this brochure at a travel agent's. Can you tell him what kind of house it is, where it is, how many bedrooms it has and how much it would cost for bed and breakfast for 7 nights?

Si su idea de vacaciones es relajarse y tomar el sol en las sierras españolas

¡BIENVENIDO A CORTIJO ROSARIO!

Cortijo Rosario es una casa de campo andaluza, con ocho habitaciones de matrimonio, cada una con baño. Hay un comedor amplio, un salón grande con chimenea y un bar bien surtido. El pueblo de Algamitas está a 20 minutos. Tiene bares, tiendas y una iglesia. Cortijo Rosario se alza con todos sus encantos en un campo de girasoles y olivares.

Precios:	Habitación y desayuno	Media pensión
3 noches	168 €	215 €
7 noches	340 €	400 €

Para información y reserva llame al número 95 57 78 45

Your friend likes the sound of it but would also like to know (a) how far away from the sea it is; (b) whether there is a garden, a swimming-pool or a terrace. How would you ask for this information in Spanish?

3 La casa de Carme

You are with Carme as she shows a friend round her new flat.

a From her description, can you draw a plan of it?
b Some pieces of furniture are in strange places. Did you spot them?

4 Checklist

Can you do the following?

a Say what kind of house you live in.
b Ask for someone's address and give your own.
c Talk about types of houses and facilities.
d Describe the rooms and furniture in your home.
e Offer someone a drink and say what you'd like.
f Ask and say what you like and don't like.

Unidad 8

En cuerpo y alma

Así se habla
Describing people
Describing your symptoms
Getting the remedy

Temas
La salud hace el hombre

Veamos de nuevo

Unidad 8

Así se habla 1

Es alto y simpático
Describing people

1

Which words would be a good description of each of these people? Work with the help of the Glossary.

| rubio/a | gordo/a | guapo/a | joven | alto/a |
| moreno/a | delgado/a | feo/a | viejo/a or mayor | bajo/a |

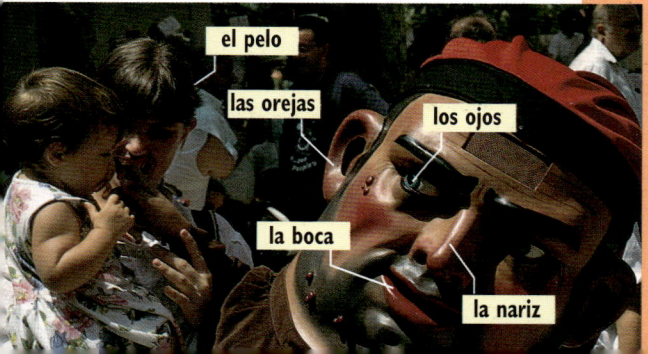

🔊 1 Now listen to four descriptions. Which person is a) young, tall, fair and very good-looking, b) older, shorter, dark and very slim?

| 1 | 2 | 3 | 4 |

Así se dice

To describe what someone looks like, say:

Es (muy) alto
   He's (very) tall
Es rubia y (bastante) delgada
   She's fair and (quite) thin
Es de mediana altura/estatura
   He/She is of medium height
No es ni delgado ni gordo
   He's neither thin nor fat

2

Describe three or four people you know using the adjectives in Activity 1.

Mi hermano es alto y rubio ...

3

Look at the pictures below and describe the features illustrated using the words in the table. Use the Glossary to check any you don't know.

el pelo		los ojos
colour	type	colour
negro	corto	negros
castaño	largo	marrones (Sp)
rojo	rizado	cafés (LA)
rubio	liso	verdes
canoso		azules
		grises

e. g. **a)** Pelo castaño, corto y rizado

Unidad 8

4 ¿Quién es quién?

Pedro has brought Isabel to a party, but she doesn't know many people there. He describes four people. Can you match their names to the people in the picture?

Así se dice

To describe someone's face and hair, say:

Tiene el pelo largo y liso
    He/she has long, straight hair
Tiene los ojos verdes
    He/she has green eyes
Tiene bigote/barba
    He's got a moustache/beard

5 Y ahora tú

You are flying to Spain tomorrow. A Spanish woman to whom you've spoken on the phone, but never met, will meet you at the airport. Can you describe what you look like to her?

Soy (alto/a) ...
Tengo ...

6 ¿Cómo son?

Can you now give a fuller description of the people in Activity 1?

V

¿Qué te parecen mis amigos?
What do you think of my friends?
me parece que ...
I think that ...
chico/a
young person

V

conocer a ...
to know (a person)
pelirrojo
red-haired
está sentado
is sitting
vamos para presentártelos
come and I'll introduce them to you

la cabeza
la pierna
el cuello
el brazo
la mano
el pie

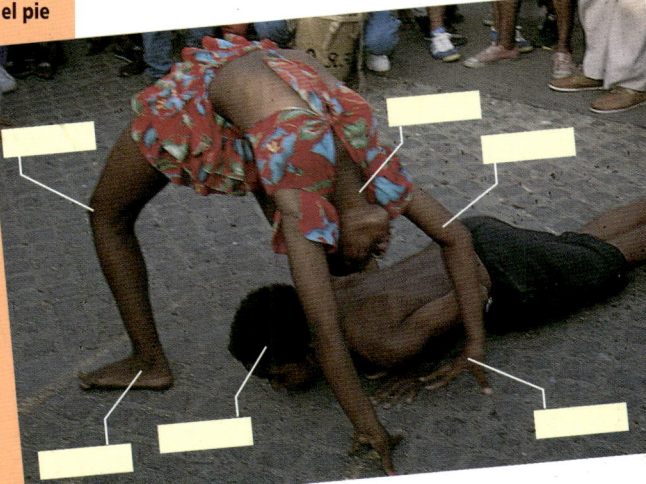

7

After the party, Isabel and Pedro are discussing the people she met there: Pepe, Teresa, Carlos and María. What does Isabel think of them? Listen and make a note.

simpático/a   inteligente
antipático/a   tonto/a
divertido/a   extrovertido/a
aburrido/a   tímido/a

8 Y ahora tú

How would you describe three or four people you know? And yourself? See also W 16 for more adjectives.

Corina es una chica ... Yo soy ...

2
Me duele la espalda

Describing your symptoms

1 El cuerpo

Can you identify which parts of the dancer's body these words relate to?

[85]

2 ¡Ay doctor! 🔊⁴

Aurora and Salvador are at the doctor's surgery in their respective countries, each with different complaints. Before you read the conversations, listen and work out which part of the body each of them is talking about.

– Hola, buenos días.
– Buenos días. ¿En qué le puedo ayudar?
– Pues, me duelen las piernas.

– Buenas tardes.
– Buenas tardes. ¿Qué le sucede?
– Me duele la cabeza. El dolor es constante. Creo que es el estrés.
– ¿Ahorita tiene dolor de cabeza?
– Sí.

Así se dice

To explain where it hurts, say:

Me duele la cabeza
   My head hurts
Me duelen las piernas
   My legs hurt

---

3 ¿Qué les pasa?

What's the matter with these people? What is each one saying?

e.g. **a) Me duele el brazo.**

Unidad 8

V

¿En qué le puedo ayudar?
How can I help you?
¿Qué le sucede/pasa?
What's the matter?
dolor
pain
ahorita
now (diminutive of **ahora**)

Estoy contento
Estoy triste

G

doler
to hurt

(See p. 91)

V

la garganta
throat
el estómago
stomach
la espalda
back
el oído
ear (internal)

V

¿desde cuándo le duele?
since when have you had this pain?
desde ayer
since yesterday
antes o después de las comidas
before or after meals
una exploración
an examination

Así se dice

With aches, pains and other symptoms, say:

Tengo dolor de cabeza, de espalda
   I've got a headache, backache
Tengo fiebre, tos
   I've got a temperature, a cough
Tengo un resfriado, catarro
   I've got a cold, catarrh

and you can also use:

Estoy enfermo/a, no estoy bien
   I'm ill, I'm not well
Estoy cansado/a, deprimido/a
   I'm tired, depressed

4

How would you say the following:

a I've got earache
b I've got a headache
c I am tired
d I've got backache
e My eyes hurt.
f I've got a cough

5 Visita al médico 🔊⁵

Nieves is in the surgery talking to a doctor. Listen as she talks and complete her medical record card.

	Estado civil:
	soltero/a casado/a divorciado/a
Nombre............................	Número de hijos............
Edad.......años	Síntomas............................
Lugar de nacimiento..........	Diagnóstico.........................
Ocupación........................	Tratamiento........................

[86]

6 Y ahora tú

Imagine you have flu (**la gripe**) and you are feeling depressed. How would you describe your symptoms to a doctor?

Me duele ... Tengo ... Estoy ...

Unidad 8

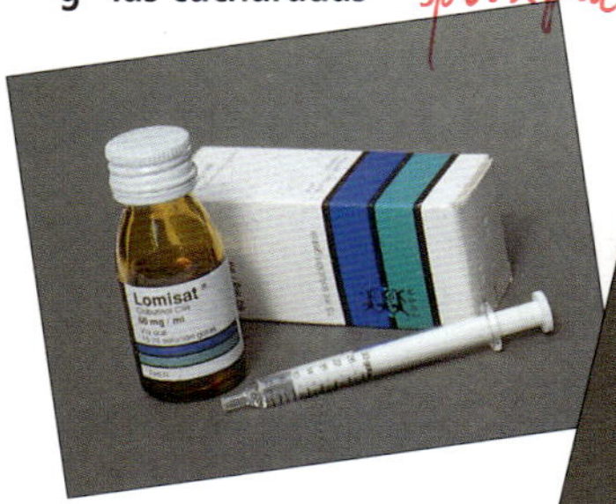

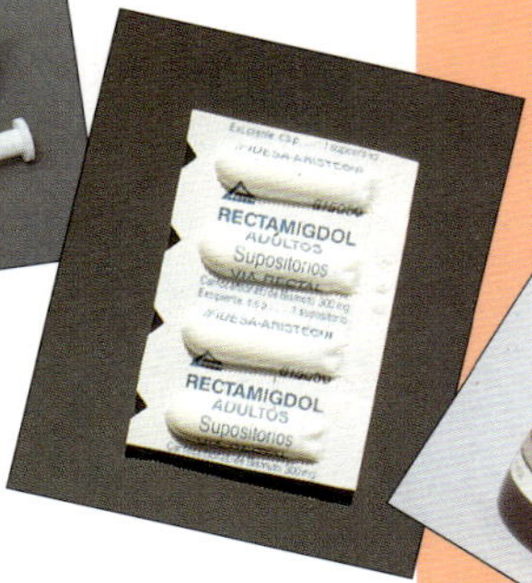

V

masticada
  chewed
quemadura de sol
  sunburn
cremita
  diminutive of **crema**
preguntita
  diminutive of **pregunta** (question)

G

deber/tener que
  to have to
  (See p. 91)

3
Tiene que tomar unas pastillas
Getting the remedy

1

Do you know the words for the ways in which medicines are packaged?

a las pastillas/los comprimidos/las tabletas
b el jarabe — *syrup*
c el ungüento/la pomada
d la crema
e las gotas — *drops*
f el sobre — *sachet*
g las cucharadas — *spoonful*

---

2 En la farmacia 🔊⁶

You will hear three customers asking a chemist for advice. Can you match the symptoms mentioned with the type of remedy he advises them to take?

1 dolor de estómago   a jarabe
2 dolor de garganta   b analgésico
3 quemadura de sol   c sobre

3 🔊⁶

Listen to the recording once more and make a note of how often each medicine needs to be taken or applied.

1 .....   2 ......   3 .....

Así se dice

To ask how you should take a medicine, say:

¿Cómo debo tomar esta medicina?
  How should I take this medicine?
¿Cómo tengo que tomar estas pastillas?
  How should I take these tablets?

The answer you might get is:

Debe tomar una pastilla antes de las comidas
  You should take one tablet before meals
Tiene que tomar una pastilla dos veces al día
  You have to take one tablet twice a day

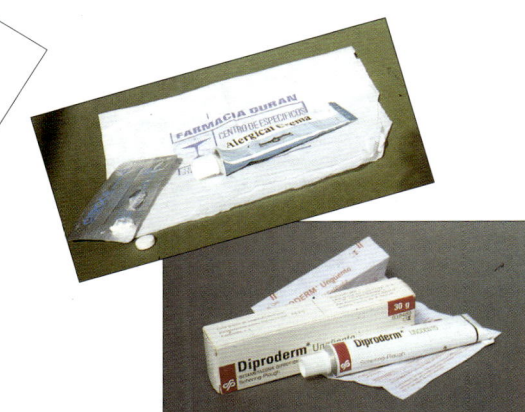

Unidad 8

4

Read the following labels and instructions. What is each medicine for and how often should it be taken or applied?

> 30 Tabletas masticables.
> Contenido por tableta: 400 mg Calcio.
> Cantidad aconsejada: 1-2 Tabletas por día.
> Ingredientes: Carbonato de Calcio, Glucosa, Sacarosa, Aceite vegetal, Emulgente E-485, esencia de limón.
> Valor energético kcalorías por 100 g = 330

> El organismo humano necesita suficiente Calcio para mantener la estructura del tejido óseo. Sobre todo en la mujer a partir de los 35 años sus huesos empiezan a perder Calcio, por lo que se aconseja la ingestión de dicho mineral.
> La dosis diaria de Calcio ha de situarse entre 800 y 1.000 mg/día que se pueden ingerir en los alimentos, como productos lácteos. Sin embargo muchas personas no alcanzan esa cantidad a través de la alimentación.
> Davitamon Calcio como complemento asegura la suficiente ingestión diaria de Calcio.

> USOS: Para el tratamiento local de afecciones de las fosas nasales, debidas a un factor alérgico, inflamatorio o infeccioso.
> DOSIS: Salvo mejor criterio del facultativo, se aplicará 2 o 3 veces diarias.
> Este es un producto de uso delicado, utilícese bajo vigilancia médica.

5 *Y ahora tú*

If friends told you they had the following complaints, what advice would you give them? Choose from this list:

beber una limonada caliente	descansar
ir al médico	hacer ejercicio
ir a la cama	hacer gárgaras

e.g. – Tengo fiebre.
– Tienes que/Debes tomar una aspirina

a **Me duele el estómago**
b **Tengo dolor de cabeza**
c **Estoy muy cansada**
d **Me duele todo el cuerpo**
e **Me duele la garganta**
f **Estoy estresado**

V
la sanidad/la salud
health

Temas

La salud hace al hombre

La Sanidad en España

Spain has both a modern and efficient public health system (**la Seguridad Social**) and private health insurance companies (**las aseguradoras médicas**). These companies insure some 5.7 million Spaniards. Some people belong to both systems. A survey in the magazine *Cambio 16* showed that Spaniards in the private and public sectors wanted rather different things from their health service:

LO QUE MÁS SE VALORA	
SEGURIDAD SOCIAL	**SANIDAD PRIVADA**
1. Médico cabecera	1. Trato personal
2. Tratamientos hospitalarios	2. Pruebas, análisis
3. Intervenciones quirúrgicas	3. Hospitalización
4. Trato personal	4. Intervenciones quirúrgicas
5. Especialistas	5. Especialistas
6. Pruebas, análisis	6. Médico cabecera
7. Hospitalización	7. Tiempo de consulta

Public health care patients are more concerned with the doctor (**el médico**) they have; those in private care with the personal treatment (**el trato**) they receive; both place high value on surgery (**la intervención quirúrgica**). What would your list look like?

Unidad 8

La salud en Latinoamérica

Latin America offers some of the best as well as some of the worst in health care. Through the 1980s, infant mortality (**la mortalidad infantil**) rose and the most powerful symbol of poverty – cholera (**el cólera**) – emerged again to claim thousands of victims in Peru as well as in other countries of the continent. The lack of clean drinking water is a constant threat to health in the poorer areas of Latin America, where the word dehydration (**la deshidratación**) has a more frightening resonance than it can ever have in the West.

Most medicine in Latin America is private. Civil servants (**funcionarios**) and other government employees will often have health insurance schemes. So will workers in the bigger industries. But for the large number of unemployed or underemployed people in the cities, most countries offer very little health care. Where there is some basic public health provision, as in Mexico, it is minimal.

The exception is Cuba whose system of public health care (**la salud pública**) is free and of a high standard. It is a sad irony that in the 1990s Cuba has had to put more and more of its medical facilities at the disposal of foreign 'health tourists' to earn precious foreign currency. And in 1994 the economic blockade so undermined the generally high level of health that neuritis (**la neuritis**), a disease of poverty that causes blindness, affected more than 20,000 people. Yet at the same time, Cuba has earned over $200 million exporting its pathbreaking vaccine against meningitis (**la vacuna contra la meningitis**).

In 1979, the new government of Nicaragua embarked on building a health care system. Between 1979 and 1981 only nine people per thousand died of malaria (**el paludismo** or **la malaria**). Before 1979 up to one third of Nicaraguans had suffered from the disease. A health campaign brought down dramatically the number of deaths from malaria, measles (**el sarampión**) and diarrhoea (**la diarrea**) caused by lack of access to clean water. By the mid-1990s, however, few of those advances had been maintained.

But new hope for controlling malaria came when a Colombian scientist, Dr Patarrayo, announced successful trials of a new vaccine. Its 70% success rate made it a breakthrough of real significance in a world where 2 million people still suffer from this terrible disease. Dr Patarrayo, and the Colombian Health Ministry, generously donated the vaccine to the World Health Organisation – WHO (**Organización Mundial de Salud – OMS**).

Unidad 8

Veamos de nuevo
Gramática

La medicina desde abajo

For some rural and indigenous communities in Latin America, popular folk and herbal medicine is still crucially important and often coexists with newer developments. As people move from the country to the city, they take their 'folk healers' (**curanderos**) with them – where they are to be found in urban markets, selling their herbs and cures. Here is part of a leaflet given out in a Mexican market by a man claiming great power for **copal** or **popochcomitl** – the resin that produces incense when it burns. According to the leaflet, burning this substance makes people feel warm and friendly towards each other.

POPOCHCOMITL

Una de las ceremonias más sencillas en apariencia y muy hermosa en realidad, es la conocida como ZAHUMACIÓN BLANCA. Esta ceremonia de Zahumación es una Ceremonia de Purificación de enorme trascendencia y significado... El humo del copal tiene la capacidad de purificar el aire, y de crear un ambiente de hermandad y amistad entre la gente congregada ... .

Se acerca la vejez

The 'syndrome' that Mario Benedetti refers to in his poem **"Síndrome"** is the onset of middle age – a familiar concern in any language!

**Todavía tengo casi todos mis dientes,
casi todos mis cabellos y poquísimas canas,
puedo hacer y deshacer el amor,
trepar una escalera de dos en dos,
y correr cuarenta metros detrás del ómnibus,
o sea que no debería sentirme viejo;
pero el grave problema es que antes
no me fijaba en estos detalles.**

V
desde abajo
from below

V
trascendencia
importance
humo
smoke
un ambiente
an atmosphere
hermandad
brotherhood
amistad
friendship

V
se acerca la vejez
old age approaches
poquísimas canas
very few grey hairs
trepar una escalera
climb a staircase
casi
almost
o sea
that is
no debería sentirme viejo
I shouldn't feel old
no me fijaba
I never used to worry

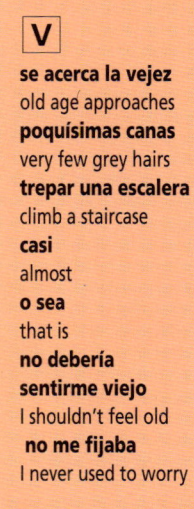

1 Ser/Estar

When describing people or things, **ser** and **estar** can both be used with adjectives, but in different circumstances. Here are some simple guidelines:

* Use **ser** for physical description and character:

Juan es alto y rubio
Juan is tall and fair
Miguel es muy simpático
Miguel is very nice
La casa es bonita
The house is pretty

* Use **estar** for describing physical state or mood:

La señora García está enferma
Señora García is ill
Estoy un poco cansado
I am a bit tired
¡Qué triste está Matilde hoy!
How sad Matilda looks today!
Estoy deprimido
I am depressed

Unidad 8

Práctica

2 You have to

To say that someone must or has to do something, use **tener que** + infinitive:

Tienes que tomar el jarabe después de comer
You must take the syrup after meals
María tiene que quedarse en la cama
Mary has to stay in bed

To advise someone what they should do, with slightly less compulsion, use **deber** + infinitive:

Debes descansar más
You should rest more
Pedro debe trabajar menos
Peter should work less

Note: When the infinitive which follows is a reflexive verb, the reflexive pronoun changes according to the subject of the first verb:

Debes acostarte más temprano
You should go to bed earlier
Tengo que levantarme a las seis
I have to get up at six

3 It hurts

To say that something hurts you can use the verb **doler**. Like **gustar** there are only two forms – **duele**, and plural – **duelen**.

The person **doler** refers to is indicated by the pronoun that goes before it; the thing or things which hurt alter the ending of the verb.

Me duele _la_ cabeza
I have a headache
¿Te duelen _los_ ojos?
Are your eyes hurting?

Note: when you refer to a part of the body, your own or somebody else's, you simply use the definite article, not the possessive adjective.

A Ser or estar?

Use either **ser** or **estar** to fill in the gaps, whichever is most appropriate:

1 María ..... nerviosa porque tiene un examen.
2 Mis estudiantes ..... cansados después del viaje.
3 Juan ..... muy antipático.
4 (Yo) ..... morena y bastante alta.
5 Mi novio ..... muy tímido y ..... siempre preocupado.
6 (Nosotras) ..... enfermas con la gripe.

B ¡Ay!

In the following sentences people describe various ailments but the parts of the body are missing. Using the clues, can you guess what the words are? Then match the symptoms to the correct course of action.

e.g. **Mi padre tiene dolor de o_d_. (oído)**
Debe ponerse unas gotas.

1 Me duelen los _ j _ _	a Debe descansar
2 Los niños tienen dolor de g _ _ _ _ _ _ a	b Debes ir al oculista
3 Me duelen mucho las p _ _ nas	c Deben ir al médico
4 Tengo dolor de c _ _ za	d Debe tomar manzanilla
5 ¡Qué dolor de _st _ _ _go tan fuerte tiene María!	e Debes tomar una aspirina

C Another day!

Naomi has a full day ahead of her. She goes through her diary and says what she (and her husband!) have to do.

e.g. **07:00: Tengo que levantarme a las siete.**

MONDAY WEEK 10

07.00 Get up
08.30 Go to work
12.00 Juan to the dentist
13.00 With cousin Alicia lunch with Sr Gómez
16.00 Go to the school
17.00 Leave work - Go shopping
18.30 Children to the optician
20.00 Juan prepares dinner - I have a rest

Unidad 8

Un paso más

1 Identikit

The police have issued this identikit picture of a man they wish to interview:

Despite some differences, you think it bears a striking resemblance to your neighbour. You phone them and describe your neighbour (below) in as much detail as you can.

2 El embarazo 🔊 7

Mari goes to see her consultant for the first pregnancy check-up. The consultant asks her about her medical history. Listen to the conversation and tick the medical problems that she has had.

a allergies
b palpitations
c nausea
d backache
e headache
f aching legs

3 Centro de Salud

You are a tour guide with a party on holiday in Mojacar. One evening several people come to you with problems: a woman has severe backache, a 5-year old feels sick, and a man has broken his spectacles. You consult the local newspaper to find out what medical services are available. How would you tell each member of the party where to seek advice?

PEDIATRA
Dra. Maria Rose
Pacientes con Seguros
Medicina General + Niños
Lunes · miércoles · jueves · viernes
10.00 - 14.00
De lunes a jueves
17.00 - 20.00
LAS TERRAZAS DE GARRUCHA
Edificio Nº4 1ªPlanta C. Tel 132 803

VEA CLARO CON
OPTICA
INDALOVISION
Reconocimientos oculares
Lentes de contacto
Gafas multifocales
Reparación de lentes
Recuerde que sólo tiene dos ojos
¡Cuídelos!
GARRUCHA, C/. Mayor, 114
Tel. 460 665

Consulta Osteopática
Una terapia natural que combina masaje y manipulación articular
Ciática, dolores de espalda, cuello y articulaciones.
Para cita llamar
ENRIQUE ARIAS
Mojácar 478 991
Almería 22 99 12

4 Checklist

Can you do the following?

a Give physical descriptions of people.
b Describe your symptoms to a doctor.
c Talk about the way you feel now.
d Ask for advice and understand remedies.
e Talk about what you have to do.

V
el embarazo
pregnancy

Unidad 9

Hoy es fiesta

Así se habla
Saying what you like doing

Dates and celebrations

Ordering drinks and snacks

Temas
El día de los muertos

Veamos de nuevo

Unidad 9

Así se habla 1

¿Qué te gusta hacer?

Saying what you like doing

1

A Mexican girl, a boy in Madrid and a woman and a man in Barcelona are saying what they like doing on Sundays. Can you match the activities with the people? Listen and say who likes doing what.

a

b

c

d

V
El Retiro
La Casa de Campo
(famous parks in Madrid)

V
Descansar

Leer y mirar películas de vídeo

Ir al parque

Estar con mis amigos

G
me gusta/ me encanta
+ leer, estudiar, escribir

(See p. 102)

2

Jesús, from Madrid, likes going to parks. How many does he go to?

– ¿Qué te gusta hacer los domingos?
– Pues ir al parque, ir al Retiro, ir al parque de atracciones, ir a Casa de Campo, ir al parque de abajo, que está cerca de nuestra casa y al parque al lado de casa.

Así se dice

To ask what a person likes doing, say:

¿Qué te/le gusta hacer los domingos?
   What do you like doing on Sundays?

To answer you can say:

(Me gusta) descansar
   (I like) to rest
(Me gusta) estar con mis amigos
   (I like) being with my friends

If you like doing something a lot, say:

Me gusta mucho ir al parque
   I like going to the park very much
Me encanta ir al cine
   I love going to the cinema

And if you don't like it at all, say:

No me gusta (nada) ir al cine
   I don't like going to the cinema (at all)

☞ Ex. A, p. 103

Unidad 9

3 Y ahora tú

¿Qué te gusta hacer los viernes por la noche?
¿Los sábados? ¿Y los domingos?
¿Qué no te gusta hacer los fines de semana?

Así se dice

To indicate what other people like doing, say:

Le gusta ir al teatro
He/She likes going to the theatre

To be emphatic about who likes doing what, say:

A mí me gusta leer pero a él no le gusta
I like reading, but he doesn't

A Juan le gusta quedarse en la cama
Juan likes staying in bed

A María y a Tere les gusta ir al parque
María and Tere like going to the park

☞ Ex. B, p. 103

4

Match the pictures to the activities and say what each person likes or doesn't like doing.

e.g. **A Sofía le gusta ir al cine.**

ir al bar
ir de compras
jugar al tenis
tocar la guitarra

Sofía

a Carlos
b Marisol
c Luis y Margarita  
d Nuna y Francisco 

V
correr to run
natación swimming

G
A mí me gusta
(See p. 103)

V
jugar to play (a sport)
tocar to play (a musical instrument)

5

Juan is asked whether he likes doing some of the things in Activities 1 and 4. Make a note of the things he likes doing. Then listen again and say how often he does those things.

e.g. **A Juan le gusta ir al cine. Va al cine una vez a la semana.**

6

Rosita is looking for a partner. Read what she says about herself. Which of the three young men on a radio phone-in would be most suitable for her?

Tengo 19 años. Soy una persona muy activa. En mi tiempo libre me gusta mucho salir. Los fines de semana me gusta ir de copas o ir a cenar en algún restaurante, ir al cine o al teatro. También me gustan los deportes. Todos los días me levanto temprano y corro en un parque cerca de mi casa. Practico también la natación en el verano y el esquí en el invierno.

1 "Me encanta el cine"
2 "Me gusta mucho quedarme en la casa"
3 "Practico la natación"

7 Y ahora tú

¿Qué te gusta hacer en tu tiempo libre?

Unidad 9

2 Fechas y festejos
Dates and celebrations

1 Los meses del año

Look at the calendar and practise saying the names of the months.

2 La fecha de hoy 4

Here are four people who cannot remember the date. Can you circle each date that is mentioned on the calendar?

V
boda
wedding
fecha de ingreso
date he joined ...

V
uno de enero,
primero de enero
(LA)
1st January

Así se dice

To ask what date it is today, say:

¿Qué fecha es hoy?
¿A qué fecha estamos? / ¿A cómo estamos?
   What's the date today?

And to answer, say:

Es el 14 de julio (de 2003)   or:
Estamos a 14 de julio (de 2003).
   It's 14th July (2003)

3 5

Nieves asks a Spanish postman what anniversaries are important for him and he mentions the ones below. Listen and note the date when each event occurs.

fecha de su nacimiento:
fecha de su boda:
fecha de ingreso a Correos:
fecha de ingreso a la oficina de trabajo actual:

4 Y ahora tú

¿Qué fecha es hoy? or ¿A qué estamos hoy?
¿Qué fechas son importantes para ti?

5

The following are all important festivals in the Hispanic calendar:

– **El día de Navidad**
– **El día de la Hispanidad**
– **El día del trabajo**
– **El día de los difuntos** (Sp)/
  El día de los muertos (LA)
– **El día de Reyes**
– **El día de los inocentes**

Can you say which date each festival falls on? Try reading each one aloud.

a **6.1**   b **1.5**   c **28.12**   d **12.10**   e **25.12**
f **2.11**

e.g. **6.1**: el seis de enero

Unidad 9

Así se acostumbra

El día de los inocentes, 28th December, is a day when you can have fun by playing tricks or jokes on people, and in some places in Latin America, it's not just a day, but a period extending until the 6th January. One 'innocent' way in which people might try to fool you is by sticking a newspaper cut-out figure on you when they greet you with a pat on your back. And if you hear a child chanting to you **'Inocente que lleva la carga y no la siente'** (Innocent person who carries a burden on his back and doesn't feel it), you'll know you've been fooled. Newspapers and radio stations, however, can play more serious jokes on people, so beware if on these days you hear that your favourite football team has lost or won. It might all be a joke.

6

Three people were asked how they celebrated Christmas (**la Navidad**), New Year's Day (**el Año Nuevo**), and their birthday (**el cumpleaños**) or name day (**el santo**). Here are their replies:

Teresa (España):
– ¿Cómo celebras la Navidad?
– Pues, en Nochebuena hacemos una comida y toda la familia viene: abuelos, tíos y primos. Comemos pavo, cordero, ternera o pescado; cantamos villancicos y hablamos. A medianoche, algunas personas van a la misa del gallo. El día 25 lo pasamos todos en casa y por la noche hay también una cena. Los regalos los damos el día de Reyes.

Miguel (España):
– ¿Cómo festejas tu santo o tu cumpleaños?
– Pues simplemente compro una tarta y me la como con mi familia o invito a mis amigos por la tarde y nos comemos unos pasteles.

Patricio (Ecuador):
– ¿Cómo celebras el Año Nuevo?
– Pues el 31 por la tarde salgo con mis amigos a ver los 'años viejos' en las calles y por la noche nos reunimos con toda la familia. Bailamos y tomamos y cuando el reloj da las doce nos abrazamos y nos deseamos felicidades. Cenamos pasada la medianoche y nos acostamos muy tarde. El primero todo el mundo descansa y mucha gente también va a misa.

7 Y ahora tú

¿Qué festejos importantes hay en tu país?
¿Cómo celebras la Navidad? ¿El Año Nuevo?
¿Y tu cumpleaños?

V
pavo
turkey
cordero
lamb
cantar
to sing
villancicos
Christmas carols
misa del gallo
midnight mass
abrazarse
to hug one another
'años viejos'
(dolls stuffed with paper and fireworks, representing well-known national and international figures – usually those not much liked by people; these dolls are burned in the streets just before midnight)

[97]

3
A beber y a picar
Ordering drinks and snacks

Unidad 9

V
bocadillo (Sp)/ **sandwich, sánduiche** (LA)
sandwich
tapas/pinchos
snacks
tortilla española
Spanish omelette
calamares
squid

V
horchata
(drink made from tiger nuts and almonds)

V
¿Cuánto le debo? = **¿Cuánto es?**

1

Here are some drinks and snacks you can get in a bar. What are they? You'll find all the words on the menu boards on the right.

e.g. **un Kas de limón** (Sp)
una ración de queso

EL MARINERO

BEBIDAS FRESCAS €
Kas Limón/naranja 1,50
Coca-Cola 1,50
Agua mineral pequeña ... 0,75
Café con hielo 1,25
Horchata 1,65
Cerveza (caña) 1,25
Mosto 0,75

BOCADILLOS y SANDWICHES
de jamón 3,00
de queso 2,50
de chorizo 2,50
vegetal 2,00

TAPAS
Calamares 2,75
Tortilla española 2,75
Queso 1,50
Gambas al ajillo 3,25

2 🔊 6

Listen to people ordering drinks in a bar in Spain on a hot summer's day, and on the menu board tick the drinks they order.

3

Now read the first two conversations you have just heard. What expression does the waiter or waitress use to take the orders? Note how the customers order their drinks.

(1)
Camarero: **Hola, buenos días, ¿qué van a tomar?**
Begoña: **Tú, ¿qué vas a tomar, María?**
María: **Yo una Coca-cola.**
Begoña: **Una Coca-cola y un mosto, por favor.**

(2)
Camarero: **Dígame.**
Victor: **Póngame un café solo con hielo y una botella de agua mineral.**
Camarero: **¿Algo más?**
Victor: **No, gracias. ¿Cuánto le debo?**
Camarero: **Tres euros.**
Victor: **Aquí tiene, gracias.**
Camarero: **A usted.**

Unidad 9

Así se dice

To take your orders the waiter might ask:

¿Qué va/van a tomar?
   What are you going to have?
Dígame
   (literally) Tell me

And you might say:

Una coca-cola, por favor
   A coke, please
Quiero una tónica, por favor
   I want a tonic water please
Ponme un café *(informal)*
Póngame un café *(formal)*
   I'll have a coffee, please

If you are with friends, you might say:

Yo ... una coca-cola y un mosto para ella
Para mí una coca-cola y un mosto para ella
   Coke for me and grape juice for her

4 Y ahora tú

You are in a bar with two friends, Julie and Patrick, who don't speak Spanish. Julie wants a beer and Patrick a coffee with ice. Order for them and also say what you'd like to have.

Camarero: **Hola buenos días, ¿qué van a tomar?**
You: ...

5 🔊⁷

Listen to Pilar ordering drinks and snacks and say whether the following statements are true (**verdadero**) or false (**falso**):

e.g. She orders two drinks. **Verdadero**

a She orders a coke for herself and a tonic water for her friend.
b She also wants something to eat.
c Two types of sandwiches are available.
d Pilar wants a cheese sandwich.
e Pilar's friend also wants something to eat.

Así se dice

To ask if a bar serves things to eat, say:

¿Tenéis *(Sp)*/**Tienen algo para comer?**
   Do you have anything to eat?

To ask what kind of sandwiches they have, say:

¿De qué son?
   What kind are they?

The answer you'll get is:

De jamón, de queso, etc.
   Ham, cheese, etc.

To express what you want, say:

Yo quiero un bocadillo de jamón
   I want a ham sandwich
(Yo quiero) uno de jamón, por favor
   I want ham, please

6 Y ahora tú

You are in El Marinero bar in Spain. See if you can complete the conversation below and say your part out loud. Can you also work out your bill from the price lists on the menu board?

Camarera: **¿Qué va a tomar?**
Tú: .....
Camarera: **Sí, hay Coca-cola, Kas limón, Kas naranja ...**
Tú: .....
Camarera: **Bien.**
Tú: .....
Camarera: **Sí, hay bocadillos.**
Tú: ......
Camarera: **Hay de queso, jamón y vegetal.**
Tú: ......
Camarera: **Sí, también. Hay calamares, jamón serrano, queso manchego ...**
Tú: ......
Camarera: **Vale. ¿Algo más?**
Tú: **No** .... ¿....................?
Camarera: **Son** ......

[99]

Unidad 9

Temas

El día de los muertos

Every year tourists gather in Mexican villages like Pátzcuaro and Mixquic to watch the ceremonies of the Day of the Dead. As night approaches, families gather to wash the graves of their dead relatives; they bring food and candles and accompany their ancestors through the night of the dead. They decorate the tomb with **sempixóchitl**, the eternal flower.

In the markets of Mexico sugar skulls appear with names across the forehead. In the Market of La Merced in Mexico City, the skulls are piled up in great pyramids.

The figure of the skeleton (**la calavera**) appears everywhere – sometimes dancing, sometimes wearing a flowered hat. **Las calaveras** have a long history in Mexico. Their most famous appearance is in the work of the great cartoonist and satirist José Guadalupe Posada. He used the skeleton figures, and the short verses that went with them, to poke fun at politicians and public figures.

**General que fue de suerte
y mil acciones ganó,
y sólo una la perdió
la que tuvo con la muerte.**

Now this general had luck on his side
A thousand wars he won
But the one he lost was when he died
(Then Death had all the fun.)

The Day of the Dead (All Souls Day) combines a native and a foreign tradition. When the Spaniards conquered Mexico, they brought their own ideas with them – for their poets and priests often wrote about the brevity of life.

Unidad 9

Carpe diem

Here are the words of the great fifteenth-century Spanish poem by Jorge Manrique "Coplas" (Couplets on the death of his father):

**Nuestras vidas son los ríos
que van a dar en la mar
que es el morir;
allí van los señoríos
derechos a acabarse
y consumirse;
allí son iguales
los que viven por sus manos
y los ricos.**

In Mexico itself even before the Spaniards came, the ancient Mexicans – the Aztecs – held very similar beliefs.

¿Acaso es verdad que se vive en la tierra? ¿Acaso para siempre en la tierra? ¡Sólo un breve instante aquí! Hasta las piedras finas se resquebrajan, hasta el oro se destroza, hasta las plumas preciosas se desgarran. ¿Acaso para siempre en la tierra? ¡Sólo un breve instante aquí!

* *What different images are used for life and death in the first poem?*
* *How is the idea of the brevity of life conveyed in the second?*

V

**allí van los señoríos
derechos a acabarse**
that's where the high and mighty all end up

V

acaso
perhaps
se resquebrejan
crack
se destroza
is destroyed
se desgarra
comes apart

La Semana Santa

Fiestas are a central part of Spanish life: they are holidays, celebrations, rituals to relive long-standing traditions. Most of them are still linked to the anniversary of the patron saint of a town (**las fiestas patronales**) or to other religious festivals. The most famous of all are probably the Easter Processions (**Semana Santa**), and particularly the week of activities in Seville. The pointed hoods of the **nazarenos** are familiar across the world; so are the great floats bearing religious figures (**los pasos**), the most famous of which is perhaps **La Macarena**, one of the Virgins of the Bullfight. The figure of the Virgin or Christ on each **paso** is elaborately dressed and jewelled as the **cofradías** compete for the honour of the best-presented figure. The **pasos** are brought out by their bearers (**costaleros**) from the various churches in the city and begin their procession (**desfile**) through the streets to the cathedral. Passionate **saetas** are sung to stop the **pasos** at various places. After congregating at the cathedral and passing through it, they return to their home churches.

[101]

Unidad 9

María Peña Álvarez sells religious objects (**reliquias**) at religious festivals in Spain. She is in her seventies and works six months of the year.

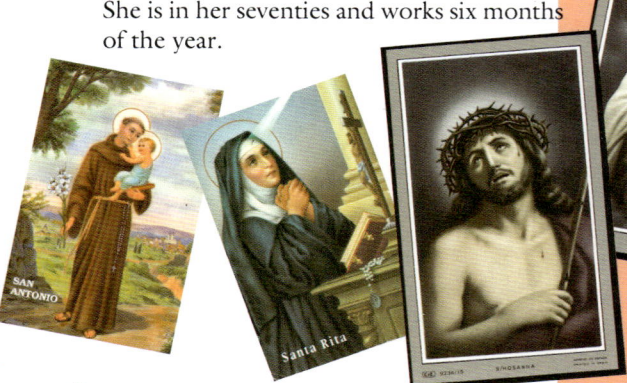

Enero:
15 y 16. Fiestas de San Antón, santo patrón de mi barrio. Como es santo patrón de los animales domésticos también llega todo el mundo con burros y bueyes y quién sabe qué. Siempre pongo un puesto allí.

Febrero:
Cádiz 5 de febrero a 4 de marzo.
Carnaval. Fiesta larga, y suprimida durante muchos años bajo Franco. Ahora la celebran de nuevo. Vendo mucho.

Abril:
Semana Santa. Siempre voy a Tobarra (Albacete). Allí la gente del pueblo pasea con tambores y toca continuamente durantes tres días. Luego a Sevilla o Granada – pues los turistas compran muchas reliquias. Me encantan mucho los Moros y Cristianos – títeres que presentan las antiguas batallas de moros contra cristianos en toda Andalucía.

Mayo:
Voy a Talavera de la Reina para el festival de San Isidro. Es una gran fiesta para los trabajadores y me encanta.

Junio:
Corpus Christi. Gran desfile y mucha devoción. ¡Es buen negocio!

* Where do you imagine María Peña would do her best business?

V

santo patrón
patron saint
quién sabe qué
who knows what
poner puesto
to set up a stall
suprimida
banned.
títeres
puppets
asistir
attend
tambores
drums

Veamos de nuevo

Gramática

1 I like dancing

In Unit 7 you saw how to use **gustar** to say you like something: **me gusta el café**; **me gustan las manzanas**. Remember that **gusta/gustan** referrred to singular and plural objects.

To say what you like doing you can use **gusta** with the infinitive of a verb.

Me gusta bailar
I like dancing
Nos gusta jugar al tenis
We like playing tennis

As always with **gustar** the subject (the person doing the liking) is indicated by the pronoun that goes before it: **me, te, nos, os** (I, you, we, you (pl)). **Le** can refer to he, she or you (**usted**), and **les** can refer to they or you (**ustedes**)

Le gusta bailar
He/ She likes *or* You like dancing
Les gusta beber el vino
They or You like drinking wine

Where there is a possibility of ambiguity, or when you want to emphasise who you are referring to, you can add an extra pronoun or use the name of the person:

A él/A ella le gusta bailar
He/She likes dancing

Unidad 9

A usted le gusta bailar
You like dancing
A Pepe/María le gusta bailar
Pepe/Maria likes dancing

Here is the complete list:

A mí me gusta	**A nosotros/as nos gusta**
A ti te gusta	**A vosotros/as os gusta**
A él/ella le gusta	**A ellos/ellas les gusta**
A usted le gusta	**A ustedes les gusta**

2 Who's it for?

Para indicates for whom something is intended or where it is going:

El café es para el señor Gómez

Or you can use it with one of the emphatic pronouns:

El café es para mí
The coffee is for me
Para mí el té, para ella el vino
The tea's for me, the wine's for her

Práctica

A *El ocio*

Argentina is a vast country with great variations in landscape and climate. The north-east is tropical and yet there are glaciers in the south; spanning the country from north to south are the Andes. On the map on the right are some of the different sports and leisure activities you can enjoy there. Can you match them with the corresponding pictures? Look up any you can't guess.

1 montar a caballo
2 esquiar
3 hacer andinismo (LA)
  hacer montañismo (Sp)
4 bailar y divertirse
5 practicar piragüismo
6 sacar fotografías
7 bucear

Can you tell a friend about two activities you like doing and then ask him whether he too likes these particular activities?

B *Mixed up*

Macarena has been collecting information on what lessons she and her classmates enjoy (if any!). Can you help her by matching up the two columns?

1 A Juan
2 A Rafael y Ana
3 A vosotros
4 A nosotras
5 Y ¿a ti Pedro

a no te gusta trabajar?
b le gusta el fútbol
c nos gusta el inglés
d os gusta la geografía
e les gusta la natación

[103]

C Odd one out

1 Which would you not eat as **tapas**?
   tortilla   calamares   infusión   ensaladilla
2 Which would you not put in a **bocadillo**?
   chorizo   naranja   queso   jamón
3 Which is never drunk with **leche**?
   café   té   sangría   chocolate
4 Which of these is not a soft drink?
   horchata   cerveza   zumo de naranja   mosto

1 La Noche Vieja

After spending Christmas with some Spanish friends, you want to take them out on New Year's Eve. Outside the market a local disco has stuck a poster advertising **el cotillón** (New Year's Eve party). Look at the poster and find out:

a how much it will cost for the three of you
b if you have to book, and if so where
c what is included in the price of the ticket
d how many people might be there

las uvas de la suerte
Spaniards traditionally eat 12 grapes at midnight to bring luck in the New Year
chocolate con churros
they drink hot chocolate with fritters very early in the morning on New Year's Day
delicias navideñas
Christmas sweets
bolsa de cotillón
party bag
saladitos
savoury nibbles

2 Agencia Cupido

The dating agency that you have just joined has sent you audio profiles of two possible contacts. After listening to them do you feel you'd like to get to know either of them any better? Can you say what some of your common interests are? In what areas would you be incompatible?

Unidad 9

3 Checklist

Can you do the following?

a Ask someone what they like doing and say what you like doing.
b Talk about dates.
c Say how you celebrate festivals and birthdays.
d Order a drink or snack.

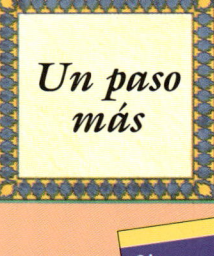

Un paso más

V
lustrar los zapatos
to polish shoes
el escaparate
shop window
aborrezco
I loathe
escupir
to spit

Gran Fiesta Noche Vieja 03

La Meca
Aguilas

1 AÑO MAS NOS AVALAN LAS 3.000 PLAZAS LIMITADAS QUE ASEGURAN UN GRAN AMBIENTE

- DELICIAS NAVIDEÑAS
- UVAS DE LA SUERTE
- BOLSA DE COTILLON
- REPOSTERIA
- SALADITOS
- FRUTOS SECOS
- BOCADILLOS VARIADOS
- CHOCOLATE CON CHURROS
- CAVA
- BOMBONES

BARRA LIBRE y COTILLON   € 50

Reservas:
en
Café-Pub COMIC
Totalmente Reformado
Tel: 976 44 81 99
y en LA MECA
Tels: 976 410976 – 976590386

Unidad 10

De viaje

Así se habla
Talking about travel
Asking about routes and times
Buying tickets

Temas
Trenes, buses, aviones

Veamos de nuevo

Unidad 10

Así se habla 1

Tomo el metro para ir al trabajo

Talking about travel

1

Match the words for each means of transport with its corresponding picture.

a el autobús/bus (LA)
b el metro/
   el subterráneo,
   'subte' (Argentina)
c el taxi
d el coche/carro (LA)
e el avión
f el tren
g el ferry

V
como estoy haciendo 'la mili'
as I am doing the military service
fuera de Madrid
outside Madrid
viaje de placer
pleasure trip

G
coger/cojo
to take
venir/vengo
to come

(See p 112)

2

Listen to three people talking about the type of transport they normally use. On the list above tick each means of transport you hear mentioned. Then listen again and find out when they use each means of transport and what purpose they use it for, if mentioned.

1 .....   2 .....   3 .....

Así se acostumbra

Spanish National Railways (**RENFE**) offer several different kinds of service. The **Talgo** and the more modern and luxurious **AVE** provide the fast intercity services, while the **Electro** covers the same routes as a stopping service. The **Tranvía** is a suburban service. Suburban trains are **trenes de cercanías**, while the **trenes regionales** serve smaller towns. There are **metro** systems in Madrid, Barcelona, Bilbao and Seville.

Así se dice

To indicate how you normally travel, say:

Cojo/Tomo/Uso el tren ...
   I take the train ...

To indicate where you are going or why, say:

... para ir al trabajo
   ... (in order) to go to work

You can also say:

Voy/vengo al trabajo en coche/ autobús/etc
   I go/come to work by car/bus/etc.
Voy a la universidad andando/a pie
   I walk to the university/ go on foot

☞ Ex. D, p. 113

3 Y ahora tú

¿Qué medios de transporte usas normalmente? ¿Para qué? ¿Cómo vas al trabajo o a clases?

4 🔊²

A Spanish woman explains why she always prefers to travel by train when she goes on holiday. Listen and read the conversation and find out why.

– Cuando vas de vacaciones, ¿vas en tren normalmente?
– Sí, normalmente voy en tren de vacaciones.
– ¿Por qué prefieres el tren?
– Me gusta viajar en tren porque es un transporte cómodo... No es caro. El precio es más o menos equivalente a otro medio de transporte ... y el tiempo también.

Así se dice

To ask about preferences, say:

¿Que medio de transporte prefieres?
  What means of transport do you prefer?
¿Qué prefieres, el tren o el autobús?
  Which do you prefer, train or coach?
¿Por qué prefieres el tren?
  Why do you prefer the train?

To answer, say:

(Prefiero el tren) porque es barato ...
  I prefer the train because it's cheap ...
... cómodo y rápido
  ... comfortable and quick

☞ Ex. A, p. 113

---

5 Y ahora tú

¿Qué tipo de transporte prefieres en la ciudad? ¿Por qué? ¿Y cuando haces viajes de larga distancia?

**Estación de Atocha
Madrid**

Talgo 200
MADRID
MALAGA

V
puedes
you can
cómodo
comfortable
cualquier otro
any other

G
preferir
to prefer
(See p. 112)

V
la estación de tren
train station
**la estación/
terminal (LA) de
autobuses**
bus station

G
poder
to be able
(See p. 112)

V
de larga distancia
long distance

2
¿Cómo puedo ir al Cabo de Gata?
Asking about routes and times

1 🔊³

Carmen is in Almería and wants to visit el Cabo de Gata, a nature reserve near the town. She is in the tourist office trying to find out how to get there. Find out how she can go and where she can leave from.

– ¿Cómo puedo ir al Cabo de Gata?
– Hay varios autobuses cada día.
– ¿Dónde puedo coger el autobús?
– Hay una estación de autobuses en el centro de la ciudad.
– Muchas gracias.
– De nada.

Así se dice

To ask how to get to a place, say:

¿Cómo puedo ir al .../ a la ...?
  How can I get to ...?
¿Cómo puedo ir de .... a ....?
  How can I get from ... to ....?

The answer you might get is:

Puede ir en tren/autobús
  You can go by train/bus
Hay autobuses/trenes
  There are buses/trains

[107]

Unidad 10

2 Go to Peru!

You are in a travel agency making enquiries about travelling in Peru. You want to go to Lima and travel on from there to some of the places in the brochure. How would you ask how to get to the following places:

a From Lima to Arequipa
b From Lima to Cuzco
c From Cuzco to Machu Picchu
d From Lima to Iquitos

Machu Picchu: La ciudad perdida

V
a partir de from
con antelación in advance
billete (Sp)/ **boleto** (LA) ticket

V
vuelo flight
avioneta light plane
durar to last

3 🔊 4

The travel agent tells you about routes, means of transport and how long it takes to get to some of the places in Activity 2. Make a note of this information for each place.

4 🔊 5

Raquel is making enquiries at the railway station in Madrid. Listen and say whether these statements are true (**verdadero**) or false (**falso**). If false, correct them. Before playing the tape, check the vocabulary on the left.

a Hay dos trenes directos para Barcelona por la mañana.
b Hay un tren a las 10.45.
c El viaje dura unas 7 horas.
d Hay servicio de restaurante en el tren.
e El billete de ida y vuelta cuesta 65 euros.
f No es posible hacer reservas por Internet.

Así se dice

If you are making travel enquiries, this is what you might say:

For general information:

Quisiera/Quiero información sobre trenes
   I'd like some information on trains

For times and timetables:

¿Tiene horario de trenes?
   Do you have a train timetable?
¿A qué hora sale/llega?
   What time does it leave/arrive?
¿Me puede decir a qué hora sale …
   …Can you tell me what time …
… el próximo autobús para Madrid?
   …the next coach for Madrid leaves?

For facilities and other inquiries:

¿Qué servicios tiene?
   What facilities does it have?
¿Se puede fumar en el autobús?
   Is smoking allowed on the bus?

Unidad 10

5 Y ahora tú

You are in Cartagena and you want to go to Bogotá by bus. You are talking to a ticket clerk on the phone. Ask what time the first bus leaves in the morning and what time it arrives in Bogotá. Ask what facilities it has and whether smoking is permitted on the bus.

3
Quería un billete de ida y vuelta
Buying tickets

1 Reservas 🔊⁶

Here is Nieves booking a seat on the train to Barcelona. When does she want to travel?

– ¿Se puede hacer reservas?
– Se puede hacer reservas siempre, hasta con 24 horas de antelación.
– De acuerdo. Pues quiero hacer una reserva para Barcelona para el viernes día ocho.

Así se dice

To ask if you can book a seat, say:

¿Se puede hacer reservas?
 Can one make reservations?

To book it, say:

Quiero reservar un asiento ...
 I'd like to book a seat ...
... para el tren de las tres...
 ... for the 3 o'clock train
para el día 7 en el Talgo de las 9 de la mañana
 ... for the 7th, on the 9 o'clock train

2 Y ahora tú

You have various trips to make by train early next week and you decide to go to the station in Madrid to book them in advance. Look at your diary and the train timetable below. What will you say to the ticket-clerk in each case?

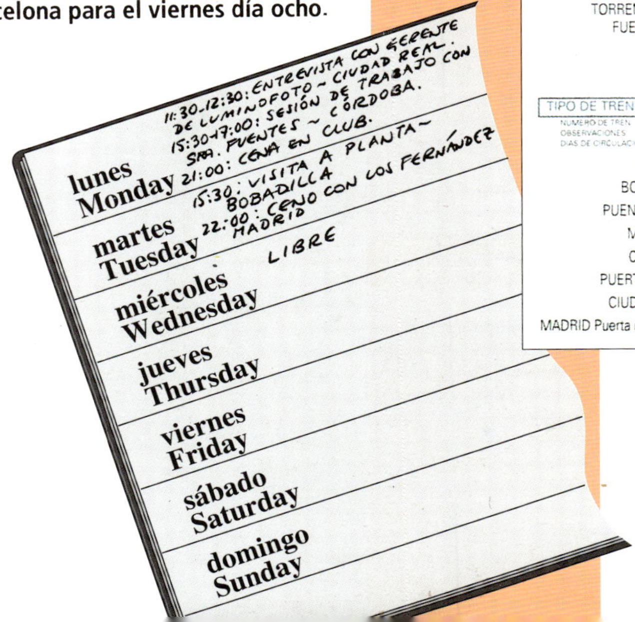

HORARIOS	MADRID - MALAGA			
TIPO DE TREN (*)	LLANO	VALLE	PUNTA	LLANO
NUMERO DE TREN	9120	9126	9130	9136
OBSERVACIONES	(1)			(2)
DIAS DE CIRCULACION	L M X J V S	L M X J V S D	L M X J V S	L M V
MADRID Puerta de Atocha	10:00	13:00	15:30	18:10
CIUDAD REAL	11:01	14:01	–	19:11
PUERTOLLANO	11:18	14:18	–	19:28
CORDOBA	12:13	15:08	17:34	20:18
MONTILLA	–	15:50	–	–
PUENTE GENIL	–	16:09	18:45	21:29
BOBADILLA	13:49	16:37	19:14	21:58
MALAGA	14:45	17:35	20:05	22:55
TORREMOLINOS	–	–	–	23:35
FUENGIROLA	–	–	–	23:50

	MALAGA - MADRID				
TIPO DE TREN (*)	VALLE	LLANO	PUNTA	VALLE	VALLE
NUMERO DE TREN	9113	9119	9133	9137	9139
OBSERVACIONES	(1)		(3)		(4)
DIAS DE CIRCULACION	L M X J V S D	L M X J V S D	L M X J V S	L M X J V S	•••••• D
MALAGA	06:45	09:30	16:10	18:50	19:40
BOBADILLA	07:29	10:14	16:54	19:49	20:35
PUENTE GENIL	–	10:42	–	20:22	21:03
MONTILLA	–	11:00	–	–	–
CORDOBA	09:06	11:52	18:26	21:30	22:06
PUERTOLLANO	–	12:41	–	22:19	22:55
CIUDAD REAL	–	12:58	–	22:36	23:12
MADRID Puerta de Atocha	11:05	14:00	20:25	23:45	00:15

lunes / Monday 11:30-12:30: ENTREVISTA CON GERENTE DE LUMINOFOTO - CIUDAD REAL. 15:30-17:00: SESIÓN DE TRABAJO CON SRA. PUENTES - CORDOBA. 21:00: CENA EN CLUB.

martes / Tuesday 15:30: VISITA A PLANTA - BOBADILLA. 22:00: CENA CON LOS FERNÁNDEZ - MADRID

miércoles / Wednesday LIBRE

jueves / Thursday

viernes / Friday

sábado / Saturday

domingo / Sunday

Unidad 10

3 Billetes de ida y vuelta
🔊 7

Pilar is at Atocha station in Madrid. Listen to her conversation with a ticket clerk and see if you can answer the following questions. Read the questions before you listen to the tape.

¿Pilar quiere ...
a – ir a Sevilla o a Cercedilla?
b – viajar el próximo martes o el próximo miércoles?
c – un billete de ida o un billete de ida y vuelta?
d – ir por la noche y volver por la noche o ir por la mañana y volver por la noche?

Así se dice

To ask for a ticket you can say:

Quisiera (comprar) un billete para (ir a) Valencia
I'd like a ticket to (go to) Valencia

For the type of ticket you want, say:

un billete de ida (y vuelta)
a single/return ticket
un billete de fumadores/no fumadores
a smoker/non-smoker

For the time you'd like to go or return, say:

Quiero ir/salir/volver a las 8 de la mañana
I'd like to go/leave/come back at 8 a.m.

For your method of payment, say:

Voy a pagar en efectivo
I'll pay cash
... con tarjeta de crédito/con cheque
by credit card/by cheque

V

de ida
single
de ida y vuelta
return
el próximo (lunes)
next (Monday)
fumador
smoker
que tenga buen viaje
have a nice trip

G

voy a pagar
I'll pay

(See G 13.3)

---

4 Y ahora tú

LA REGIONAL V.S.A
MEDINA CAMPO – VALLADOLID

SALIDAS VALLADOLID	SALIDAS MEDINA
SABADOS	
8,30	8,30
10,30	10,30
13,30	13,30
15,00	15,00
18,00	18,00
19,30	19,30

You are in Valladolid and you want to visit Medina del Campo, which is on one of Valladolid's wine routes. You want to go on Saturday to spend the day there, but you need to be back in Valladolid by 8 p.m. on the same day. The journey time by coach is 30 minutes. Look at the bus timetable and choose suitable departure times from Valladolid and back.

🔊 8 Imagine you are now at the ticket window at the bus station in Valladolid. You've said you want a ticket for Medina del Campo. Now listen to the clerk and answer his questions.

Unidad 10

Temas

Trenes, buses y aviones

"El tren"

Antonio Machado, the great Spanish poet, recalled some of his own feelings about travel.

**Yo para todo viaje
– siempre sobre la madera
de mi vagón de tercera –
voy ligero de equipaje.
Si es de noche, porque no
acostumbro a dormir yo,
y de día, por mirar
los arbolitos pasar,
yo nunca duermo en el tren,
y sin embargo voy bien.
¡Este placer de alejarse!
Londres, Madrid, Ponferrada,
tan lindos...para marcharse.**

(Antonio Machado, *Poesías completas*, Austral, Madrid, 1963, p.92)

* *Are the feelings that Machado expresses about travel positive or negative?*

Los buses

The bus has a central place in the life of many Latin Americans. Railway lines are few and far between – and the train is often the slowest way to travel. So people normally move from place to place by bus. And there is an enormous amount of movement and a great variety of buses to carry them. A high proportion of the urban population are recent immigrants. They still have contacts in their home villages, and will often return there. At the same time, growing numbers are travelling from remote places to the towns and cities, and sometimes to other countries from there. It is a continent of constant movement!

Within the cities the crowded buses vie with taxis and one another for space in the streets. The range of vehicles is enormous; from the elegant luxury buses (**autocares de lujo**, **púllman**, **góndolas** in Chile) to the often dilapidated and sometimes positively dangerous vehicles with wooden seats and plenty of standing room (**autobuses de segunda clase**). Inner-city buses have as many names as there are types of bus: **el bus** or **autobús** is a general term, but in Mexico it is called **el camión** and in Chile it is called **el micro**, in Cuba and the Canary Islands **la guagua**, in Peru **el ómnibus**. They vary enormously in quality too – from the pick-up trucks with wooden benches in Nicaragua, to the modern Línea 100 of Mexico City. If the bus is too crowded, then you can always try the collective taxis, or minibuses, which ply the long central avenues of most cities – **el colectivo**, **la combi**, as they are sometimes called. What is certain is that in the fast-expanding cities, a growing population with its need to find work wherever it is available will ensure an increasing travelling public in every direction.

Unidad 10

Los grandes viajes en tren

One of the great train journeys of the world is along the Central Railroad of Peru, the highest normal gauge railway in the world. From Lima it carries the traveller up its zig-zag route to Huancayo, at 3 271 metres above sea level. It is in every sense a breathtaking journey – as the oxygen bottles carried on every train can testify!

Building on the railway began in 1870, under the direction of Henry Meiggs, an American engineer. Its aim was to link the mining areas of the Central Valley. The thousands of men who built the railway worked in appalling conditions, and there was precious little pay even for those who survived the diseases or the bitter cold that claimed so many victims.

The journey begins at Lima's station **Desamparados** (it means 'The Unprotected'). The train moves out of the characteristic mist (**la garúa**) of the city, to the sudden greenness of Chosica, and across la Quebrada de Verrugas named after the plague of warts (**verrugas**) that killed many of the labourers. The track rises to its highest point – the freezing open wastes (**puna**) of Ticlio, at 4 758 metres above sea level – then down to the mining town of La Oroya dominated, like any other mining town, by the winding-gear and the wagons that carry coal and copper to the coast. The journey ends, eleven hours later, at the beautiful market town of Huancayo.

Veamos de nuevo

Gramática

1 Radical-changing verbs

The verb **preferir** (to prefer) looks like this in the present tense:

prefiero	I prefer	**preferimos**	we prefer
prefieres	you prefer	**preferís**	you prefer
prefiere	he, she prefers	**prefieren**	they prefer
	you prefer (formal)		you prefer (formal)

You will notice that the **e** in the infinitive **preferir** becomes **ie** in the singular forms and in the 3rd person plural, including **ustedes**. This makes it a radical-changing verb (see **querer**, Unit 5, p.57).

Other verbs which behave in the same way include: **querer**, **tener**, **empezar**, **comenzar**, **divertirse**, **venir**.

Note: **tener** and **venir** are also unusual in the first person singular: **tengo** and **vengo**.

Poder (to be able) is another radical-changing verb:

puedo	I can	**podemos**	we can
puedes	you can	**podéis**	you can
puede	he, she can	**pueden**	they can
	you can (formal)		you can (formal)

Here the **o** in **poder** becomes **ue** in the singular and the 3rd person plural.

Unidad 10

Other verbs behaving in this way include: **acostarse**, **volver**, **dormir**.
(For more on radical-changing verbs see G 9.2 and G 17.)

2 Se puede

Se puede can be used in a range of different ways, to express what is possible and what is allowed.

(1) Possibility: as in the English 'you can, one can':

Se puede tomar el tren o el autobús
You can take the train or the bus

(2) Permission: as in the English 'one may do something' or 'it is allowed':

¿Se puede hacer una reserva?
Can one make a reservation?
No se puede fumar
Smoking is not allowed

3 Further uses of para

We saw in Unit 9 how **para** is used to say for whom something is intended: **El café es para mí**.

In this unit it is used for direction and purpose:

Un billete para Salamanca
A ticket to Salamanca
El tren para Valencia
The train to (or for) Valencia
Tomo el tren para ir al trabajo
I take the train (in order) to go to work

Note that when **para** is used to express purpose it is normally followed by an infinitive.

Práctica

A El transporte

Each member of Clara's family prefers a different means of transport. Can you fill in the blanks with the right form of **preferir**.

En mi familia, cada uno ..... un modo de transporte diferente. Mis padres ..... la rapidez del avión. Mi hermano Juan es estudiante y ..... viajar con sus amigos en bicicleta; en cambio Alicia y Ana ..... ir en tren. Yo, por el contrario ..... la comodidad del coche. Y tú ¿qué .....?

B No se puede

Here is a sign stating that smoking is not allowed. Can you write signs saying what is not allowed in the following cases?

| a) photography | b) eating | c) paying with a credit card |
| d) entry | e) drinking the water | f) swimming |

C Mystery destination!

Find the Spanish words which are missing from the following sentences. The first letters put together will give you the name of a famous Spanish town.

	Inicial
1 ¿A qué hora ..... el tren para Valencia?	...
2 Cojo el tren en la	...
3 Quisiera un billete de ida y	...
4 Uso el metro para ..... al trabajo	...
5 ¿A qué hora ..... el tren de León?	...
6 Allí tiene ..... parada de autobuses	...
7 El ..... llega al aeropuerto de Lima	...

D Coming and going...

Finish the sentences using the right form of each verb:

1 (Yo) ..... a clase pronto (*venir*)
2 Margarita y su marido ..... de vacaciones a Canarias (*ir*).
3 ¿Cómo ..... vosotros a la oficina? (*venir*)
4 Las chicas y yo ..... siempre el metro (*coger*)
5 Este ferry ..... a Barcelona (*ir*)

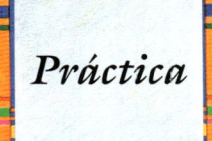

Unidad 10

Un paso más

1 Excursión con guía

While on holiday in Barcelona, you decide to go sightseeing. You have heard about the magnificent monastery of Montserrat near Barcelona and you enquire at the hotel about it. Can you ask the following:

a If there are guided tours to Montserrat.
b How to get there.
c How much it costs.
d What time you leave and return.
e If you have to book in advance.

2 El ferry

You are still in Barcelona and you'd like to take your family on a trip to Palma de Mallorca. You read the **Trasmediterránea** brochure and work out:

a How much it costs for two adults and two children (with or without a cabin)
b If it's cheaper to buy a return fare
c What discounts there are for children
d What time the ferry leaves on a Friday
e What time it leaves Palma on a Tuesday

3A 🔊 9

You are at Santa Justa railway station in Sevilla waiting for a train to Madrid when you hear three announcements on the loudspeaker. Work out the following:

Tren	procedente de	con destino a	vía
Train	coming from	going to	platform
1			
2			
3			

Which is your train?

3B

You are at Barajas airport in Madrid waiting for a flight to London. Work out the following three announcements:

Vuelo	compañía	procedente de	destino	puerta
Flight no.	airline	coming from	going to	gate
1				
2				
3				

Which is your flight?

4 Checklist

a Say how you travel to work.
b Say which means of transport you prefer.
c Ask how to get to a place.
d Ask and understand about departure times.
e Ask if you can make a reservation.
f Say you'd like a return ticket.

TRASMEDITERRANEA

Travesía	20.06 / 11.09.03 * 17.06 / 18.09.03		12.09 / 16.10.03	
	Hora	Día • Day • Jour • Tag	Hora	Día • Day • Jour • Tag
Barcelona–Palma	13.00	• • J V • •	13.00	• M • • • • •
	23.30	L M X J V S D	23.30	L M X J V S D
Palma–Barcelona	13.00	L M X • V S D	13.00	• M • • • S •
	23.30	• • X J V • D	23.30	L M X J V • D

TARIFA GENERAL DE PASAJEROS

ACOMODACIONES	TRANSPORTE MARÍTIMO	TARIFA PORTUARIA	TOTAL
Camarote doble ocupado x 2	92,30	10	102,30
Camarote cuadruple ocupado x 4	42,30	3	45,30
Butaca Turista (Ferry)	25,30	3	28,30

TARIFAS REDUCIDAS

1. TARIFA IDA Y VUELTA
Pasajeros
– 15% DESCUENTO
Acomodaciones: Todas
Trayectos: Península/Baleares e interinsulares/Baleares e interinsulares canarias, excepto Jet-Foil.

MENORES
– Hasta dos años sin cumplir: gratis.
– De dos a doce años cumplidos la mitad del precio del adulto.

NOTA. ESTAS TARIFAS PUEDEN SER MODIFICADAS SIN PREVIO AVISO.

Puesta a punto 2

1 ¿A qué hora?

Make sentences using the appropriate form of the verbs and writing out the times in full.

e.g. Piluca 7.15 am (empezar)/
     4.00 pm (terminar)
     Piluca empieza el trabajo a las siete y cuarto y termina a las cuatro.

a Yo – 7.00 am (levantarse)/
    11.00 pm (acostarse)
b El partido de fútbol – 3.00 pm (comenzar)/
    4.45 pm (terminar)
c Marta y Sergio – 9.00 am (ir a la oficina)/
    7.30 pm (volver a casa)
d Patricia – 8.45 am (venir)/
    5.30 pm (regresar)
e Marisa – 9 am (hacer la limpieza)/
    7.30 pm (prepara la cena)
f Los toros – 5 pm (comenzar)/
    7.00 pm (acabar)

2 Ser or Estar

Complete the sentences with the correct form of **ser** or **estar** as appropriate.

1 El salón ..... grande y alegre.
2 Yo no ..... enferma.
3 La casa de Matilde ..... enfrente del banco.
4 Mis padres ..... simpáticos.
5 ..... las cuatro de la tarde.
6 Vosotros, ¿..... muy cansados?

3 Los billetes

The following sentences have been jumbled up. Put them in the correct order to make a conversation.

a De ida y vuelta, segunda clase, no fumador.
b Hay el TALGO que sale a las 4.30 y el AVE que sale a las 6.15.
c Muy bien. ¿Cuándo quiere viajar?
d Quisiera dos billetes para Málaga.
e El próximo martes por la tarde.
f Son 62,35 euros.
g ¿Ida o ida y vuelta?
h Prefiero el TALGO de las 4.30, ¿cuánto es?

4 Sopa de letras

Find the fifteen words hidden in this grid – vertically, horizontally, diagonally and even backwards. They come under the following headings: transport, parts of the body and rooms of a house.

A	U	T	O	B	U	S	H	L	N	B	A
S	L	C	O	C	I	N	A	R	E	R	C
E	S	P	A	L	D	A	B	R	Ñ	A	O
C	O	M	E	D	O	R	I	F	M	Z	M
A	O	O	G	A	M	O	T	S	E	O	U
B	S	F	I	N	B	G	A	R	A	J	E
E	I	A	E	D	A	A	C	S	E	E	L
Z	L	P	L	R	S	F	I	Y	F	N	A
A	L	R	T	O	R	C	O	C	H	E	S
E	A	V	I	O	N	Y	N	S	W	P	R

5 ¿Dónde?

In which places are the following sentences said?

a in a house   b at the chemist
c in a bar   d at the station

1 Por favor, una tapa de calamares y una cerveza.
2 Quisiera un billete de ida para Valencia.
3 El salón está enfrente de la cocina.
4 Hay que cambiar de tren.
5 ¿Tiene algo para el dolor de cabeza?
6 ¿Hay bocadillos?

6 ¡Qué familia!

Your new neighbours, Mr and Mrs Pirúlez, seem to be rather striking. Which of the phrases below would you apply to each of them?

e.g. **El señor Pirúlez tiene el pelo corto .....
es simpático .....**

La señora Pirúlez tiene ..... /es .....

rubio   pelo largo   alto   delgada   fría
simpático   morena
ojos verdes   pelo corto   ojos azules
delgado   antipática   barba   extrovertido

Puesta a punto 2

7 Mistakes

Each of the following sentences has a mistake. Find the mistake and write the correct version.

e.g. *A María, nos gusta el café.*
     A María, le gusta el café.

a ¿Qué hora son?
b Mi amigo y yo prefiero el café.
c Teresa quiere a vivir en Madrid.
d Yo tienes el pelo largo y liso.
e Juan está enferma.
f A Martín gusta jugar al tenis.
g Quiero una billete de ida y vuelta para Alicante.
h El salón es amplia y bonita.
i Me duele mi espalda.

8 Puesta a punto oral

From your hotel room you want to book a flight to Bogotá. You ring Tierra, Mar y Aire Travel Agency.

a Greet the operator and enquire about times of flights to Bogotá.
b Say you want a single ticket for Saturday morning.
c Ask the price.
d Give your name, and say that you are at the Hotel Caribe, room 537.
e Ask what time you have to be at the airport.

Unidad 11

Nos quedamos para el festival

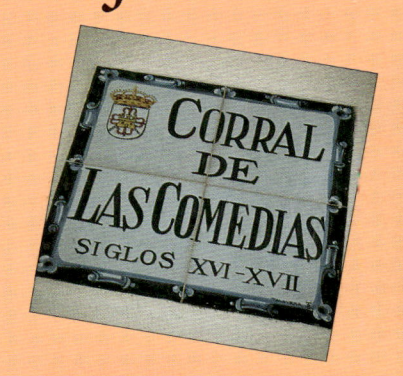

Así se habla

Booking a hotel room

Checking in and out. Making complaints

What's on and where to buy tickets

Temas

El gran teatro del mundo

Veamos de nuevo

Unidad 11

Así se habla 1
¿Tienen una habitación libre?
Booking a hotel room

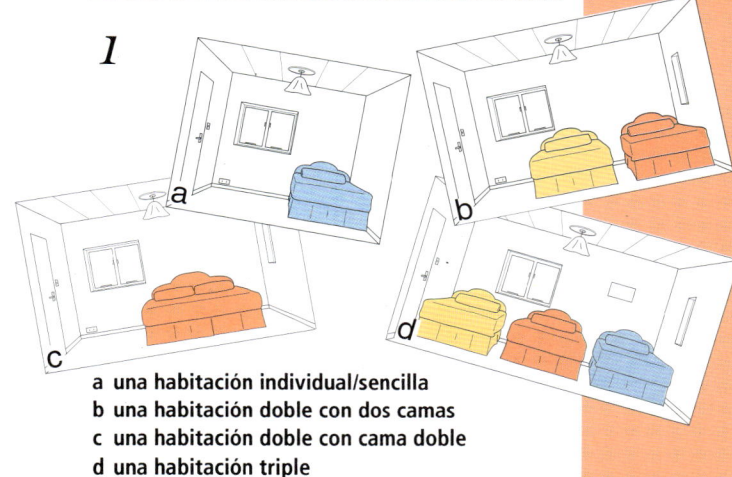

1

a una habitación individual/sencilla
b una habitación doble con dos camas
c una habitación doble con cama doble
d una habitación triple

🔊 ¹ Raquel is planning to go to Barcelona for a short visit and she needs to book a hotel room. Listen to her making enquiries on the phone and read the conversation. Find out the type of room she wants, when she wants it for, the price per night and what it includes.

– Muy bien.
– ¿Cuál es el precio de la habitación?
– 78 euros por noche. Está incluido el desayuno en el precio.
– Bueno, pues ¿puedo hacer una reserva?
– Sí, ¿a nombre de quién, por favor?
– A nombre de Raquel González.
– Raquel González. Muy bien.
– Pues muchas gracias, ¿eh?
– Vale, hasta luego.
– Hasta luego.

V
quería saber si
I'd like to know if
el desayuno está incluido
breakfast is included

V
incluir
to include

Así se dice

To find out if a room is available, say:

¿Tiene una habitación libre?
Do you have a room?

To specify what kind of room you want, say:

Quiero/Quisiera (reservar) una habitación individual...
I'd like a single room ...
...con baño/con ducha
...with a bath/with a shower

To indicate when you want it or for how long, say:

... para el fin de semana/para tres noches
... for the weekend/ for three nights
... para el 10 de marzo
... for 10th March *or:*
... del 16 al 30 de marzo
... from 16th to 30th March

To ask the price of the room, say:

¿Cuál es el precio de la habitación?
What's the price of the room?

To find out if breakfast or taxes are included, say:

¿Está incluido el desayuno?
¿Están incluidos los impuestos? *or:*
¿Qué incluye el precio?
What does the price include?

[118]

2

	T.B.*	T.A.*
Habitación individual / Chambre individuelle / Single room / Einzelzimmer	55 EUROS	71 EUROS
Habitación doble / Chambre double / Double room / Doppelzimmer	67 EUROS	91 EUROS
Habitación triple / Chambre triple / Triple room / Zimmer für 3 Personen	90 EUROS	123 EUROS
Habitación doble-sala / Chambre double avec salon / Double room with lounge / Doppelzimmer mit wohnraum	111 EUROS	153 EUROS
Desayuno / Petit déjeuner / Breakfast / Frühstück	6,61 EUROS	6,61 EUROS
Comidas / Repas / One meal / Mittag- oder abendessen	8,41 EUROS	8,41 EUROS
Pensión completa / Pension complète / Full pension / Vollpension	19,92 EUROS	19,92 EUROS
Media pensión / Demi-pension / Half pension / Halbpension	15,03 EUROS	15,03 EUROS
Parking / Parking / Garage / Parkplatz	GRATUITO · GRATUIT FREE · KOSTENLOS	

*T.B.: 1/1 AL 30/6 1/10 AL 31/12   *T.B.: DU 1/1 AU 30/6 DU 1/10 AU 31/12
*T.A.: 1/7 AL 30/9   *T.A.: DU 1/7 AU 30/9

HOTEL ZARAUZ

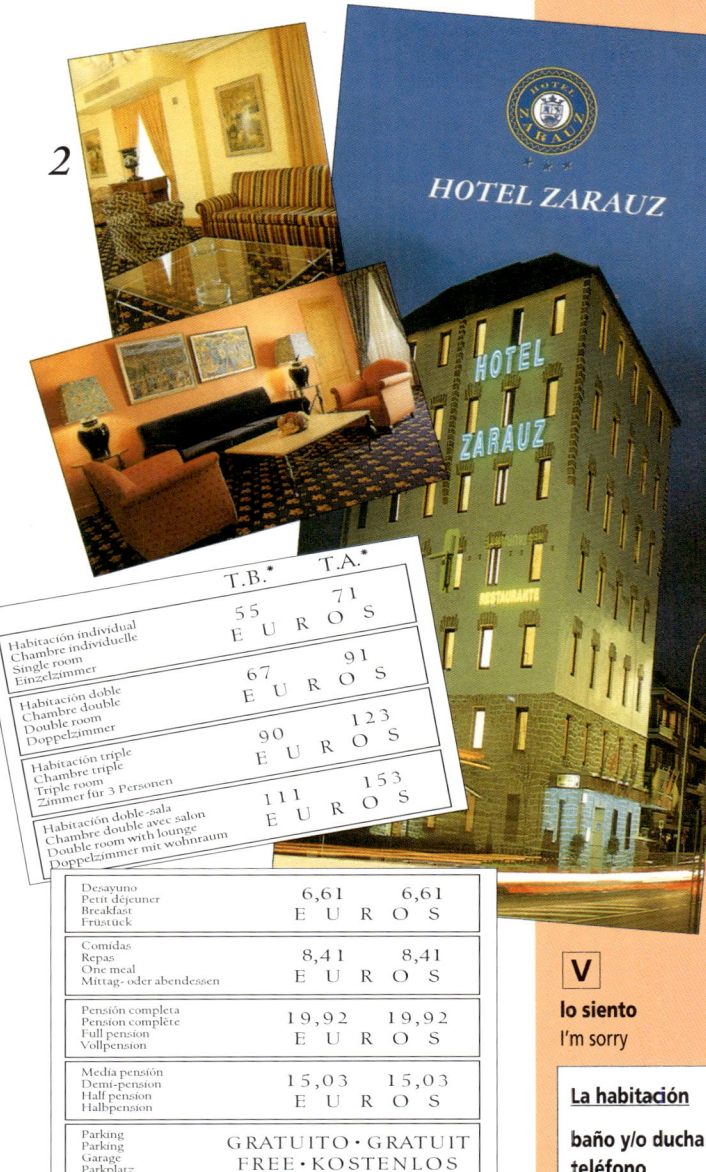

Martin and his wife are planning to take their two teenage daughters to Guipuzcoa at the end of May. How much does it cost at the Hotel Zarauz for two double rooms including breakfast?

3 ¿Qué quieren? 🔊²

Listen to three people asking for rooms. What kind of room does each person want? Do they actually get it?

1.....   2.....   3.....

Así se acostumbra

The range of accommodation in the Spanish-speaking world is enormous: from exclusive five-star hotels (**hoteles de cinco estrellas**), to inexpensive guest houses (**pensiones** or **casas de huéspedes**) or lodgings (**hospedajes**) which offer only basic amenities. It includes **hostales** (small, often family-run hotels), **albergues juveniles** (youth hostels), **residencias** (hostels) and **moteles**. Be warned that **un motel** in some countries in Latin America is not for the family, but for romantic encounters! Also at the top of the range in Spain are the luxurious **paradores nacionales** – usually historic buildings that have been converted into hotels; in some areas of Latin America old farmhouses have been converted into **hosterías** for the same purpose. There are also cottages (**casas rurales**) and flats (**apartamentos**) to let (**de alquiler**).

4 ¿Qué servicios tiene?

Match the facilities with their symbols.

V
lo siento
I'm sorry

La habitación

baño y/o ducha
teléfono
hilo musical
televisión
aire acondicionado
calefacción

El hotel

restaurante
bar
cafetería
discoteca
tienda
piscina
peluquería
salón social
aparcamiento (Sp)/estacionamento (LA)
pista de tenis (Sp)/cancha de tenis (LA)

5 🔊³

Listen to a receptionist describing hotel and room facilities to a customer and make a note of them. Also find out if room service (**servicio de habitaciones**) is available.

Hotel facilities: .....
Room facilities: .....
Price per night: low season high season

6 *Y ahora tú*

You've just arrived in Zaragoza with another couple and after going round the town you find a hotel.

a Tell the receptionist that you'd like a single room with a shower for two nights for yourself, and a double room with a double bed for four nights for your friends.
b Ask the price of each room and whether breakfast is included.
c Ask if the rooms have air-conditioning and find out if the hotel has a restaurant.

2
¿Tiene una reserva a nombre de Cobos?
Checking in and out. Making complaints

1 🔊⁴

Ana has booked a room in a hotel in Costa Rica. Listen and read her conversation with the receptionist as she checks in. What information does she have to write in the booking form? Where is room 2097?

Unidad 11

V
temporada baja
low season
temporada alta
high season

V
me pone
put
firma
signature
subiendo las gradas
up the steps

– Buenos días.
– Buenos días.
– Tengo una reserva.
– Sí señora. ¿A nombre de quién?
– Me llamo Ana Cobos.
– Sí, señorita. Aquí está. Aquí tengo la reserva.
– Muy bien.
– Señorita, me pone aquí su dirección ... número de pasaporte, su firma aquí, y aquí, y su tarjeta de crédito, por favor.
– De acuerdo.
– Señorita, su habitación es la 2097. Está subiendo las gradas, a mano derecha, y bienvenida.

Así se acostumbra

The terms **señorita** (Miss), **señora** (Mrs) and **señor** (Mr) are commonly used to address people in formal situations and as a mark of respect. In a hotel or shop, for example, they are equivalent to 'Sir' or 'Madam' – **Sí, señora** (Yes, madam). In some parts of Latin America, professional titles such as **ingeniero**, **arquitecto**, and **licenciado** (a person with a university degree) are also used as respectful terms of address.

Así se dice

When you arrive at a hotel having booked you could ask:

¿Tiene una reserva (Sp)/ **reservación** (LA) ...
... a nombre de Cobos?
   Do you have a booking for Cobos?

Or you could say:

Tengo una habitación reservada...
   I've booked a room ...
... (a nombre de Cobos)
   ... (in the name of Cobos)

2 Y ahora tú 🔊 5

Imagine you've just arrived in San José de Costa Rica. You've booked a hotel room for four nights. You go to the hotel and speak to the receptionist. Start as follows; then listen to the receptionist's questions and reply accordingly.

You: **Buenas tardes. Tengo una habitación reservada.**
Receptionist: ...

What room number were you given?

3 Making complaints

Some hotel facilities are not always as they should be. Here are some of the common things that you might want to complain about. What are they? Use the Glossary if you need to.

No hay ...	No funciona ...	... está(n) sucio/a(s)
... agua caliente	... la ducha	las toallas .....
... jabón	... la nevera	las sábanas ....
... papel higiénico	... la calefacción	el baño ...
... toallas	... el aseo/servicio	la habitación ...

4 Apartamento-hotel 'desastre'

All is not well when Marco arrives at the apartment he has rented for his holiday. Can you say what the problems are?

Unidad 11

V
forma de cancelar la cuenta
way of paying the bill

V
la factura
the invoice/the bill
la llave
the key

5 A la hora de salir 🔊 6

Two hotel guests are checking out. Can you say in each case how much the bill comes to, whether it's inclusive, and how the guests intend to pay? The beginning of each dialogue is given below.

<u>Room no. 206</u>
– Hola, buenas tardes.
– Buenas tardes.
– Quería mi cuenta, por favor.
– Sí, ¿me permite la llave?

<u>Room no. 55</u>
– Hola, quiero pagar la habitación.
– ¿Me puede decir su habitación, por favor?
– Cincuenta y cinco.
– Un momento, por favor. Aquí tiene la factura.

Así se dice

To indicate you want to pay your bill, say:

Quiero/quería pagar mi cuenta *(Sp)*/
cancelar mi cuenta *(LA)*
   I'd like to pay my bill

To ask what the bill includes, say:

¿Qué incluye la factura?
   What does the bill include?
¿Incluye impuestos?
   Does it include taxes?
¿Está el IVA incluido?
   Is VAT included?

6 Y ahora tú

a After checking in to a hotel room, you find that there is no hot water, there aren't any towels and the central heating isn't working. How do you complain about it to the receptionist?
b Next morning you want to leave. Tell the receptionist you'd like to pay your bill and give your room number.

[121]

Unidad 11

3 ¿Dónde puedo conseguir entradas?

What's on and where to buy tickets

1 Eventos y espectáculos

It is festival time in Almagro. Which of the events on the list are featured in the programme below?

a una corrida de toros
b un festival de teatro
c una exposición de pintura
d un espectáculo de danza
e un partido de fútbol
f un festival de cine
g un concierto

2 ¿Qué hay para ver?

Listen to a man asking for information at the tourist office in Almagro and make a note of two or three of the events mentioned.

3

Say which of the events in Activity 1 you like or dislike.

(No) me gustan los partidos de fútbol.

4

Raquel too is in Almagro and is being given some information about the **festival de teatro**. Listen, read the conversation and say whether the statements below are true or false.

V
la taquilla (Sp)/
la boletería (LA)
ticket office

Mujer: **El festival da comienzo el día 6 de julio y se clausura el 31. Hay distintas representaciones en distintos sitios.**
Raquel: **Las entradas ¿dónde las puedo conseguir?**
Mujer: **Las entradas, se pueden conseguir en el Hospital de San Juan de Dios, en la calle San Agustín número 23. Y el precio de las entradas, pues es de veinte euros para todas las obras en todos los sitios.**
Raquel: **¿Y las entradas se pueden reservar, o las tengo que comprar el mismo día en la taquilla?**
Mujer: **No. Se pueden reservar. Incluso hay un teléfono para ello que es el 926 88 22 00.**

a The festival lasts more than 3 weeks.
b You can buy tickets at two places.
c Tickets are at different prices.
d You can only buy tickets on the day of the performance.
e You can book by telephone.

XVII Festival d'Almagro
del 6 al 31 de julio

PLAZA MAYOR
CONCIERTOS DE BANDAS DE MÚSICA,
PASOS Y ENTREMESES,
COMEDIA DEL ARTE,
"EL RETABLO DE MAESE RODRIGO" Y
FOLKLORE INTERNACINAL DE TURQUIA,
PERÚ Y UCRANIA
Todos los días de actuación a las 21'00 h.

PALACIO DE LOS FUGGER
**EXPOSICIÓN DE PINTURA DE
ARSENIA TENORIO**

JARDINES DE LA PLAZA MAYOR
"GALERIA DE FAMOSOS"

**HOSPITAL DE
SAN JUAN DE DIOS**
"EL MÉDICO DE SU HONRA"
de Calderón de la Barca
COMPAÑÍA NACIONAL DE TEATRO
CLÁSICO
del 7 al 17 (miércoles 13, descanso)

Unidad 11

Temas

El gran teatro del mundo

Así se dice

To ask what there is to see or do, say:

¿Qué hay para ver o hacer?

To ask where to buy tickets, say:

¿Dónde puedo conseguir entradas ...
   Where can I buy tickets
...(para el concierto)?
   ... (for the concert)?

To ask where an event takes place, say:

¿Dónde es el concierto?
   Where is the concert?

The answer will normally be the name of a building rather than an address:

Es en la Casa de la Cultura
   It's in the Casa de la Cultura

5 *En la taquilla*

Listen to Ana buying tickets for a theatre festival. Complete the conversation.

– Hola, buenas tardes.
– ¿Puedo comprar entradas para el festival de teatro aquí?
– Sí.
– ¿Qué precio tienen las entradas?
– El precio de las entradas es de .....
– Quiero ..... .
– Aquí tiene.
– Pagaré al contado.
– Muy bien.
– Aquí tiene.
– Muchas gracias, y aquí tiene el cambio.

6 *Y ahora tú*

You want to attend one of the events in Activity 1. Decide which one and prepare the questions you'd ask to find out about it:

a where to buy tickets for the event,
b how much the tickets are,
c when the show or event starts and ends,
d where it takes place.

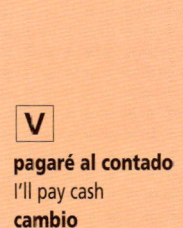

V

pagaré al contado
I'll pay cash
cambio
change

El teatro español

Spain's **Siglo de Oro** (Golden Century) was rich in many ways. When Spain conquered Mexico in 1519, it acquired some of the world's biggest deposits of precious metals, and in 1532 added the gold and silver of the Incas to its stock. This great wealth financed the Emperor Charles V's plans for expansion. It was also a century rich in culture. The Emperor was a great patron of the arts, and painters like El Greco came to Seville and Madrid to work. In this atmosphere Spanish theatre was born.

It was an actor-writer called Lope de Rueda who first laid planks on barrels in the courtyards of inns (**corrales**) and presented theatre for the people. There had been theatre at court, of course, but this was the first time that ordinary people were able to have access to plays (**comedias**) and the short comic sketches (**pasos**) that were put on during the intervals. By 1584, there were three official theatres in Spain, though the courtyards still drew the noisy, intolerant crowds to watch the racier kind of plays –like Tirso de Molina's ***El Burlador de Sevilla*** (*Trickster of Seville*), which brought the figure of Don Juan into the public eye for the first time. The crowd's favourite playwright, though, was Lope

Unidad 11

XVII Festival d'Almagro

CORRAL DE COMEDIAS
"EL BURLADOR DE SEVILLA"
de Tirso de Molina
THEATRE DE L'EPÉE DE BOIS DE LA CARTOUCHERIE DE PARIS
del 15 al 17
días 15 y 16 en Español
día 17 en Francés

Man of La Mancha

It was another great writer of the Golden Century, Miguel de Cervantes (1547–1616) who called Lope de Vega "**un monstruo de la naturaleza**" (a monster of nature) because he was so productive. But it was Cervantes who gave birth to La Mancha's most famous son, the Knight of the Sad Face Don Quijote de la Mancha, and his equally famous squire Sancho Panza.

Somewhere around 1605, a nobleman (**un hidalgo**) of La Mancha, Don Alonso Quijano, decides to launch his own crusade against the evil in the world. His elderly horse becomes a knight's charger called Rocinante and a local peasant girl, the unwilling object of his attentions, is transformed in his mind into his princess and patron, Dulcinea. Armed with a horse, some armour and a cause, all the newly-christened Sir Quijote, Wandering Knight (**caballero errante**), now needs is a squire to go with him. The wily peasant Sancho Panza is offered wages and food and agrees to set out with him. While Sancho sees a real world of peasants, inns, greedy girls and drunken, overbearing men, Don Quijote sees only what he believes to be there. His imagination is shaped by his reading of stories about knights and damsels in distress. Windmills are giants waving their arms in mock defiance; wine barrels are insolent enemies. Don Quijote takes them all on – to the amusement of all those who watch and mock. At first Sancho joins in the laughter, but later comes to share some of his master's values – honour, nobility, high-minded love. It is one of the beautiful ironies of the book that Sancho begins to believe in his master's world just as Don Quijote comes to realize that he has deluded himself, and dies in deep disillusion.

Cervantes wrote about La Mancha as it was, but he also explored the themes of deception and self-deception, which are far more modern and universal concepts.

de Vega (1562–1635). He was an extraordinary man. He began writing plays at the age of ten; when he died he left behind at least 1,500 theatrical works despite having lived a life that would have exhausted most people. He had a series of tempestuous love affairs, took religious orders in middle age, was secretary to four noblemen, and ran several businesses. Yet in later life, as he faced one personal tragedy after another, he was churning out two plays a week! They weren't all good plays, of course; but they were full of life and wit. One of the most famous, *Fuenteovejuna*, shows how a peasant community faced up to a corrupt and brutal local official and exposed him to the Emperor – who, as the fount of all wisdom, ensured that justice was done. Other great writers followed Lope's example. Calderón de la Barca (1600–1681) wrote even more than Lope, ranging from comedy sketches to great tragedies like *La vida es sueño* (*Life is a dream*).

Unidad 11

Veamos de nuevo
Gramática

Práctica

V
actuación
theatre performance
sesión
cinema performance

1 Past participles

In this unit you have met words such as **reservado** (reserved) and **incluido** (included). These words are past participles, and are used here with **estar** to indicate that something has been done.

| La habitación está reservad**a** | The room is booked |
| El coche está reservad**o** | The car is booked |

When this occurs the past participle behaves like an adjective, agreeing with the noun in gender and number.

Past participles of regular verbs:
Verbs ending in -ar: -ado
          reserv**ar**   reserv**ado**
Verbs ending in -er, -ir: -ido
          barr**er**   barr**ido**
          inclu**ir**   inclu**ido**

2 Conseguir (e → i)

As well as the radical-changing verbs you saw in Unit 10, there is a third group where the vowel change is from -**e** to -**i**. **Conseguir** (to obtain), **seguir** (to follow) and **pedir** (to ask for) belong to this group.

sigo	seguimos
sigues	seguís
sigue	siguen

A ¿Servicio incluido?

Before going to Madrid you contacted a hotel to book a room and also to make some additional requests. What questions might you have asked to get the following answers?

1 Sí, tenemos. ¿Con ducha o con baño?
2 93 euros por noche.
3 Sí, señora. Tiene una mesa reservada.
4 No, señora. No hay entradas reservadas para el festival.
5 Sí, señora, un Renault Clio. ¿Está bien?

B Guía del Ocio

Look at the cuttings from Andalucia's *El Giraldillo* (*What's on*). Which events do the following descriptions refer to?

1 Hay dos sesiones, a las 19.30 y a las 22.30
2 Es en Jerez el día 10 a las 21h
3 Hay dos actuaciones solamente: el 2 y el 3
4 Hay exposición de un famoso pintor nacido en Málaga
5 Termina el día 3 de noviembre
6 Se presentan cuatro películas del mismo director
7 La música es de Arriaga, Freire y Hoyos

CINE

EL ALLEN DE LOS 80
Ciclo organizado por el Aula de Cultura de la Facultad de Derecho en el que se da un repaso a la obra de Woody Allen en su última época.
Durante el mes de noviembre.
Día 12: LA ROSA PURPURA DEL CAIRO, v.o.s.
Día 13: DIAS DE RADIO (doblada).
Día 14: HANNA Y SUS HERMANAS, v.o.s.
Día 15: DELITOS Y FALTAS (doblada).
Todas las proyecciones a las 19 h. en el Salón de Actos del PABELLON DEL URUGUAY, Sevilla. Entrada gratuita.

TEATRO

LA IMPORTANCIA DE LLAMARSE ERNESTO. Comedia de Oscar Wilde que representa el TALLER DE TEATRO MUNICIPAL BASTILIPO. Días 21 y 22 de diciembre a las 21 h. en el Salón de Actos de la CASA DE LA CULTURA. Organiza: Ayuntamiento de El Viso del Alcor.

SOY UN SINVERGÜENZA, de Pedro Muñoz Seca, a cargo de la AGRUPACIÓN ALVAREZ QUINTERO. Hasta el 23 de diciembre en el TEATRO IMPERIAL, Sierpes, Sevilla. Secciones a las 19,30 y 22,30 h.

¿QUE HAGO CON MI MUJER?, Comedia de Pedro Osinaga, desde el 25 de diciembre al 6 de enero. TEATRO IMPERIAL, Sierpes, Sevilla. En dos sesiones, a las 19,30 y 22,30 h.

CURSOS TALLERES

DEPORTE
SEVILLA

ESCUELA DE VELA. Cursos de vela ligera para iniciarse en el mundo del mar. Cursos de siete días, desde el 27 de diciembre. Organiza: Karacol Ocio y Viajes. Imager, 6, 3º. 41003 Sevilla. Tel. 95/421 00 €2.

KUNG-FU. Dos semanas, desde el 3 de diciembre en horario de 18 a 19,30 h. Asociación Cultural El Patio, Moratín, 7, Sevilla. Tel. 421 41 11.

DANZA

CORDOBA

BALLET DE EUSKADI. Día 15 de diciembre (por confirmar) a las 21 h. en el GRAN TEATRO DE CORDOBA. Programa: Giselle.

GRANADA

BALLET DE EUSKADI. Día 13 de diciembre a las 21 h. en el TEATRO MUNICIPAL ISABEL LA CATOLICA, Granada.

SEVILLA

SUEÑOS FLAMENCOS. Reestreno del Ballet de Cristina Hoyos desde el día 30 de octubre hasta el 4 de noviembre en función única. TEATRO LOPE DE VEGA, Sevilla. Patrocinado por el Pabellón de Andalucía de la Expo '92. **Programa:** Seguiriya (lamento), Farruca (sobriedad), Bamberas (ensueño), Tangos (misterio), Taranto (pasión), Alegrías (compás), Soleá por bulerías (solera), Bulerías (júbilo). **Dirección:** Cristina Hoyos. **Coreografía:** Cristina Hoyos, Manolo Marín. **Música:** Arriaga, Freire, Hoyos.

MUSICA

ZARZUELA
HUELVA

COMPAÑIA LIRICA ESPAÑOLA. Compañía estable que busca la renovación de nuestro género lírico en su aspecto visual y escénico. Dirección musical: Pascual Ortega. Dirección: Antonio Amengual. Días 2 y 3 de noviembre a las 19 y 21,30 h. en el GRAN TEATRO, Huelva. Organiza: Patronato Provincial del Quinto Centenario del Descubrimiento de América y Ayuntamiento de Huelva.

FLAMENCO en los CLAUSTROS DE SANTO DOMINGO
Durante el mes de noviembre se realizarán los siguientes actuaciones.
Jerez. A las 21 h.
Día 3: Recital de Baile, con JOAQUÍN GRILO.
Día 10: Recital de Guitarra.
Día 17: Recital de Cante a cargo de JOAQUÍN JIMÉNEZ "Salmonete".
Día 24: Recital de Baile a cargo de MARÍA DEL MAR MORENO.

Organiza: Ayuntamiento de Jerez.

EXPOSICIONES

MALAGA

GRABADOS DE PICASSO EN LA PROVINCIA. Del 3 al 7 de noviembre. Todos los días de 18 a 22 h. en la Sala de Exposiciones de la CASA DE LA CULTURA, Antequera. Organiza: Diputación Provincial de Málaga.

EL RETORNO DE LOS DINOSAURIOS. hasta el 3 de noviembre en el CASINO DE LA EXPOSICIÓN, Sevilla. Todos los días de 10 a 14 h. y de 16 a 20 h. Muestra elaborada por el Museo de Ciencias de la Fundación Caixa de Pensiones.

C ¿Adónde ir?

To repay hospitality, you'd like to take members of your host's family out to a show, but they all have different interests.

Abuela: **No me gusta la música pop pero me gusta el flamenco.**
Sobrina: **Me encantan las ciencias naturales, los deportes y la música.**
Padres: **Nos encanta todo tipo de danza, sobre todo la española.**
Hermano: **Estudio deportes. No me gusta la zarzuela, pero me gusta la danza.**

1 Looking again at the *Guía del Ocio*, is there any one show you could all go to?
2 Where would you yourself like to go?

1 La carta 🔊 10

You and your family want to spend a few days in Spain and you have written to the Hotel Alfonso X to book rooms.

```
Hotel Alfonso X        Birmingham, a 8 de mayo de 2003
Calle Trapería
Murcia
España

Muy Sres. míos:
   Quisiera reservar una habitación doble y dos
individuales para cuatro noches a partir del 28.
Quiero habitaciones con baño completo y aire
acondicionado. ¿Me pueden confirmar el precio por
noche? Me gustaría saber también qué servicios
ofrece el hotel. ¿Hay piscina? ¿Tiene restaurante?
¿Qué actividades hay en la zona?
   Nuestra dirección es: Mr & Mrs Gough, 1 City Road,
Quinton, Birmingham, Inglaterra, Teléfono: (0121)
453 7769
   En espera de su pronta respuesta, les saluda
atentamente.
                Stuart Gough
```

a While you were out a message from Hotel Alfonso X was left on your answering machine. Listen to the recording and work out if all your questions were answered.
b Write a reply to the hotel to confirm the booking (**confirmar la reserva**) using the model above.

V
Muy Sres. míos Dear Sirs
Les saluda atentamente Yours faithfully
vista al mar sea view

Un paso más

Rent a car Murcia
Alquile un coche desde 33,54 €/día
Mínimo 7 días

INCLUYE:
Kilometraje ilimitado.
Seguro al vehículo (con franquicia de 150€)
Entregas / Recogidas dentro de la Provincia.
NO INCLUYE I.V.A.

Signos de Especificación
DA Dirección Asistida AC Aire acondicionado R Radio

CONDICIONES
• Pago: tarjeta de crédito o bono.
• Edad mínima 21 o 25 años según grupo y permiso de conducir 1 año.

	GRUPO / MODELO GROUP / MODEL	SEMANA WEEK	DÍA EXTRA EXTRA DAY
A	Nissan Micra Peugeot 106 3 p.	150,25 €	30,00 €
B C	Renault Clio 5 p. Peugeot 106 DIESEL 5 p.	197,40 €	39,50 €
D F	Renault 19 Peugeot 306 DIESEL	324,00 €	64,80 €
G	Nissan Almera Peugeot 405	462,00 €	92,40 €
M	Mercedes Combi 9 Plazas	487,20 €	97,44 €

2 Quiero alquilar un coche

You are in Murcia, and want to hire a car. At the hotel they give you a leaflet about car hire (**coches de alquiler**).

a Read the information and say if the following statements are true (**verdadero**) or false (**falso**)
  i You can pay by credit card.
  ii You can rent a car for one day.
  iii The price includes unlimited mileage.
  iv VAT is included.
  v The Renault Clio has power steering.
b You go to the **Rent a car** offices in Murcia. Can you do the following?
  Say you want to hire a car for a week.
  Ask if a Renault 19 is available and find out if insurance (**seguro**) is included.

3 Checklist

Can you do the following?

a Ask if the hotel has a double room for the night.
b Say you want a room with shower, television and sea view.
c Ask what facilities the hotel has.
d Say you want three tickets for the match.
e Ask times and prices of a film show.

Unidad 12

Estuve en Acapulco

Así se habla

Saying where you usually go on holiday

Saying what you did

Saying when you did something

Temas

Hay muchas maneras de escaparse

Veamos de nuevo

Unidad 12

Así se habla 1

¿Dónde sueles ir?
Saying where you usually go on holiday

Así se acostumbra

In the heat of the summer (**el verano**) Spaniards desert their towns for the beach or countryside with their families. Popular summer resorts (**centros de veraneo**) are along the Mediterranean coast and in the north, San Sebastián or Santander. Some people prefer to stay in small villages or to go camping in the **Sierra de Cazorla**, **los Pirineos** or **los Picos de Europa**.

Así se dice

To find out where someone usually goes on holiday, say:

¿Dónde sueles ir de vacaciones?

To answer, say:

Suelo ir a la playa/al lago
   I usually go to the beach/to the lake
Me gusta/encanta ir a la montaña
   I like/love going to the mountains

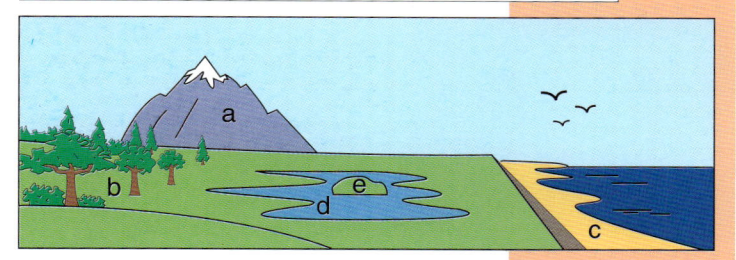

G
soler (+ ir, etc)
to usually (+ go, etc)
(See Ref G 17)

1 Centros de veraneo

Match names for places to the pictures.

| la playa/el mar   la montaña   el campo   el lago   la isla |

2 🔊 ¹

Antonia asks Hernán, the Colombian coffee farmer, and Noelia, a Spanish student, where they usually go on holiday. Do they like the same things?

Antonia: ¿Dónde sueles ir de vacaciones?
Hernán: Me encanta el mar. Me gusta mucho la ensenada de Málaga que es por los lados del Departamento del Valle, cerca de Buenaventura. Cuando quiero algo más sofisticado me gusta ir a Cartagena o San Andrés.
Antonia: ¿Dónde sueles ir de vacaciones?
Noelia: Pues suelo ir a la playa. Este año me voy a ir a Matalascañas, Huelva.

V
la ensenada
bay, cove
me puedo dar el lujo
I can afford to
solo/sola
alone/on your own

3

Where do these people usually go on holiday?

e.g. **María suele ir al campo en Francia** or **A María le gusta ir ...**

Francia — María
Grecia — Juan y Teresa 
Irlanda — Gloria, Pedro y Elvira
Los Alpes suizos — Carlos y Pepe

[128]

4 Y ahora tú

¿Dónde sueles ir de vacaciones? ¿Con quién sueles ir?

5 ¿Dónde fuiste? 🔊 ²

Five people are asked where they went on holiday last year (**el año pasado**) or last time (**la última vez**). Number the places as you hear them mentioned. The first dialogue is printed for you.

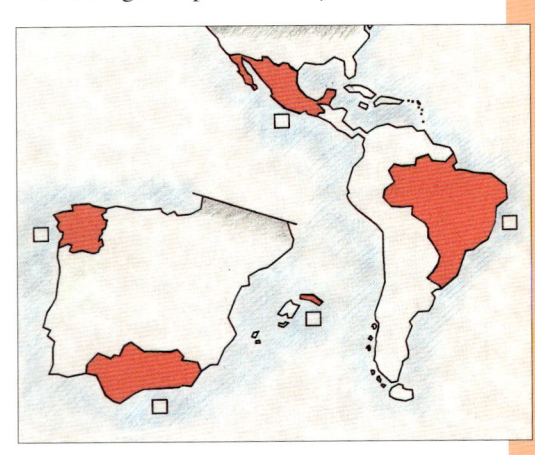

– ¿Dónde fuiste de vacaciones el año pasado?
– Fui a Acapulco.

G
ir/fui
estar/estuve
(See p. 135)

V
pasar
to spend

V
buenísimo
very good (from **bueno**)

Así se dice

To ask where someone went, say:

¿Dónde fuiste?

And to answer, say:

Fui a Acapulco
   I went to Acapulco
Estuve en Acapulco
   I was in Acapulco

To ask how it was, say:

¿Qué tal (Acapulco)?/¿Cómo te fue?

And to answer, you can say:

Muy bien/estupendamente/increíble
   Excellent/ fantastic
Lo pasé fenomenal/fabuloso
   I had a great time

6

Ask the people in Activity 3 where they went last year. What did they reply?

e.g. – María, ¿dónde fuiste el año pasado?
     – Fui al campo/Estuve en el campo.

7 🔊 ³

Listen again to some of the people in Activity 5. What were their holidays like? Can you match the place each person went to with its description?

	Menorca	Brasil	Galicia	México
fenomenal (Sp)				
estupendamente				
increíble				
buenísimo				
muy bien				
muy relajado				

8 Y ahora tú

Describe your holiday to a Spanish friend. You went to the Canary Islands (**las islas Canarias**) by plane (**en avión**) with two friends for a week and had a great time.

Unidad 12

2
Comí en El Panecillo
Saying what you did

G
visitar/visité
comer/comí
subir/subí

(See p. 135)

V
acabo de regresar
I've just returned
quizá
perhaps
ya te contaré
I'll tell you about it

V
refugio
mountain hut

V
recorrí I explored
vi I saw

Así se dice

To describe what you did, say:

Visité iglesias
   I visited churches
Comí en El Panecillo
   I had lunch on El Panecillo
Subí al refugio
   I climbed to the mountain hut

If you liked something, say:

Me gustó/me encantó
   I liked it, loved it

If you didn't like it, say:

No me gustó
   I didn't like it

1

Read about Rosa Elena's holiday and answer these questions:

Caracas, 23 de abril de 1995

Querido Juan:
Hola, ¿qué tal? Espero que bien. Yo acabo de regresar de mis vacaciones en Ecuador. Lo pasé estupendamente. La primera semana estuve en Quito. Es una ciudad muy pintoresca y me gustó mucho. Visité iglesias y museos y fui a muchos restaurantes: comí en El Panecillo, una colina en la parte colonial. También fui al Cotopaxi y subí al refugio. La segunda semana la pasé en Galápagos. Las islas son maravillosas. ¡Me encantaron! Fue quizá lo mejor del viaje.
Bueno, ya te contaré más de mi viaje. Escríbeme pronto.
Abrazos,
Rosa Elena

1. How long did she stay in Ecuador?
2. Did she have a good time?
3. What did she do in Quito?
4. What is the name of the mountain she climbed?
5. What place in Ecuador did she like best?

2 *Y ahora tú*

Imagine you were lucky enough to go to Ecuador for a short holiday: You went to Quito and Cuenca. In Quito you visited the old part of the town (**el casco colonial**) and you went to the Museo del Banco Central. In Cuenca you bought some jewellery (**joyas**) and you went to the river. You ate '**mote pata**' (a type of soup) there. You liked Cuenca very much. Describe your holiday to a friend.

3

Last summer Juan Carlos visited Carzola, a national park in Andalucía. His wife describes what he did:

– **Pues se bañó, recorrió el parque, anduvo en bicicleta, comió, visitó todos los lugares de interés, vio los ríos, vio los animales, sacó fotos, subió a las montañas del parque ...Lo pasó muy bien.**

4 Now listen to Juan Carlos himself describing his experiences. There are two things his wife said he did which he doesn't mention. Can you say what they are?

Unidad 12

Así se dice

To describe what someone else did, say:

Se bañó
   He/She bathed
Comió
   He/She ate
Subió a las montañas
   He/She climbed the mountains

4

Look at the letter in Activity 1 once more. Can you describe to a friend what María Rosa did in Ecuador?

5

Carlos and Jajana were married last month and went to Acapulco for their honeymoon. Here they are describing some of the things they did. Which of the following activities did they try?

a bailar; b tomar el sol; c cenar;
d nadar; e bucear; f esquiar

Así se dice

To indicate what you did with someone else, say:

Bailamos
   We danced
Comimos
   We ate
Subimos
   We climbed

6 Y ahora tú

You and your friend went on holiday together. Write a letter to another friend describing some of the things you did together. Refer to Activity 1 to see how to start and finish your letter.

V
bucear
scuba-diving

G
leer/leyó

3 ¿Qué hiciste ayer?
Saying when you did something

1

Andrés has been told to take some exercise and watch his diet. You will hear him telling his wife María Rosa what he did yesterday while she was away. Can you put the sequence in the right order?

Leí un libro	Me duché
Fui al supermercado	Tomé un zumo
Me levanté temprano	Fui a la piscina
Volví a casa	Desayuné

Así se dice

To describe a sequence of events, say:

Primero me duché
   First I had a shower
Después/luego tomé un zumo
   Afterwards, I had some juice
Y por último leí un libro
   And finally, I read a book

2

But he wasn't telling his wife the truth. Looking at the pictures, can you say what he really did?

e.g. **Se levantó a las diez**

3 Y ahora tú

Can you explain to your friend what you did yesterday? Start from the time you got out of bed: **Me levanté a las ...** How did your friend or partner spend his/her day?

4

Match the expressions of time on the left with their English equivalents.

1	ayer	a	last year
2	anteayer	b	last night
3	anoche	c	yesterday
4	la semana pasada	d	last month
5	el mes pasado	e	the day before yesterday
6	el año pasado	f	last summer
7	el verano pasado	g	last week

5

Carlos was surprised by his bank balance. Can you explain how he spent his money? Today is Monday, 3rd May.

e.g. **Cenó en un restaurante italiano anteayer.**

Teatro de la Opera
2 de abril de 2002
Carmen
Butaca   3.000 pesos

Restaurante La Traviata
1º de mayo de 2002
Cena para dos   10.000

Supermercado LA FAVORITA
2 de mayo de 2002
Carnes..... 3.000
Legumbres.... 1.500
Pan......... 500
Vinos....... 2.000
Total....... 7.000

Calama BAR RESTAURANTE
1 cerveza   500
5 ron con cola   1.800
Total   2.300
28 de abril de 2002

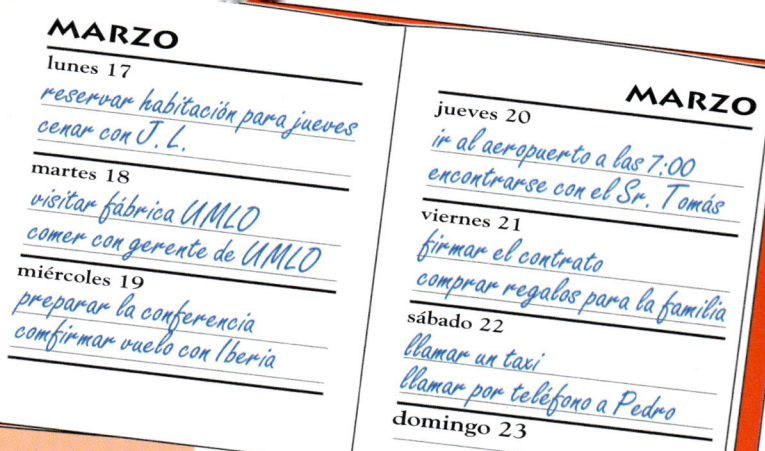

MARZO

lunes 17
reservar habitación para jueves
cenar con J. L.

martes 18
visitar fábrica UMLO
comer con gerente de UMLO

miércoles 19
preparar la conferencia
confirmar vuelo con Iberia

MARZO

jueves 20
ir al aeropuerto a las 7:00
encontrarse con el Sr. Tomás

viernes 21
firmar el contrato
comprar regalos para la familia

sábado 22
llamar un taxi
llamar por teléfono a Pedro

domingo 23

6

Today is Sunday, 23rd March. How did María Rosa spend her working week?

e.g. **El lunes pasado reservó habitaciones**

7 🔊 7

Carmen speaks to three couples in Mexico. Listen and find out what each couple did. The first conversation is printed below.

Pareja 1 ... ...   Pareja 2 ... ...   Pareja 3 ... ...

¿Qué hicieron ayer?
– Esquiamos un rato, este, fuimos a comer, nadamos, eh, en la tarde ... y este, estuvimos en un bar toda la ..., hasta las doce de la noche.

V
andar (Sp)
caminar (LA)
walk

estudiantina/tuna
student band

G
hacer/hiciste
(See p. 135)

Así se dice

To ask someone what they did, say:

¿Qué hiciste/hizo ayer?
¿Qué hicisteis/hicieron ayer? *(plural)*
  What did you do yesterday?

To answer, say:

Ayer por la tarde fui/fuimos ...
  Yesterday afternoon I/we went ...
La semana pasada/el mes pasado visité/visitamos ...
  Last week/last month I/we visited ...

8 Y ahora tú

Can you describe two interesting things you did last week and say exactly when you did them?

Temas

Hay muchas maneras de escaparse

Unidad 12

Apart from weekends, it is the summer months that provide an opportunity to escape the routines of everyday living. Millions of Spaniards still go to the resorts of the Costa Brava, the Costa del Sol and the Canary Islands for the sun and the sand. But growing numbers are seeking out the Pyrenees and the southern mountain range of the Sierra Nevada for activity holidays. Latin America, too, has its traditional summer resorts – Punta del Este in Uruguay, for example, Viña del Mar in Chile and of course Acapulco, in Mexico.

Acapulco tiene dos caras

Acapulco's population is now more than a million. In winter and spring it is packed with tourists crowded into its 16 kilometres of beautiful beaches. In the summer it is unbearably hot, which is why the wealthier houses and expensive hotels sit high on the cliffs overlooking the sea. Acapulco was developed as a resort for U.S. tourists in the late forties by Conrad Hilton and the Mexican president Miguel Alemán. They profited greatly from the project but not everyone did. Acapulco is set in the poorest state of the Mexican Republic – Guerrero – a region of hills and deep valleys, bandits and the direst poverty. A few streets away from the beach and its lights and night life is a much poorer, dimly-lit city where Acapulco ends and Guerrero begins.

En busca del pasado

In recent years, travellers have turned their interest to another America – the Mexico and Peru of the past. The extraordinary civilizations of pre-Columbian America – Aztecs, Mayas, Incas among them – were overwhelmed and destroyed by the Spanish invaders. But many of their monuments and buildings remain. Not far from Cancún are the wonderfully intact temples and

La huida al mar

El puente means 'the bridge'; but it has another, more important meaning – 'the long weekend', when official holidays combine to include a Friday and a Monday. The roads from the cities are jammed with cars and buses escaping the city for a few days. All roads lead, eventually, to the place in the country (**la casa de campo**), the beach (**la playa**) or the mountain campsite (**el camping de montaña**).

Picos de Europa - España

V
la huida
escape

V
en busca de
in search of

buildings of the Mayan city-states – Chichen Itza, Palenque – deep in the rain forest of Tabasco, Tulum and Uxmal, witnesses to a civilization that began its decline before the Spaniards came. Anáhuac was the name the Aztecs gave to their empire, whose centre was in the Valley of Mexico. The pyramids of the ancient city of Teotihuacan still remain, and were there long before the Aztecs came in the fourteenth century. The remains of the great capital city of Mexico, razed to the ground by the avenging Cortés, have in recent years risen again from the rubble – and the Main Temple (**Templo Mayor**) stands at the centre of Mexico's capital city. In Peru, the magnificent city of Machu Picchu has attracted thousands to its mountain fortresses. Here the Incas mounted their final resistance to the Spanish colonizers in 1571, before they were finally overwhelmed. Their descendants still live in the high sierras.

También hay otras salidas

In every city in Spain and Latin America small boys juggle tennis balls or tin cans with their feet. Football (**el fútbol**) gives them their heroes – and their dreams of a different life. The great teams are legend – Real Madrid and Barcelona have played host to the greatest players. In Argentina Boca Juniors had the same legendary status – and the players became national heroes, like the complex and contradictory Diego Maradona. Elsewhere, too, the road out of the poorest quarters runs through sportsfields and stadiums. In Central America and Cuba, baseball (**el béisbol**) opens doors that are normally firmly closed. The U.S. Leagues are well staffed with pitchers and batters from the Dominican Republic, Cuba, Puerto Rico. Boxing (**el boxeo**) has drawn crowds across Latin America, and some of the lower weights have produced fine fighters like Mexico's Roberto Durán.

Jack Johnson

V
confundo
I confuse
ajedrez
chess
alfil
bishop
peón
pawn
tablero
board
recuerdo
I remember
guardar
to keep

Raúl González

Conchita Martínez

Sport provides an escape in two different ways for those without means or influence looking for success; and for those who live that success at one remove through the careers of people much like themselves. From Spain have come some of the finest golfers (Ballesteros and García), tennis players (Ferrero, Moyà, Martínez) and footballers (Raúl, Mendieta). Nicolas Guillén, perhaps Cuba's most popular poet, remembers his own childhood heroes. Who would yours be?

"Deportes"

¿Qué sé yo de boxeo,
yo, que confundo el jab con el upper cut?
Y sin embargo, a veces
aún desde mi infancia
como una nube inmensa desde el fondo de un valle,
sube, me llega Johnson,
el negro montañoso
el dandy atlético magnético
.....
¿Qué sé yo de ajedrez ?
Nunca moví un alfil, un peón.
Tengo los ojos ciegos
para el álgebra, los caracteres griegos
y ese tablero filosófico
donde cada figura es una interrogación.
Pero recuerdo a Capablanca.
.....
Niño , jugué al béisbol.
Amé a Rubén Darío, es cierto,
con sus violentas rosas.
Pero allá en lo más alto de mi sueño
un sitio puro y verde guardé siempre
para Méndez, el pítcher – mi otro dueño.

(from *La paloma del vuelo popular*, 1958)

Veamos de nuevo

Gramática

1 Talking about the past

There are several ways of talking about the past in Spanish. If you are talking about what you did, or describing an event (or sequence of events) that occurred at a specific time in the past, use the Preterite tense.

Anoche cené en el restaurante
Last night I had dinner in the restaurant
El lunes pasado visitaron el Prado
Last Monday they visited the Prado
Primero se levantó y luego tomó el desayuno
First he got up and then he had breakfast

The patterns of endings of verbs in the three groups are as follows:

visitar (to visit)	**comer** (to eat)	**subir** (to climb)
visit*é*	com*í*	sub*í*
visit*aste*	com*iste*	sub*iste*
visit*ó*	com*ió*	sub*ió*
visit*amos*	com*imos*	sub*imos*
visit*asteis*	com*isteis*	sub*isteis*
visit*aron*	com*ieron*	sub*ieron*

As you can see, there is one form of endings for **-ar** verbs and another for **-er**/**-ir** verbs. As always, some very common verbs have irregular preterite forms. Those you have met in this unit include: **estar**, **hacer** and **ir**. Their Preterite forms are as follows:

Unidad 12

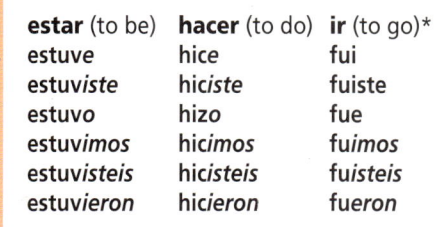

estar (to be)	**hacer** (to do)	**ir** (to go)*
estuve	hice	fui
estuv*iste*	hic*iste*	fuiste
estuvo	hizo	fue
estuv*imos*	hic*imos*	fu*imos*
estuv*isteis*	hic*isteis*	fu*isteis*
estuv*ieron*	hic*ieron*	fueron

Note: **ir** and **ser** have exactly the same forms in the preterite tense.

Práctica

A Unas vacaciones estupendas

You were interested to hear from Carlos who has been on holiday with Mari Carmen in Nerja (Málaga):

Estuve en Nerja de vacaciones. Me gustó muchísimo. La primera semana nadé mucho, tomé el sol, y un día buceé con el club local. Mari Carmen y yo jugamos al tenis en las pistas del hotel. ¡Ella ganó siempre! La segunda semana alquilé un coche y en dos ocasiones fuimos a la Sierra Nevada – esquiamos en Pradollano. ¡La sierra está a sólo 80 kilómetros de la playa! La última noche cenamos en Jardines Neptuno, un restaurante que es también sala de fiestas de Granada. Allí bailamos en la fiesta flamenca. ¡Lo pasé fenomenal!

Can you tell a mutual friend about Carlos's holiday?

B Matchmaking

Match the two parts of each sentence to make sense.

1 Ayer, Juan y María
2 La semana pasada, yo no
3 Anoche, Marta
4 El sábado, tú
5 Arancha y yo
6 Vosotros

a salisteis anteayer ¿no?
b viste el musical *Drácula* ¿verdad?
c salimos de copas la otra noche
d comí en casa
e vio el fútbol en la televisión
f comieron con sus padres

[135]

Unidad 12

Un paso más

1 Matalascañas

Imagine you went to Matalascañas for a weekend break with your family. Afterwards you tell your friends about it. Use the map on p. 129 to describe where you went and what you did.

e.g. **El viernes fuimos al Parque Nacional de Doñana, vimos muchos animales**

2 El diario de a bordo

Here is part of Christopher Columbus's log of his first voyage across the Atlantic.

a When did Columbus sail for America, and from where?
b How long did it take him to reach the Canary Islands?
c Why did they spend time on the islands?
d Why was 26th September a frustrating day?
e What happened on 3rd October?
f What clues were there that land was near?
g What happened on 12th October?

V
rumbo course
carabela caravel
leña firewood
alga marina seaweed
se quejaron complained
un himno de gracias a hymn of thanks

3 Por México

Listen to Carlos and Jajana talking about their visit to Taxco and Acapulco in Mexico. Are the following statements true (**v**) or false (**f**)?

	V	F
a Carlos y Jajana were in Taxco to see the procession.		
b They did not buy anything in Taxco.		
c They walked around the town of Acapulco.		
d They went to a bar, a restaurant and a cinema.		
e At the restaurant Carlos only had a salad.		

4 Checklist

Can you do the following?

a Say where you usually go on holiday.
b Ask someone where they went on holiday and say where you went.
c Ask someone what they did and how it went.
d Say what you did and when you did it.

---

3 de agosto: Salimos de Palos en la madrugada, rumbo a occidente. Vamos con tres carabelas – la Niña, la Pinta y la Santa María.

5 de agosto: Navegamos 50 millas. ¡No está mal!

13 de agosto: Anoche llegamos por fin a las islas Canarias.

12 de septiembre: Estuvimos en las islas varios días porque tuvimos que reparar las carabelas. Hicimos provisión de agua fresca, leña y verduras. Finalmente, anoche salimos de La Gomera.

14 de septiembre: Algunos de los hombres de la Niña vieron un gran pájaro blanco que pasó cerca del navío.

17 de septiembre: Después de tres semanas de viaje, los hombres están ansiosos. Alguien vio algas marinas.

26 de septiembre: Martin Alonso dice que vio una gran isla, pero luego desapareció.

3 de octubre: Los hombres se quejaron mucho. Insistieron en volver a La Gomera. Estuvimos varias horas en discusiones. Al final aceptaron seguir – unos días más.

8 de octubre: La tierra está cerca. Vimos pájaros y alga marina, y uno de los hermanos Pinzón vio flores en el mar.

12 de octubre: ¡Bendito sea Dios! A las dos de la madrugada se escuchó el cañón indicando que hay tierra a la vista. Juan Rodríguez de Triana fue quien vio la tierra esta vez. Cantamos juntos un himno de gracias. Llegamos por fin a Las Indias.

(Adapted from *The Journal of Columbus' First Voyage*)

Unidad 13

Cuando era joven

Así se habla

Saying what sports you liked when you were younger

Saying what you used to do; what people were like

Contrasting the present with the past

Temas

En La Pampa argentina

Veamos de nuevo

Así se habla 1

¿Practicas algún deporte?

Saying what sports you liked when you were younger

Sarasketa

Goitia

1

Which sports listed below are not among the activities on offer at this country club?

EL PARAÍSO Country Club

la natación	el baloncesto	el voleibol	el fútbol
el golf	el tenis	el ciclismo/la bicicleta	la equitación
correr	el atletismo	el squash	
la pesca	el esquí	el montañismo	

Now say which of these sports you like or dislike.

e.g. **Me gusta la natación pero no me gusta el squash.**

Así se acostumbra

The Basques have given the Spanish-speaking world one of its most spectacular sports – **jai alai** – or **pelota vasca**. In a long three-sided court (**el frontón**), two (or sometimes four) players catch a ball in a long crescent-shaped basket (**la cesta punta**) attached to their hands. The small hard ball never slows down, and reaches great speeds as it is smashed from wall to wall. It can be played with rackets too or with the hands – by far the most painful version! Traditionally, players wore a white shirt and trousers and the red Basque beret, but nowadays the beret has been replaced by a helmet. In the spectators' gallery, bets fly as money is stuffed into a hollow ball and thrown around as the game progresses.

2

Listen to Patricia and Alberto, two young Spaniards. Can you say which sports they play and when they practise them?

Patricia: ..... Alberto: .....

Así se dice

To ask someone if they play a sport, say:

¿Practicas algún deporte? *or:*

¿Qué deportes practicas?
What sports do you play?

To say what you play:

Practico la natación, el baloncesto, etc.
I go swimming, play basketball, etc.
No practico ningún deporte
I don't play any sports
Nado
I swim
Juego al fútbol/baloncesto, etc.
I play football, basketball, etc.
Me gusta nadar/la natación
I like swimming

Unidad 13

Lorena Ochoa, la campeona infantil

Es jalisciense, apenas tiene 12 años y va a entrar al libro Guinness. A partir de 1989, Lorena ha sido cinco veces campeona mundial infantil de golf y la más pequeña en ganar esta distinción. Practica el golf desde los 3 años de edad. A los 5 años empezó a recibir entrenamiento con Barry Willardson, un reconocido maestro de golf, y a los 8 ganó el primer campeonato mundial infantil de golf que se juega en San Diego, California.

– Cuando llego al campo – dice la niña – empiezo a tirar bolas y luego me concentro; después veo a mi oponente. Lo más importante en el golf es la concentración, junto con la relajación.

Lorena posee muchos premios y actualmente cursa la secundaria. Su proyecto es realizar una carrera universitaria y obtener una beca para una escuela de golf en Estados Unidos.

(Adapted from an article in the Mexican magazine *Actual*, No. 16, enero, 1995)

3

Lorena Ochoa es famosa. ¿Por qué?

Now answer these questions.

a What important things happened in Lorena's life when she was 3, 5 and 8?
b Why did she get into the *Guinness Book of Records*?
c What two things did she think were important for a successful game?
d What were her plans for the future at the time of the interview?

V

jalisciense
from Jalisco, Mexico
mundial
world
ganar
to win
tirar
to throw
premio
prize
una beca
scholarship

G

ser/yo era
tener/yo tenía
gustar/
me gustaba(n)

(See p. 145)

4 Y ahora tú

A ¿Practicas algún deporte? ¿Cuándo? ¿Te gusta el squash? ¿el tenis? ¿la natación?
B ¿Te gusta asistir a partidos de fútbol? ¿a carreras de ciclismo? ¿a campeonatos de tenis o de natación? ¿a carreras de caballos?

5 🔊 ²

Isabel talks about what sports she enjoys now and what she enjoyed when she was younger. Listen and read. Have her preferences changed?

– ¿Practicas algún deporte?
– Me gusta la natación, pero ahora no hago ningún deporte.
– Y cuando eras más joven, ¿te gustaban los deportes?
– Sí, cuando tenía quince años me gustaba el judo. Participé en dos campeonatos y gané un tercer puesto en uno de ellos – la medalla de bronce. En la escuela también me gustaba hacer gimnasia.

Así se dice

To ask someone what they liked doing when they were younger, say:

Cuando eras más joven/pequeño/a, ...
    When you were younger, ...
... ¿te gustaban los deportes?
    ...did you like sports?
Cuando tenías doce años, ¿te gustaba el tenis?
    When you were twelve, did you like tennis?

To say what you liked doing:

Cuando era pequeño/a, me gustaba correr
    When I was a child, I liked running
Cuando tenía doce años, me encantaba el fútbol
    When I was twelve, I loved football

6 Y ahora tú

Cuando eras más joven, te gustaba:
a) ¿ir a la piscina?   b) ¿ir a la escuela?
c) ¿hacer deberes?   d) ¿jugar con los vecinos? e) ¿jugar al fútbol o al tenis?

¿Qué otras cosas te gustaba hacer?

2
Los sábados salía con mis amigos
Saying what you used to do; what people were like

1 🔊 ³

Antonia remembers her college days. Listen, read and answer the questions.

a What was her timetable at the university?
b Where did she have lunch? And dinner?
c Did she go out during the week?
d What did she do at weekends?

Por la mañana iba a clases a la universidad. Empezaba a las 8:30 y terminaba a las 2:00 de la tarde pues estaba en el grupo de la mañana. Iba a casa a comer y por las tardes estudiaba. A veces salía con amigos hacia las 6:00 y regresaba a las 10:00 para cenar. Mis padres eran muy estrictos y me controlaban mucho y entonces tenía que estar de vuelta a las 10:00. Los fines de semana siempre salía con amigos. Íbamos a un bar a charlar y tomar algo juntos o íbamos a casa de un amigo para una fiesta o al cine.

Unidad 13

V
deberes homework
vecinos neighbours

G
empezar/ yo empezaba
tener/yo tenía
salir/yo salía
ir/yo iba
(See p. 145)

V
estar de vuelta to be back

V
como as
molestar to tease
reírse de to laugh at
pelea fight
yo les pegaba beat them up
aficiones favourite activities
aficionado fan

Así se dice

To talk about what you were in the habit of doing, say:

Iba a clases a la universidad
  I used to go to classes at the university
Empezaba a las 8:30
  I used to begin at 8:30
A veces salía con amigos
  Sometimes I'd go out with friends
  ☞ Ex. A, p. 145

2

Here is part of an interview with Andy García, the Cuban-born actor, in which he describes some aspects of his school years as an exile in the U.S.

- ¿Y cómo fueron tus primeros años en los Estados Unidos?
- Como éramos exiliados, los primeros años resultaron difíciles. En el colegio nos molestaban y se reían de nosotros. Como yo era un poco pequeño para mi edad, era muy sensible y estaba ansioso por defenderme. Cuando alguien hacía un comentario despectivo, había pelea. Yo les pegaba únicamente por seguridad.

- ¿Y cuáles eran tus aficiones entonces?
- Me gustaban las películas de James Bond y era un gran aficionado de Sean Connery. Montaba a caballo y me encantaba el baloncesto.

(Adapted from *Woman*, 25 de octubre 1994)

a Did he have a hard time at school? Why?
b What did he enjoy doing?

Unidad 13

3 Y ahora tú

A ¿Qué hacías en tu tiempo libre cuando eras adolescente?
B ¿Adónde ibas de vacaciones cuando eras pequeño/a? ¿Qué hacías?
C Recuerdas tu primer trabajo. ¿Cómo era un día típico?

4 ¿Cómo era?

Antonia is describing one of her teachers. What was he like? Did she like him?

– ¿Recuerdas a alguno de tus profesores?
– Recuerdo al profesor de literatura canadiense. Se llamaba Donald y era canadiense.
– ¿Cómo era?
– Pues, era alto, rubio y muy guapo. Llevaba gafas y siempre estaba muy elegante. Y era buen profesor. Era muy estricto con nosotros pero sus clases eran muy interesantes.

> **Así se dice**
>
> To describe what someone looked like, say:
>
> **Era alto/a**
>   He/she was tall
> **Llevaba gafas**
>   He/she wore glasses
> **Era muy estricto**
>   He/she was very strict
>
> ☞ Ex. C, p. 146

5

Can you describe your former teachers? The first one has been done for you.

a Era bajo y calvo. Tenía bigote largo y andaba siempre de mal humor. Daba clases de matemáticas ¡y no entendíamos nada!
b .....
c .....

6 Y ahora tú

A ¿Cómo era tu mejor amigo/a de la infancia?
B ¿Te acuerdas de alguno de tus profesores? ¿Cómo era? ¿Era simpático?

3
Antes y ahora
Contrasting the present with the past

1 🔊 4

Miguel went to college in Spain but now he is doing his final year in London. Read his description of what his daily routine used to be. Then listen to him saying what it is now and make a note of three or four things that have changed and two that are the same.

– Antes, cuando estaba en España, yo me levantaba sobre las nueve de la mañana y me tomaba un café con leche y bollos y luego me iba a la facultad hasta la una y media de la tarde. Volvía a mi casa, comía sobre las tres y descansaba un rato. Sobre las cuatro y media o las cinco volvía a la facultad y me quedaba hasta las ocho o nueve. Luego volvía a casa, cenaba, leía un poco, estudiaba un poco, veía un poco la tele y me acostaba.

V
bollos bread rolls

Unidad 13

Así se dice

To contrast what you did before with what you do now, say:

Antes me levantaba a las nueve
   Before, I used to get up at 9:00
Ahora me levanto a las ocho
   Nowadays I get up at 8:00
Antes me tomaba un café con leche
   Before, I used to have a white coffee
Ahora no desayuno
   Nowadays I don't have breakfast

2

A worker on an **estancia** in Argentina describes what life used to be like and some of the changes that have occurred.

– ¿Cómo era la vida en la estancia antes?
– Hace 26 años la vida aquí era mucho más rigurosa en el sentido horarios. Los horarios se respetaban al máximo. Existía la hora de almuerzo, la hora de descanso, la hora del té. Hoy en día no existe el tema del almuerzo, es más elástico. También tenemos más confort: tenemos ventiladores, tenemos electricidad, tenemos heladeras que antes no las teníamos. Nos bañábamos en la laguna; ahora tenemos pileta, tenemos una cantidad de cosas. El campo antes estaba poblado; ahora está despoblado.

Can you list six things that have changed?

e.g. **Antes la vida era mucho más rigurosa. Ahora es menos rigurosa**

3

Listen to Antonia describing her neighbourhood. What has changed in the last fifteen years?

G
hay/había

Así se dice

To describe what a place used to be like, say:

Hace 10 años, era más tranquilo
   Ten years ago, it was quieter

To describe what there used to be there, say:

Había un restaurante
   There was one restaurant
No había muchos coches
   There weren't many cars

4

Here is the living-room in a farmhouse as it would have looked a hundred years ago. But there are six mistakes. Can you spot them?

e.g. **Hace 100 años no había lámparas de escritorio.**

5 *Y ahora tú*

A ¿Puedes describir cómo era tu casa antes y cómo es ahora?
B ¿Y tu barrio?

Temas

En La Pampa argentina

Los gauchos

The wide grasslands called the **Pampas** have always been the heartland of Argentina. Today they sustain sixty per cent of the population, contain most of its industries, and supply the majority of its exports. In the mid sixteenth century, Spanish colonisers abandoned their horses and cattle there; four hundred years later, the descendants of those animals became the chief source of Argentina's wealth. First they provided leather and dried meat; later, when refrigerated shipping was able to carry it to Europe, fresh meat was transported to Paris, London and Madrid.

The cattle were tended by herders and cattlemen called **gauchos**, skilled horsemen of independent mind who grazed their animals along the entire length of the immense grass plains. The **pampa** was their common land: in these early days, it was an open place and there were few fences dividing one estate from another. After Argentina's declaration of independence from Spain in 1816, Buenos Aires began to grow and trade with Britain, France and Germany increased. As the city expanded, its attention turned to the **pampas** – and the wealth that they were capable of producing. A vagrancy law (**ley de vagancia**) was passed – directed against those nomadic herdsman who until now had roamed the **pampas** freely. When arrested, they were forced to serve in frontier patrols whose task it was to drive back all those – Indian peoples or free herdsmen – who laid any claim to the land. The battle was waged on the frontier (**la frontera**) between enclosed and open land and as the line was pushed further and further into the interior of the country, fences (**los cercos**) began to make their appearance. The days of the **gaucho** were numbered: in the decades that followed, more and more of the grasslands came under the control of individuals and companies connected to the city. By the 1860s, the native peoples had been driven back and the **gauchos** were on the verge of disappearing – their way of life coming to an end as they became wage-earning employees on the new modern ranches.

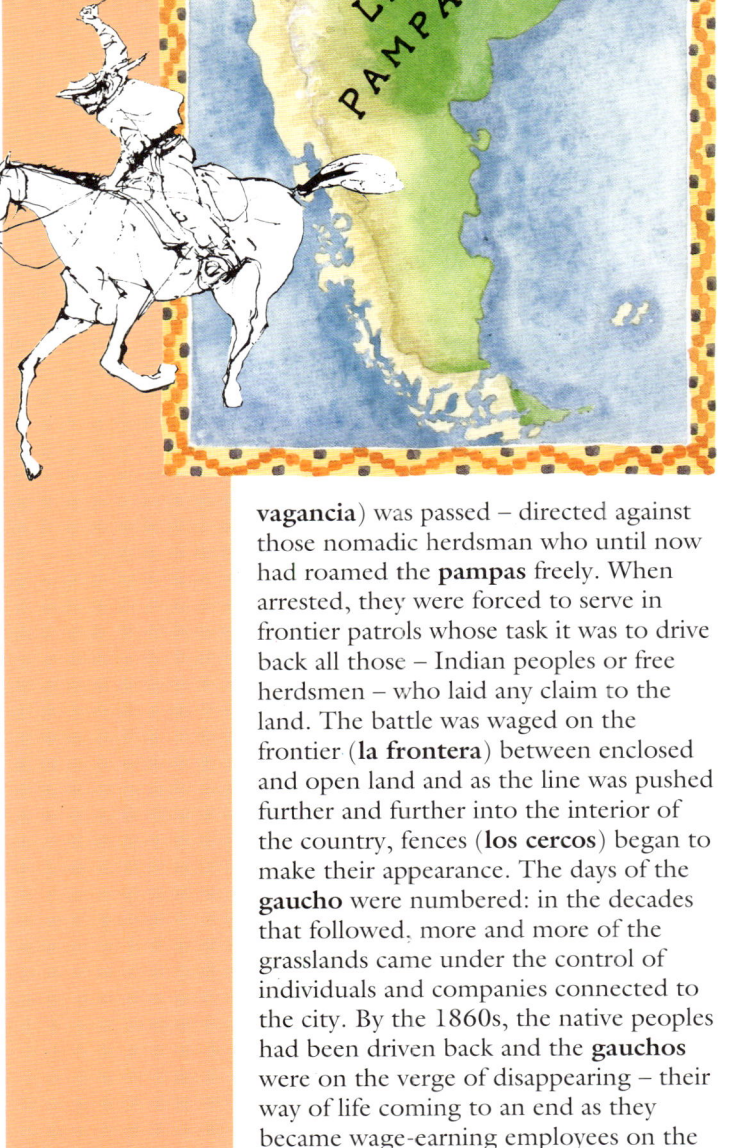

El último gaucho

In 1872 the first part of the epic poem *Martín Fierro* appeared. Written by the journalist and politician, José Hernández, its hero Martín narrates his own life in his own way – though it was a story typical of all those whose way of life was becoming obsolete as the fences, and later the railways, transformed the pampas.

Playing his guitar by a lonely camp fire, Martín remembers life as it was on the pampa:

**Yo he conocido esta tierra
En que el paisano vivía
Y su ranchito tenía
Y sus hijos y mujer ...
Era una delicia el ver
Cómo pasaba sus días.**

But all that ended as he was arrested after a brawl and sent to the frontera. For three years he endured the terrible conditions – the arbitrary cruelty of the officers, the Indian raids – until he could stand no more and deserted. But when he returned home, there was no sign of his wife or his family. Argentina was changing and the pampa was no longer his home.

**¡No hallé ni rastro del rancho;
Sólo estaba la tapera!
Por Cristo, si aquello era
Pa' enlutar el corazón
Yo juré en esa ocasión
Ser más malo que una fiera**

Martín Fierro was now an outlaw and a fugitive. His adventures in the desert, the death of his companion Cruz – another deserter – and his eventual acceptance that his old life was no longer possible, are told in the ballad style of the old gaucho singer-storytellers. The final act sees Fierro go to the city, to find his long lost sons. But when he sees how people live in Buenos Aires, he knows that he has no place there. Gathering his family around him he returns to the wilderness.

V

no hallé ni rastro
I found no trace
la tapera
roof
enlutar
to wrap in mourning
juré
I swore
una fiera
a wild beast
abriré
I will open
pa' seguir
to follow

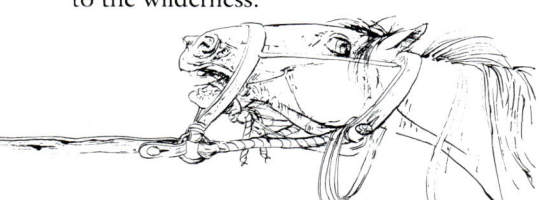

Yo abriré con mi cuchillo
el camino pa' seguir

El gaucho que llevo en mí

Fierro disappeared into the wilderness at the end of Part 2 of the poem published in 1879. By then there were no gauchos left, other than those who survived (and still survive) by herding sheep and cattle in the harsh and empty landscapes to the south of the pampas – in Patagonia. For the pampas were now part of modern agriculture, and the herders worked for wages on other people's farms. Where did the gauchos go? Some went to the city in search of work, and stayed, merging with a population most of whom were recent arrivals from Europe. The nostalgia for rural life crept into the words of the tangos that were becoming the music of Buenos Aires. With time, the real life of the gauchos was forgotten; instead a new figure emerged, a mythical herdsman who came to symbolise an idealised national identity – like Ricardo Guiraldes' Don Segundo Sombra, a kind of wise man of the pampa whose eyes were fixed on the distant horizon because **'tenía alma de horizonte'** (he had the horizon in his soul).

Unidad 13

Veamos de nuevo
Gramática

Práctica

Imperfect tense

There are three main situations in which the imperfect tense is used:

1) To describe what what was going on over time, without indicating when it started or finished:

Cuando era joven, vivía en Bilbao
When I was young, I lived in Bilbao

2) To speak about habits in the past:

Salía de casa a las nueve cada sábado
I used to leave the house at nine every Saturday

3) To describe something or someone in the past:

Hace veinte años no había muchos coches
Twenty years ago there were not many cars
Era un hombre alto; llevaba un sombrero gris
He was a tall man; he was wearing a grey hat

Most Spanish verbs are regular in the imperfect and are formed as follows:

andar (to walk)	**leer** (to read)	**vivir** (to live)
and*aba*	le*ía*	viv*ía*
and*abas*	le*ías*	viv*ías*
and*aba*	le*ía*	viv*ía*
and*ábamos*	le*íamos*	viv*íamos*
and*abais*	le*íais*	viv*íais*
and*aban*	le*ían*	viv*ían*

There are only three verbs which do not follow this regular pattern:

ser	**ver**	**ir**
era	veía	iba
eras	veías	ibas
era	veía	iba
éramos	veíamos	íbamos
erais	veíais	ibais
eran	veían	iban

A

Pablo remembers how he used to spend his weekends. How would you describe the activities of Pablo and his friends to another person who didn't know them?

Cada sábado íbamos a jugar fútbol; a veces llegábamos tarde y bastante sucios a casa, y teníamos que bañarnos rápidamente, porque por la noche siempre salíamos a tomar una copa con nuestra familia. Era una diversión bonita, pues trabajábamos mucho durante la semana y esperábamos con impaciencia el partido del sábado. El domingo lo dedicábamos a trabajar en el jardín, y nos dormíamos temprano porque el lunes empezábamos el trabajo de nuevo.

B Antes y ahora

Choose a sentence from the second list which makes sense as a sequel to the first, and complete it with a suitable verb:

1 Ahora tienen una casa en la ciudad
2 Ahora van a la universidad
3 Ahora tengo cuatro hijos
4 Ahora jugamos con computadores
5 Hoy día vemos la televisión

a Antes no ..... familia
b Antes ..... en el campo
c Antes ..... libros
d Antes ..... la radio
e Antes ..... a clases en la escuela

C

Lurking suspiciously in your garden you saw a young man of about 20 to 25, tall and thin, with long dark hair and wearing glasses. Can you describe him to the police?

1 Querida Claudia

This letter from a grateful reader appeared recently in a magazine's problem page.

> Te escribo porque mi vida ha cambiado completamente – gracias a ti y a tu revista. Hace cinco años yo era un hombre completamente infeliz. Tenía muchos problemas personales y comía y bebía demasiado. Mi trabajo empezaba a empeorar. Mis amigos me decían que debía tomar unas vacaciones; pero yo insistía que no pasaba nada. Un día te escribí una carta; tu consejo fue: toma unas vacaciones en la playa y haz deporte. Fui a la playa; aprendí a pescar. Y ahora soy campeón nacional de pesca. ¡Gracias!

Can you talk about a problem which you had and which you have overcome?

2 La mujer de ayer y hoy

A middle-aged male journalist is reflecting on the changing place of women in Spanish society:

– Mi generación es testigo del contraste de las mujeres que vivían antes y las mujeres profesionales de hoy. Durante la época franquista ninguna mujer casada respetable trabajaba. Las solteras de clase baja trabajaban como criadas o en sectores textiles. Las jóvenes de clase media si trabajaban era para encontrar marido. Las chicas de antes se conformaban con ser sirvientas, secretarias, costureras o dependientas; hoy quieren ser juezas, ingenieras, directoras generales o pilotas de aviación. ¿Qué está pasando? Se trata de una discreta y lenta revolución social, la liberación de la mujer. Las mujeres antes dependían económicamente de sus padres o maridos; ahora con su trabajo tienen independencia económica y personal.

(Adapted from *El País Semanal*, 13/7/1993)

Are the following sentences true or false?

1. Respectable women in Franco's time did not go out to work.
2. Middle-class women were always career-orientated.
3. Today's women want jobs as judges, engineers, company directors and airline pilots.
4. The liberation of women has happened very quickly in Spain.

3 El ganadero de Trujillo

Matilde is interested in finding out what life is like nowadays for a family in the cattle-raising business? What can you gather about their way of life as it used to be? Do you think it has changed for the better?

4 Checklist

Can you do the following?

a Say what sports you do and what you liked doing when you were young.
b Ask someone where they used to live and say where you lived.
c Say what you were in the habit of doing.
d Describe what you looked like when you were fourteen.
e Contrast what life is like now with the way it used to be.

Unidad 13

Un paso más

V

el ganadero
cattle breeder
a ver quien apostaba más
for the highest bid
la trashumancia
movement of cattle from the south to the north of Spain
las pieles
skins

V

franquista
of General Franco
solteras
single women
criadas
maids
de clase media
middle class
se conformaban
were resigned
costureras
seamtresses

Unidad 14

Las estaciones y el tiempo

Así se habla
Talking about the weather
Making comparisons
Saying which is the longest or the most expensive

Temas
La tierra es frágil

Veamos de nuevo

Así se habla 1

¿Qué tiempo hace?
Talking about the weather

Unidad 14

V
temporada/época
season/time
lluviosa
rainy
seca
dry
llover
to rain

1 Las estaciones

Countries in the temperate zone (**la zona templada**) of both northen and southern hemispheres have four distinct seasons:

el invierno   **la primavera**

el otoño   **el verano**

1 However, when it is winter in Spain, it is summer in Argentina. Listen to a woman explaining when summer comes where she lives. Which hemisphere does she come from?

2

Countries nearer the equator in the tropical zone (**la zona tropical**), do not have four seasons. How many do they have, and what are they? Listen and find out about Costa Rica and Ecuador.

– ¿Cuántas estaciones hay en Costa Rica?
– Estaciones, no tenemos definidas. Hay una temporada lluviosa, una temporada seca.
– ¿En qué meses llueve?
– De mayo a octubre más o menos.

– ¿En Ecuador cuántas estaciones hay?
– Dos estaciones: la época lluviosa y la época seca. La época lluviosa empieza a partir del mes de diciembre hasta mayo, y la época seca de junio hasta el mes de noviembre.

> *Así se dice*
>
> *To ask about seasons, say:*
>
> **¿Cuántas estaciones hay?**
>   How many seasons are there?
> **¿Cuándo es el invierno/verano/etc.?**
>   When is winter/summer/etc.?
>
> *And to answer, say:*
>
> **El invierno es de diciembre a marzo**
>   Winter is from December to March
> **Hay ..... estaciones**
>   There are ..... seasons
> **No hay estaciones definidas**
>   There aren't well-defined seasons
> **Hay una temporada lluviosa y una temporada seca**
>   There is a rainy season and a dry season

3 Y ahora tú

¿Hay estaciones definidas en tu país?
¿Cuántas estaciones hay? ¿Cuándo son?

Unidad 14

4 El tiempo

Which phrases relate to the above pictures?

Hace sol	Nieva/Está nevando
Hace viento	Llueve/Está lloviendo
Hace calor	Hay neblina/niebla
Hace frío	Hay heladas

5 🔊³

Listen to an Ecuadorian and a Spaniard describing the weather in the area where they live and tick the expressions above as you hear them mentioned. Then listen again and say which seasons are mentioned and what the weather is like in each case.

Así se dice

To ask about the weather, say:

¿Cómo es el invierno?
  What's the winter like? *or:*
¿Qué tiempo hace (en invierno/ hoy)?
  What's the weather like (in winter/ today)?

And to answer, say:

Hace (mucho/bastante) frío/calor, etc.
  It's (very/quite) cold/hot, etc.
Llueve/nieva, etc.
  It rains/it snows, etc.
Está lloviendo/está nevando
  It's raining/it's snowing
Hay niebla/neblina
  It's foggy/misty
Está nublado/despejado
  It's cloudy/clear
Hay temperaturas altas/bajas ...
  There are high/low temperatures ...

[G]
está + nevando/lloviendo,
(See p. 156)

[V]
pegajoso
sticky

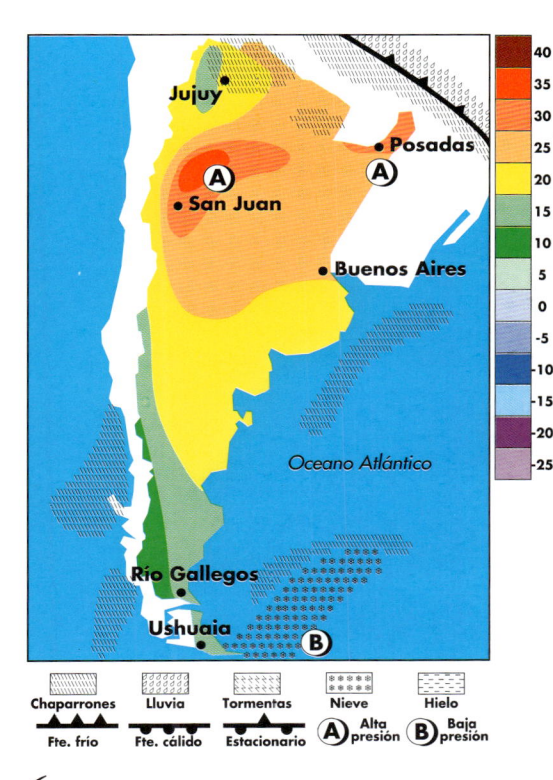

6

Today is 20th October. What is the weather like in different parts of Argentina?

e.g. En Córdoba hace un poco de calor.

a En Río Gallegos ...   d En Ushuaia ...
b En San Juan...   e En Jujuy ...
c En Buenos Aires ...   f En Posadas ...

7

Here are three people's views of the climate of particular regions of Spain.

a Which areas have extreme weather conditions?
b In which area does it rain a lot?

> El clima en el País Vasco es húmedo, muy húmedo, con temperaturas medias; llueve todo el año. Durante el verano hace calor pero es un calor pegajoso. En el invierno es húmedo también, no suele nevar. Nieva solamente en las montañas.

> El clima en Madrid es bastante diferente, dependiendo de la época del año. En verano hace mucho, mucho calor, y en invierno mucho frío. No hay un paso intermedio entre el calor y el frío.

> El clima de Extremadura es muy extremado. Entonces son los inviernos fríos y los veranos calurosos. Lo propio de un clima extremado, ¿no?

8 Y ahora tú

A ¿Qué tiempo hace hoy?
B ¿Cómo es el verano en tu país? ¿Y el invierno? ¿Y la primavera? ¿Qué temperatura hace?

2
En la costa el clima es más suave
Making comparisons

1 🔊 4

Read and listen to Carme describing the varied climate of Cataluña. Then answer the questions.

El clima, pues, depende bastante de la zona. Las ciudades o pueblos que están más cerca de la costa, el clima es más suave tanto en invierno como en verano. Luego está la parte de Lleida, que es el clima más continental, más seco – un clima más duro tanto en invierno como en verano. Mucho calor y bastante frío. Luego están los Pirineos. también el clima es ... es más extremo. Es donde, para ver nieve en Cataluña, tienes que ir a los Pirineos porque en otras partes es muy difícil. Luego en general llueve bastante poco. Llueve más al norte, por Girona o en el norte de Lleida, pero ... La parte sur, en Tarragona, es más seca ...

a Where is the weather milder?
b Where is it harsher?
c Where does it rain more?
d Where is the weather more extreme?
e Where is it drier?

Así se dice

To compare things, say:

Hace más frío en el norte que en el sur
It's colder in the north than in the south
Hace menos frío en el sur
It's less cold in the south
Llueve más/menos en el norte
It rains more/less in the north
El clima es más/menos suave/seco ...
The climate is more/less mild/dry ...
... más caluroso en el sur que en el norte
... hotter in the south than in the north

2

Look at the weather map of Argentina in Section 1. Now compare the weather in autumn between:

a San Juan and Buenos Aires
b Rio Gallegos and Posadas
c Buenos Aires and Ushuaia
d the south of the country and the centre
e the north of the country and the centre

e.g. **Hace más calor en San Juan que en Buenos Aires** or:
   El clima es más caluroso en San Juan que en Buenos Aires

3 Y ahora tú

¿Qué tiempo hace en tu país? ¿Dónde hace más calor? ¿Dónde llueve más?

Unidad 14

V
Lleida (catalán) = Lérida
Girona (catalán) = Gerona
Catalunya (catalán) = Cataluña

G
más/menos + adjective + **que**
verb + **más/menos**
más/menos + noun

(See p. 156)

V
el clima
climate

Unidad 14

Así se acostumbra

The Spanish-speaking world embraces an incredible diversity of climate and landscape. In Spain there is snow all year round in the Pyrenees and the Sierra Nevada; at the same time the heat is extreme on the Castilian plain and at the beach resorts of the far south. Latin America includes every kind of climate. The southernmost part of the continent, in southern Chile and Argentina, touches the Antarctic; yet northern Chile also contains the Atacama desert. The bitter cold of the high Andes contrasts with the sweltering Amazon rain forest which occupies much of the territory of Peru, Ecuador and Colombia. And most of Central America, Colombia and Venezuela are tropical regions.

Lacandon Forest, Guatemala

4

Three people were asked which they liked better – country or city, beach or mountains.

¿Te gusta más la playa o la montaña?
¿Te gusta más estar en el campo o la ciudad?

Listen to their answers. Which does each prefer?

5 Y ahora tú

Here are some well known cities and some words to describe them. Can you compare one with another?

| grande/pequeño | antiguo/moderno | limpio/sucio |
| bonito/feo | interesante/aburrido | |

a Oxford ..... Los Ángeles
b Londres ..... México (D.F.)
c Nueva York ..... Buenos Aires
d Toledo ..... Los Ángeles
e Madrid ..... Barcelona

e.g. **Oxford es más antiguo que Los Ángeles**

V
mejor better
peor worse
chévere nice, fine (LA)
apretado oppressive
libre free

6

Juan (below) had his photo taken with two of his classmates and a teacher. How do they compare in age and size?

e.g. **¿Quién es más joven, Juan o Federico?**
     Juan es más joven que Federico.

Can you compare some of the others:

a ¿Quién es más alto, Miguel o Federico?
b ¿Quién es más guapo, Juan o Miguel?
c ¿Quién es más delgado, Juan o Federico?
d ¿Quién tiene más pelo, Federico o Pilar?
e ¿Quién es mayor, Miguel o Federico?

V
mayor older
menor younger

Miguel   Pilar   Federico   Juan

Unidad 14

V
el árbol tree
la pintura painting

V
orquídea orchid
especies types, species
algunas some

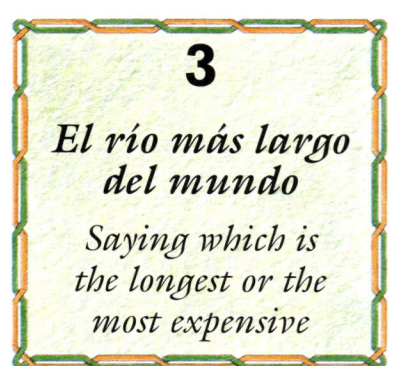

3 El río más largo del mundo

Saying which is the longest or the most expensive

1 La más bella del mundo

"Espejo, espejo, ¿quién es la mujer más bella del mundo?"

Can you match the following?

1 El río más largo del mundo	a Everest
2 La montaña más alta del mundo	b Nilo
3 El árbol más viejo del mundo	c Mona Lisa
4 El cuadro más famoso del mundo	d paella
5 El plato español más conocido	e Sequoia americana

2 🔊[6]

Two people say what they think are the longest rivers and the biggest and smallest Spanish-speaking countries in the world. Note down their replies, one of which is wrong! Which one?

	Speaker 1	Speaker 2
El río más largo del mundo		
El país más grande de habla hispana		
El país más pequeño de habla hispana		

Así se dice

To ask which is the longest/biggest, etc, say:

¿Cuál es ...
   Which is ...
... el río más largo (de tu país)
   ... the longest river (in your country)?
... la ciudad más grande (del mundo)?
   ... the biggest city (in the world)?
¿Cuál es la mujer más joven?
   Who is the youngest woman?
¿Cuáles son los hoteles más caros?
   Which are the most expensive hotels?
¿Quién es el mejor pianista?
   Who is the best pianist?

To answer you can say:

El río más largo/ la ciudad más grande es ...
   The longest river/the biggest city is ...
La mujer más joven es ...
   The youngest woman is ...
Los hoteles más caros son ...
   The most expensive hotels are ...

3 Y ahora tú

¿Cuál es la ciudad más grande de tu país?
¿El río más largo? ¿La montaña más alta?

4 🔊[7] La más bonita

Platystele

Cattleya Digbyana

Brassia Longissima

Óscar Rodríguez Quiroz works in the Botanical Gardens of the University of Costa Rica, with special responsibility for orchids. Listen and read his description of his work, then answer the questions.

Unidad 14

a How many species of orchid are there in Costa Rica?
b How many species of orchid are there in the world?
c According to Óscar Rodríguez which is the most beautiful, which is the largest and which is the smallest orchid?

5

Look again at the picture in Section 2, Activity 6. Can you say who is the tallest, the youngest, the oldest, the best looking and the most interesting person in the picture?

> ### Así se dice
>
> To ask what someone likes best, say:
>
> **¿Qué hotel/ playa te gusta más?**
> Which hotel do you like best?
>
> To answer you can say:
>
> **El Hotel Paraíso es el que más me gusta**
> **La Playa Arena es la que más me gusta**

6 *Y ahora tú*

A ¿Qué lugares te gustan más de tu pueblo/ciudad? ¿Qué tienda te gusta más? ¿Qué parque te gusta más?
B ¿Qué otras cosas te gustan más?

Temas
La tierra es frágil

La ruta verde

The Iberian peninsula is criss-crossed by drovers' paths (**las cañadas**), some more than a thousand years old. Once, shepherds and herders moved their animals along them – often using routes marked out by more ancient migrations – taking them from summer to winter pastures (**la trashumancia**). Today, they are a network for a very different group of travellers – the 'ecotourists'. Project 2001, an EU-supported plan for the protection of these routes and pathways, will take the hardier traveller across hundreds of miles of varied and impressive territory. The plan is that the ancient paths will begin to be used again by an agricultural collective with permanent herds of animals based at the beginning of each route. Every year the animals will travel the whole distance, keeping the paths open and in use. When this green network (**la gran ruta verde**) is finally in place, it will link 150 areas of special ecological interest – and enable walkers, riders and cyclists to travel from the Pyrenees to Gibraltar and back. On their way they might see some of the species of animals and birds today under threat across the Iberian Peninsula – such as the bearded vulture or lammergeyer (**el quebrantahuesos**), a bird of prey

Unidad 14

close to extinction because of the fall in numbers of cattle using the mountain paths across the Pyrenees; the night heron (**el martinete**) whose river habitats have been destroyed by major engineering works; the Iberian lynx (**el lince ibérico**) whose isolation from the animal paths has brought the number of living cats to below 1000; and the aquatic birds disappearing as the wetlands of Castilla–La Mancha are destroyed by intensive farming and drought.

Paisaje tropical

Eduardo Galeano's story shows with delicate irony how the Amazonian rainforest is fighting a losing battle with the twentieth century.

Por las aguas del Amazonas avanza lentamente el barco. Rara vez aparece alguna choza en la selva enmascarada por marañas de lianas, y algún niño desnudo saluda a los navegantes con la mano. En la cubierta, repleta, alguien lee la Biblia en voz alta, pero la gente prefiere reír y cantar mientras botellas y cigarrillos pasan de boca en boca.

Un periodista suizo viaja en este barco. Lleva horas observando a un viejo pobretón y huesudo, que pasa todo el tiempo abrazado a una gran caja de cartón y no la suelta ni para dormir. A mitad de camino, en medio de la selva, el viejo desembarca. El suizo lo ayuda a bajar la gran caja de cartón y entonces, entreabriendo la tapa, espía; dentro de la caja, envuelta en celofán, hay una palmera de plástico.

(adapted from Eduardo Galeano: *Memorias del fuego III: El siglo del viento*, Siglo XXI, Madrid, 1990, p. 269)

Destrucción del medio ambiente

Latin America has had its landscape transformed more than once. The giant Amazon rain forest (**la selva amazónica**) stretches out from Brazil into Peru,

Las cañadas

V

rara vez
rarely
choza
shack
enmascarada
masked
por marañas
by tangles
la cubierta
the deck
lleva horas
for hours he's been
viejo pobretón y huesudo
wretched, emaciated old man
caja de cartón
cardboard box
no la suelta
he won't let go
entreabriendo la tapa
opening the lid a little
palmera
palm tree

Colombia, Venezuela and Guayana. But it is losing great swathes of deep-breathing trees every day. Forty million hectares have been cut down to make way for cattle ranches and to provide farmland for landless people, the forest being destroyed by slash and burn methods – even though when the trees are cut down the soil very quickly loses its nutrients and its fertility. In the rain forest of southern Mexico, acid rain (**la lluvia ácida**) eats away at the inscriptions of the ancient Maya cities like Palenque. In Central America the cattle ranches producing meat for export have eroded the soil and taken much of the food-producing land (**las tierras de pan llevar**). In Chiapas, Mexico, the expansion of cattle-raising (**la ganadería**) has threatened the farming land of the indigenous population – which led to the uprising of January 1994.

Unidad 14

It is the cities that most clearly show the impact of pollution (**la contaminación ambiental**). In May 1990 Santiago, Chile, was declared to be in a State of Environmental Emergency. Mexico City, at 2240 metres above sea level, suffers hugely from the carbon monoxide belched out by the millions of cars that clog the city streets using highly leaded petrol. Most of the major capitals of Latin America have banned one sixth of all cars from the streets for one day a week. But it will take much more than that to turn the tide.

(Based on Duncan Green: *Faces of Latin America*, Latin America Bureau, London, 1991, chapter 3)

España gráfica

This table shows the degree of air and water pollution in Spain's main regions, and the state of the land.

* *Which regions suffer from sea and river pollution? Which regions do not suffer from air pollution*

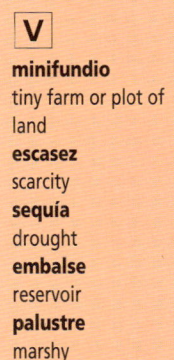

V
minifundio tiny farm or plot of land
escasez scarcity
sequía drought
embalse reservoir
palustre marshy

Región	Suelo	Agua	Aire
Andalucía	Desiertos	Contaminación ríos y costa	Sequía Contaminación industrial (Huelva)
Aragón	Desertización	Escasez de agua en río Ebro	—
Asturias	—	Agua muy contaminada:	Contaminación urbana minería e industrial (Avilés-Gijón)
Baleares	—	Contaminación de costas	—
Canarias	Volcánico/Desértico	Escasez	—
Castilla-León	—	Contaminación de embalses	—
Castilla-La Mancha	Desertización	Desecación zonas palustres	—
Cataluña	—	Agua muy contaminada ríos y costas	Contaminación urbana e industrial (Barcelona, Tarragona)
Extremadura	Erosión	Muy escasa	—
Galicia	Minifundios	—	Contaminación industrial
Madrid	—	Contaminada	Contaminación urbana
Murcia	—	Contaminación ríos y costa	—
País Vasco	—	Alta contaminación (Bilbao)	Contaminación urbana e industrial
Valencia	—	Contaminación ríos y costas	Contaminación rural y urbana

Unidad 14

Veamos de nuevo
Gramática

1 Talking about the weather

To ask about the weather the usual question is:

¿Qué tiempo hace?

Hace + noun is used to reply:

Hace sol, hace mucho calor
Hace bastante frío, hace viento

Several other common verbs are also useful in describing the weather:

| **llover** (to rain): **llueve** | **nevar** (to snow): **nieva** |
| **granizar** (to hail): **graniza** | **helar** (to freeze): **hiela** |

En invierno, nieva en las montañas
In winter, it snows in the mountains

Or you can use **hay**:

e.g. **Hay escarcha** It's frosty
     Hay niebla   It's foggy

2 Está nevando

To describe something that is happening as you speak, or to emphasise that something is going on over time, you can use a different form of the present tense – **está corriendo** (he is running), for example. Here you use **estar** + the present participle of the verb, formed as follows:

| **-ando** (-ar verbs): | nevando, trabajando, etc. |
| **-iendo** (-er/-ir verbs) | lloviendo, haciendo, subiendo |

Hoy está nevando en las montañas
Today it is snowing in the mountains
Estoy preparando la cena
I'm getting the dinner ready

3 Making comparisons

To compare two people or things you use **más** (more) or **menos** (less).

más alto/a que   taller than
menos caro/a que less expensive than

Más and **menos** can be used with a noun, an adjective or a verb.

<u>1) with a noun</u>:
En Sevilla hace más calor que en Bilbao

<u>2) with an adjective</u>:
Juan es más alto que Paquita
Tenerife es menos húmedo que Galicia

<u>3) with a verb</u>:
En mi pueblo llueve más que en el tuyo

To indicate that something is the longest/the highest, etc. you say:

el río más largo (del mundo)
the longest river (in the world)

To say what you like most or least:

El autor que más me gusta es ...
La bebida que menos me gusta es ...

Note: If you want to say that something is very good/bad, etc. without necessarily making a comparison with anything else, you can add the suffix **-ísimo**:
buenísimo, muchísimo, etc.

El clima del Caribe es buenísimo

There are four irregular comparatives/ superlatives:

menor (younger) **el/la menor** (the youngest)
mayor (older)   **el/la mayor** (the oldest)
mejor (better)   **el/la mejor** (the best)
peor (worse)   **el/la peor** (the worst)

Es el mejor escritor que hay

Unidad 14

Práctica

A Las estaciones

Some words are missing from these sentences about the seasons. Can you fill them in?

30 - nieva - frío - calor - hiela - sol - llueve - abril - viento - 15 - frío - tormentas - suave

1 En verano hace mucho ..... y ..... . La temperatura es de unos ..... grados. A veces hay ..... .
2 En otoño hace bastante ..... y hace ..... . La temperatura normal es de ..... grados.
3 En invierno ..... y ..... . Hace muchísimo ..... con temperaturas de 5 grados bajo cero.
4 En la primavera la temperatura es .... mucho, sobre todo en el mes de ..... .

B Compara

In a holiday brochure are two hotels which both look attractive. Compare them and make a note of the following:

a Which is bigger?
b Which has more bedrooms?
c Which has more facilities?
d Which is less expensive?
e Which is nearer the beach?

e.g. El hotel Mar es más grande que el Playa Sol

> **Hotel Mar (***)**
> Situado a cinco minutos de la playa y a veinte del centro de la ciudad, tiene 236 habitaciones. El hotel también dispone de salón social, dos piscinas: una cubierta y una al aire libre; dos restaurantes y un jardín infantil. El precio por habitación es de 87 euros por noche.
>
> **Hotel Playa Sol (***)**
> Está en el centro de la ciudad, a quince minutos de la playa, dispone de 189 habitaciones. Tiene peluquería, gimnasio y restaurante. La piscina es de tamaño olímpico. El precio de la habitación es de 79 euros.

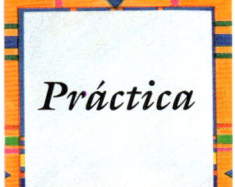

C Charlando

You have just phoned a friend in Madrid and discussed what you were both doing. When you put the phone down fragments of the conversation are still in your head. Can you put them together so that they make sense?

1 Hola Alicia, ¿qué estás haciendo?
2 ¿Y los niños?
3 Y ¿qué tiempo hace?
4 Aquí está lloviendo

a Están viendo la televisión
b ¡Qué pena!
c Estoy preparando la cena
d Buenísimo, hace mucho calor. ¿Y con vosotros?

Un paso más

V
el punto knitting
el bricolaje DIY

1 La vela es más sencilla

You are comparing notes with a friend about how interesting/boring (**interesante/aburrido**), easy/difficult (**fácil/difícil**) useful/useless (**útil/inútil**), simple/complicated (**sencillo/complicado**) cheap/expensive (**barato/caro**) certain activities are. How would you rate the following?

<u>Pasatiempos:</u>
la jardinería el punto el bricolaje el ajedrez

<u>Deportes:</u>
el ciclismo el alpinismo la vela el esquí

<u>Idiomas:</u>
el ruso el alemán el español el inglés

e.g. El español es más fácil que el ruso.

Now can you say which you like the most and which you like the least out of all these activities?

e.g. El pasatiempo que más me gusta es la jardinería

Unidad 14

2 Zonas húmedas de la Mancha

A friend has given you the following information about the wetlands of La Mancha, an area of Spain that UNESCO has declared **Reserva de la Biosfera**. Read about the two routes that you could take and answer the questions.

a Which route would you take if you like canoeing?
b And if you are interested in water birds?
c What are the best months to see migrating birds?
d Why is the area so important ecológicamente?

Ruta Verde 1 – Entre Alcázar de San Juan y Villacañas
Una ruta ideal para el senderismo pasa por muchas lagunas protegidas. Se pueden observar las gaviotas reidoras y los aguiluchos laguneros. Una vegetación esteparia rodea las lagunas, donde hay liebres, avutardas y sisones.

Ruta Verde 2 – Zonas húmedas estacionales
Este recorrido pasa por Manjavacas, que tiene especial importancia por las aves migratorias, con máxima concentración en los meses de marzo y abril. Posibilidades ecoturísticas: combinación tren-bicicleta y descenso del río Cigüela en piragua.
Mejor época del año: otoño, invierno y primavera.
Valores naturales: Es la principal concentración de humedades de la Península Ibérica.

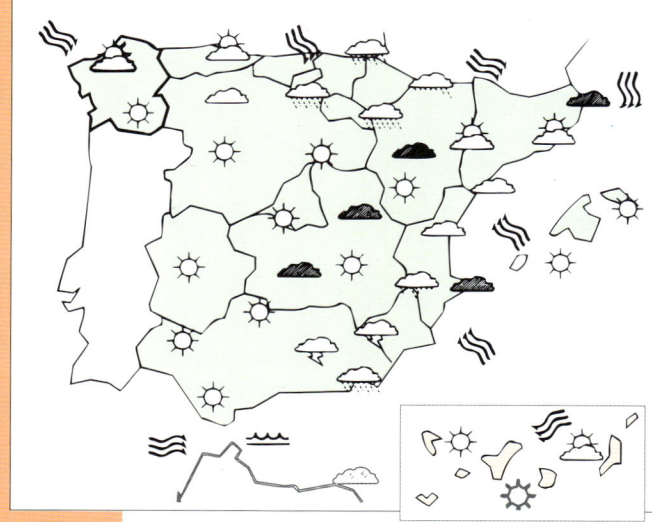

V
el senderismo
walking, hiking
la laguna
pond
la gaviota reidora
black-headed gull
el aguilucho lagunero
pool eaglet
la liebre
hare
la avutarda
great bustard
el sisón
little bustard

3 El tiempo

Despejado | Nub./Clar. | Cubierto | Lluvia
Chubascos | Llovizna | Tormenta | Heladas
Niebla | Nieve | Viento | Marejada

Before going camping in the north of Spain with your family, you listen to the forecast on the radio. Listen, check the weather in the areas marked on the map, and decide if the weather is suitable.

4 Checklist

Can you do the following?

a Ask and talk about climate and seasons.
b Ask about the weather and say what it's like in your area.
c Compare two people or objects.
d Ask and say which is the longest, the best, which you like most, etc.

Unidad 15

Pasó hace mucho tiempo

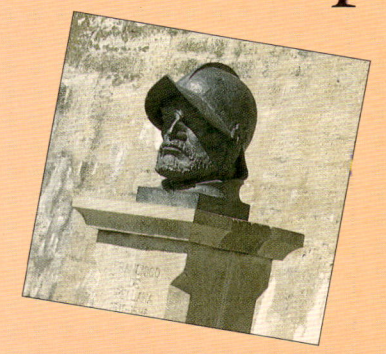

Así se habla
Telling your life story
Saying how long ago and how long for
Talking about history

Temas
De Extremadura salieron

Veamos de nuevo

Unidad 15

Así se habla 1
Nací en Badalona
Telling your life story

1 🔊¹

Mario Posla, an expert working for 'OIT' (Organización Internacional del Trabajo), gives an account of his life. Listen and match the events he describes with the places where they took place.

Nací en …	Estados Unidos
Pasé a …	Guatemala
Viví cuatro años en …	América
Viví algunos años en …	Guatemala
Trabajé como experto en …	El Salvador
Trabajé como jefe de misión en …	Italia
Pasé dos años en …	El Salvador
Pasé tres años en …	México

Así se dice

To describe the main events in your life, say:

Nací en Italia (en 1950)
 I was born in Italy (in 1950)
Pasé dos años/mi infancia en …
 I spent two years/my childhood in …
Viví/estudié en …
 I lived/studied in …
Me casé/me divorcié/me volví a casar en …
 I got married/got divorced/remarried in …

V
nacer to be born
jefe head/boss
pasar to spend (time)
pasar a to go to

G
nacer/yo nací
tener/yo tuve
casarse/me casé

(See Unit 12, G 10)

2

COMPAÑÍA DE SEGUROS CONTINENTAL

Nombre: Jordi Moliner
Lugar de nacimiento: Badalona, Cataluña
Fecha de nacimiento: 18 de julio de 1957
Estudios: Arquitectura, Universidad de Barcelona (1974-1982)
Profesión: Arquitecto
Estado civil: Casado   Fecha: 1980
Número de hijos: Dos

COMPAÑÍA DE SEGUROS CONTINENTAL

Nombre: Antonio González
Lugar de nacimiento: Badalona, Cataluña
Fecha de nacimiento: 14 de abril de 1955
Estudios: Arquitectura, Universidad de Barcelona (1973-1982)
Profesión: Arquitecto
Estado civil: Casado   Fecha: 1984
Número de hijos: Uno

Look at the personal details of two Spanish architects who are in partnership and answer these questions:

a ¿Quién es mayor?
b ¿Cuántos años estudiaron para ser arquitectos?
c ¿Quién se casó primero?
d ¿Quién tiene más hijos?

How would each describe his life? Use the following verbs:

nacer, estudiar, empezar/terminar la carrera, casarse, tener hijos.

e.g. Jordi: 'Nací en Badalona el 18 de julio de 1957'.

3 🔊²

Now listen to one of the architects talking about his life. Can you say whether it is Jordi or Antonio?

Unidad 15

4

Isabel Allende, menuda y graciosa, es la mujer que en su natal Chile intentó una vez ser corista; abuela de tres nietos, la autora siempre comienza a escribir sus libros el 8 de enero.
– Yo nací en Lima por casualidad; pero en realidad soy chilena – declara.
Tuve un padre que desapareció sin dejar recuerdos y mi madre fue el norte de mi infancia. Tal vez por eso me resulta más fácil escribir sobre las mujeres. Sobrina del asesinado presidente Salvador Allende, Isabel se fue a vivir a Venezuela, donde continuó su carrera de periodista que empezó a los 17 años. Allí se enamoró de un músico y terminó su largo matrimonio con Michael, padre de sus hijos. En Caracas se volvió escritora.

Trabajaba 12 horas dando clases en un colegio y cuando regresaba a casa escribía en una pequeña máquina portátil hasta muy tarde. Así comenzó un 8 de enero *La casa de los espíritus*. Esta novela, muy biográfica, dio origen a la película coproducida por Dinamarca, Alemania y Portugal.
Las obras de Isabel Allende giran en torno a su vida y a personas cercanas a ella. En *La casa de los espíritus*, Clara, el personaje principal, es su abuela. En *El plan infinito*, lo es William, su segundo marido y en *Paula*, su hija quien murió en Madrid víctima de una rara enfermedad.

(Adapted from *Actual*, January, 1995).

Read this extract from an interview with the well-known Latin-American writer Isabel Allende, and say whether these statements are true (**verdadero**) or false (**falso**).

a Isabel Allende es chilena.
b Isabel tiene recuerdos de su padre.
c Su madre tuvo mucha influencia en su vida.
d Se enamoró de un músico a los 17 años.
e Fue periodista antes de ser escritora.
f Empezó su carrera como escritora en Venezuela.
g Su obra es autobiográfica.

5 De periodista

Imagine Mario Posla has come to your town. Using the information in Activity 1, can you write a short description of his life for the *Gaceta hispánica*? Start like this:

Nos visita Mario Posla, un experto de la OIT. Mario Posla nació en Italia ...

V
menuda
slight
corista
chorus girl
norte
guide
cuaderno
notebook
girar en torno
to revolve around

6

Javier   Lucía

What kind of life might the two people above have lived? Write an imaginary biography of Lucía or Javier, by answering the following questions:

¿De dónde es? ¿Cuál es su trabajo? ¿Dónde nació? ¿Dónde pasó su niñez/juventud? ¿Estudió una carrera? ¿Cuándo empezó a trabajar?
¿Se casó? ¿Tuvo hijos?

7 Y ahora tú

Imagine you are telling your children or grandchildren about your life.

¿Cuándo naciste? ¿Dónde pasaste tu infancia? ¿En qué año empezaste y en qué año terminaste la escuela?
¿Cuándo empezaste a trabajar? etc.

2

Nos casamos hace tres meses

Saying how long ago and how long for

1 🔊³

Two couples in Acapulco are asked about their married life. Make a note about:

a how long they have been married
b where they got married
c where they met, if mentioned

The first part of each conversation is printed for you on the next page.

Carmen: ¿Ustedes están casados?
Mujer: **Sí, ya, ya hace mucho.**
Carmen: ¿Cuánto tiempo hace que se casaron?
Hombre: **Veinticinco años ...**

Isabel: ¿Está casado?
Hombre: **Sí, y tenemos una familia grande.**
Isabel: ¿Cuántos años lleva casado?
Hombre: **Treinta y dos el día de hoy.**

Así se dice

To ask someone how long ago they did something, say:

¿Cuánto tiempo hace que te casaste?
   How long ago did you get married?
Hace veinte años que me casé
Me casé hace veinte años/en 1975
   I got married twenty years ago/in 1975

To find out how long someone has been doing something, say:

¿Cuánto tiempo llevas ...
   How long have you been ...
... casado/a?/en Madrid?/trabajando?
   ... married?/in Madrid?/working?

To ask where you met someone, say:

¿Dónde conociste a tu marido/mujer?
   Where did you meet your husband/wife?

To answer, say:

Lo/la conocí en ...
   I met him/her in ...

2 🔊 4

María Elena is from Ecuador, but she lives and works in England. Can you ask her the following questions?

a How long ago she got married
b Where she met her husband
c How long ago she left Ecuador
d How long she's been teaching in London

Now listen and find out how she answers.

EL NOVIAZGO *Fecha a fecha*

ENCUENTRO
Junio 1992: Rocío Jurado y Ortega Cano se conocen en la consulta del doctor Mariscal.

ADMIRADOR
13 de agosto 1992: Ortega Cano asiste al espectáculo Azalbache en Sevilla, donde actúa Rocío.

RUMORES
18 de septiembre 1992: Ortega Cano asiste al cumpleaños de Rocío. Torea en Málaga. Después de la corrida va a Madrid y aparece en el chalé de ella. Empiezan los rumores de un posible noviazgo.

CUMPLEAÑOS
23 de diciembre 1992: Rocío organiza una fiesta por el cumpleaños de Ortega Cano en un tablao de moda.

DIVORCIO
6 de marzo 1993: Rocío y su marido, Pedro Carrasco, se divorcian.
Nochevieja 31 de diciembre 1993: En Cali, Colombia, la pareja brinda por el nuevo año. Rocío solicita la nulidad de su primer matrimonio.

NULIDAD
18 de abril 1994: Rocío obtiene la nulidad y anuncia su boda para fines del año en la iglesia de La Macarena.

NEGATIVA
26 de octubre de 1994: El cura de La Macarena no acepta casarles.

NUEVA FECHA
20 de noviembre de 1994: Anuncian nueva fecha de matrimonio: el 17 de febrero de 1995

COGIDA
5 de enero 1995: Ortega Cano sufre una herida grave en una corrida en Cartagena de Indias y va al hospital.

SALIDA
17 de enero 1995: Sale del hospital acompañado de su novia y de su madre.

VUELTA
26 de enero 1995: La pareja regresa a España. Continúan los preparativos.

FINAL FELIZ
17 de febrero: Rocío y Ortega Cano se casan y ofrecen una gran recepción en la finca Yerbabuena.

Chronicle adapted, from revista *Tiempo* Febrero 95

V
consulta surgery/practice
tablao a flamenco club
herida wound

G
conocer a to meet
(See p. 167)

V
enseñar to teach

3 ¡Una boda comentada!

Read about the much discussed engagement (**el noviazgo**) and wedding (**la boda**) of two Spanish celebrities: the singer Rocío Jurado and José Ortega Cano, the bullfighter (**el torero**).

a Where did Rocío and José meet?
b When did their relationship become public?
c What difficulties did they have to overcome before they could get married?

4

Your friend has missed the details of this famous wedding. Can you fill him in?

e.g. **Rocío Jurado y Ortega Cano se conocieron en la consulta del ... en junio de 1992.**

5 Y ahora tú

Answer about yourself or pretend you are somebody else if you wish:

A **¿Cuánto tiempo llevas estudiando español?** or **¿Cuánto tiempo hace que empezaste a estudiar español?**
B **¿Trabajas? ¿Dónde trabajas? ¿Cuánto tiempo llevas trabajando allí?**

Unidad 15

3
Extremadura, cuna de conquistadores
Talking about history

1

Trujillo is the town in Extremadura where many of the **conquistadores** came from. The brochure below describes its history. Can you say whether:

a Trujillo was built between two rivers.
b The town has had different names.
c It came under Christian rule in the 14th c.
d The Plaza Mayor is the focal point.
e The Palacio de la Conquista was built by Francisco Pizarro.

> Trujillo está situada al sur de la meseta central cacereña. Se construyó entre dos grandes ríos del oeste peninsular, Tajo y Guadiana. Sus orígenes se remontan a seis siglos antes de la era cristiana. Fue 'Turgalium' para los romanos y 'Torgiela' para los árabes. Los cristianos la reconquistaron en 1232 y se convirtió en 'Truxellum', hoy Trujillo.

> Trujillo es conocida como la cuna de los conquistadores por la gran cantidad de personas ilustres que allí nacieron: Francisco Pizarro, conquistador del Perú y fundador de Lima; García Paredes, fundador de Ciudad Trujillo en Venezuela; Francisco de Orellana, descubridor del río Amazonas y muchos capitanes que participaron en la conquista del Nuevo Mundo.

> La Plaza Mayor de Trujillo es el centro de la ciudad. En ella se encuentran las iglesias la de la Sangre y la de San Martín. En el centro está la estatua ecuestre de Francisco Pizarro, el Palacio de la Conquista, construido por Hernando Pizarro, y el Palacio de Chaves – Cárdenas.

2

Isabel is in Trujillo, visiting some of the places mentioned above. Listen and find out where she is.

V

se remontan a
go back to
cuna
cradle
estatua
statue

Así se dice

To describe when a place was built, say:

Trujillo se fundó entre dos ríos
    Trujillo was founded between two rivers
La iglesia se construyó/se restauró en 1627
    The church was built/restored in 1627

☞ Ex. A, p.167

3

These important historical or literary figures are all relevant to the New World. Busts of some of them have been erected in one of the rooms of the Javier de Salas museum in Trujillo. Listen to the guide and tick the names you hear mentioned.

Bartolomé de Las Casas (1470-1566)
Defensor de los indígenas

Sor Juana Inés de la Cruz (1651-1695)
Poetisa mexicana

Simón Bolívar (1783-1830)
El Libertador de América

José de San Martín (1778-1850)
Líder de la independencia de Argentina y Chile

Rubén Darío (1867-1916)
Escritor nicaragüense

Pablo Neruda (1904-1973)
Escritor chileno

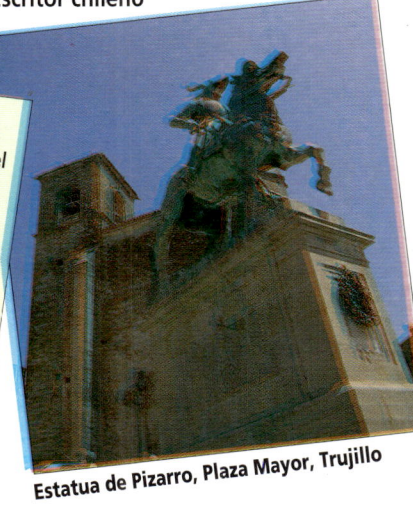

Estatua de Pizarro, Plaza Mayor, Trujillo

Unidad 15

Así se dice

To indicate who someone was and what he did, say:

Bartolomé de Las Casas ...
... fue un fraile español ...
  ...was a Spanish friar
... que defendió a los indígenas
  ... who defended the Indians
Fue obispo de Chiapas
  He was bishop of Chiapas
Nació en Sevilla en 1470
  He was born in Seville in 1470
... y murió en Madrid en 1566
  ... and died in Madrid in 1566

4

Say who the people in Activity 3 were, where and when they were born and when they died.

5 *Y ahora tú*

A Think of the name of someone important in the history of your country.

¿Quién fue? ¿Cuándo nació/murió?

B Name one important building in your town/country.

¿Cuándo se construyó?

C **¿Cuándo se fundó tu pueblo o tu ciudad?**

G
ser/fue
nacer/nació
morir/murió

(See p. 166)

Cortés

Temas

De Extremadura salieron

Two men from Extremadura (**extremeños**) became central figures in the history of Latin America. Hernán Cortés and Francisco Pizarro, sometimes called conquerors (**conquistadores**), both led their army of Spaniards into the territory of great empires in the New World. Both met an emperor – for whose death they were finally responsible.

Cortés en México

Cortés was born in Medellín in 1485. In 1504, at nineteen, he sailed with an expedition bound for the Americas. Settling at first in the island colony of Santo Domingo, he later sailed to Cuba with the expedition of Diego Velazquez. He had already grown wealthy, and his new position of influence in Cuba made him richer still. But the persistent rumours of even greater treasures led him to join several expeditions along the Mexican mainland before disembarking, on Good Friday, 21st April 1519, at what became the port of Veracruz. When envoys came bearing gifts from the Aztec Emperor Moctezuma, Cortés conversed with them through his interpreter, Doña Marina; she later became his lover and reverted to her own name, Malinche. Cortés soon realized that the Aztecs were unpopular rulers, and that many of the

Unidad 15

subject peoples they dominated would gladly ally with Spain against them. Four months later, Cortés began to march towards the centre of the country. On the night of 18th October 1519, at the ceremonial city of Cholula, Cortés heard rumours that the Aztecs were plotting to kill him. He attacked first, leaving thousands dead. In this way, Cortés both preempted the attack and persuaded the indigenous armies that resistance to Spain would be useless. His army of 500 now swelled with the soldiers of the enemies of Moctezuma – and it was a column of tens of thousands that came over the peak of the Popocatépetl volcano to look down on the marvellous Aztec capital – Tenochtítlan. One of Cortés' soldiers (Bernal Diaz) described the city:

"Mudos de hermosura, los conquistadores cabalgan por la calzada. Tenochtitlan parece arrancada de las páginas de Amadís, cosas nunca oídas, ni vistas, ni aún soñadas. El sol se alza tras los volcanes, entra en la laguna, y rompe en jirones la niebla que flota. La ciudad, calles, acequias, templos de altas torres, se despliega y fulgura."

(Eduardo Galeano: *Memorias del Fuego I: Los nacimientos*, Siglo XXI, Madrid, 1991, p. 79.)

Cortés was popular with his men, but absolutely ruthless with those who defied his authority. In his accounts to the King explaining his actions (the **Cartas de Relación**) he was careful to say that he was the servant of God and the Emperor – yet he became a virtual emperor himself in the colony of New Spain. With so much at stake, there were rebellions against him – he put them all down without quarter. When his enemies won the ear of the emperor in Spain, he returned to Spain where he died in 1547, still arguing his case. His lover Malinche became a byword in Mexico for betrayal to a foreign power (**malinchismo**).

V

mudos de hermosura
struck dumb by the beauty
cabalgar
to ride
la calzada
the causeway
Amadís
Amadís of Gaul (a novel of chivalry widely read at the time)
rompe en jirones
breaks into strands
acequias
canals
desplegarse
to unfold
fulgurar
to shine

V

unos cuantos
a few
vergüenza
shame
entregamos
we surrendered
grandeza
greatness
quedamos
we remained
el maleficio
the curse
brindar
to offer

Pizarro

Gabino Palomares' wonderful song describes the whole history of Mexico under Spanish tyranny as Malinche's curse: "La maldición de Malinche".

Iban montados en bestias
Como demonios del mal
Iban con fuego en las manos
Y cubiertos de metal

Fue por el valor de unos cuantos
Que se opuso resistencia
Y cuando vieron correr la sangre
Se llenaron de vergüenza

En ese error entregamos
la grandeza del pasado
y en ese error nos quedamos
trescientos años esclavos

Y nos quedó el maleficio
de brindar al extranjero
nuestra fe nuestra cultura
nuestro pan nuestro dinero

(Gabino Palomares and Amparo Ochoa: "Maldición de Malinche" (Palomares)

Pizarro en el Perú

While Cortés, at the age of 36, was subduing a great empire, Francisco Pizarro, at 41, was having less success. He was involved in several expeditions to what is now Panama, none of which were very successful. But he persevered, and in 1528 returned to Spain to seek the King's licence to explore to the south. He arrived at court as Cortés was giving his extraordinary accounts of the conquest of Mexico; so Pizarro had little difficulty in persuading people to join his proposed expedition. It was a difficult project, but rumours of golden places and golden men (Eldorado) kept up the spirits of his men until 1532 – when Pizarro, now aged over 50, came face to face with the awesome power of the Incas. They met at Cajamarca – Pizarro, the brusque, illiterate but wily soldier of fortune and Atahualpa, emperor of the

Incas. Pizarro had 132 men, Atahualpa an army of thousands. But Pizarro made up for his small numbers by capturing and imprisoning the Inca after a surprise attack in the town's central square.

Pizarro had arrived, by accident not design, at a fortunate moment. The Inca empire embraced 6 000 kilometres of territory, from central Chile to northern Ecuador; it was efficient, centralised, and linked by great highways where couriers (**chasquis**) carried messages at extraordinary speed along the high mountain range. But when the Spaniards came, it was locked in a dispute between two people both aspiring to the imperial throne – Atahualpa and his half-brother Huascar. Atahualpa probably thought that the Spaniards, with their horses and their weapons, could add weight to his own challenge for power. When Pizarro demanded that he fill his cell with gold and silver, he did so at speed – and sealed his own fate, especially when Pizarro saw the gold-leaf-covered walls of the Inca capital of Cuzco. With so much wealth at stake, Pizarro could never allow the Inca to resume his place. In the end, Pizarro had him killed. In the years to come, many of those who had accompanied him fought one another over the spoils of Conquest, and Pizarro himself fell victim to his enemies – killed in Lima, capital of the new Spanish colony, in 1541.

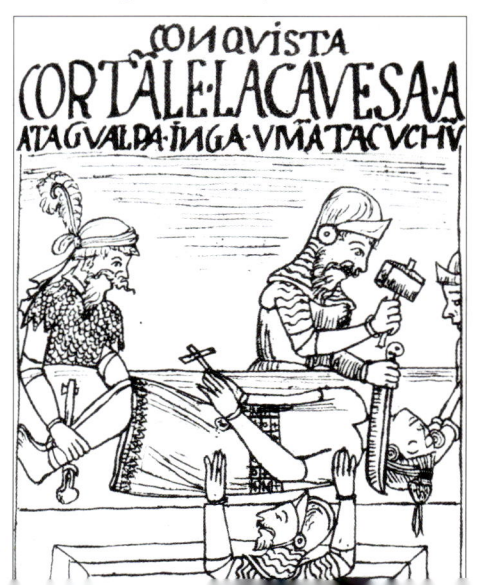

The execution of Atahualpa

Unidad 15

Veamos de nuevo
Gramática

1 More about the past

You have already met the preterite tense in Unit 12. As you have seen in this unit, you can use also the preterite to talk about historical or personal events in the past.

Aprendí español en Salamanca
I learned Spanish in Salamanca

Useful irregular verbs include: **ser** (to be) – which has the same form as **ir** (see Unit 12), **venir** (to come) **morir** (to die), and **tener** (to have)

Salvador Allende fue el presidente de Chile
Salvador Allende was president of Chile
Alicia vino del Perú
Alicia came from Peru
Franco murió en 1975
Franco died in 1975

venir	**morir**	**tener**
vine	morí	tuve
viniste	moriste	tuviste
vino	murió	tuvo
vinimos	morimos	tuvimos
vinisteis	moristeis	tuvisteis
vinieron	murieron	tuvieron

2 How long ago

To say how long ago, use **hace**:

Hace cinco años que me casé or:
Me casé hace cinco años

Unidad 15

3 How long for

If you want to say for how long a situation has existed, there are two common ways of doing it:

a) use **llevar** + time:
Llevo un año en Madrid
I have been in Madrid for a year
b) use **desde hace** with the present tense of the verb:
Trabajo en Madrid desde hace un año
I have been working in Madrid for a year

If you want to say for how long you have been doing something, use **llevar** + time + the present participle of a verb:

Llevo dos años estudiando
I have been studying for two years
Ana lleva dos meses trabajando
Ana has been working for two months

4 Conocer

Conocer means to know people or places.

¿Conoces a Juan? – Sí, conozco a Juan
Do you know Juan? Yes, I know Juan
¿Conoces Madrid? – No, no conozco Madrid
Do you know Madrid? No, I don't ...

It can also mean 'to get to know' and thus 'to meet' (i.e. for the first time):

Conocí a María en España
I met María in Spain

Note that between **conocí** and the person you need an **a** which you don't translate. Whenever any verb has a person as a direct object (as opposed to an animal or a thing) you must remember to use what is called the personal **a**. Apart from **conocer**, other useful verbs that have people as objects are: **ver** (to see), **visitar** (to visit), **buscar** (to look for), **esperar** (to wait for) and **llamar** (to phone).

Visité a tu tía ayer
I visited your aunt yesterday but:
Visité el hospital ayer
I visited the hospital yesterday

5 Him or Her

If you want to replace the name of a person with a pronoun such as 'him' or 'her', you use **lo** or **le** for 'him', and **la** for 'her'. Look at these examples:

¿Conoces a Juan? ¿Lo conoces?
Do you know him?
Conocí a mi esposa en Acapulco.
La conocí en Acapulco.
I met her in Acapulco

For more on object pronouns see Unit 18, p. 200.

6 Se construyó

To say something was done, without saying by whom, you can use a reflexive **se** where English uses the passive:

La casa se construyó en 1500
The house was built in 1500
La ciudad se fundó en 1492
The city was founded in 1492

Práctica

G
convertirse (e/i)

A *Historia de dos ciudades*

Cartagena in Spain took its name from the north African city of Carthage and gave its name in turn to Cartagena in Colombia. Can you put the verbs in brackets in the correct form, using **se**?

Hay dos ciudades llamadas Cartagena. La Cartagena de España (fundarse) en el siglo ocho antes de Cristo. (Volverse) a fundar en el año 223, en tiempos de Asdrúbal. (Convertirse) en uno de los puertos más importantes del Mediterráneo. La Cartagena de Colombia (empezarse) a construir en el siglo XVI. El pirata Francis Drake destruyó su primera catedral en 1586, pero finalmente la nueva catedral (terminarse) en 1610. En ese mismo año (registrarse) otro acontecimiento importante; (mandarse) a San Pedro Claver a Colombia para ayudar a los esclavos. Murió en 1654 y 60 años más tarde (construirse) una iglesia en su honor. Y en el siglo XIX (liberarse) a los esclavos finalmente.

B ¿Hace cuánto tiempo ...?

These are some snippets of conversation heard in a bus queue. Can you report what was said to the person behind you, using **hace**.

e.g. **Son las cuatro y espero el bus desde las dos. Hace dos horas que espera el bus.**

1 Son las cuatro y espero el bus desde las dos.
2 Son las doce y el desayuno fue a las ocho.
3 Es 1995 y me casé en 1991.
4 Hoy es viernes y espero a Manuel desde el martes.
5 Ahora es diciembre y llegué en marzo.

C A busy day

Can you say what you did yesterday?

a you saw your mother; b telephoned your brother; c visited your aunt; d met your friend and e last night you saw your brother.

e.g. **Ayer, vi a mi madre.**

1 ¿Conoces la historia?

Three Spaniards are asked about important historical dates. The following dates are mentioned. Can you match the events with the dates on the right? Then check your answers on the recording.

¿Cuándo fue...?

* la invasión de los musulmanes a España	1975
* la Revolución Francesa	1936
* el Descubrimiento de América	711
* el inicio de la Primera Guerra Mundial	1992
* el inicio de la Guerra Civil española	1975
* la muerte de Franco	1492
* la venida de la democracia a España	1914
* la EXPO de Sevilla	1789

2 Pilar Miró

Pilar Miró was a famous Spanish television director who died in October 1997. Think how you might have asked her about the following in an interview before she died:

Unidad 15

V
realizadora
director
el ente televisivo
official television
malversar fondos
misappropriate funds
procesar
to put on trial

Un paso más

10 COSAS SOBRE
Pilar Miró

1. Nació en Madrid el 20 de abril de 1940.
2. Su mejor compañera de la infancia fue una gata.
3. En 1957 empezó Derecho en la Universidad Central de Madrid, con la misma promoción del rey Don Juan Carlos, con quien mantiene amistad.
4. Con 23 años fue la primera mujer realizadora de dramáticos en televisión.
5. Aunque de niña quería ser misionera, Pilar ha realizado trabajos más lucrativos: directora general de Cinematografía (1982) y directora general del Ente Público (1986).
6. En 1979 fue procesada por injurias a la Guardia Civil a raíz de la película *El crimen de Cuenca*. En 1989 se la acusó de malversar fondos públicos.
7. Obtuvo el Oso de Plata del Festival de Cine de Berlín por *Beltenebros*.
8. Lee el *ABC*, le gusta la ópera y odia el queso.
9. Ha sido operada dos veces a corazón abierto.
10. Soltera, tiene un hijo de 13 años: Gonzalo. ■

F. J. Gil

(a) her past history (when she was born, where she spent her childhood, where and what she studied, when she got her first job, what problems she encountered, etc.);
(b) her lifestyle at the time (if she was married, and if so for how long, if she had any children, how long ago they were born, what work she was doing, when did she take up her current post, etc.)

3 The article

In the course of your research about Pilar Miró, you come across this article about her. Does the text answer all your questions? Now prepare your own report as if you were describing her to a TV audience.

4 Checklist

Can you do the following?

a Say what were the main events of your life.
b Ask someone how long ago he/she got married.
c Say when and how you met your partner/ your best friend.
d Say how long you have been living where you are now/in your present job.
e Tell a friend about key dates in the history of your country.

Puesta a punto 3

1 Making sense

Put the words in the correct order to make sentences.

a ir al encanta teatro Me
b ¿habitación es de precio la Cuál el?
c funciona las ducha están toallas sucias y La no
d ¿entradas puedo Dónde las conseguir?
e una noches individual para habitación dos Quiero
f ¿cine en Qué para hay ver el?
g que Fernando más es alta Julia

2 Crucigrama deportivo

Horizontal
1 Animales del rugby argentino.
3 Deporte de cinco jugadores muy popular en España.
4 Deporte que cuenta con Venus y Serena Williams entre sus estrellas.
7 Hockey sobre hierba y – – – – –.
8 M – – – – r un 6 en fútbol.

Vertical
1 – – – – – – vasca.
2 Argentina fue campeona en 1978 y 86.
3 Deporte número uno en Cuba y Venezuela.
5 El Rey de España compite en su barco de – – – –.
6 Ver 8 horizontal.

3 Cervantes

Complete the text using the preterite of the appropriate verb from the list below. The first one is done for you.

nacer morir perder ser hacer casarse publicar luchar regresar

V
luchar
to fight

Miguel de Cervantes Saavedra **nació** en Alcalá de Henares en 1547. ..... sus estudios en Madrid. A los veintitrés años, siendo soldado, ... en la batalla de Lepanto, donde ..... un brazo. Durante cinco años ..... prisionero en Argel. ..... a España y ..... con Catalina de Salazar y Palacios. ..... su primera obra *La Galatea* en 1588 y su extraordinaria novela *Don Quijote* en 1605. Finalmente, ... el 23 de abril de 1616.

4 El mejor

Complete this chart with the correct form of the adjectives.

	comparativo	superlativo
largo	más largo	el más largo
bueno	_____	_____
_____	peor	_____
pequeño	_____	_____
_____	más caro	_____

5 ¡Qué tiempo!

Match the phrases with the appropriate season.

| Spring | Summer | Autumn | Winter |

hace calor   nieva   hay niebla   hiela mucho
hay tormentas   hace buen tiempo   hace viento
hace mucho frío   está nublado   hace sol   llueve

6 Tal como éramos

Make sentences by matching phrases from the two sets. Write the correct forms of the verbs in parentheses.

a Me levantaba a las siete
b A mi hermano le gustaba la leche
c Los chicos jugaban al fútbol en la playa
d Carmen estudiaba enfermería
e Mi madre cocinaba en casa
f Veía películas españolas

i   y las chicas ..... (nadar) en el mar
ii   y ..... (trabajar) en una farmacia
iii pero Marta y yo ..... (preferir) la horchata
iv   pero los domingos nosotros ..... (ir) a los restaurantes
v   cuando ..... (ir) al cine
vi   pero mi hermano ..... (levantarse) a las once

7 Where? What? Who?

Write the questions to these answers.

a _____
   No practico ningún deporte.
b _____
   Mis padres suelen ir a la playa de vacaciones.
c _____
   Lo pasó fenomenal en Acapulco.
d _____
   Nos casamos hace nueve años.
e _____
   Isaac Peral construyó el primer submarino.
f _____
   La conocí en una fiesta de cumpleaños.

8 What's missing?

Complete each sentence with the missing word.

a A nosotros ...... gusta el mar.
b Los domingos íbamos .... cine.
c No me gusta ..... el fútbol.
d El Amazonas es más largo ..... el Orinoco.
e Me casé ..... dos años.
f En verano, los niños ..... acostaban tarde.
g ¿Cúando conociste a tu mujer?. ..... conocí en 1986.
h Juan tiene 20 años y su hermana Marta 12. Juan es .... que Marta.

9 Puesta a punto oral

You ring a Mexican hotel to book a room. Do the following:

– give your name and say that you want to book a double room with a shower.
– say it is for two weeks (8–22 July) and you want half board.
– ask the price and if you can pay by credit card.
– ask them to confirm the booking by post
– give your full address and phone number

Unidad 16

¡A comer!

Así se habla
Ordering food in a restaurant

Saying what you eat every day

Describing recipes

Temas
La comida es cultura

Veamos de nuevo

Unidad 16

Así se habla 1

Para mí un gazpacho
Ordering food in a restaurant

1 🔊¹

This is the menu at **Rincón de Paco**, a Spanish restaurant. Can you find the following? Use a dictionary if necessary.

a two types of soup	b two types of cold starters
c three types of meat	d seafood dishes
e three ways in which potatoes can be served	
f two ways in which meat can be prepared	
g one vegetarian dish	

Rincón de Paco

Entradas frías
Cóctel de mariscos ....12,40 €
Espárragos vinagreta ....8,20 €
Melón con jamón ....5,50 €
Entremeses variados ....6,40 €

Pastas, Sopas y Verduras
Macarrones con tomate ....5,50 €
Gazpacho ....6,10 €
Sopa de ajo ....6,10 €
Judías verdes con jamón ....6,10 €

Paella especial mixta,
carne, ave y marisco ....7,30 €

Ensaladas
Mixta: lechuga, tomate, cebolla, aceitunas ..5,50 €
Ensalada Rincón de Paco ....6,70 €

Pescados, carnes y aves
(Guarnición de patatas fritas, al vapor, o puré de patatas)
Merluza en salsa verde ....10,60 €
Filete de ternera a la plancha ....13,60 €
Bistec a la parrilla ....9,40 €
Chuletas de cordero lechales ....9,40 €
Pollo al ajillo ....7,00 €
Cochinillo a la brasa ....8,80 €
Caldereta de cordero ....7,00 €

V

¡Buen provecho!
Enjoy your meal!

V

guarnición de (Sp)
served with
caldereta
stew
a la plancha, a la parrilla, a la brasa
grilled
al ajillo
in a garlic sauce

---

2 🔊²

Listen to a group of friends ordering a meal at the **Rincón de Paco**. On the menu tick the dishes ordered, and also make a note of the drinks they ask for.

Así se dice

To order different courses, say:

De primero (Sp)/De entrada (LA) yo quiero …
    As a starter, I'd like …
De segundo/De plato fuerte a mí me apetece …
    As the main course, I'd like a/an …
De postre, me gustaría …
    For dessert, I'd like …

To order drinks, you can say:

De beber/de tomar (LA), un agua mineral
    To drink, mineral water

Así se acostumbra

Each region in Spain and Latin America has its own dishes and special tastes. Soups, for example, are many and varied: two traditional Spanish ones are **el gazpacho andaluz** – a cold vegetable soup and **sopa castellana** – one of the different varieties of garlic soup. In Latin America, too, the list is endless: examples include the Mexican **sopa de tortilla** – made with chicken, chilli and tomato and served with fried tortilla and avocado, and **el sancocho** from the Andean region – made with potatoes, yucca and beef.

Unidad 16

3 Y ahora tú

Imagine you are having lunch at the **Rincón de Paco**. What would you order as a starter and as a main course? And to drink? How would you order?

4 🔊 ³

The customers at the restaurant are having their starters. What do they think of them?

– ¡Ay! los macarrones están buenos ¿eh?
– Huy, el gazpacho ¡qué rico!
– ¿Está fresco?
– Sí, está buenísimo.
– Las judías se nota que son de aquí, ¿eh? ¡Están buenísimas!
– ¡Qué rico!

Así se dice

To express delight, displeasure, etc. you could say:

¡Ay! ¡Huy, qué rico!/¡Qué asco!
    It's delicious!/It's horrible!
El gazpacho está rico/delicioso/horrible
    The gazpacho is good/delicious/horrible
Las judías están buenas/buenísimas
    The green beans are good/excellent

---

5 Y ahora tú

Your Latin American friends have invited you for dinner. You want to compliment your hosts on their cooking. What would you say in these situations?

a The soup is excellent.
b You love the chicken/fish/salad.
c You find the wine very good.

6 🔊 ⁴

Listen to the waiter listing the desserts they have got today. Can you tick the items he mentions on the dessert menu? Also make a note of what the customers order. Does everyone want a dessert?

V
natillas
custard
helado
ice cream
tarta (Sp)/**torta** (LA)
tart, cake

V
¡Qué rico!
How delicious!
se nota
one can tell

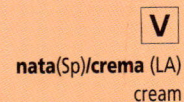

tierna/
tender

V
nata(Sp)/**crema** (LA)
cream

Postres

Natillas .... 8,20 €
Flan de la casa .... 8,20 €
Helados variados .... 8,00 €
Tarta de café .... 8,50 €
Fruta de la temporada .... 5,40 €
Queso manchego con uvas .... 8,50 €

Tarta de manzana

Así se dice

To ask what desserts they've got, say:

¿Qué helados tiene?/hay?
    What ice-creams have you got?
¿Qué sabores tiene?/hay?
    What flavours have you got?
¿Qué tartas/frutas tiene?/hay?
    What cakes/fruit have you got?
Hay de vainilla, nata y chocolate
    There is vanilla, cream and chocolate

---

7 Y ahora tú

You are still at the **Rincón de Paco** and it's time to order a dessert. What would you choose? How would you order it? Also, for the benefit of some English friends who don't speak Spanish, ask what type of ice cream and fruit they've got.

Unidad **16**

2
La comida diaria
Saying what you eat every day

1 El desayuno

Here are some breakfast dishes from around the Hispanic world. Can you say what they are?

un chocolate
un vaso de leche
una taza de café con leche
huevos fritos
huevos revueltos
huevos pasados por agua/a la copa (LA)
tostadas
cereal
bollos (Sp)/pan con mantequilla

Así se acostumbra

As with other meals, breakfast takes many different forms across the Hispanic world. For a Spaniard it might consist of a cup of coffee or chocolate and toast or fritters (**churros**), although some people nowadays prefer a bowl of cereal. In many parts of Latin America, breakfast is traditionally a more substantial affair: you might start with fresh fruit (**papaya**, **melón**, **sandía**, **piña**); in the northern part of Mexico, you might be offered **huevos rancheros** – fried eggs with tomato sauce, served on a tortilla base, or **chilaquiles** – made with chile, onions and cheese. Beans (**frijoles**) are also eaten for breakfast in some areas in Central and South America, and in the coastal region of Ecuador, **arroz con menestra** (rice with lentil or bean stew) and **plátano verde asado** (grilled bananas) would be normal dishes. In many places, however, people simply have coffee, tea or chocolate with bread or toast.

2 [5]

An Ecuadorian, a Spaniard and a Mexican talk about what they normally have for breakfast. Can you say what it is in each case? The first one is printed for you.

1 **Ecuatoriana**
– Un desayuno típico varía de acuerdo al sitio ¿no? La costa, por ejemplo, un arroz con menestra y un ... carne, un calentado como se llama; un verde, que es el plátano verde asado, un café negro y un jugo de naranja. Que es el ... los productos que hay en la costa. En la sierra es el café en leche con pan, mermelada, muchas veces y una rodaja de fruta.
2 **Español**
3 **Mexicano**

Unidad 16

Así se dice

To ask what people normally eat, say:

¿Qué desayunas normalmente?
What do you normally have for breakfast?
¿Qué comes/almuerzas normalmente?
What do you normally have for lunch?
¿Qué cenas normalmente?
What do you normally have for dinner?

And to answer, say:

**Normalmente desayuno ...,
como/almuerzo ...**
I normally have ... for breakfast/lunch

3 *Y ahora tú*

¿Qué desayunas tú normalmente?
¿Qué desayunan otras personas en tu país?
¿A qué hora desayunas?

4 *La comida*

A Basque woman describes a typical Spanish lunch (**la comida, el almuerzo**). As you can see, it is more than a meal; the after-lunch conversation (**la sobremesa**) is at least as important as the meal itself.

> Aquí todo se hace en torno a la mesa. Uno se sienta a comer a las dos de la tarde y hasta las ocho puede estar sentado en la mesa, durante horas y horas y horas. O sea ya no es sólo el comer, es todo el ritual que se crea en torno a la comida, ¿no?, y todo lo que supone una comida.

How long can lunch last?

V
garbanzos
chickpeas

V
comer = almorzar
(LA)

V
en torno
around

5 🔊 [6]

Two people are asked what they have for lunch. What do they reply?

Ion ...   María ...

Así se acostumbra

In recent years, with the rapid growth of towns and cities and changes in working hours, eating habits have also changed for large numbers of people. There is often no time to go home for lunch or to spend long hours at the restaurant. Many people opt for **la comida rápida**, which might consist of **hamburguesas**, **perros calientes** (hot dogs) or different types of **bocadillos** and **sándwiches**, as well as local dishes, such as **tacos** in Mexico, **arepas** in Venezuela and Colombia, or **empanadas** (pasties) and **ceviches** (raw fish or shell-fish marinated in lemon juice) in the other Andean countries.

6 🔊 [7]

Three Spaniards say what they usually eat when they want fast food. Do they have similar tastes?

7 *Y ahora tú*

¿Qué comes al mediodía? ¿Te gustan las hamburguesas y otros tipos de comida rápida? ¿Y qué cenas? ¿Qué tipo de comida te gusta en general? ¿Te gusta la comida italiana, china, etc.?

[175]

3 Se sazona con sal y pimienta
Describing recipes

1

Here is a list of common verbs employed in cooking. Match the verbs in Spanish with their English equivalents.

a cocer	b cortar	c picar	to add	to stir	to season
d añadir	e sazonar	f freír	to crush	to mix	to chop
g machacar	h remover	i batir	to beat	to cook	to cool
j enfriar	k calentar	l mezclar	to cut/slice	to fry	to heat

2

Which of the verbs from Activity 1 could you use with the following ingredients?

e.g. **Se pica el perejil**

V
mediano medium sized
picado chopped
diente de ajo garlic clove
miga de pan bread crumbs

V
remojada soaked
exprimida pressed

V
el perejil parsley

G
freír/se fríe(n)
servir/se sirve(n)
calentar/se calienta(n)
cocer/se cuece(n)

Unidad 16

3 Receta española 🔊 8

Your Spanish friend gives you a recipe for **gazpacho gitano**. Listen and make a note of the ingredients.

4

You made some notes about how to make this soup, but they are a bit jumbled. Can you make sense of them by numbering the steps? Three have been done for you.

1. Se machacan los ajos pelados con un poquito de sal
4. Se mezcla todo bien hasta formar una pasta
3. Se añade la miga de pan previamente remojada y exprimida
7. Se enfría
6. Se sazona con sal y pimienta
5. Se añade agua fría poco a poco y se remueve
2. Se añade el aceite y se bate
8. Antes de servir, se añaden los tomates y el pepino

🔊 9 You want to check whether you have got this right, so you phone your friend and she gives the recipe to you again. Did you get it right?

Así se dice

To describe recipes or other processes, say:

Se machacan los ajos
  You crush the garlic
Se añade sal al gusto
  You add salt to taste

Unidad 16

5 Receta latinoamericana

Guacamole

A friend would like to make **guacamole** and asks you for a recipe. You find one in a cookery book:

Ingredientes:
una cebolla
2 dientes de ajo
1 limón
2 aguacates grandes pelados y cortados en trocitos
una pizca de sal

Primero picar la cebolla y pelar y cortar los aguacates en trocitos. Rallar el limón y luego sacar el jugo. Después poner la cebolla, el ajo, el jugo y la ralladura del limón y los aguacates en la licuadora. Añadir sal. Servir inmediatamente.

Can you tell your friend how to make it?
Se pica la cebolla ...

6 Y ahora tú

Can you describe the recipe of a dish or a drink you like? Start with a list of ingredients. Use a dictionary to help you.

V
aguacate
avocado

Temas

La comida es cultura

The smells and tastes that identify the cooking of the Hispanic world each carry a history. Behind a simple list of ingredients lie stories, great movements of population, meetings and conflicts.

Los gustos de España

Madrid's eighteenth-century bar owner Tío Lucas made the cheapest possible dish for the workers who frequented his bar:

Judías del tío Lucas
"Se fríe tocino en aceite y se añaden judías, cebollas, ajo, perejil, comino, laurel, sal y pimentón. Se cuecen cuatro horas mínimo."

What were once the staples of the poor – chickpeas (**garbanzos**), haricot beans (**judías**), lentils (**lentejas**) – are now the food of rich and poor alike. But the real taste of Spain comes from herbs like coriander (**cilantro**) or parsley (**perejil**), spices like pepper (**pimienta**), cumin (**comino**) or cinnamon (**canela**), and sweet peppers (**pimientos**). All of these came into southern Spain with the Arabs who also introduced oranges, lemons and almonds (**almendras**). Olive oil, the fruit of the olive groves first planted during the Roman occupation, is liberally used. And the Romans took the vines as far north as **La Rioja**, where the best of Spanish wines are still produced.

Unidad 16

Hombres de maíz

Before the Spaniards came, the world of Indian America was delivered from hunger by the discovery of maize (**el maíz**). Nobody knows where it originated – only that it grew on small plots (**las milpas**) everywhere in America. On an average plot in Mexico, a family could cultivate in 200 days enough maize and beans (**frijoles**) to live on for a year; they could then devote the rest of their time to crafts or other activities. Small wonder that Aztec myth described five ages of human development – the last of which was the age of maize. The maize was eaten on the cob (**elote**) or pounded into dough (**nixtamal**) for the ever-present tortilla. The Mayas also grew maize and squash (**zapote**) and beans in the stubble of the fields. In the Andes, maize was grown on the steep slopes and irrigated terraces of the high sierra. It was eaten as a young and tender vegetable (**choclo**) or mashed into a potent drink (**chicha**).

Today, the staple product of America is grown across the world – but it is the United States that dominates world production – and world consumption of the **tortilla** in its many incarnations – **taco**, **tostada**, **enchilada** among others.

Taco de pollo (México)
"Se hace la masa de maíz, se prepara en un comal. Luego se unta crema o aguacate y se añaden pedazos de carne de pollo. Se enrolla y se come con cebollitas."

Tamales (estilo Michoacan, México)
"Se prepara una masa de trigo o de maíz; se hierve media hora. Luego se prepara una salsa de jitomate, ajo, chile verde y cebolla y se rellena la masa. Luego se envuelve en una hoja de plátano y se cuece al vapor."

V
los campesinos peasants
sembrar to sow
dueños owners
empréstitos extranjeros foreign loans
competir to compete
el pequeño cosechero the small farmer

Las repúblicas bananeras

Bananas (**los plátanos**) have marked the history of Latin America like few other commodities. By the 1540s this Caribbean fruit had spread to Central America; it was soon part of the cooking of every country in the Hispanic world. The yellow banana is eaten as a fruit – the green **plátano verde** as a vegetable. It is eaten raw, fried in slices or as chips; its leaves are used to wrap and cook the filled dough in **tamales**. Bananas began to be eaten by Europeans and Americans at the end of the last century. Out of the growing market emerged one of the most powerful multinational companies in Central America – the United Fruit Company which was formed by the merger of the Boston Fruit Company and another enterprise. It became the owner of large tracts of land throughout the region, a manipulator of governments and controller of markets.

Ernesto Cardenal, the Nicaraguan poet, recalled the Company's role in Central America in his poem "**Hora cero**".

**Los campesinos hondureños traían el dinero en el sombrero
cuando los campesinos sembraban sus siembras
y los hondureños eran dueños de su tierra.
Cuando había dinero
y no había empréstitos extranjeros
... y la compañía frutera no competía con el pequeño cosechero.
Pero vino la United Fruit Company
con sus subsidiarias la Tela Railroad Company
y la Trujillo Railroad Company
aliada con la Cuyamel Fruit Company
la United Fruit Company
con sus revoluciones para la obtención de concesiones
y exenciones de millones en impuestos de importaciones y exportaciones....**

Unidad 16

Veamos de nuevo

Gramática

1 Giving advice and instructions

When a set of instructions is given as in a cookery book or manual, you will often find that the verbs are in the infinitive:

Pelar y cortar las patatas
Peel and chop the potatoes
Machacar el ajo y añadir sal
Crush the garlic and add salt

However, when relaying the instructions to someone in person, you normally use **se** with the third person singular or plural:

Se pelan y se cortan las patatas
(You) peel and cut the potatoes
Se machaca el ajo y se añade sal
(You) crush the garlic and add salt

Some radical-changing verbs often used in the language of cookery are:

hervir/se hierve; freír/se fríe; cocer/se cuece; servir/se sirve; calentar/se calienta.

2 Useful cooking terms

The following prepositions are much used in menus and recipes:

de: what something is made of:

**sopa de tomate   helado de fresa
granizado de café macedonia de frutas**

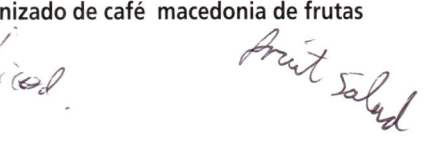

con: what has been added:

**huevos con patatas   melón con jamón
bonito con tomate** (tuna with tomato sauce)

al/a la: <u>Either</u> how it is cooked:

a la plancha (grilled)   **a la brasa** (barbecued)
al horno (baked)

<u>Or</u> in a way particular to a region:

callos a la madrileña (tripe Madrid style)
bacalao a la vizcaína (cod Basque style).

3 Exclamations

The Spanish language is full of exclamations, expressions of delight or disgust, happiness, excitement or sadness. For example, talking about food:

¡Qué rico! ¡Está buenísimo! How wonderful!
¡Qué sabroso! How tasty!
¡Qué asco! How horrible!

Other common expressions include:

¡Qué maravilla! How wonderful!
¡Qué guapo/a! How handsome/pretty!
¡Qué pena! What a shame!
¡Qué bien! Great! **¡Qué suerte!** What luck!
¡Qué horror! How awful/terrible!

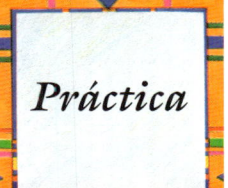

Práctica

A Odd one out

Spot the odd one out:

1 tortilla   manzanilla   paella   costillas
2 merluza   besugo   ternera   bonito
3 sidra   vino blanco   cerveza   jamón
4 flan   natillas   helados   empanada
5 sopa   consomé   calamares   gazpacho
6 cerdo   cordero   bistec   trucha

B ¡Qué .....!

Give your reaction to these prompts:

1 Hay una mosca en la sopa.
2 Me tocó la lotería ayer.
3 Para comer tenemos paella.
4 ¡Mira a ese chico!
5 El autocar chocó con un coche.

Unidad 16

C En el restaurante

Can you make sense of the following dialogue between a waiter and his client by rearranging the order of the questions and answers?

1	Buenos días	a	¿Tiene el menú del día?
2	¿Para cuántas personas?	b	Luego, chuletas de cerdo
3	Pase por aquí	c	¿Tiene una mesa libre?
4	¿Y de beber?	d	Para una persona
5	¿De segundo?	e	De primero, sopa de ajo
6	Aquí tiene. ¿Qué va a tomar?	f	Una cerveza

D ¿Cómo se hace la sangría?

A friend is giving a party and wants to make **sangría**. You find this recipe in a Spanish cookery book; can you tell him how to make it?

Sangría
1 litro de limonada
500 gr. de melocotón
2 limones en rodajas
1 manzana o 1 pera (opcional)
750ml. de vino tinto
200 gr. de azúcar

Cortar los melocotones en trozos y los limones en rodajas. En una fuente de cristal, añadir todos los ingredientes y remover bien. Poner la fuente en el frigorífico. Servir con cubitos de hielo.

1 What's in a dish?

Here is a recipe for **Marmitako**, a well-known Basque fish stew.

1 cebolla
2 pimientos verdes
2 tomates maduros
1kg de patatas
1kg de bonito
1 vaso de vino blanco
sal y pimienta

Se pican la cebolla y los pimientos. Se quita la piel de los tomates. Se calienta el aceite en una olla, se fríe primero la cebolla y el pimiento. Se añaden las patatas en dados y se vuelve a freír todo. Se cubre con agua por 10 minutos y se corta el atún en dados. Se hierve por tres minutos, y se añade finalmente vino blanco seco.

V
una fuente
large bowl

V
palmitos palm hearts
pescando fishing
el bufete selection of dishes

Un paso más

V
bonito bonito, tuna
en dados diced

Could you choose a dish which you know very well and describe the ingredients to a Spanish friend? Start **Lleva ...** And then try to describe how to make it?

2 ¿Dónde comemos?

You are on holiday in La Manga and you want to take your family to a restaurant. Which one will you choose, bearing in mind that your husband hates fish, your mother-in-law loves seafood, the children only like meat, and you want to try some Spanish delicacies?

MARISQUERIA - RESTAURANTE
EL PEZ ROJO
BALCON del MEDITERRANEO
Vivero de Langostas
Parrilladas
Dorada a la sal
Paellas y Caldero
Paseo Marítimo
Teléfono 563 109
CABO DE PALOS
D. García

Los Churrasc
Fundado en 1977

Cocina Regional de La Huerta y de La Mar
Le recomendamos nuestra especialidad. Pava con Pelotas, el delicioso Churrasco, Bacalao a lo Don Bibiano, o nuestra especial y única Leche Asada y los tradicionales Cordiales de la Casa.
Comedores privados en Bodega, lejos del mundanal ruido...
Amplia y cómoda barra

3 Todo con langostinos 🔊 10

Listen to Carmen at a restaurant in Cartagena de Indias during the **Festival de langostinos**, Everything seems to be with prawns! Listen to her conversation with the waiter, and find out three ways to serve them.

4 Checklist

Can you do the following?

a Order a starter and a main course from a set menu.
b Talk about what you eat and drink normally.
c Ask about the ingredients of a dish.
d Understand a simple recipe and explain to a friend how to cook it.

Unidad 17

Sueños y deseos

Así se habla

Talking about your dreams and ambitions

Giving instructions and commands

Talking about what you like to wear

Temas

Las aparencias y las ilusiones

Veamos de nuevo

Unidad 17

Así se habla 1

¿Qué quieres ser?

Talking about your dreams and ambitions

1

a **b** **c**

Here are three people talking about their dreams. Can you link each speaker to one of the pictures? Listen and read.

(1)
– ¿Qué quieres ser?
– Quiero ser una gran actriz y también quiero cantar y bailar al mismo tiempo.

(2)
– ¿Qué te gustaría hacer en el futuro?
– En el futuro me gustaría actuar tanto en la televisión como en el teatro y el cine.

(3)
– ¿Tienes un sueño?
– Tengo muchos sueños, muchos sueños ... por ejemplo, me gustaría vivir en un acantilado, con gaviotas, y con el ruido del mar, y con una escalera que bajara a una pequeña playa ...

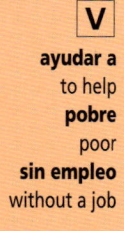

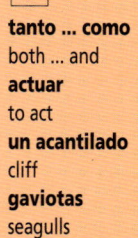

V
ayudar a to help
pobre poor
sin empleo without a job

V
tanto ... como both ... and
actuar to act
un acantilado cliff
gaviotas seagulls

Así se dice

To ask what someone would like to be or to do, say

¿Qué quieres /te gustaría ser/ hacer?

And to reply you could say:

Quiero ser cocinero
 I want to be a cook
Me gustaría actuar en el teatro
 I'd like to act in the theatre

You could also ask and answer:

¿Tienes un sueño?
 Do you have a dream?
Sí, mi sueño es ser actor
 Yes, my dream is to be an actor

2

Sometimes people dream about a different way of life, or about changing their life. Can you match the dream to the people described below?

e.g. **El estudiante de medicina.**
 "Quiero curar a los enfermos."

1 El estudiante de medicina.
2 La abuela de setenta años.
3 Este hombre lleva un año sin empleo.
4 La joven que trabaja de voluntaria en un centro comunitario.
5 La madre de seis niños.
6 Este hombre tiene familia pero es pobre.

a "Quisiera ir a una playa desierta."
b "Me gustaría tener mucho dinero."
c "Me gustaría tener algún trabajo."
d "Quiero ayudar a los pobres."
e "Quisiera ser joven otra vez."
f "Quiero curar a los enfermos."

3

Listen to a fuller version of the first interview from Activity 1. What else would the young woman like to do?

Unidad 17

4

Look at the pictures above and say what each of these people wants to be in the future.

e.g. **Quiere/Le gustaría ser campeona de patinaje**

5 *Y ahora tú*

¿Tienes algún sueño? ¿Qué te gustaría hacer?
¿Te gustaría cambiar tu vida?

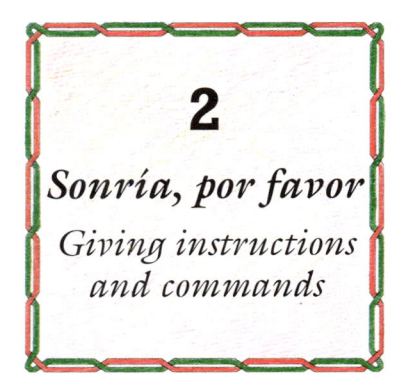

2

Sonría, por favor

Giving instructions and commands

1

Luisa is a young woman with an ambition to be a fashion model. Can you place the pieces of dialogue in the right places in the strip at the top of the next column?

" Pase al estudio entonces. Tiene que hacer un ensayo".
"Quiero ser modelo. Voy a preguntar en esta agencia".
"¿Qué quisiera hacer?"
"Me gustaría ser modelo".
"Muchísimas gracias".

2 🔊³

Luisa has her first photo session immediately. Listen to the photographer's instructions, and match each instruction with the appropriate picture.

V
sonría
smile
coja
take
el suelo
floor
más arriba
higher up
hacia la pared
towards the wall
lentamente
slowly

1. Luisa, levante la cabeza y sonría por favor. Bueno. Ahora coja el vaso y beba el agua.

2. Bueno, Luisa. Ahora acuéstese en el suelo y levante el brazo. Así, así un poco más arriba. Perfecto. Gracias. Ahora levántese.

3. Luisa, siéntese en esa silla – muy bien. Un momento. Perfecto.

4. Ahora Luisa – por favor vaya hacia la pared. Claro cuidado – muy lentamente. Fabuloso. Y venga aquí otra vez.

Unidad 17

Así se dice

If you want to tell someone to do something, you say formally – with **usted** *expressed or understood:*

Levante (usted) el brazo
   Lift your arm
Beba (usted) el agua
   Drink the water
Sonría (usted)
   Smile!
Acuéstese/levántese/ siéntese
   Lie down/ get up/ sit down
Vaya hacia la pared/Venga aquí
   Go towards the wall/ Come here

Informally - with **tú** *expressed or understood:*

Levanta el brazo
   Lift your arm
Bebe el agua
   Drink the water
¡Sonríe!
   Smile!
Acuéstate/levántate/siéntate
   Lie down/get up/sit down

3

Your son is still in bed and is clearly going to be late for school unless he hurries. Using the familiar form of address, can you tell him to get up, eat his breakfast, finish his homework, drink his milk, and RUN to school.

4

Here is part of the running script for your current film whose star is a Spaniard. Can you very politely give him his instructions?

> "Go towards the bus, get in, sit down, wait a few minutes then get off the bus."

G
Tome/toma
Cruce/cruza
Siga/sigue

G
levante, beba, sonría
(See p.189)

G
ir/vaya, venir/venga
(See p. 189)

G
levanta, bebe, sonríe
(See p.189)

V
los deberes
homework
correr
to run

V
subir
to get on (a bus)
bajar
to get off

---

5 *Y ahora tú*

A friend rings you from your nearest railway station wanting to know how to get to your house. Can you give him instructions? You might want to tell him to catch a bus or taxi, or, if it is within walking distance, to give him directions for getting there on foot.

3
Me gusta el vestido rojo
Talking about what you like to wear

1

Which words for clothes are illustrated in the picture?

sombrero   chaqueta/saco (LA)
zapatos   zapatillas (Sp),
traje   zapatos de deporte
camiseta   falda
vaqueros/ blue jeans   pantalones cortos
pantalones   vestido
camisa   blusa

Unidad 17

2 🔊 4

In an interview Luisa was asked some questions about her clothes. Listen and read. How does she dress when she's unhappy? And what does she like to wear when she's at home on her own?

– ¿Qué ropa te gusta ponerte?
– Pues, depende del momento; cuando me siento triste o deprimida, casi siempre me pongo ropa negra - vestido negro, zapatos negros – o por lo menos vestido oscuro.
– ¿Y cuando las cosas van bien?
– Entonces me pongo algo de color vivo. También me encantan los blue jeans y las camisetas, y casi siempre llevo zapatillas blancas.
– ¿Y qué te pones en casa cuando estás sola?
– ¿La verdad? Pues una vieja camisa de hombre y pantalones cortos. Siempre ando descalza.

Así se dice

To ask what people like to wear you say:

– ¿Qué ropa te gusta ponerte?
– Pues, depende del momento; cuando me siento triste o deprimida, casi siempre me pongo ropa negra - vestido negro, zapatos negros – o por lo menos vestido oscuro.
– ¿Y cuando las cosas van bien?
– Entonces me pongo algo de color vivo. También me encantan los blue jeans y las camisetas, y casi siempre llevo zapatillas blancas.
– ¿Y qué te pones en casa cuando estás sola?
– ¿La verdad? Pues una camisa vieja de hombre y pantalones cortos. Siempre ando descalza.

V
la ropa clothes
ponerse to put on (clothes)
llevo I wear
deprimida depressed
oscuro dark
las cosas van bien things are going well
descalzo/a barefoot

V
desnudo naked

V
cita date, appointment

3

These two models are wearing very different clothes. Can you say who is wearing what?
e.g. **Luisa lleva ...**
    Jorge lleva ...

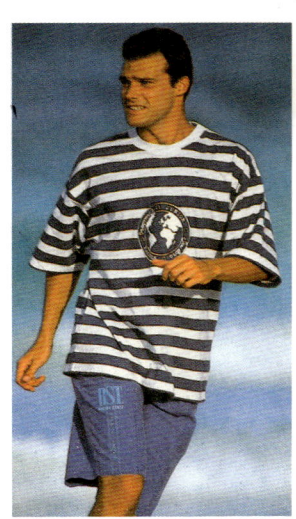

4 🔊 5

At the weekend most people like to get out of their working clothes. These three people have their own preferences. Listen and tick on the grid who prefers what.

	Speaker 1	Speaker 2	Speaker 3
shorts			
jeans			
t-shirt			
tennis-shoes			
barefoot			
naked			

5 *Y ahora tú*

¿Qué ropa llevas ahora? ¿Qué te pones cuando sales a comer en un restaurante/ cuando tienes cita por primera vez con alguien?

Unidad 17

Temas

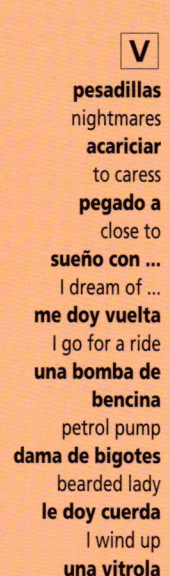

Las apariencias y las ilusiones

Así se acostumbra

In Latin America colourful local dress is often still worn in country areas by the indigenous peoples (**los indígenas**). The Maya peoples of Guatemala and Mexico, for example, or the people of southern Mexico still wear the embroidered blouse (**huipil**) and the skirt (**pollera**) with its many starched petticoats beneath, and the Otavaleños in Ecuador have incorporated modern technology into their daily life but have mostly retained their traditional dress. The warm blanket (**poncho**) is made of alpaca in Peru and Colombia and is called **ruana**. The woven hats (**chuyos**) of Bolivia and the felt hats of Ecuador are a practical necessity in the intense cold of the mountain night.

6

Listen to this description of the clothes someone is wearing and make a note of as many of them as you can.
Can you guess who is being described here? See unit 13, Temas, for a clue.

V
pesadillas nightmares
acariciar to caress
pegado a close to
sueño con ... I dream of ...
me doy vuelta I go for a ride
una bomba de bencina petrol pump
dama de bigotes bearded lady
le doy cuerda I wind up
una vitrola gramophone
los anteojos glasses
un ataúd coffin

V
botas boots
cuero leather
cinturón belt
tela fuerte thick material
pañuelo scarf, kerchief

Sueños y pesadillas

A young Nicaraguan wrote this love poem about a girl in his neighbourhood. What is she like and what does he wish for?

Yo quisiera ser como el viento
para poder acariciar
el pelo rubio de esa muchacha,
o como el pantalón tallado
tan pegado a sus piernas.
Por eso no quisiera salir del barrio
para verla.

(Alex Donald Lumbi: from *Poems of love and revolution*: NSC, London, 1983.)

Nicanor Parra is a Chilean poet who looks at the most ordinary and everyday experiences. Would you say the poem spoke more of dreams or of nightmares?

Sueño con una mesa y una silla
Sueño que me doy vuelta en automóvil
Sueño que estoy filmando una película
Sueño con una bomba de bencina
Sueño que soy un turista de lujo ....

Sueño con una dama de bigotes
Sueño que voy bajando una escalera
Sueño que le doy cuerda a una vitrola
Sueño que se me rompen los anteojos
Sueño que estoy haciendo un ataúd
Sueño con el sistema planetario

(Nicanor Parra: from *Antipoemas*, Seix Barral, Barcelona 1976. p.142)

Unidad 17

Diseñadores famosos

The Basque designer Balenciaga became a byword in the 1960s for the grandest evening dresses with their characteristic sweeping lines. Balenciaga left Spain in 1936, at the beginning of the Spanish Civil War and went to Paris, where he set up his first workshop a year later. There he learned his fine tailoring and his daring design techniques. But he always regarded fashion as an art form rather than a commercial activity and refused to attend press showings or photo calls. He died in 1972 – and unusually for a publicity conscious industry, his name was known, but not his face.

Balenciaga's most famous pupil, Paco Rabanne, had none of his master's aversion to publicity. His metallic dresses and space helmets were the signs of a revolution in fashion. Agata Ruiz de la Prada has taken Spanish design in even more adventurous directions. Toni Benitez and Valverde, on the other hand, have dressed the wealthiest families of Spain – Valverde designed the Infanta Elena's wedding dress in 1995. And out of Sevilla and Barcelona have come some of the most exciting and adventurous developments in Spanish fashion – a long way from Balenciaga!

And from Latin America, Carolina Herrera, a Venezuelan designer now living in New York, numbers among her customers many well-known American women. Her designs are noted for their elegance and simplicity.

La vestimenta también habla

Clothes are sometimes more than simple dress. The clothes people wear (**la vestimenta**, **la indumentaria**) can also be a mark of identity, a symbol of defiance or pride.

Los españoles

Since the end of the Franco regime, the suppressed nationalities have once again begun to express themselves in language, dress and custom. In 'el País Vasco', for example, on ceremonial occasions women wear a red skirt with a black stripe (**falda roja con raya negra**), a black bodice (**corpiño**) and apron (**delantal**) and a three-pointed scarf on their head. The men wear white shirts and trousers with the familiar red sash (**fajín**) and red beret (**boina roja**). In Cataluña a similar costume is capped by the red cap (**birretiña**) which more than anything else symbolises Catalunian nationhood. Andalucía has adopted for itself the dress of the gypsy – the polka-dot dress, the tasselled shawl for women; the short jacket, tight trousers and low-crowned broad-brimmed hat called the **sombrero de cordobés** for men.

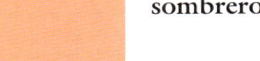

Los mayas

The Maya communities of Guatemala still wear their national dress with pride. Their clothing, together with their language, customs and religion, is a symbol of their identity and the history that links them to a past that stretches back beyond the Spanish Conquest. When the Spaniards first colonised the Maya lands, they wove cloth to replace the native textiles. But the colours and designs of Maya dress are their own, and the Spanish weaving techniques have now merged with the older ways of making cloth. The many different and dispersed Maya communities successfully resisted the conquerors until the last was

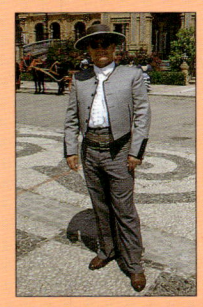

Unidad 17

taken in the late seventeenth century. But they survived culturally despite many more attempts to crush and destroy their culture. Their bright and distinct clothing testifies to the fact that it has survived.

Los otavaleños, Ecuador

Otovalo has produced clothes for centuries. The Incas admired Otovaleño textiles, and when the Spaniards came they built new clothing factories there. When the colony ended, English cloth flooded the market and the Otovalo weavers found themselves with few clients among the poor of Ecuador. But history has its ironies – and the Otovalo weavers began to manufacture fabrics like the foreign imports, buying small plots of land with their profits. From the 1930s onwards, the indigenous peoples organized to win back their land and to end the practice of obligatory labour (**huasipungo**) owed to the landowners. There were agrarian reforms – but they did little to improve the conditions of the Indians. Only Otovalo benefited from the changes, as the local textiles found a growing market among tourists and others.

Zoot Suits

For young Mexican Americans in California, the style of the 1940s was the zoot suit. It was a stylish long draped suit with baggy, narrow-bottomed trousers, striped sweaters underneath and two-tone shoes; a ducktail haircut completed the outfit. It was a challenging way of dressing, but it was also a group identity. The young men who wore them – the **pachucos** – were taking pride in their difference, and perhaps also making a gesture towards a society they felt had discriminated against them. In the charged atmosphere of 1943, groups of young Mexican-Americans clashed with servicemen in the streets of the barrio. The incidents were known as the Zoot Suit Riots.

Veamos de nuevo

Gramática

Unidad 17

1 Telling someone what to do

To tell someone to do something you can use the command or imperative. It has two different forms: the formal (for **usted**) and the informal (for **tú**). For **usted** take the first person (**yo** form) of the present tense and replace the final -o with an -e (-**ar** verbs) or an -a (-**er** and -**ir** verbs).

levantar	beber	subir
levante	beba	suba

For **tú** take the second person singular of the present tense and remove the final -s:

levanta	bebe	sube

Most verbs are entirely regular in the imperative. A few have irregularities:

	tú	*usted*
decir:	di	diga
tener:	ten	tenga
ir:	ve	vaya
venir:	ven	venga
hacer:	haz	haga
poner:	pon	ponga
ser:	sé	sea

Any reflexive or object pronouns are added to the end of the verb:

¡Levántate! ¡Levántese!	Get up!
¡Acuéstate! ¡Acuéstese!	Go to bed!
¡Dime! ¡Dígame!	Tell me!

2 Different meanings of llevar

You have already met two different meanings of the verb **llevar**.

a) With expressions of time to mean 'how long for':

Llevo estudiando español un año
I've been studying Spanish for a year

b) In describing recipe ingredients:

La salsa lleva ajo y perejil
The sauce has got garlic and parsley in it

In this unit it is used to describe what someone is wearing:

Lleva pantalones y jersey
She is wearing trousers and a sweater
Juan lleva gafas
Juan has glasses

3 Talking of dreams

In this unit you have seen how to express your dreams and ambitions with different degrees of passion and realism:

Quiero viajar por todo el mundo
I want to travel the world
Me gustaría ser jugador de fútbol
I'd like to be a footballer
Quisiera ser millonaria
I'd like to be a millionaire
Mi sueño es ser actor
My dream is to be an actor

Práctica

G
regar (ie)
cerrar (ie)

A Don't forget!

You are going on holiday leaving your teenage son to follow in a couple of days. You make this list of things for him to do before he leaves the house. Can you also tell him in person?

e.g. **Desenchufa la televisión**

1 desenchufar la televisión
2 regar las plantas
3 sacar las basura
4 dejar las llaves a la vecina
5 apagar las luces
6 ¡cerrar la puerta!

B To the rainforest

You work at a hotel in Ecuador and you need to give your guests tips for an excursion. Can you write a note for your guests making these into instructions?

1. Llevar una camisa de manga larga para protegerse de los mosquitos
2. Ponerse repelente de insectos en manos y cuello
3. Llevar un sombrero
4. Ponerse zapatos cómodos
5. Seguir al guía todo el tiempo

e.g. **Lleve una camisa ...**

1 Day dreaming

On a televison chat show you are asked to talk about your dreams and ambitions. Given the chance, whom would you like to meet and why? (politician, artist, pop-singer, historical figure, etc.) Where would you like to live and what kind of house would you like to have? What parts of the world would you like to visit and why?

e.g. **Me gustaría conocer a ... porque ...**

2 Espartaco el torero

Espartaco is a famous Spanish bullfighter who retired in 2001. In this extract from an interview a few years ago, he talked of some aspects of his life. Read it and decide if these statements are true or false.

a His real name is Juan Antonio Ruiz.
b He comes from a poor background.
c He always wanted to be a bullfighter.
d He became a professional bullfighter at the age of 16.
e He is not a family man.
f His ambition is to rear bulls.

Fue un niño pobre. Su padre fue torero también pero no tuvo éxito y Juan Antonio Ruiz no era un niño que soñaba con ser torero. Se enamoró de la profesión solamente cuando se hizo matador de toros. Tomó la alternativa con sólo 16 años y pronto alcanzó la fama y la riqueza. Ahora tiene una finca ganadera de 800 hectáreas a 35 kilómetros de Sevilla, pero invierte en locales, en pisos, en bienes que producen las rentas que necesita para la finca y la ganadería.

Ahora con 28 años, este hombre menudo, que sonríe enseñando unos dientes de niño, sueña despierto con llegar a ser un tranquilo rentista rodeado de su mujer y sus hijos.

– ¿Comprarse una finca es un sueño de torero?
– Hay mucha gente que quiere tener una finca, pero de cultivo. Sólo los toreros soñamos con una finca con toros y para eso es necesario tener muchas hectáreas. Porque nuestra ambición no es tener tierras; es tener toros.

(Adapted from *El País*)

3 La maleta

Now listen to four people saying what they put in their suitcases. What does each one always take? Which item is mentioned but not listed below? What essentials would you pack?

**zapatillas de deporte   ropa   bronceador
traje de baño   shorts   bolsa de aseo
cepillo de dientes**

4 Checklist

Can you do the following?

a Ask someone what they would like to be.
b Talk about your ambitions and dreams.
c Talk about what you like to wear.
d Tell someone how to do something.

Unidad 17

Un paso más

V

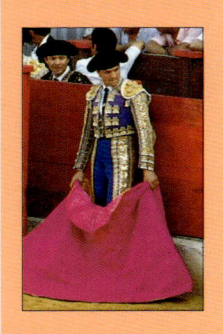

se enamoró
he fell in love
tomar la alternativa
to become a professional bullfighter
alcanzó
he achieved
finca ganadera
cattle ranch
invierte
he invests
sueña despierto
he daydreams
rentista
a man of independent means
de cultivo
arable

[190]

Unidad 18

De compras

Así se habla
Making plans and suggestions

Buying clothes

Buying souvenirs and bargaining

Temas
Manos juntas

Veamos de nuevo

Así se habla 1

¿Qué vas a hacer el fin de semana?
Making plans and suggestions

1

Listen and read the following conversation and find out whether these statements are true or false.

a Isabel wants to go shopping.
b Maite is free all Saturday.
c They decide to go on Saturday morning.

Isabel: ¿Qué vas a hacer el sábado por la mañana?
Maite: Nada especial, ¿por qué?
Isabel: Necesito comprar un par de cosas en el centro. ¿Quieres venir conmigo?
Maite: El sábado por la mañana, pues no puedo, tengo una cita en la peluquería, pero por la tarde estoy libre.
Isabel: El sábado por la tarde ... sí, vale. Estupendo.

Así se dice

To find out about someone's plans, ask:

¿Qué vas a hacer mañana?
  What are you going to do tomorrow?
¿... la semana próxima/que viene?
  ... next week?

To answer, say:

Nada especial
  Nothing much
Voy a descansar/levantarme tarde
  I'm going to rest/get up late

Unidad 18

G ir a + infinitive
(See G 13.3)

2

Complete the chart of expressions referring to the future:

mañana	....
mañana por la mañana	tomorrow morning
....	tomorrow afternoon
mañana por la noche	....
el sábado que viene	next Saturday
....	next Sunday
el fin de semana que viene	....
la semana que viene	....
....	next month
el año que viene	....

See W 17 for more expressions of time.

3

Today is Tuesday. You want to ask Maite for a drink or a coffee, so you need to check whether she is free. How would you ask her what she is planning to do tomorrow, Friday evening, or next weekend?

4

Look at Maite's diary. How would she reply to your questions in Activity 3? Remember today is Tuesday.

a ¿Qué vas a hacer mañana?
b ¿Qué vas a hacer el viernes por la noche?
c ¿Qué vas a hacer el próximo fin de semana?

lunes
a.m. _____
p.m. _____

martes
a.m. _____
p.m. _____

miércoles
a.m. *clases*
p.m. *biblioteca*

jueves
a.m. *piscina*
p.m. *clases*

viernes
a.m. *10:00 cita con médico*
p.m. *fiesta en casa de Juan*

sábado
a.m. _____
p.m. _____

domingo
a.m. *misa*
p.m. *comida en casa de Pepe*

5

Can you tell a friend what Maite is going to do on Thursday and Sunday?

El jueves Maite va a ir a ...

6 *Y ahora tú*

¿Qué vas a hacer mañana? ¿Qué vas a hacer el próximo fin de semana? ¿Y el próximo mes? ¿Y el verano que viene?

> *Así se dice*
>
> *To invite someone to do something with you, say:*
>
> **¿Quieres venir/ir de compras conmigo?**
> Do you want to come/go shopping with me?
>
> *And to reply, say:*
>
> **Sí, vale. ¡Estupendo!**
> Yes, that's fine. Great!
> **No puedo. Tengo un examen/una cita con ...**
> I can't. I have an exam/ an appointment with ...

7

Listen to three invitations and complete the chart below:

	¿Dónde?	¿Cuándo?	¿Puede?
1			
2			
3			

8 *Y ahora tú*

A You're planning to go to these places at the weekend:

a) el cine; b) el teatro; c) la discoteca;
d) el parque.

Decide when you'd like to go. Ask different friends whether they want to come with you.

Unidad 18

V
la familia política
parents-in-law

G
poder/puedo

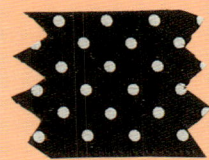

de lunares

de/a rayas

de/a cuadros

B On your answerphone are messages from four of your friends inviting you to go out with them to various places today. Check your diary and plan your replies.

martes
11 a.m. cita con el dentista
2–5 clases en la universidad
8 p.m. cena con parientes políticos
miércoles

2 ¿Puedo probármelo?
Buying clothes

1 *Colores y diseños*

What colour is each sock?

azul   verde oliva   blanco/a   negro/a
malva   rosa/rosado/a (LA)
azul marino   amarillo/a   rojo/a   gris

[193]

Unidad 18

2 En la tienda de ropa

How would you say you want the items in this catalogue?

e.g. **Quiero el vestido rojo.**
Quiero la camisa azul a cuadros

3 🔊 4

Mercedes is in a clothes shop (**una tienda de ropa**) in Barcelona. Listen and answer these questions.

a What does Mercedes want to see?
b In what colours is that item available?
c What colour does she want?
d Is it the right size for her?

– **Hola, buenas tardes.**
– **Hola.**
– **Por favor, ¿podría enseñarme el jersey rojo que hay en el escaparate?**
– **Sí, aquí lo tiene.**
– **¡Es muy bonito! ¿En qué colores más lo tiene?**
– **En rojo, en azul marino y en malva.**
– **Por favor, sáqueme uno en azul marino. ¿Puedo probármelo?**
– **Sí, pase aquí al probador. ...**
– **Me queda muy bien.**

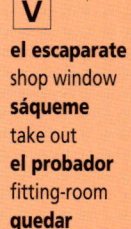

G
lo/la/los/las

V
el escaparate
shop window
sáqueme
take out
el probador
fitting-room
quedar
to fit/suit

Así se dice

These are some of the things you might want to say or ask when buying clothes:

Quiero comprar una camisa blanca
  I'd like to buy a white shirt
¿Podría enseñarme el jersey rojo ...
  Can you show me the red sweater ...
... que está en el escaparate?
  ... in the window?
¿Puedo probarme este jersey/esta blusa?
  Can I try on this sweater/blouse?
¿Puedo probármelo/la/los/las?
  Can I try it/them on?
¿En qué otros colores lo/la/los/las tiene?
  What other colours have you got?
Me queda bien/mal ...
  It fits me well/doesn't fit me ...
... grande/pequeño/corto
  It's too big/small/short for me   *or*
Me quedan grandes/flojos/estrechos
  They are too big/loose/tight for me
Me lo/la/los/las quedo/llevo
  I'll take it/them

4 Quiero un vestido negro

Luisa sees a dress she likes and wants to try it on. Can you follow the sequence of events and say what she tells the shop assistant for each frame?

Unidad 18

1 ...   2 ...
3 ...   4 ...

How would she ask how much it costs?

5

You are in a shop looking at the clothes in Activity 2. Practise asking whether you can try on some of them and whether they have them in other colours.

e.g. **¿Puedo probarme esta camisa?** or
¿Puedo probármela?
¿La tienen en otros colores?

6 ¿De qué material es?

Here are some words to describe what clothes and accessories are made of:

lino linen	**seda** silk	**algodón** cotton
lana wool	**paja** straw	**piel** (Sp) / **cuero** (LA) leather
ante suede	**oro** gold	**plata** silver

What might the following items be made of? Look up the new words in the dictionary.

a un anillo	b un vestido	c unos zapatos
d un cinturón	e una chaqueta	f una corbata
g unos calcetines	h una camisa	i una bufanda
j un sombrero		

e.g. **un anillo de oro**

7 🔊 5

Listen to two people buying different things. Can you note down what each one buys, the characteristics of each item and the price?

	item	characteristics	price
1			
2			

8 Y ahora tú

A You see a pair of trousers you like. How do you ask: a) If you can try them on? b) Whether they've got them in other colours? c) Whether they are made of wool?

B After you have tried on a pair, you do the following: d) Say you like them and that they fit you well; e) Ask how much they are; f) Say you'll have them

3
Quiero comprar un recuerdo
Buying souvenirs and bargaining

1

Carmen visited Cartagena de Indias and San José de Costa Rica. Before leaving, she went to a souvenir shop in each place. These are some of the things she found there.

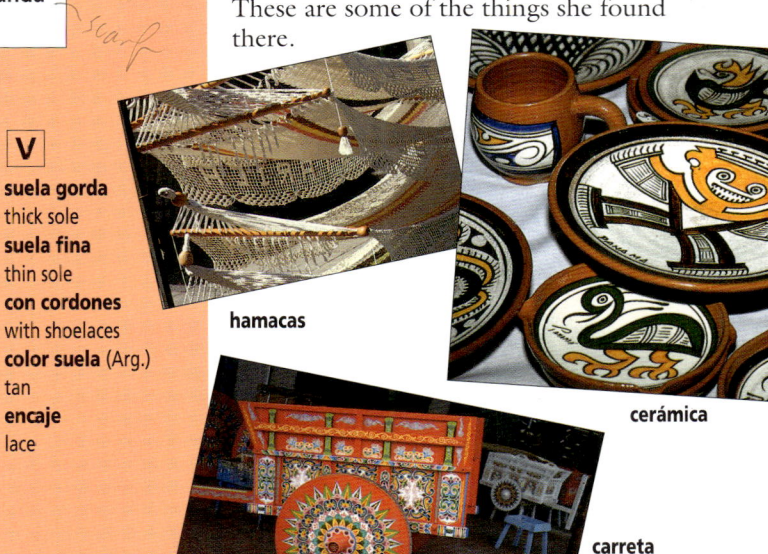

hamacas

cerámica

carreta

V
suela gorda
thick sole
suela fina
thin sole
con cordones
with shoelaces
color suela (Arg.)
tan
encaje
lace

6 Listen to the recording and find out which souvenirs can be found in Cartagena and which in San José.

Así se acostumbra

The colourful **carreta** has become Costa Rica's unofficial national emblem. These wooden carts, pulled by oxen, were used to take coffee, sugar-cane and other goods from the farms and plantations to the market in the town. Today, brightly coloured miniatures are sold everywhere as souvenirs.

2 **7**

Now listen to the rest of the conversation in the souvenir shop in Cartagena and find out what Carmen buys.

3 El regateo **8**

Maira is in an outdoor market in Ecuador and she's trying to bargain for the musical instrument she wants to buy. Does she manage to get a reduction?

– ¡Me gusta! ¡Me parece lindo! Y ¿qué tal? ¿Qué instrumento es éste?
– Éste se llama ... zampoña.
– Zampoña, ¡ah! ¿Y cómo suena la zampoña?
– Lindo está.
– ¿Y qué precio tiene ésta?
– Dieciocho.
– ¡Oh! Pero eso sí que está caro ¿eh? Oye y ... ¿y en cuánto me dejarías éste? porque éste me gustó.
– Son originales. Yo trabajo originales.
– Sí, ¿tomarías quince?
– Bueno, bueno.
– Ya, gracias. Entonces me das una de ésas.

V
tambores
drums
collares
necklaces
cuadros
paintings

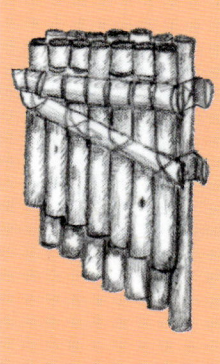

V
¿Qué es esto?
What's this?

Así se dice

To bargain, ask:

¿En cuánto lo/la deja(s)?
  What's your price?
¿Me hace(s) una rebaja?
  What discount can you give me?
¡Está caro/a! *(LA)*/**¡Es caro!** *(Sp)*
  It's expensive!

Así se acostumbra

Bargaining or **el regateo** is very common in markets and street selling, but not in supermarkets or shops. A useful tip is to offer much less than the original price and gradually move up to a price that is acceptable to the seller. Another tip is not to show any particular interest in the item you want to buy and perhaps even find fault with it. You can say '**¡Es muy caro!**', '**No me gusta mucho el color**' or '**Me queda grande**'.

Unidad 18

Temas

Manos juntas

4 Y ahora tú

You are in Ecuador and you want to buy a woven handbag (**una shigra**).

A Ask how much it costs and try and see whether you can get a reduction.
B You don't get a reduction, but since you really like it and you know it's quite cheap, you decide to buy it. Say you'll take it.

leaf, petal

V
corregiré
I'll correct
bolígrafo
ball pen
aumentará
will grow
las arcas
the coffers

shigra

La industria de las artesanías

No matter how remote a community may be, at the end of the twentieth century the familiar products that appear on market stalls everywhere – the Coca Cola, the plastic bucket, the Nike shoes and printed T-shirts – will all be there. When it comes to clothes, for example, no local weaver or tailor can compete with the cheap cotton imports or the mass-produced acrylic cardigans and sweaters that flood the market.

> **"Ya todos saben para quien trabajan"**
> Traduzco un artículo de Esquire
> sobre una hoja de Kimberley Clark Corp.,
> en una antigua máquina Remington.
> Corregiré con un bolígrafo Esterbrook
> Lo que me paguen
> aumentará en unos cuantos pesos las arcas
> de Carnation, General Food, Heinz,
> Colgate-Palmolive, Gillette
> y California Packing Corporation.

(José Emilio Pacheco, *Tarde o Temprano*; Fondo de Cultura Económica, Mexico, 1980, p.76)

* *Could you write a similar poem about your own daily life?*

Unidad 18

The likelihood is that local people will be selling these products on their stalls rather than their own. They might have been manufactured in the Far East, or perhaps in Latin America itself by women sewing in basement workshops. Ironically, in Latin America as elsewhere in the world, it is tourism that keeps the handicrafts industry alive – Western tourists who buy the woven hats and blankets (**mantas** or **frazadas**), the pottery (**la cerámica**), the figurines (**las figuritas**), the wooden furniture (**los muebles de madera**), the handmade silverware (**la platería**) It is tourists, too, who buy the 'authentic' relics from the historic sites of ancient America – even if the clay is still wet from the workshop where it was made hours before. Yet that demand has served to revive ancient skills and forgotten knowledge. That is the irony – that the craft skills are not necessarily traditions surviving from the past – they may be a new industry!

Gabriela Mistral, for example, the Nobel Prize winning Chilean poet, lamented the passing of the old skills over fifty years ago.

"Nocturno de los tejedores viejos"

**Se acabaron los días divinos
de la danza delante del mar
y pasaron las siestas del viento
con aroma de polen y sal
y las otras en trigos dormidas
con nidal de paloma torcaz**

**Tan lejanos se encuentran los años
de los panes de harina candeal
disfrutados en mesas de pino,
que negamos, mejor, su verdad,
y decimos que siempre estuvieron
nuestras vidas lo mismo que están,
y vendemos la blanca memoria
que dejamos tendida al umbral**

(From *Antología de Gabriela Mistral*; Ed. Costa-Amic, Mexico, 1967, p.82)
* *Do you think she might be idealising the past?*

V
tejedores weavers
se acabaron they have ended
trigos corn(fields)
nidal de paloma torcaz the turtle dove's nest
harina candeal wheatmeal flour
disfrutados enjoyed
negamos we deny
tendida al umbral hanging in the doorway

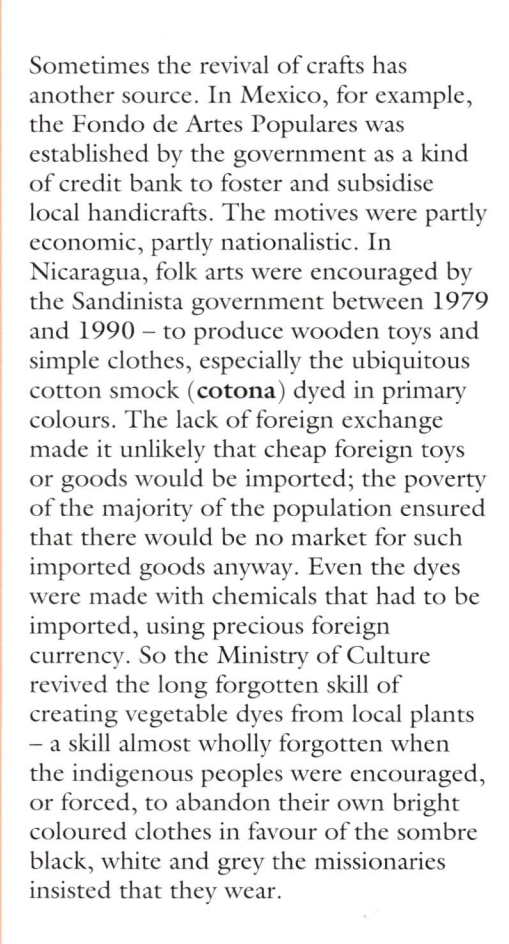

Sometimes the revival of crafts has another source. In Mexico, for example, the Fondo de Artes Populares was established by the government as a kind of credit bank to foster and subsidise local handicrafts. The motives were partly economic, partly nationalistic. In Nicaragua, folk arts were encouraged by the Sandinista government between 1979 and 1990 – to produce wooden toys and simple clothes, especially the ubiquitous cotton smock (**cotona**) dyed in primary colours. The lack of foreign exchange made it unlikely that cheap foreign toys or goods would be imported; the poverty of the majority of the population ensured that there would be no market for such imported goods anyway. Even the dyes were made with chemicals that had to be imported, using precious foreign currency. So the Ministry of Culture revived the long forgotten skill of creating vegetable dyes from local plants – a skill almost wholly forgotten when the indigenous peoples were encouraged, or forced, to abandon their own bright coloured clothes in favour of the sombre black, white and grey the missionaries insisted that they wear.

Las arpillerías

Nothing could be less sombre than the patchworks (**arpillerías**) so typical of Chile. For the majority of Chileans, 1975 was a terrible year. The military coup two years earlier had brought in a brutal military rule, and for many people great poverty as well as fear. While there was little to relieve their distress, the soup kitchens provided by some church organisations in Santiago at least

Unidad 18

provided food for the children and a resting place for their mothers, many of whom were still searching for family members who had 'disappeared'. They began to bring scraps of material (**recortes de género**), and to form out of them simple, direct and colourful pictures reflecting their daily life – the patchwork pictures or **arpillerías**.

One woman remembers her first piece:

"Recuerdo claramente mi primera arpillería ...me veo como mujer joven, con mi hijo en brazos. Después de eso, grandes nubes con alambradas y vi a mi hijo saliendo de ellas."

The subject-matter was always their reality; but these patchworks served a double purpose, as self-expression and as a means of earning a little money by selling them – which also helped to make their situation more widely known. But above all it was their own work and their own tradition that they brought to life again.

La cooperativa

Cooperatives have often been one option for groups of people working in the countryside, or in workshops, to combine their skills and resources. As a bigger unit, and – as history has shown – accepting that in exchange for a degree of control over work they may have to accept lower wages, they hope to survive in a world of very big fish. One of the most successful has been in the Basque Country.

V
alambradas
wires

Mondragón was a prosperous town in the years before the Spanish Civil War. Then the Basque Country was bombed and devastated by Franco's Nationalist army and air force. When the war ended, Franco banned the Basque language and subjected the whole area to systematic repression. The young priest José María Arizmendi left Spain at the war's end along with thousands of other Basque refugees. When he returned in 1943 to the parish of Mondragón he found it far poorer than it once had been. Trade unions were forbidden and the workers at the local factory, Unión Carrejera, worked in very poor conditions. Among the apprentices to whom he gave classes were five who decided to ask the factory management for more worker participation. When this was refused they set up their own plant, Ulgor, making paraffin heaters (**calentadores de querosén**) and cookers (**hornos**). In 1959 they and others formed their own bank, the Caja Laboral Popular, to provide the funds and investment the government was still refusing.

By 1980 Mondragón embraced 80 industrial cooperatives with 18,000 members making everything from machine tools to buses. Its management was elected at a general assembly of all members. It provided welfare for the elderly and children, and technical training for young people without regard to gender. The cooperative built its own houses and opened its own retail stores; and established openly the **ikastolas** or Basque language schools which had already operated secretly in Mondragón and elsewhere.

Unidad 18

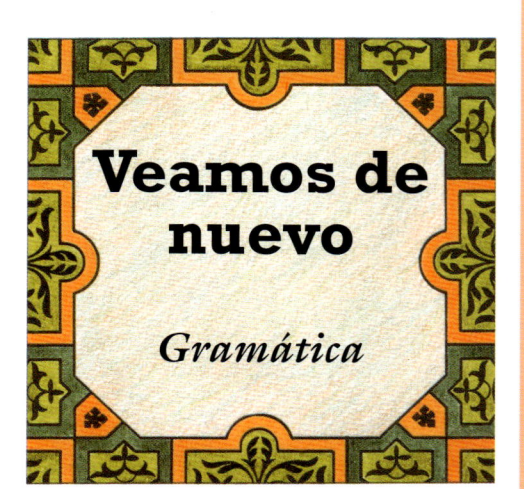

Veamos de nuevo
Gramática

1 Voy a visitar a mi madre

To talk about your plans and what you are going to do you can use **ir a** + infinitive:

Voy a ir de compras
I am going to go shopping
Teresa va a pasar una semana en Ávila
Teresa is going to spend a week in Avila
Juan va a levantarse temprano
Juan is going to get up early

2 Me lo quedo

To be more economical in conversation, you often use pronouns such as **lo, la, los, las** to refer to the object you are talking about. When shopping, if you decide to buy something you can say: **me lo quedo** (I'll have it) or **me los quedo** (I'll have them). Which pronoun you use depends on whether the thing referred to is masculine or feminine, singular or plural:

	masculine	feminine
it	lo	la
them	los	las

el pantalón: *lo* compro
los zapatos: *los* compro
la camisa: *la* compro
las camisetas: *las* compro

3 Position of direct object pronouns

These pronouns usually come before the verb:

¿Las camisas? – Sí, me las llevo/las compro
The shirts? Yes, I'll take them/I'll buy them

However, when they occur with an imperative, they are added on to the end of it:

¿Las camisas? – ¡Cómpralas!
The shirts? Buy them!

¿El café? – ¡Bébelo!
The coffee? Drink it!

With an infinitive they can be placed either before or after:

¿Las camisas? Voy a comprarlas
¿Las camisas? Las voy a comprar
The shirts? I am going to buy them

For a complete list of direct object pronouns see G 4.3.

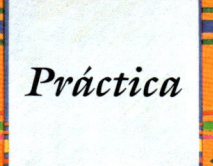

Práctica

A Mil y una excusas

Miguel, the office bore, asks Conchita if she will go out with him next week. However Conchita does not want to go and tells him she is too busy. Work out what her excuses are.

e.g. **Mañana   ir al dentista**

No puedo, mañana voy a ir al dentista

1	martes:	Marta y yo – jugar al tenis
2	miércoles:	llevar a mis padres al aeropuerto
3	jueves:	ir de compras
4	viernes:	el jefe y yo – tener una reunión
5	sábado:	lavarme el pelo
6	domingo:	visitar a la abuelita

Unidad 18

Un paso más

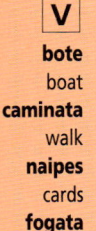

B Sí, lo compro

You've been looking at clothes in a shop and you've decided what to buy. Answer the shop assistant's questions:

1 ¿Quiere la camisa? Sí, la quiero.
2 ¿Va a comprar los zapatos? No, no .....
3 ¿Quiere los pantalones? No, ...
4 ¿Va a comprar las gafas? Sí, ...
5 ¿Quiere la corbata? No, ...
6 ¿Va a comprar las sandalias? No, ...

Así se acostumbra

If you are in Spain and want to buy clothes and shoes, the following tables of sizes will be useful.

Talla de ropa

Estados Unidos:	6	8	10	12	14	16	18	20	22
Inglaterra:	8	10	12	14	16	18	20	22	24
España:	36	38	40	42	44	46	48	50	52

Número de zapato

Estados Unidos	4½	5½	6½	7½	8½	9½	10½	11½	12½
Inglaterra	3	4	5	6	7	8	9	10	11
España	36	37	38	39	40	41	42	43	44

Medida de cuello

Estados Unidos	14	14½	15	15½	16	16½
Inglaterra	14	14½	15	15½	16	16½
España	36	37	38	39	40	41

To talk about clothes sizes you can say:

Mi talla es .../Soy talla 44

To talk about shoe size you can say:

Gasto (Sp)/calzo (LA) el número 38

It is also common to find clothes in sizes small (**pequeña**), medium (**mediana**), large (**grande**). Sometimes in Latin America they refer to them as **talla S (ese)**, **M (eme)** , **L (ele)**, and **XL (equis ele)**.

V
bote boat
caminata walk
naipes cards
fogata bonfire

C ¿Qué talla usa?

You need an entirely new outfit. Describe each item you need and say what size you take.

e.g. **Quisiera comprar una chaqueta, soy talla 42.**

1 Misahuallí Jungle Hotel

Imagine you are working as a guide in Quito, Ecuador. Some tourists inquire about this advertised excursion to Misahuallí, a town in the rainforest.

Misahuallí Jungle Hotel
Ramírez Dávalos 250
Quito, Ecuador
Tel. 500-200-043

5:30	Salida del bus interprovincial hacia el Tena (6 horas). Ascenso a las cumbres de la cordillera oriental de los Andes y luego el descenso a la intrigante selva amazónica.
12:00	Llegada a la ciudad del Tena. Traslado a Misahuallí y llegada al hotel
13:30	Almuerzo: Exquisitos platos
15:00	Excursión en bote por el río Misahuallí, caminata por la selva
17:30	Regreso al hotel
19:00	Cocktail de presentación y bienvenida.
19:30	Cena
20:30	Disfrute de buena música, juegos de naipes y una fogata romántica en la playa del río

Tell them how you will travel, how long it will take, when you will leave, and what you will see.

e.g. **Vamos a salir a las 5.30 de la mañana**

Unidad 18

2 Compradores a la carta

MAYA
Centro de todas sus compras.

SANTA CRUZ DE TENERIFE
CANDELARIA, 31 Tel. 922 24 76 84

Planta 5.ª	CONFECCION SEÑORA Y NIÑOS · MODA JOVEN · TIEMPO LIBRE LENCERIA · PIEL Y COMPLEMENTOS · ZAPATERIA BOLSOS · OPORTUNIDADES
Planta 4.ª	CONFECCION CABALLERO · MODA JOVEN · TIEMPO LIBRE ARTICULOS DE DEPORTE · ZAPATERIA · MALETAS PIEL Y COMPLEMENTOS
Planta 3.ª	ARTICULOS DE REGALOS · MANTELERIAS · CRISTALERIA ELECTRODOMESTICOS · VAJILLA · CUBERTERIA · ALFOMBRAS RELOJES DE PARED Y DESPERTADORES MAQUINAS DE COSER · LISTAS DE BODA
Planta 2.ª	SONIDO · TELEVISION · VIDEO · MAQUINAS DE ESCRIBIR CALCULADORAS · INFORMATICA · CAR-STEREO · ORGANOS Y PIANOS · DISCOS · CASSETTE Y COMPACT DISC
Planta 1.ª	FOTOGRAFIA · APARATOS DE MEDICINA · TEODOLITOS MICROSCOPIOS · NIVELES · RELOJERIA · JOYERIA · BISUTERIA PLUMAS · BOLIGRAFOS · ARTICULOS FUMADOR · GAFAS DE SOL PERFUMERIA · COSMETICA
Planta BAJA	JUGUETES · WHISKY · LICORES · TABACOS · BOLSOS DE VIAJE ROPA DE CAMA Y HOGAR · PERFUMERIA DE BAÑO

You are in the Maya department store in Santa Cruz de Tenerife. Read the store guide. Which floor do you go to if you need to buy: sunglasses, sandals, a sweater for your father, a toy for your nephew and a film for your camera.

3 Jarapas

Níjar, a small village in the province of Almería, is famous for articles made from old clothes – **las jarapas**. In **la tienda de recuerdos** (souvenir shop) listen to the shopkeeper talking about Níjar's traditional crafts, and answer the following:

a What articles are made from **jarapas**?
b How long have they been making them?
c What other craft is Níjar known for?
d What colours are used for this craft?
e Apart from crafts, what other attractions does Níjar offer?

4 Checklist

Can you do the following?

a Ask someone what their plans are and say what you intend to do.
b Invite someone to go out with you.
c Ask for what you want in a clothes shop.
d Talk about colours, shapes and sizes.
e Buy a souvenir in a market and try to get a bargain.

Unidad 19

¿Has visto la última película?

Así se habla

Saying what you have or haven't done

Describing what has happened

Recalling childhood memories

Temas

La construcción del sueño

Veamos de nuevo

Así se habla 1

Esta semana no he hecho mucho

Saying what you have or haven't done

1

A teacher and a student are talking about what they have done this week. Which of the two has spent more time at home?

¿Qué has hecho esta semana?

A Pues he hecho muchas cosas – he visto algunos vídeos en casa, he leído un par de libros, he ido al bar con unos amigos y al cine con mi novia; he jugado al tenis, he ido a dar un paseo, y pues ... nada más.

B ¿Esta semana? No he hecho mucho. Veamos... he hecho limpieza general de arriba abajo, he tirado un montón de periódicos, ropa vieja, cosas que no me servían. ¡Ah! También he preparado la ropa para mi amiga que va a tener un bebé – el moisés y las camisetitas y todo eso.

Así se dice

To describe what someone has or hasn't done during a period of time, say:

Esta semana ...
   This week ...
... he preparado la ropa ...
   ... I've prepared the clothes ...
No he hecho mucho hoy
   I haven't done much today
He leído un par de libros este mes
   I've read a couple of books this month

V
dar de comer
   to feed
recoger
   to pick up
contestador automático
   answering machine

V
tirar
   to throw away
limpieza general
   spring-cleaning
de arriba abajo
   from top to bottom
el moisés
   Moses basket

V
todavía
   yet

G
yo he preparado
el/ella ha preparado

(See G 12.1)

hacer/hecho
leer/leído
ver/visto

(See G 12.2)

Unidad 19

2 ¿Qué ha hecho Luis hoy?

Luis was asked to look after his neighbours' flat while they were away for the weekend. Look at what he has been asked to do and say what he has or hasn't done.

dar de comer al perro y al gato ✓
regar las plantas
recoger el correo ✓
abrir las ventanas ✓
sacar a pasear al perro
escuchar los mensajes en el contestador automático

3 Y ahora tú

¿Qué cosas interesantes/aburridas/necesarias has hecho hoy/esta semana/este año?

4

Ana and Miguel are looking at the cinema guide. Which film are they planning to see? Listen and read.

– ¿Y has visto "Hable con ella"?
– Sí, la vi la semana pasada.
– ¿Qué te pareció?
– Pues, me gustó mucho.

El Pianista
un film de Roman Polanski

El pianista polaco de origen judío Wladyslaw Szpilman interpreta un tema de Chopin en la radio nacional de Polonia mientras la aviación alemana bombardea la capital. Szpilman y toda su familia se ven obligados a dejar su casa y todo lo que les pertenece para trasladarse al ghetto de Varsovia.

– ¿Y has visto "El Pianista"?
– No, no la he visto. Dicen que es buena.
– Pues, yo tampoco la he visto todavía. Podemos ir a verla el fin de semana que viene.
– Muy bien, vale.

Unidad 19

Así se dice

To ask whether someone has done something, say:

¿Has visto/leído/comido ...?
  Have you seen/read/eaten ...?

And to answer, say:

Sí, he visto/leído/comido ... (dos veces)
  Yes, I've seen/read/eaten ... (twice)
No, no he visto/leído/comido ... (todavía/nunca)
  I haven't seen/read/eaten ... (yet/ever)
No, nunca he comido ...
  No, I've never eaten ...

Or, if you want to say when you did something, say:

Sí, lo/la vi/leí la semana pasada
  Yes, I saw/read it last week

To ask for an opinion, say:

¿Qué te pareció?
  What did you think of it?

And to answer:

Me pareció muy buena/malísima
  I thought it was very good/very bad
Me gustó mucho
  I liked it very much

5

Imagine you and your friend are looking at this week's film guide. Ask your friend whether he/she has seen one of the latest films and say which films you have or haven't seen.

6 *Y ahora tú*

Answer these questions about yourself:

A ¿Has estado en París/Madrid/Nueva York?
B ¿Has probado la comida mexicana/española/china?
C ¿Has esquiado/buceado/subido a una montaña?

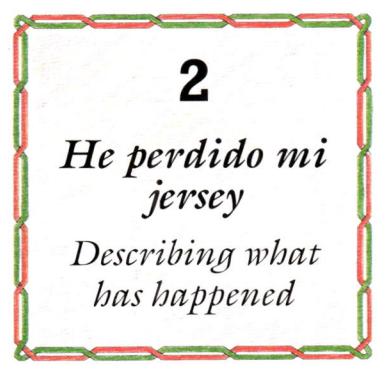

2
He perdido mi jersey
Describing what has happened

1

Jorge has left a sweater on a station platform, so he goes to the lost-property office (lost and found). Listen and read to find out what his sweater was like and whether it has been handed in.

– Hola.
– Hola, buenas tardes.
– He perdido mi jersey y quería saber si lo habéis encontrado.
– ¿Dónde crees que lo dejaste?
– Pues creo que en el andén número seis, en los asientos que hay al lado.
– Sí, un momento ... ¿Y cómo era?
– Era azul con blanco.
– Sí, en el libro aparece un jersey de color azul con blanco.
– ¡Pues sí!
– Perfecto, has tenido suerte. Lo tenemos aquí.
– Ah, pues muchas gracias.

V
dejar to leave
la suerte luck

Oficina de objetos perdidos

Unidad 19

Así se dice

If you have lost something, you can say:

He perdido mi bolso/cartera
 I've lost my handbag/wallet

You might be asked:

¿Qué tenía en el bolso?
 What did you have in your handbag?
¿Cómo era?
 What was it like?

And to answer, you could say:

Era un bolso grande de color marrón
 It was a big brown handbag
Tenía un broche dorado
 It had a golden clasp
Llevaba dinero y tarjetas en el bolso
 The bag had money and cards in it

2 🔊 4

Carme has left something on the coach from Valencia. Listen to her conversation and answer these questions:

¿Qué ha perdido? ¿Dónde lo dejó? ¿Cuándo? ¿A qué hora? ¿Cómo era? ¿Lo tienen en la oficina de objetos perdidos?

3 Y ahora tú

Imagine you have lost your briefcase (**el maletín**) and your scarf (**la bufanda**) at the station. You go to the **oficina de objetos perdidos**. Say what you have lost and describe the objects.

V
cartera (Sp),
billetera (LA)
wallet

V
**quiero poner
una denuncia**
I want to report
a crime
robar
to steal
contar
to tell
autores
perpetrators
pegar el tirón
to snatch

4 En la comisaría

Nieves was mugged in the street. Two men on a motorbike snatched her handbag and fled. By chance someone managed to photograph them. What do they look like? What are they wearing?

5 🔊 5

Nieves is now at the police station making a statement. Which details does she not get right in her description of the muggers? Listen and read. The first part is printed for you.

– Buenos días. Quiero poner una denuncia.
– Buenos días. Cuénteme lo que le ha pasado.
– Me han robado el bolso en la calle.
– ¿Sabe dónde, en qué lugar ha sido?
– Aquí, en la Calle Mayor de Carnicerías.
– ¿Conocía usted a los autores?
– Eran dos chicos jóvenes.
– ¿Qué iban, en un ciclomotor, en un coche, andando … ?
– Iban en una motocicleta roja.
– Motocicleta roja. ¿Sabe cómo iban vestidos?
– Llevaban, uno llevaba, el que me ha pegado el tirón, llevaba pantalón vaquero y camiseta negra, y el otro le he visto la cami … una camiseta verde. […]

Unidad 19

V
una mochila
rucksack
el bolsillo
pocket
una maleta
suitcase
ruedas
wheels

Así se dice

If you want to report a theft, you say:

Quiero poner/presentar una denuncia
Me han robado el bolso/la cámara
  My handbag/camera has been stolen

6

At the police station there are a number of stolen objects. How would their owners describe them?

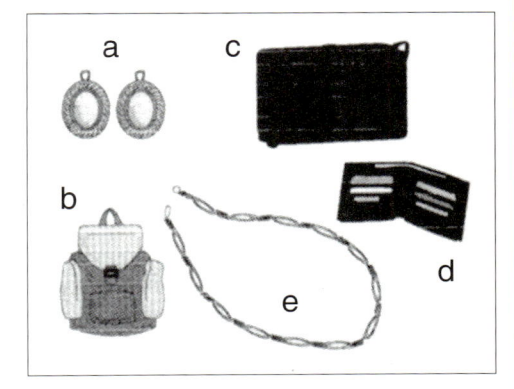

e.g. **Me han robado unos pendientes. Eran de oro, con una perla.**

Can you match each line of his description with one of the following pictures?

a ...y cayeron los dos encima de mí
b ... íbamos en un caballo mi padre, mi hermano y yo, y yo iba el primero
c ... nací en un pueblo pequeñito
d ... entonces nos caímos

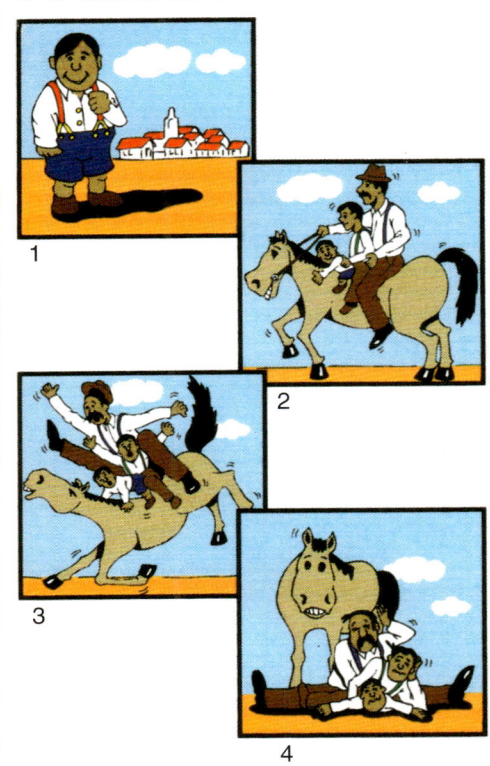

V
caerse
to fall

3
Íbamos en un caballo
Recalling childhood memories

1

Esteban, a Spanish teacher, recalls an event from his chilhood, which made a big impression on him. Here his story is told in pictures:

🎧 6 Now listen to Esteban describing the event and check your answers.

– ¿A qué edad comenzó a obsesionarte la palabra?
– Desde antes de escribir me obsesionaron mucho las palabras de mi abuela. Ella decía cosas extraordinarias ...
– Qué tanta influencia tuvo tu abuela en tu formación?
– El esposo de mi abuela, mi abuelo, era un coronel de las guerras civiles de fines de siglo pasado que tuvo actuaciones notables. Yo vivía en un mundo de las mujeres; él era el único hombre en una casa llena de mujeres. Cuando llegué yo era el segundo hombre, pero estaba entre las mujeres y lo veía a él desde el punto de vista de las mujeres y me daba cuenta que nadie le hacía caso. El mundo aquel y el mundo entero giraban alrededor del sol por determinación de las mujeres. Y claro, el centro de ese universo de mujer era la abuela. La abuela, que se llamaba Tranquilina, era una persona muy intranquila y muy móvil. Desde entonces me formé la impresión de que son las mujeres las que mueven el mundo ...

(Por Silvia Lemus, *Diario Hoy* 8/2/94)

2

In an interview, Gabriel García Márquez, the great Latin American writer, recalls some childhood memories. Read the text above and answer these questions:

a Who had a great influence in his life? In what way?
b What conclusion did he reach about women?

3 *Y ahora tú*

Which people or places from your childhood do you remember well? What were they like?

e.g. **Me acuerdo de mi abuela. Era muy alegre. Me acuerdo de la casa de mi abuela. Era grande y tenía ...**

V

punto de vista
point of view
darse cuenta
to realise
hacer caso
to pay attention
el mundo aquel
that particular world

V

acordarse de
to remember

Temas

La construcción del sueño

Antonio Gaudí

Barcelona in the 1880s and 1890s underwent a great transformation. The 1881 Exhibition marked the growth of industry and the arrival of new migrants from the rest of Spain to work there. This was the first leap into the modern world. In art and architecture, though, the word "modern" seemed to mean something very different.

The name most closely linked to this new modernity was Antonio Gaudí. The new houses and streets of the Ensanche (the new extension to the city) were built to a design and with a common style. The plan was for elegant symmetrical streets where the designs of street-lamps, doorways and benches matched the elegant interior of the new apartments. And all were built in the new style – art nouveau – which brought nature back into architecture and interior decoration. Gaudí's early designs for chairs, for example, rejected all straight edges in favour of curves and sweeping lines – they seem to have no regard for practicality or even stability. Whether he was designing furniture or buildings, his structures give an impression of constant movement.

Gaudí built two blocks of flats, the Casa Milá and the Casa Batlló. The roof

Unidad 19

of the Casa Milá turns chimneys and vents into a kind of urban jungle in concrete and stone. That sense is there again in the Parc Güell, with its huge curving creatures in mosaic and the forests of leafless concrete trees that sweep around the park. It is a fantasy landscape. And the sweeping curves in iron and plaster on the facades of the Barcelona apartment blocks mimic the concrete forest in their turn.

But the best known of all Gaudí's works, and the project that became the obsession of his life, was the great cathedral of La Sagrada Familia, unfinished in his lifetime and still in the process of completion today. He began work on the eight towers (there were originally to be twelve, one for each apostle) in 1903, helped as always by his aristocratic sponsor Güell and sponsored by his native city. But the money ran out and Gaudí's star began to fade. When he was knocked down by a Barcelona tram in 1926, at first nobody recognised him, because for more than ten years he had lived in a shed on the cathedral site and rarely left it. He died in hospital two days later, and the whole city turned out for his funeral. Arguments rage about this huge, eccentric and self-indulgent monument. George Orwell hated it; others love it. But it is evidence of an extraordinary imagination which saw no line between art and architecture, sculpture and engineering.

Recuerdos

Memory may bring pain or it may bring comfort; in these poems there are different responses to the past. How do they differ?

"Para recordar"

**Recordás el viejo patio
de nuestra casa en el pueblo
donde un geranio sembró
nuestra madre y nunca ha muerto
con sus manos cariñosas
de mujer nicaragüense
con las mismas que amasó
el pan que hoy todos comemos.

Recordás también al viejo
construyendo sus marimbas
y mar adentro cantando
su sueño de marinero
todo aquel malabarismo
de navegar contra el viento
para ganar el futuro
hay que soñarlo primero.

Y hoy que andamos los caminos
y hay ceniza en nuestro pelo
nuestros hijos han crecido
como crecen los recuerdos
recuerdos para escribir
en la mitad del sendero
para recordar también
es preciso estar despierto.**

(Luis Enrique Mejoa Godoy : "Yo soy de un pueblo sencillo": KKLA 010 1982. Amsterdam)

V

recordás = recuerdas
sembró
planted
cariñosas
loving
amasó
made the dough
marimbas
wooden xylophones
malabarismo
juggling
navegar contra el viento
to sail into the wind
ceniza
ash
crecido
grown
la mitad del sendero
half way along the road
es preciso
you must

"(The spires of) La Sagrada Familia are the extreme of artifice, yet they also resemble stalagmites, or the crags and crevices of lonely mountains. They appear to be as solid as Gothic cathedrals, yet they are hollow structures, as light as candles dripping wax"

(Carlos Fuentes: *The buried mirror*; Andre Deutsch, London, 1992; p.331)

No puedo recordar
qué nos dijimos
cómo pasó.
Eran largos mis trajes.
Me peinaba de moño.
Pasó.
Eso fue todo,
cuando yo era inocente.
....
Sentada en mi colina
veía atardecer. Era terso el paisaje:
azul morado,
azul espeso.
Habría sido difícil no amar
con ese tiempo,
ese paisaje
y mi inocencia.
Comencé a conocerme...

(And later as a woman, as a mother)

No me encuentro por días.
Paso delante del espejo
sin reflejar mi imagen.
No tengo tiempo de conversar conmigo.
Ni falta me hago a veces.
Vivo cuando me premian
con puestas de sol
y risas de mi niño.
Acepto pleitos, insomnios, desengaños.
No puedo tolerar la indiferencia...
No es la vida esperanza
es más volátil,
más precisa.
Un algo menos que el amor,
un algo más que la jornada.

(Claribel Alegría: *Aprendizaje*: Ed. Universitari de El Salvador, San Salvador, 1970, p.41/2)

Unidad 19

V

me peinaba de moño
I did my hair in a bun
colina
hill
terso
smooth and shining
morado
purple
habría sido
it would have been
ni falta me hago a veces
sometimes I don't even miss myself
premiar
to reward
puestas de sol
sunsets
pleitos
quarrels
desengaños
disappointments
la jornada
the daily toil

Veamos de nuevo

Gramática

1 Perfect tense

The Perfect tense is another way of talking about the past in Spain – the Preterite is generally preferred in Latin America. It is formed with the present tense of **haber** and the past participle of the main verb:

haber		past participle
he	hemos	terminado
has	habeis	perdido
ha	han	vivido

It is used to describe very recent events, or what has happened during a period of time that includes a reference to the present:

Esta semana he trabajado mucho
This week I have worked hard

You saw in Unit 11 (p. 125) how the regular past participles are formed:

-**ar** verbs: -**ado**   **hablado**, **terminado**
-**er** and -**ir** verbs: -**ido**   **bebido**, **vivido**

When used to form the Perfect tense, past participles do not change.

Here are some common irregular ones:

abrir/abierto	morir/muerto
decir/dicho	poner/puesto
escribir/escrito	romper/roto
hacer/hecho	ver/visto

With reflexive verbs the pronoun is always placed before the part of **haber**:

Me he lavado el pelo
I (have) washed my hair

2 Expressions of time

The following expressions of time are often used with the Perfect tense.

1 hoy; esta semana/este mes/este año
   Este año he viajado a España dos veces
   This year I have been to Spain twice
2 ya (= done already, by now)
   Ya han encontrado la maleta
   They have already found the suitcase
3 todavía/aún ... no (= still, yet to be done)
   Todavía/ aún no la han encontrado
   They haven't found it yet
4 nunca/no ... nunca
   (never, not ever)
   Nunca he estudiado ruso
   I have never studied Russian

See W 20 for a fuller list of time expressions.

A Flash de noticias

Can you put these news headlines into the perfect tense?

1 **El rey visita la catedral de Sevilla.**
2 **Esta mañana José María Aznar se entrevista con el primer ministro británico.**
3 **Un elefante se escapa del zoo municipal.**
4 **Hoy comienza la Vuelta ciclista a España.**
5 **Esta semana, el director Almodóvar estrena una nueva película.**
6 **Este mes tenemos escasez de agua en toda Andalucía y Levante.**

e.g. **El rey ha visitado la catedral de Sevilla.**

B ¿Qué tal te ha ido?

It's been a bad day! When you get home in the evening you tell your partner all about it ... Put the verbs in brackets in the correct form using the Perfect tense.

¡Menos mal que no estabas aquí! (Tener) un día terrible. Por la mañana, (levantarse) todos tarde, y (desayunar) corriendo, por eso (romper) varios platos. Luego, de camino al colegio de los niños, el coche (pararse) ¡No tenía gasolina! Así es que (llegar) tarde al trabajo. ¡La jefa estaba enfadada! En todo el día no (parar) de recibir llamadas, así es que no (hacer) mucho trabajo. En medio de todo eso (llamar) la escuela diciendo que Juanito se sentía mal. Y para colmo tu madre (telefonear) diciendo que viene a cenar. ¡Casi me muero!

Start: **He tenido un día terrible ...**

C Mi maleta aún no ha llegado

At Alicante airport, you overhear a passenger complaining that his suitcase has not arrived. Match the questions and answers to make a dialogue.

1 ¿En qué vuelo viajaba?
2 Sí un momento ¿a qué hora ha llegado?
3 Muy bien. ¿Cómo era la maleta?
4 ¿Qué llevaba en la maleta?
5 ¡Ah! Me dicen que ya ha llegado

a Ropa, una bolsa de aseo, y regalos
b Era grande, negra y de cuero
c En el IB345 procedente de Londres
d ¡Qué suerte!
e A las catorce treinta y cinco

1 Joan Manuel Serrat

The catalan singer Joan Manuel Serrat has been popular with young and old for many years. This article appeared in the Spanish magazine *Women* just after the release of his album "**Nadie es perfecto**".

Serrat ocupa un primer lugar dentro de la 'Nova Cançó Catalana'. Hoy en día, es uno de los cantantes que tiene mayor difusión y éxito. Su repertorio ha contado desde siempre con una gran gama de música, desde la tradicional catalana a canciones adaptadas de composiciones de grandes poetas:

Unidad 19

Práctica

Un paso más

V
difusión distribution
la gama range

Antonio Machado, Miguel Hernández, Rafael Alberti. Pero su mayor éxito ha sido con sus proprias canciones: "Cançó de matinada", "Paraules d'amor" y "La Tieta".

Recientemente, ha lanzado un nuevo disco "Nadie es perfecto" dedicado a la gente, toca temas humanos y pretende incitar a la revolución. Joan Manuel comenta que "la parte de creación ha sido más dura que en cualquier otro disco; la grabación en cambio, ha sido la más agradable. Me he dejado llevar y he hecho una crónica sobre la gente, de sus problemas, de sus esperanzas".

a What is the range of his repertoire?
b In which field is he most successful?
c The work of which major poets does he adapt?
d What was the name of his new record at the time, and what was its theme?

He andado muchos caminos,
he abierto muchas veredas;
he navegado en cien mares
y atracado en cien riberas.

(Antonio Machado: *Soledades*)

2 *Manos del Uruguay* 🔊 7

Listen to Elena, one of the workers of the Co-operative 'Manos del Uruguay'. The Co-operative promotes jobs for women in the knitting industry, giving them training, skills and a salary.

a What details of her family does Elena give?
b How long has she been working with Manos?
c Why did she start to work?
d What benefits has she obtained from working at Manos?

Unidad 19

V
toca temas
it touches on themes
grabación
recording
dejarse llevar
to let oneself go
esperanzas
hopes

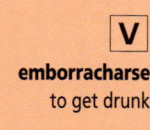

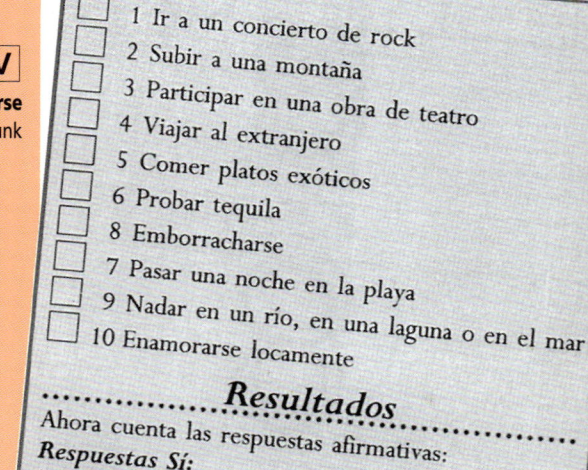

V
emborracharse
to get drunk

V
veredas
paths
navegado
sailed
atracado
landed
riberas
shores

V
hilandera
spinner
capacitación
training

3 ¿Eres una persona aventurera?

A recent test in the magazine *Lecturas* claims to enable you to judge how adventurous you are. Have you ever done any of the things mentioned? Answer in Spanish.

e.g. No, no he ido nunca a un concierto de rock.
Sí, he ido a un concierto de rock alguna vez/muchas veces etc..

Sí
☐ 1 Ir a un concierto de rock
☐ 2 Subir a una montaña
☐ 3 Participar en una obra de teatro
☐ 4 Viajar al extranjero
☐ 5 Comer platos exóticos
☐ 6 Probar tequila
☐ 8 Emborracharse
☐ 7 Pasar una noche en la playa
☐ 9 Nadar en un río, en una laguna o en el mar
☐ 10 Enamorarse locamente

........*Resultados*........

Ahora cuenta las respuestas afirmativas:
Respuestas Sí:
8–10 Eres una persona extrovertida y aventurera. Te dejas llevar por tus pasiones.
4–7 Te gusta la aventura, pero tienes los pies en la tierra.
1–3 No te gustan mucho los riesgos. Estás contento/a con tu vida sin necesidad de la aventura.

4 Checklist

Can you do the following?

a Ask someone what he/she has done in the last week and say what you have done.
b Ask someone what recent films he/she has seen and say what films you have seen.
c Make a report about something which you have lost or had stolen.
d Describe what it was like.
e Tell someone about a childhood memory.

Unidad 20

Te llamaré mañana

Así se habla
Talking on the phone
Making arrangements to go out
Talking about plans and intentions

Temas
Unidos en la lengua

Veamos de nuevo

Unidad 20

Así se habla 1

¡Dígame!
Talking on the phone

1

Listen and read the following extract from a telephone conversation. Which expressions mean the following:

a Is ... there?
b Hello?
c Speaking. Who is it?
d It's ... here.

1 ¡Dígame!
2 ¿Está Ana?
3 Sí, soy yo. ¿Quién es?
4 ¡Ah! Hola Ana, soy Pepe.

Así se dice

To answer the phone, say:

¡Dígame!
  Hello?

To ask to speak to someone, say:

¿Está Juan, (por favor)?
  Is Juan there (please)?
¿Puedo hablar con Ana?
  Can I speak to Ana?

If someone asks to speak to you and you answer the phone, say:

Sí, soy yo
  Yes, speaking

G
dejarle (a él/ella)
dígale (a él/ella)

(See p. 222 and G 4.4)

Así se dice

To ask the caller to hold on, say:

Un momento, por favor. Ahora se pone
  Hold on, please. He/she's coming

If the person called is not there, say:

No, no está
  No, he/she's not in
No puede ponerse en este momento. Está en la ducha
  He/she can't come to the phone at the moment. He/she is in the shower

Other useful expressions are:

¿De parte de quién?/¿Quién habla?
  Who's calling?/Who's speaking?
¿Puedo dejarle un recado?
  Can I leave him/her a message?
¿Quiere dejar recado?
  Do you want to leave a message?
Dígale que me llame/que llame a Pedro
  Tell him/her to ring me/to ring Pedro

2

Complete these telephone conversations with the right phrases, then listen and check your answers against the recording.

(1) – .....
  – ¿Está Juan, por favor?
  – Sí, ... ¿Quién habla?
  – Ah, hola Juan. Soy Leticia.
  – Hola Leticia. ¿Qué tal?
  – Bien, ¿y tú?

(2) – ¡Dígame!
  – ¿..... .... Rosa María?
  – Un momento, ahora se pone.

(3) – ¡Diga!
  – ¿Está Raquel, por favor?
  – No, no está. ¿..... ....?
  – De Paco.
  – ¿..... .... ?
  – Sí, dígale que voy a estar en casa, que me llame.
  – Muy bien.

Unidad 20

Así se acostumbra

Telephone expressions vary across the Spanish-speaking world. When you answer the phone in Spain, the most common expressions are '**¡Dígame!**' ('tell me'), or '**¡Diga!**' ('say it'), but you might also hear '**¿Quién es?**' ('who is it?') and sometimes '**¿Sí?**'. In Latin America, on the other hand, you might hear '**¿Bueno?**' '**¿Hola?**' or '**¿Aló?**'. When Spaniards want to identify the caller, they ask, '**¿Quién habla?**' or '**¿Quién es?**' whereas some Latin Americans might ask '**¿Con quién hablo?**' ('who am I speaking to?'). Instead of '**Soy yo**', in Latin America you might hear '**Con el mismo/la misma**' ('with the same'). If you dial the wrong number, in Spain you might hear, '**No, no es aquí, se ha equivocado**', and in some parts of Latin America, '**Está equivocado.**'

3

Here are the summaries of four telephone conversations. Listen and write the number of the conversation each summary refers to.

- a ... The person has got the wrong number. ☐
- b ... The woman is going to go and fetch the person called. ☐
- c ... The person called cannot come to the phone because he/she is in the shower. ☐
- d ... The person called answers the phone. ☐

4 Y ahora tú

Can you play both parts in the telephone conversations above – the caller (blue circles) and the person receiving the call (red circles)? Follow the instructions.

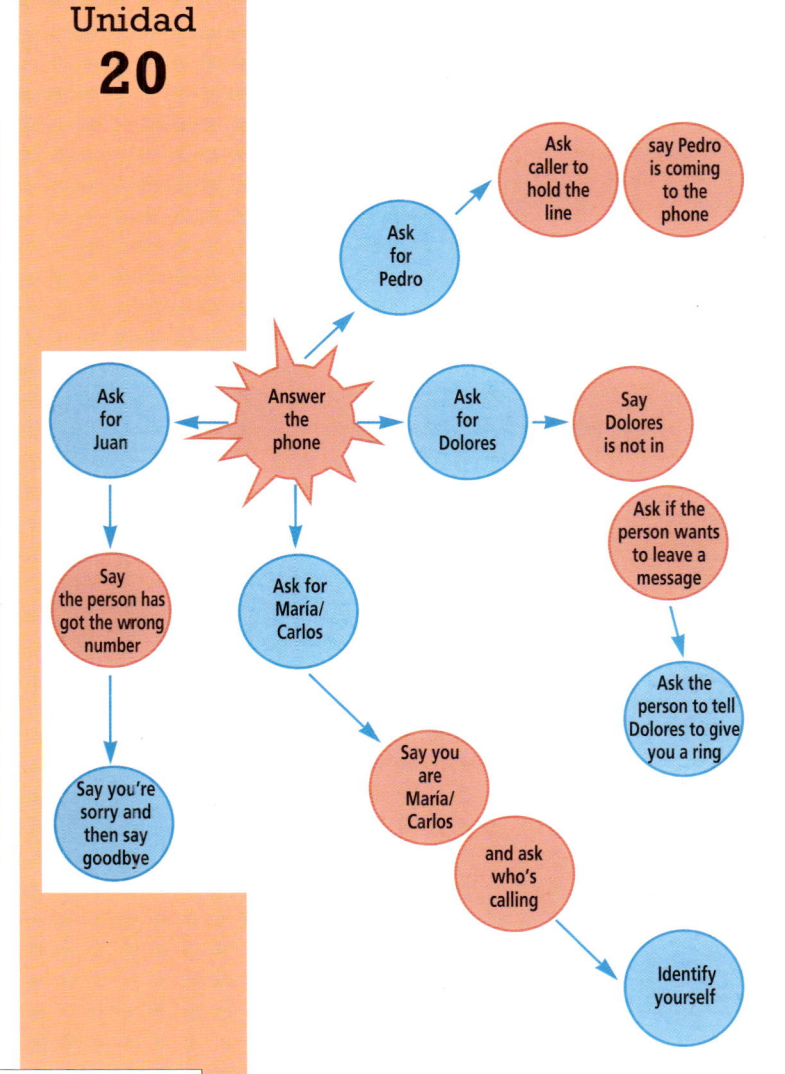

5 Phoning the office

Lucía Montes is trying to speak to Mr Martínez. Listen and find out whether she gets through to him.

– Seguros Continental, buenos días.
– ¿Me puede poner con el señor Martínez?
– ¿De parte de quién?
– De la señora Montes.
– Sí, un momentito que le paso.
– Lo siento, está comunicando. ¿Quiere esperar o quiere llamar más tarde?
– Espero.

Unidad 20

quedar not in dictionary as "to meet"?

Así se dice

To ask the operator to put you through to somebody else, say:

¿Me puede poner con ... ? (Sp)/
¿Me comunica con ... ? (LA)
  Can you put me through to ... ?
¿Me puede poner con el señor Martínez?
  Can you put me through to Mr Martínez?

Some replies you might get would include:

Está comunicando (Sp)/**Está ocupado** (LA)
  The line is engaged
Un momentito que le paso
  Hold on a moment. I'll put you through
No contestan
  There's no reply

6

Listen to the receptionist at an advertising firm dealing with two calls. Do the callers manage to get through to the person they want to speak to.

The caller wants to speak to:	Is he/she able to do so?
☐ La Sra Carmen Pérez ...	
☐ El Sr Figueroa ...	

G
tener que
to have to

2
¿A qué hora quedamos?
Making arrangements to go out

1

Ana and Noeli are discussing with another friend what to do at the weekend.

a Where are they probably going to go?
b What are their alternative plans?
c When and where are they going to meet?

– ¿Qué vamos a hacer este fin de semana?
– A mí me gustaría ir al cine.
– Yo prefiero ir a la playa.
– Bueno, podemos quedar para ir por la mañana a la playa, y a la tarde al cine.
– ¿Y si hace malo?
– Si hace malo nos quedamos a la mañana en el pueblo de compras, y a la tarde vamos al cine.
– Buena idea.
– ¿Quedamos a las nueve?
– Vale, pues quedamos ¿en dónde?
– A las nueve en mi casa.
– Vale, hasta mañana.
– Hasta mañana.

Así se dice

To propose doing something, say:

¿Qué vamos a hacer el sábado?
  What shall we do on Saturday?
Yo prefiero/me gustaría ir al cine
  I'd prefer/like to go to the cinema
¿Por qué no vamos a la playa?
  Why don't we go to the beach?
No puedo. Tengo que ir de compras
  I can't. I have to go shopping

[216]

Unidad 20

Así se dice

To make arrangements, say:

¿A qué hora quedamos?
  What time shall we meet?
¿Te va bien a las dos?
  Is two all right for you?
¿Quedamos a las dos?
  Shall we say two o'clock?
¿En dónde quedamos?
  Where shall we meet?
¿Quedamos en mi casa?
  Shall we meet at my house?

2

Listen to three people discussing what to do and complete the chart:

Proposed activity	Agreed?	Arrangements
1		
2		
3		

3 *¿Quieres ir al cine?*

Carlos asks four of his friends to go to the cinema with him, but they are all very busy. What do they reply?

e.g. **No puedo, tengo que …**

1 2 3 4

4 *Y ahora tú*

It is Friday morning and you are chatting to a colleague at work. She suggests going out for lunch together. Tell her you can't and say why. Suggest going for a drink/meal in the evening, and propose a time and a place to meet.

G
procuro llegar …
  I try to get …

Así se acostumbra

La puntualidad: People around the Hispanic world have the reputation of not being very punctual. Of course, it is difficult to make generalizations – there are some people for whom punctuality is very important and others for whom it is not. And there are events where punctuality is expected, such as business meetings or appointments, and others where the opposite is true. When you agree to meet someone, for example, you might be told '**Quedamos entre las cinco a las cinco y media**' ('I'll see you between 5 and 5:30') and you might decide to turn up at 5:20. Don't be surprised, however, if in some places you are invited for dinner at 7 p.m., but are not expected to arrive before 8 p.m. with dinner taking place around 9 p.m. or later.

5

Four people are asked whether they usually arrive on time for appointments and whether punctuality is important to them:

¿Sueles llegar a tiempo?/¿Sueles ser puntual?
¿Es importante la puntualidad?

A Listen to the recording and complete the chart:

¿Llegan a tiempo?	¿La puntualidad es importante?
Speaker 1	
Speaker 2	
Speaker 3	
Speaker 4	

B Answer the same questions about yourself.

Unidad 20

3
Llegaré en el vuelo 30
Talking about plans and intentions

1

Isabel's brother, Luis, who lives in Caracas, is flying over and coming to stay with her. Yesterday he sent her a fax with some details of his itinerary. Read it and find out the following:

a when he's arriving
b which airline he's flying with
c what he's going to do tomorrow night

```
¡Hola! ¿Qué tal?
Espero que bien.
Saldré de Caracas el
miércoles a las 10:15
y llegaré el jueves
a las once en el vuelo
730 de Viasa. ¿Podrás
venir a recogerme?
Te llamaré mañana por
la noche para
confirmarlo. ¿Vale?
Abrazos,
         Luis
```

Así se dice

To talk about your plans, say:

Llegaré el jueves a las once
   I'll be arriving at eleven on Thursday
Te llamaré mañana
   I'll phone you tomorrow
Hablaremos el sábado
   We'll speak on Saturday.

---

2 🔊 9

Luis has arrived and Isabel has organized various activities for the weekend. Listen and find out what they will be doing.

e.g. **Por la mañana primero iremos a ... y luego ...**

3 *Y ahora tú*

You are travelling to Madrid to visit a friend. You phone her the day before your departure to let her know when exactly you're arriving, but she's not in. Leave a message on the answering machine saying what time you are leaving, when you'll arrive in Madrid and which airline you are flying with. Tell her you'll take a taxi from the airport.

4 *Buenos propósitos*

The end of the year is approaching and Teresa is making new year resolutions. What does she say she will do?

e.g. **a) Dejaré de fumar.**

G
ir/yo iré
/nosotros iremos

V
dejar de fumar
to give up smoking
romper con su novio
to break up with your boyfriend

G
llegar/llegaré
salir/saldré
poder/podré

(See p. 221 and G 13)

Unidad 20

Temas

Unidos en la lengua

"Cuento"

Today I thought I'd call home
  so I got on the telephone
and said: "Operator, please give me
  AZTLAN person to person"
She replied: "Sorry sir, still checking"
after 2 minutes
  She asked me to spell it
So I did - A-Z-T-L-A-N
.....
She said, is this some kind of joke
I said: "No, you know
  where it is"
She said "Sir I cannot
  take this call..."

(Carlos Cumpian: "Cuento" in T. Empringham (ed) *Fiesta in Aztlan*:, Capra Press, Santa Barbara California 1982, p. 114)

Aztlan is almost certainly an imaginary place. But for many Mexican Americans, Spanish-speaking but resident in the United States, Aztlan symbolises their roots in a Mexico that existed before the Spanish Conquest, in the Aztec world and the Toltec and Olmec civilizations that preceded it.

    Part of what is today the United States once belonged to Mexico: Arizona and Colorado, for example, were sold to the United States for $15 million in 1843. Texas seceded from Mexico and became an independent state in 1846 – and was immediately absorbed into the growing U.S.A. Los Angeles (originally called El Pueblo de la Reina de los Angeles) was founded in 1781 by Mexicans moving northwards into California Today's Mexican Americans are descendants of the original inhabitants of those areas, and only became strangers in their own country because of a shifting border. From the nineteenth century onwards, poor Mexicans travelled north to look for work, usually in the countryside, where there was always seasonal work for fruit pickers, but also in the mines and as domestic labour in the cities. Their position was always precarious – few of them had official papers, so they could very easily be sent back across the Rio Grande (the river that marked the border between Mexico and the United States) when the picking season ended. Then they would swim back again for the next season – that is why they became known as 'wetbacks' or **espaldas mojadas**.

    By 1990 there were 22 million **latinos** (people of Hispanic origin) in the United States – nine per cent of the total population, and at least 13 million of them were born in the U.S. Not all were of Mexican origin – **chicanos**. In New York, for example, the Spanish-speaking population is predominantly from Puerto Rico – occupied by the United States in 1899 and incorporated as **un estado asociado** (a dependency) a few years later. In Florida there had always been a

Cuban community – it is only 90 miles away from the island, after all. The leader of Cuba's independence movement (1895–98), José Martí, enjoyed the enthusiastic support of the Cuban tobacco workers living there. After the Cuban Revolution of 1959, the population grew dramatically – and today, the Cuban-Americans of Miami are an important component of the Hispanic population of the United States. More recently they have been joined by other groups – from the Dominican Republic, for example, and more recently from Central America, as large numbers of refugees fled the social conflicts of the 1980s. And there are growing numbers of other Latin Americans seeking work and a better life.

Despite the discrimination this community has suffered and continues to experience in places, their presence has greatly enriched the culture of the United States. From the 1930s onwards Latin music drew an enthusiastic and growing audience for the 'mambo kings' of the city clubs (Johnny Pacheco, Machito, Tito Puente, Desi Arnaz). When their music began to mix and mingle with other Caribbean rhythms, **salsa** (the sauce) was born – and produced new stars like Ruben Blades and Celia Cruz. The traditional **norteña** music of Mexico was played at the celebrations of Mexicans living in Texas and became **tex-mex** as brilliantly expounded by Flaco Jiménez among others. The Spanish voice was heard in the rock chorus too with Santana, Los Lobos and Gloria Estefán.

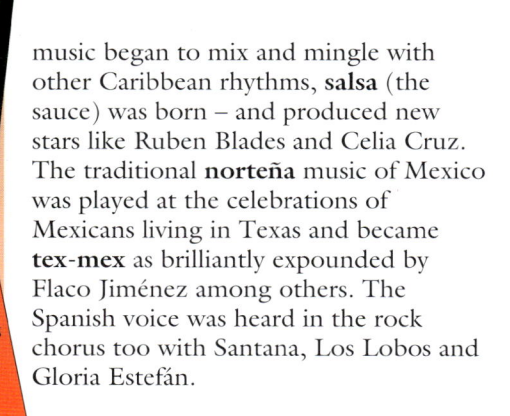

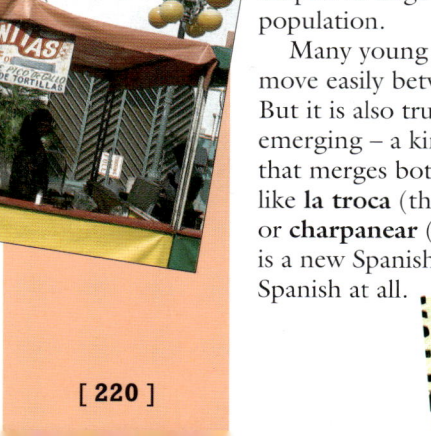

Hablando a voces

These are all North American voices – yet many of them speak or have spoken in Spanish. Today most speak both languages. And that is a matter of pride. The younger generation of Hispanics have English as their first language – yet they are fiercely committed to retaining their links with a Mexican or Latin American past and celebrating their culture. To do so, the Spanish language becomes a precious resource, the medium through which all these other loyalties are expressed. In recent years the number of Spanish-language TV and radio stations, publications and newspapers has grown. Spanish is now an official language in many schools, and there are active bilingual education programmes across the U.S. To understand the significance of this, it is worth recalling that until 1970 it was forbidden to use Spanish as a medium of teaching in Los Angeles, for example, despite its large Hispanic minority population.

Many young people are learning to move easily between both languages. But it is also true that a new dialect is emerging – a kind of combined language that merges both and produces words like **la troca** (the truck), **picar** (to pick), or **charpanear** (to sharpen). Perhaps this is a new Spanish – perhaps it is not Spanish at all.

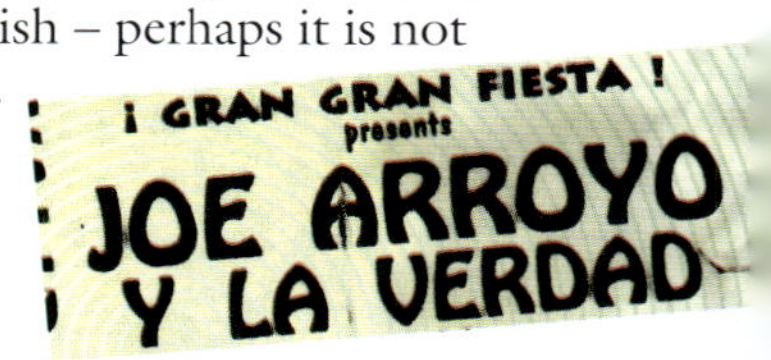

Unidad 20

"Third World Theme"

with savoring eyes
con los ojos saboreando
and trembling fingers
y trémulos los dedos
partimos el pan
we broke the bread
y no alcanzó para todos
 -not enough to go around-

de esta mesa alguien
se acostará con hambre
from this table tonight
somebody will go hungry
señor presidente
President Paleface
¿qué nos aconseja…?
what shall we do for tomorrow…?

"Chicanita flor de Campo"

Que sea yo linda-linda
para ti
pero no con adornos falsos
eyes tinted
lips painted
hair waved and perfumed
sino por estas
tortillas de cariño
que amaso
día tras día

(Angela de Hoyos: from *La palabra americana*. Originally in Tino Villanueva: **Chicanos – Antología histórica y literaria**, Fondo de Cultura Económica, Mexico, 1980.)

"TORMENTA"

Veamos de nuevo
Gramática

1 Talking about the future

In Unit 18 you learned to talk about the future using **ir a** + infinitive – **voy a comprar**, for example. You can also use the future tense, which is formed as follows:

llegar	*beber*	*vivir*
llega**ré**	bebe**ré**	vivi**ré**
llega**rás**	bebe**rás**	vivi**rás**
llega**rá**	bebe**rá**	vivi**rá**
llega**remos**	bebe**remos**	vivi**remos**
llega**réis**	bebe**réis**	vivi**réis**
llega**rán**	bebe**rán**	vivi**rán**

The endings, which are the same for all three verb groups, are added to the infinitive.

Llegaré en el ferry de las 12
I'll arrive on the 12 o'clock ferry
Beberemos a su salud
We will drink to his health
Berta vivirá en Madrid dos años
Berta will live in Madrid for two years

Some verbs are irregular in the future, but only in the stem, not in the endings. Here are some common ones:

decir/diré   querer/querré
haber (hay, habrá) saber/sabré
hacer/haré   salir/saldré
poder/podré   tener/tendré
poner/pondré   venir/vendré

Unidad 20

V
tocar la lotería
to win the lottery

If you want to refer to the very near future, you sometimes use the present tense in Spanish instead of the future.

Te veo después de comer
I'll see you after lunch
¿A qué hora llegas?
What time will you arrive?

2 *¿Puedo dejarle un recado?*

The pronoun **le** may be used in Spanish to mean 'him' or 'her', as the indirect object of the verb – **puedo dejarle un recado** (literally, can I leave him/her a message). See G 4.4 for the full list of indirect object pronouns.

3 Expressions of time

Here are some common expressions often used with the future tense:

mañana; pasado mañana
el lunes próximo/que viene
la semana próxima/que viene

For a fuller list see W 20.

A *Cada loco con su tema*

Your office manager, Don Joaquín, is going to be away all day on Tuesday and has left a memo for his employees. Can you say what everyone will be doing, using the future tense of the following verbs: **preparar, llevar, ir, comer, escribir, tener, estar**.

AVISO A TODO EL PERSONAL

El martes estaré en Sevilla

1. El Sr. Jiménez ..... el café a las once y media
2. El Sr. López ..... las cartas a Correos
3. Paco y Luis ..... a buscar a los nuevos clientes y
4. ..... con ellos en el restaurante
5. Matías ..... el informe para Benítez
6. Todos ..... permiso para terminar el trabajo a las cuatro.

El miércoles ..... de nuevo en la oficina.

Joaquín Ochoa

Un paso más

Práctica

B Madame Fifí

In the '**Parque de Atracciones**' in Madrid you visit Madame Fifí, the fortune-teller. This is what she says after looking in her crystal ball. Put the verbs in the future tense.

Tienes un futuro muy brillante: (casarse) muy pronto, (tener) diez hijos – cinco niñas y cinco niños. Te (tocar) la lotería y no (necesitar) trabajar más. (Viajar) por todo el mundo y (visitar) a tus amigos de Finlandia. Finalmente (perder) todo el dinero en el casino. No (saber) que hacer, así es que me (visitar) otra vez. ¡Hasta pronto!

1 La cita

You are planning a business trip to Madrid to visit a new client. Can you complete your part of the dialogue?

Señorita: **Cofrusa, buenos días, ¡dígame!**
You: (Greet the person, and say that you want to speak to la señora Gómez.)
Señorita: **¿De parte de quién?**
You: (Say your name and where you are ringing from.)
Señorita: **La señora Gómez no está. ¿Quiere dejarle un recado?**
You: (Say that you will be in Madrid next week, and you'd like to visit her on Monday at 10 o'clock.)
Señorita: **Muy bien. Pero no tengo la agenda de la señora Gómez. Confirmaremos la cita más tarde por teléfono. ¿De acuerdo?**
You: (Say fine, and give your international phone number.)
Señorita: **Muchas gracias. Adiós.**

2 La llamada [10]

While you were away from the office, señora Gómez has rung to confirm the meeting. Listen to the message on the answering machine. When will she see you, and at what time? Write a memo to your boss stating all the details of the meeting.

3 Llamar por teléfono

You have just arrived at Madrid airport, and want to telephone home. The information leaflet at the airport gives you the information you need.

La mayoría de las cabinas telefónicas instaladas en Madrid admiten monedas de 5, 10, 20 y 50 céntimos y de 1 y 2 euros. También es posible usar tarjetas telefónicas, que se pueden comprar en estancos, en correos y en algunas gasolineras y se pueden recargar en los cajeros automáticos.
Para llamar a otros países desde España, debe marcar el prefijo 00, luego se marca el indicativo del país que quiere llamar, el prefijo correspondiente de la ciudad y el número del abonado. Por ejemplo: Si Vd quiere hablar con el número 508 47 36 de Milán, marque:

Comunicaciones Internacionales

00	+39	+02	+508 47 36
línea internacional	indicativo de Italia	indicativo de Milán	número del abonado

a Which coins can be used in a public phone box?
b Where can you buy phone cards in Spain?
c To make an international call, what do you do after dialing 00?

Unidad 20

V

locutorios
operator-controlled telephone booths
marcar
to dial
el indicativo
code
abonado
subscriber

V

disfrutar
to enjoy
destacar
to highlight

4 Tenerife

Imagine you are a counter clerk at a travel agency. A client who has booked a holiday in Tenerife rings you up to ask for details of her holiday package. You use part of this leaflet to explain her itinerary:

Las Cañadas de Teide y El Valle de la Orotava

Día 1 Valencia–Tenerife
Salida de Valencia en vuelo especial con destino a Tenerife. Llegada al hotel.

Días 2 al 7 Tenerife:
Se queda en el hotel, en régimen de pensión completa, con el tiempo libre para admirar los preciosos paisajes isleños y disfrutar de las maravillosas playas de estas Islas Afortunadas. Hay un programa completo de excursiones, entre las que destacamos: Las Cañadas de Teide y El Valle de la Orotava. Para efectuar las oportunas compras, debe ir a Santa Cruz de Tenerife. Por las noches puede asistir a algunos de los innumerables espectáculos en el Puerto de la Cruz.

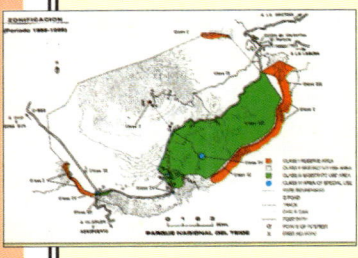

e.g. **Saldrá de Valencia ...**

5 Checklist

Can you do the following?

a Phone someone and ask to leave a message.
b Fix an appointment.
c Make an arrangement to meet someone.
d Talk about your future plans and intentions.

Puesta a punto 4

1 En el restaurante

Complete the conversation by filling in the missing words.

Camarero: Buenos días, ¿qué va a .... ?
Cliente: De ...... una sopa de pescado
Camarero: Muy bien, y ¿de ..... plato?
Cliente: Pollo y ensalada.
Camarero: De .....
Cliente: Agua ...... con gas
Camarero: ¿Desea algo de ......?
Cliente: Sí, tarta al whisky.
Camarero: Muy .... Ahora mismo se lo traigo todo.

2 Clasifica

Below are the ingredients for **paella**, **tortilla** and **sangría**, but they have been mixed up. Can you sort them out?

limones pimientos azúcar arroz huevos azafrán patatas pollo limonada melocotones cebollas mariscos vino tinto

3 Lo, la, los, las

You are shopping for clothes. Follow the example to tell the assistant exactly what you want (and remember that adjectives and nouns have to agree).

e.g. pantalones – grande
     Los quiero más grandes.

a jersey – largo
b falda – ancho
c zapatos – estrecho
d camisas – pequeño
e vestido – moderno
f chaqueta – grande

4 Diario de un futbolista

Make sentences by putting the words in the correct order.

a hemos semana Esta jugado Barcelona en
b El ha Barça partido perdido el ¡bien qué!
c He un gol Barça contra marcado el
d han muchos Hoy aficionados al partido venido
e El está entrenador nosotros contento con
f bien entrenamiento jugado En el no he

5 La fiesta

You are helping a friend to organise a 40th birthday party for her husband. She checks with you that everything is in order. Follow the example for your replies.

e.g. ¿Has mandado las invitaciones?
     (v) Sí, ya las he mandado
     (x) No, todavía no las he mandado

a ¿Han traído las flores? (v)
b ¿Ha llevado Silvia los regalos a tu casa? (x)
c ¿Has recogido la tarta de cumpleaños? (x)
d ¿Han organizado tus vecinos la música? (v)
e ¿Ha llegado tu padre para la fiesta? (v)
f ¿Habéis hecho tú y Fernando la compra? (v)

6 El cupón de la ONCE

While in Spain, you bought a ticket for the National Lottery run by **ONCE**, the organisation for the visually impaired. You win the big prize (**el gordo**) of 1.5 million euros. You note down some ideas of what you will spend the money on. Now describe your plans to a curious journalist, using the future tense.

V
el entrenador
coach
el entrenamiento
training

e.g. **Vamos a viajar por Europa**
    Viajaremos por Europa

a Vamos a viajar por Europa.
b Voy a conducir un Rolls-Royce.
c Mis hijos van a poder disfrutar con una nueva moto.
d Vamos a celebrar con una gran fiesta para toda la familia.
e No voy a pensar en mi trabajo, sólo en el ocio.
f Voy a ponerme un traje elegante.
g Vamos a tener un profesor de gimnasia individual.
h Voy a construir una nueva casa para la familia.

7 ¡Dígame!

Fill in the gaps using the words below, then match phrases from the two sets to make up a telephone conversation.

**quedamos sábado soy tal quieres
en media puerta vas hora**

a ¿Está Jaime? ..... Alicia.
b Muy bien. Jaime ¿qué ...... a hacer el sábado?
c Buena idea. ¿A qué ..... es?
d Muy bien. ¿Quedamos de seis y ..... a siete?
e En la ..... del Teatro.

i Voy a un concierto. ¿..... venir?
ii A las siete ..... el Teatro Real
iii Muy bien. Hasta el ......
iv Hola Alicia. ¿Qué .....?
v Vale. Pues ¿dónde ..... ?

8 ¿Qué servicio?

The following people each have a problem. What services from the telephone directory would they need?

Puesta a punto
4

e.g. "El Sr. Martínez se ha roto una pierna."
    – servicio de ambulancias

a "El Sr. Martínez se ha roto una pierna."
b "Mi coche está averiado en la carretera de Valencia."
c "No sé a que hora llega el autobús de Castellón."
d "Las paquetes que enviaron mis padres no han llegado."
e "El gato de Federico se ha subido a un árbol."
f "Me han robado la maleta en el aeropuerto."
g "¿A qué hora llega el tren de Valencia?"

9 Puesta a punto oral

If you visit Argentina and Uruguay you'll have the opportunity to drink the herbal tea **mate**. **Mate** is very much part of people's lives. It is brewed in a gourd (**una calabaza**) and people drink directly from it using a straw called **una bombilla**, and circulate it. Look at the pictures and descriptions. Then tell a friend how to prepare it.

e.g. **Primero pon ....**

1 Poner yerba mate en la calabaza
2 Incorporar un poco de agua fría
3 Calentar agua a punto de hervor
4 Añadir el agua al mate y azúcar al gusto
5 Beber con la bombilla
6 Volver a llenar con agua

Answer Key
(Units 0–4)

Unit 0

Section 1 (p 2)
Ex.2 1d. 2a. 3e. 4b. 5c.

Section 2 (p 2–3)
Ex.2. a Buenas tardes. b ¡Hola! ¿Qué tal? c Buenos días. d Buenas noches.
Ex.3 One was very well (muy bien) and the other was terrible (fatal).
Ex. 4 1 formal a.m. 2 informal. 3 formal, afternoon or evening.
4 informal. 5 formal, evening. Ex. 6 1a ¡Hola! ¿Cómo estás? – Muy bien, ¿y tú? b – Bueno, adiós. Hasta luego./2a Buenas tardes. – Buenas tardes. ¿Cómo está? b – Bueno, ya me voy. Adiós, buenas tardes.

Práctica (p 4)
A 1 ¡Hola! ¿Qué tal? 2 Buenas tardes. ¿Cómo está? 3 Adiós, buenas noches. 4 Hasta luego. B 1 Disculpe, no le entendí. 2 Gracias. Muy amable. 3 Gracias. Muy agradecido. 4 Perdón.

Unit 1

Section 1 (pp 6–7)
Ex. 1 Marco Antonio Castillo Morán; Raquel; María Florencia Ferrari.
Ex. 2 a ¿Cómo te llamas? – Carlos Silva (boy). b ¿Cúal es su nombre? – Antonia Sánchez (young woman). b ¿Cómo se llama? – José Valbuena (old man). Ex. 4 Julio, Hernán, Matilde, Isabel, José, Ana. Ex. 5 Matilde Muro; Hernán Sierra Nieto; José Julio Toaquiza Vega. Ex. 7 Carreras y Caballé (opera singers); Guevara (freedom fighter); Gaudí (architect); Cervantes (writer); Buñuel (film director). Ex. 8 B-O-R-J-K-U-E-Z.

Section 2 (pp 8–9)
Ex. 1 Venezuela, Colombia, Ecuador, el Perú, Bolivia, Chile, Argentina, Paraguay, Uruguay, Panamá, Guatemala, El Salvador, Honduras, Cuba, Puerto Rico (USA), Chile, Costa Rica, Santo Domingo, México, España.
Ex. 2 Venezuela, Costa Rica, Ecuador, Chile, Panamá, Guatemala, Uruguay, Paraguay, Argentina, México. Ex. 3 México; Distrito Federal.
Ex. 5 a Adriana: México, México. b Silvia: San José, Costa Rica. c Alicia Carolina: Tejada, El Salvador and San Francisco, California. d Carmen: Salamanca, Salamanca. e Carmen Rosa: Viña del Mar, Chile and Madrid.
Ex. 6 Adriana es de México y vive en México D.F. Silvia es de San José, Costa Rica. Alicia es del Salvador y vive en San Francisco, California. Carmen es de Salamanca y vive en Salamanca. Carmen Rosa es de Viña del Mar, Chile y vive en Madrid.

Section 3 (pp 9–10)
Ex. 1 a Giovanni – italiano b José – español. c Kate – inglés. d Françoise – francés. e Helmut – alemán. Ex. 2 Santander; un poquito de inglés y un poquito de italiano. Ex. 3 Me llamo Giovanni y hablo italiano. Me llamo José y hablo español. Me llamo Kate y hablo inglés. Me llamo Françoise y hablo francés; Me llamo Helmut y hablo alemán. Ex. 5 a Begoña: País Vasco, vasco y español. b Linda: Suecia, sueco, inglés, un poquito de alemán y español. c Fátima: Salamanca, español, portugués, francés. d Simona: Italia, español, francés, italiano. Ex. 6 Begoña habla vasco y español. Linda habla sueco, inglés, un poquito de alemán y español. Fátima habla español, portugués, francés. Simona habla español, francés, italiano.

Práctica (pp 13–14)
A 1 Me llamo Ricardo. 2 ¿Cuál es su nombre? 3 Hablo un poco de español. 4 Soy de Sevilla. 5 ¿Cómo se escribe? 6 Yo vivo en Salamanca. 7 Su nombre es Paco. B 1b. 2e. 3a. 4c. 5d. C 1 hablan. 2 es. 3 vivo. 4 hablo.

Unit 2

Section 1 (p 16)
Ex. 2 a español. b ecuatoriano. c argentino. Ex. 3 2 mexicana. 4 francesa; 5 inglés. 7 canadiense. Ex. 4 ¿De qué nacionalidad es usted? a Soy chilena. b Soy español. c Soy catalana. Ex. 6 a iv. b i. c ii. d iii. e v. Ex. 7 a Pierre es francés. b Giovanna es italiana. c Stephen es norteamericano. d Clare es inglesa. e Costas es griego.

Section 2 (p.17–18)
Ex. 1 1g. 2c. 3b. 4d. 5a. 6e. 7f. 8h. Ex. 2 2 secretaria. 4 pintor. 6 recepcionista. Ex. 3 1 médico. 2 pintora. 3 carpintero. 4 secretaria. 5 cocinera. 6 estudiante. Ex. 4 a ¿A qué te dedicas? ¿A qué se dedica? b ¿Qué haces? ¿Qué hace? Ex. 6 Cristina es pintora. Marco Antonio es médico. Felipe es carpintero. Marisa es secretaria. Mónica es cocinera. Andrés es estudiante. Ex. 8 a Sandra trabaja en una óptica y estudia enfermería. b Yaseña trabaja de recepcionista y estudia administración. c Alicia trabaja cuidando niños y estudia diseño. Ex. 9 a Es carpintero pero trabaja de dentista. b Es médico pero trabaja de cocinero. c Es policía pero trabaja de pintora.

Section 3 (p 19–20)
Ex. 4 Carmen and Ion. Ex. 5 a I. b F. c I. d F. Ex. 8 Tiene tres hijos; uno de doce, otra de diez, y otro de tres años.

Práctica (pp 23–24)
A 1 es. 2 eres. 3 es. 4 soy. 5 tienes. 6 tiene. B 1 Pierre es de Lyon. Es francés y habla francés. 2 Patricia es de Buenos Aires. Es argentina y habla español. 3 Jill es de Nueva York. Es norteamericano y habla inglés. 4 Isabella es de Roma. Es italiana y habla italiano. 5 Antonio es de Barcelona. Es español y habla español. C 1 Betty, ésta es mi abuela. 2 Ana, ésta es mi madre. 3 Claudia, ésta es mi hermana, Federica. 4 Guillermo, éste es mi hijo. D 1 ¿Cuántos años tiene Alicia? 2 ¿De dónde es? 3 ¿Cuál es tu nacionalidad? 4 ¿A qué te dedicas? 5 ¿Cuántos hermanos tiene? E 1 dónde. 2 Ecuador. 3 no. 4 tú. 5 irlandés. 6 soy. 7 trabajo. 8 abuela. Answer: Dentista.

Unit 3

Section 1 (pp 26–27)
Ex. 1 1f. 2a. 3d. 4b. 5c. 6e. Ex. 3 Es muy bonito, muy tranquilo y muy alegre. Ex. 4 1 bonito, grande, acogedor. 2 antiguo, bonito, aburrido. 3 bonito, bonito, bonito. Ex. 6 México: bonito, divertido, cálido. San Sebastián: grande, turística, famosa. Almagro: turístico, artístico, antiguo. Ex. 7 La ciudad de México es muy bonita, muy divertida y muy calida. El pueblo de Almagro es turístico, también es artístico, es un pueblo antiguo. La ciudad de San Sebastián es muy grande, muy turística y muy famosa. Ex.9 a It is a big city (ciudad grande) of around 4 million inhabitants (cuatro millones de habitantes). b University students, business, tourism and conferences (universitarios, negocios, turismo y congresos). c There are 3 universities (hay tres universidades). d The area round the Plaza Mayor is the old part (la parte antigua). e It's an up-to-date, lively and dynamic city (actual, viva y dinámica).

Section 2 (pp 28–29)
Ex. 2 El ayuntamiento – el hotel – la oficina de correos – la casa de cultura – el juzgado – el bar – el hospital – el teatro – el cine – la residencia – la casa de ancianos. Ex. 3 It is small (Es un pueblo muy pequeño). Its main buildings are: dos iglesias, siete bares, cinco restaurantes, dos tiendas de comestibles, un estanco, un supermercado, una tienda de ropa. Ex. 4 a En San Telmo hay dos iglesias. b una plaza. c dos restaurantes. d una escuela. e tres galerías. f dos museos.

Section 3 (pp 30–31)
Ex. 1 a Perdone, ¿hay un hotel por aquí? b En la calle San Nicolás y en la avenida J.F. Kennedy. Ex. 2 a En correos. b En la platería. c En una tienda de comestibles. d En una farmacia. e En un banco. Ex. 3 ¿Hay una platería cerca de aquí? ¿Me puede decir si hay una tienda de comestibles por aquí? Perdone, ¿hay una farmacia por aquí? ¿Me puede decir si hay un banco cerca?

Práctica (p 35)
A hay un castillo, un hospital, una biblioteca, un cine, unos restaurantes, unos hoteles, y una oficina de Correos. B 1d. 2c. 3e.4b. 5a. C 1 No, es muy acogedor. 2 No, son limpias. 3 No, es bonita. 4 No, es divertida. 5 No, es alegre.

Unit 4

Section 1 (pp 38–39)
Ex. 1 Mi casa – la calle principal – la tienda de ropa - la tienda de comestibles – la farmacia – la lavandería – la parada de autobuses. Ex. 1.3 a La tienda de comestibles está al lado de la tienda de ropa. b El parque está detrás de la tienda de ropa. c La tienda de ropa está entre la farmacia y la tienda de ropa. d El hotel está lejos de la farmacia. Ex. 4 a ¿Dónde está Correos? ¿Dónde está la iglesia? ¿Dónde está el estanco? b Está enfrente del hotel. Está en la esquina, enfrente del convento. Está al lado de la lavandería. Ex. 5 a cerca del hotel. b en la plaza de san Pedro. c enfrente del hotel. d muy lejos de aquí.

Answer Key
(Units 4–6)

Section 2 (pp 39–41)
Ex. 1 **a** un horario de trenes. **b** un plano. **c** un mapa. **d** un horario de trenes. **Ex. 4** 34 treinta y cuatro; 46 cuarenta y seis; 57 cincuenta y siete; 66 sesenta y seis; 77 setenta y siete; 88 ochenta y ocho; 99 noventa y nueve. **Ex. 5** winning numbers: 28, 44, 66, 39, 17; big prize: 88; viaje para dos a la capital de España; excursiones a Toledo y otros lugares de interés cerca de Madrid. **Ex. 6 a** Segovia. **b** 81 km northwest of Madrid. **Ex. 7** El Escorial: 49 km northwest; Guadalajara: 56 km; Ávila: 115 km; Navacerrada 50 km northwest; Cuenca 167 km; Segovia 81 km.

Section 3 (pp 41–42)
Ex. 2 a first street on the right. **b** fourth on the left. **c** third on the right and then straight on. **d** three streets along and on the left. **Ex. 3** Cathedral: A. Town hall: D. Library: E.

Práctica (pp 46–47)
A No estoy en casa. Marco y Juan están en el parque y María está en la universidad. José Luis y yo estamos en el supermercado. Si quieres comer, el queso está en la nevera y el pan está en la mesa. ¡Hasta luego! **B 1** cerca de la catedral. **2** enfrente del banco. **3** en la Plaza Mayor. **4** detrás del colegio. **5** delante del hotel. **C 1** La segunda calle a la izquierda, en la plaza. **2** Todo recto, 100 metros a la derecha. **3** La primera a la derecha, y luego todo recto. **4** En esta calle, 50 metros a la izquierda. **5** La segunda calle a la derecha, enfrente de la biblioteca

Unit 5

Section 1 (pp 50–51)
Ex. 1 El pan – el jamón – el queso – los huevos – el aceite – el vino – las patatas o papas – las patatas fritas – el arroz – las galletas – las sardinas. **Ex. 2** Begoña: pan – jamón – vino; Miguel: patatas – queso – aceite. **Ex. 3 a** Me da una barra de pan? **c** Quiero una barra de pan. **c** Quería jamón de York. **Ex. 5** Begoña: una barra de pan, jamón serrano, una botella de vino. Miguel: un kilo y medio de patatas, quinientos gramos de queso, una botella de aceite. **Ex. 6** una botella de vino, un bote de mayonesa, una lata de jamón, una paquete de patatas fritas, una botella de aceite. **Ex. 9** el pan en la panadería; las verduras en el mercado; la carne en la carnicería; las bebidas en el mercado; los pasteles en la pastelería; el pescado en la pescadería. **Ex. 10** Compro **a** carne en la carnicería; **b** pescado en la pescadería. **c** cebollas en el mercado; **d** pasteles en la pastelería. **e** chorizo en la charcutería.

Section 2 (pp 52–53)
Ex. 2 Sandías – melones – naranjas – manzanas – tomate – pera – melocotón – coliflores – pepino – cebolla – patatas – puerros – plátanos – zanahoria. **Ex. 3 a** Ah, como medio kilo. **b** Me da dos kilos. **c** Quisiera un kilo, por favor. **Ex. 4** 1 kilo de pimientos; 1 kilo de tomates; ½ kilo de cebollas; ½ kilo de pepinos. **Ex. 6 a** cuatrocientos cuarenta y dos; **b** ciento veinticinco; **c** seiscientos; **d** mil cuatrocientos diez; **e** quinientos treinta y dos; **f** trece mil doscientos cincuenta.

Section 3 (p 54)
Ex. 1 A siete el kilo. **b** El kilo de mangos está a catorce pesos. **c** A cuarenta y cinco el kilo. **Ex. 2** ¿A cómo son las patatas? Quiero dos kilos./¿A cómo están las manzanas? Quiero medio kilo./¿A cómo está el kilo de queso? Quiero doscientos cincuenta gramos./¿A cómo es el kilo de jamón? Quiero quinientos gramos. **Ex. 3 c** 12,20 (euros). **a** 20 (pesos). **b** 17,50 (pesos) **e** 15.000 (pesos) **d** 7,35 (euros) **Ex. 4** Tomates a 1,49 € kilo, 3 kilos = 4,47 €. Patatas a 0,75 € kilo, 2 kilos = 1,50 €. Manzanas a 1,59 € kilo, medio kilo = 0,80 €. Queso a 15,90 € kilo, doscientos cincuenta grms. = 3,98 €. Jamón a 16,20 € kilo, quinientos grms. = 8,10 €. Total = 18,85 €. 'Son dieciocho euros con ochenta y cinco, por favor'.

Práctica (pp 57–58)
A 1 ¿Cuántos huevos hay en la caja? **2** ¿Cuántas sardinas hay en la lata? **3** ¿Cuántas botellas de vino hay en la caja? **4** ¿Cuántos chocolates hay en la caja? **5** ¿Cuántas naranjas hay en la bolsa? **6** ¿Cuántas cerillas hay en la cajita? **B 1** Me da esta caja de huevos. **2** Quiero esa lata de sardinas. **3** Quisiera esa caja de botellas de vino. **4** ¿Me da esta caja de chocolates? **5** Me da esa bolsa de naranjas. **6** Me da esa cajita de cerillas. **C 1** quiere. **2** quiere. **3** quiero. **4** quieres. **5** quieren.

Puesta a punto 1 (pp 59–60)
1 a iv. **b** vi. **c** i. **d** v. **e** vii. **f** viii. **g** ii. **h** iii. **2 a** está. **b** son. **c** es. **d** es. **e** están. **f** está. **g** soy. **3 a** Mi barrio es muy alegre. **b** ¿Qué hay en tu ciudad? **c** Hay un hotel por aquí? **d** Mi pueblo tiene un restaurante, una iglesia y muchos bares. **e** La iglesia está al lado del Ayuntamiento. **f** ¿Dónde está la oficina de turismo? **4** Nationalities: español, francesa, argentino, inglés, mexicana, italiano, vasco. Languages: español, inglés, italiano, vasco. Professions: recepcionista, profesor, cocinera, pintor, estudiante. Places: Correos, hotel, farmacia, bar, parque, iglesia. Descriptions: moderno, antigua, pequeño, grande, acogedor, artístico. Food: tomate, lechuga, melocotón, jamón, manzana. **5 A** es; vive; tiene; trabaja; está; tiene; son; hablan; van; tienen; viven; trabajan. **B** Me llamo Maruja Serrano. Soy de Málaga en el sur de España. Vivo con mi marido en Torremolinos. Tengo cincuenta y tres años. Trabajo en una oficina. Juan, mi marido, está jubilado. Tiene sesenta y siete años. Hablamos inglés. Hablamos francés cuando viajamos a Francia. Tenemos dos hijas y un hijo. Nuestros hijos viven en las afueras de Madrid, pero trabajan en el centro. **6 a** españoles. **b** francesas, sevillanas. **c** inglés, irlandesa. **d** tranquilo, antiguo. **e** bonita, cálida. **7** ¿Qué desean?/¿A cómo está ...?/(15,90 €)/¿Algo más?/(1,39 €)/ ¿Algo más?/dos paquetes ... una botella/¿Cuánto es?/Son (22,64 €). **8 a** ¿Cómo te llamas? ¿De dónde eres? **b** ¿Habla usted inglés? **c** ¿Cómo te llamas? **d** ¿Tienes un mapa de Madrid? **e** ¿Tiene hijos ¿Qué edad tienen? **f** ¿Va usted de compras al mercado? **g** Señoras ¿pueden describir su ciudad, por favor? **h** ¿Qué fruta tiene?

Unit 6

Section 1
Ex. 1 a limpiar la casa. **b** preparar la cena. **c** lavar la ropa. **e** fregar los platos (Spain), lavar los platos (LA). **Ex. 4** Limpio la casa y barro el patio una vez a la semana, preparo la cena todas las noches, lavo la ropa dos veces a la semana, nunca plancho. **Ex. 5** Cocino, lavo y seco los platos y preparo la ensalada. **Ex. 7** Ana: lee el periódico todos los días y escribe cartas cada fin de semana. Come chocolate una vez a la semana al menos. Habla por teléfono varias veces al día. Bebe vino cada día. Jorge: bebe vino todos los días. Habla poco por teléfono, pero escribe cartas todos los días. Come chocolates una vez al mes. Lee el periódico los fines de semana. **Ex. 8** ¿Preparas la cena? ¿Cocinas? ¿Barres la casa? ¿Lavas la ropa? ¿Friegas los platos? ¿Sacas la basura?

Section 2 (pp 63–64)
Ex. 1 b son las diez. **a** es la una. **c** son las dos en punto. **Ex. 2 a** las nueve. **b** las doce (mediodía). **c** las cinco. **d** las once (las veintitrés). **Ex. 3 a** 07:00. **b** 10:00. **c** 13:00. **d** 16:00. **Ex. 4 a** ¿Qué hora es? **a** Son las tres y diez. **b** Son las dos y media. **c** Son las cinco y cuarto. **d** Son las diez y treinta y cinco. **e** Son las doce menos diez. **f** Es la una y veinte. **g** Son las ocho menos cuarto. **h** Son las ocho y cinco. **Ex. 5 a** What time is the film "En el Nombre del Padre". **b** There are performances at: 16:00, 18:45, 21:00.

Section 3 (pp 65–66)
Ex. 1 The housewife gets up at 6.45 and goes to bed at midnight; the soldier gets up at 7 o'clock and goes to bed at 10. **Ex. 3** Me baño y me maquillo/Me ducho y me afeito. **Ex. 4** a7. b4. c5. d1. e9. f6. g8. h8. i2. **Ex. 5** Se levanta a las siete de la mañana y desayuna, sale de casa a las ocho y va a clase, come a las dos, termina las clases hacia las seis de la tarde y vuelve a casa, cena sobre las nueve o nueve y media, se acuesta alrededor de la doce.' **Ex.7** Julia.

Práctica (pp 69–70)
A ceno, cenas, cena, cenamos, cenáis, cenan; lavo, lavas, lava, lavamos, laváis, lavan; leo, lees, lee, leemos, leéis, leen; vivo, vives, vive, vivimos, vivís, viven. **B** limpiamos la casa ... prepara la comida ... barre el patio y saca la basura ... yo preparo un pastel ... lava y plancha toda la ropa ... arreglan sus habitaciones ...yo paso todo el día en la cama. **C a** Yo como carne, pero Juanita come solamente verduras. **b** No bebemos vino. Preferimos cerveza. **c** No, yo no leo nunca, pero mi hermana lee muchos libros. **d** Mi marido y yo vemos la televisión por la noche después de cenar. **D a** iii. **b** vii. **c** iv. **d** i. **e** vi. **f** v. **g** ii.

Answer Key
(Units 7–10)

Unit 7

Section 1 (pp 72–73)
Ex. 1 1c. 2a. 3d. 4b. **Ex. 2 a** En un piso, two people. **b** En una casa, three people. **Ex. 5 a** garaje. **b** aire acondicionado. **c** calefacción. **d** ascensor. **e** número de habitaciones. **f** amueblado. **g** área/zona o distrito. **h** tipo de vivienda.

Section 2 (pp 74–75)
Ex. 1 e el dormitorio. **f** el baño. **c** el cuarto de estar. **b** el comedor. **a** el living. **Ex. 2 a** 2 bedrooms. **b** 1 bathroom. **c** el comedor: es lo más lindo; el dormitorio principal: es una parte muy antigua de la casa; el baño: es un baño muy grande. Tiene su propia chimenea. **Ex. 4** 1 2 habitaciones, 1 baño, sala, cocina. 2 4 habitaciones, 2 baños, cocina, patio, y jardín. 3 3 habitaciones, sala, estudio, cocina y comedor. 4 2 habitaciones, 1 baño, sala, cocina, y patio. **Ex. 5** En el comedor: la mesa, sillas. En el living: el sillón, el sofá, el escritorio. En el dormitorio: la cama, el armario.

Section 3 (pp 75–77)
Ex. 2 a Olga wants a coffee. **b** con leche, con un poco de azúcar, con unos cubitos de hielo. **Ex. 4** No, they do not like the same things; Rosa likes tea, coffee, infusions such as camomile tea and mint tea; Juan likes weak coffee, does not like infusions, likes tea with lemon or sugar but not milk.

Práctica (p 81)
A Ana, ¿te gusta el té? – Sí, me gusta./Alberto, ¿te gusta el té? – No, no me gusta./Pepe y Marta, ¿os gusta el té? – Sí, nos gusta mucho./Jaime, ¿te gusta el café? – No, no me gusta./Ana, ¿te gusta el café? – Sí, me gusta mucho./Alberto, ¿te gusta el café? – Sí, me gusta./Pepe y Marta, ¿os gusta el café? – Sí, nos gusta. Jaime, ¿te gustan las galletas? – No, no me gustan./Ana, ¿te gustan las galletas? – Sí, me gustan./Alberto, ¿te gustan las galletas? – Sí, me gustan./Pepe y Marta, ¿os gustan las galletas? – Sí, nos gustan mucho./Jaime, ¿te gustan los pasteles? – Sí, me gustan./Ana, ¿te gustan los pasteles? – No, no me gustan./Alberto, ¿te gustan los pasteles? – No, no me gustan./Pepe y Marta, ¿os gustan los pasteles? – Sí, nos gustan mucho. **B a** quiere tomar. **b** quiero estudiar. **c** queremos trabajar. **d** quieren comer. **e** quieren comprar. **C** Mi piso está en la calle Serrano … es bastante grande. La cocina es amplia y soleada; está enfrente de … Los muebles … son modernos y prácticos. … a la derecha está el dormitorio principal y a la izquierda está el salón. … es espacioso y alegre. El sofá es cómodo … La cama está en el centro… a cada lado están las mesillas de noche. El dormitorio es muy abrigado.

Unit 8

Section 1 (pp 84–5)
Ex. 1 a alta, guapa, rubia. **b** vieja, morena, gorda. **c** bajo, delgado, feo. **d** joven, gordo. No 4: young, tall, fair and good-looking; No 3: older, shorter, dark and very slim. **Ex. 3 a** el pelo castaño, corto y rizado. **b** el pelo corto y liso, los ojos negros, la boca grande. **c** el pelo largo, moreno, y rizado, los ojos azules. **d** el pelo rubio, largo y liso, los ojos azules. **Ex. 4** 1 Pepe. 2 María. 3 Teresa. 4 Carlos. **Ex. 6 a** Tiene el pelo largo y rubio. **b** Tiene el pelo canoso. **c** Tiene el pelo corto. **d** Tiene el pelo corto y rizado. **Ex. 7** Teresa y Maite son muy simpáticas y divertidas. Pepe es tímido e inteligente. Carlos es antipático.

Section 2 (pp 85–7)
Ex. 2 Aurora: her legs (las piernas). Salvador: his head (la cabeza). **Ex. 3 a** me duele el brazo. **b** me duele la espalda. **c** me duelen los oídos. **d** me duele el estómago. **e** me duele la garganta. **Ex. 4 a** Tengo dolor de oído. **b** Tengo dolor de cabeza. **c** Estoy cansado/a. **d** Tengo dolor de espalda. **e** Me duelen los ojos. **f** Tengo tos. **Ex. 5** Nieves Martínez Carrión, 27, married, 3 children, stomach-ache.

Section 3 (pp 87–8)
Ex. 2 1c. 2a. 3b. **Ex. 3** 1 después de las comidas. 2 tres veces al día durante cinco días. 3 la crema dos o tres veces al día, el analgésico una tableta cada seis horas. **Ex. 4** 1 Calcium for healthy bones, 1-2 tablets a day. 2 Nose drops, 2-3 times a day. **Ex. 5 a** beber una limonada caliente. **b** ir al médico. **c** descansar. **d** ir a la cama. **e** hacer gárgaras. **f** hacer ejercicio.

Práctica (p 91)
A 1 está. 2 están. 3 es. 4 soy. 5 es, está. 6 estamos. **B** 1b. 2c. 3a. 4e. 5d. **C** Tengo que ir al trabajo. Juan tiene que ir al dentista. Alicia y yo tenemos que comer con el señor Gómez. Tengo que ir a la escuela. Tengo que ir de compras. Los hijos tienen que ir a la óptica. Juan tiene que preparar la cena.

Unit 9

Section 1 (p 94-5)
Ex. 1 a Ir al parque. **b** Estar con amigos. **c** Leer y mirar películas de video. **d** Descansar. **Ex. 2** Five parks. **Ex. 4 a** A Carlos le gusta tocar la guitarra. **b** A Marisol no le gusta ir de compras. **c** A Luis y Margarita les gusta ir al bar. **d** A Nuna y Francisco no les gusta jugar al tenis. **Ex. 5 A** Juan le gusta ir al cine. Va al cine una vez a la semana. Le gusta ir al teatro. Va al teatro una vez al mes. No le gusta ir de compras. No le gusta hacer deporte. **Ex. 6** 3 Ramón (possibly).

Section 2 (pp 96–7)
Ex. 2 25 June; 10 April; 18 September; 5 February. **Ex. 3** Su nacimiento: 24 de junio de 1941. Su boda: 13 de noviembre de 1966. Su ingreso en Correos: 28 de febrero de 1966. Su ingreso en la oficina actual: 18 de julio de 1966. **Ex. 5 a** el seis de enero (el día de los Reyes). **b** el uno de mayo (el día del Trabajo). **c** el veintiocho de diciembre (el día de los inocentes). **d** el doce de octubre (el día de la Hispanidad). **e** el veinticinco de diciembre (la Navidad). **f** el dos de noviembre (el día de los Difuntos/de los Muertos (LA).

Section 3 (pp 98–9)
Ex. 2 1 Una coca-cola y un mosto. 2 Un café solo con hielo, y una botella de agua mineral. 3 Dos coca-colas en botella. **Ex. 3** ¿Qué van a tomar? ¡Dígame! ¿Algo más? **Ex. 5 a** falso. **b** verdadero. **c** falso. **d** falso. **e** falso.

Práctica (pp 103–4)
B A 1b. 2e. 3d. 4c. 5a. **C** 1 infusión. 2 naranja. 3 sangría. 4 cerveza.

Unit 10

Section 1 (pp 106–7)
Ex. 2 1 el autobús; siempre. 2 el metro; para ir a trabajar por las mañanas. 3 el tren; cuando va a Málaga los fines de semana. **Ex.4** She prefers the train because it's comfortable (cómodo), inexpensive (no es caro) and reasonably quick.

Section 2 (pp 107–9)
Ex. 1 by bus (en autobús); from the bus station in the city centre (la estación de autobuses en el centro de la ciudad). **Ex. 2 a** ¿Cómo puedo ir de Lima a Arequipa? **b** ¿Cómo puedo ir de Lima a Cuzco? **c** ¿Cómo puedo ir de Cuzco a Machu Picchu? **e** ¿Cómo puedo ir de Lima a Iquitos? **Ex. 3 a** Arequipa by plane (an hour and a quarter), train or bus (16 to 20 hours). **b** Cuzco by plane direct (an hour), train or bus to Arequipa then change (16 hours to train from Arequipa to Cuzco). **c** Machu Picchu by bus or train from Cuzco (about four hours) (or walk!). **d** Iquitos by plane only. **Ex.4 a** Falso. **b** Falso. **c** Verdadero. **d** Verdadero. **e** Falso. **f** Falso.

Section 3 (pp 109–10)
Ex. 1 She wants to travel: el viernes día ocho. **Ex. 3 a** ir a Sevilla. **b** el próximo miércoles. **c** un billete de ida y vuelta. **d** ir por la mañana y volver por la noche.

Práctica (p 113)
A cada uno prefiere … mis padres prefieren … mi hermano prefiere … Alicia y Ana prefieren … yo prefiero … tú prefieres. **B a** No se puede hacer fotos. **b** No se puede comer. **c** No se puede pagar con tarjeta de crédito. **d** No se puede entrar. **e** No se puede beber agua. **f** No se puede nadar. **C** 1 sale (S). 2 estación (E). 3 vuelta (V). 4 ir (I). 5 llega (L). 6 la (L). 7 avión (A). **D** 1 vengo. 2 van. 3 venís. 4 cogemos. 5 va.

Puesta a punto 2 (pp 115–6)

1 **a** Yo me levanto a las siete y me acuesto a las once. **b** El partido comienza a las tres y termina a las cinco menos cuarto. **c** Marta y Sergio van a la oficina a las nueve y vuelven a casa a las siete y media. **d** Patricia viene a las nueve menos cuarto y regresa a las cinco y media. **e** Marisa hace la limpieza a las nueve y prepara la cena a las siete y media. **f** Los toros comienzan a las cinco y acaban a las siete. 2 1 es. 2 estoy. 3 está. 4 son. 5 Son. 6 estáis. 3 d, c, e, b, h, g, a, f. 4 autobús; cocina; espalda; comedor; estómago; garaje; coches; avión; cabeza; silla; habitación; brazo; salón; ferry; tren. 5 1c. 2d. 3a. 4d. 5b. 6c. 6 El señor Pirúlez tiene el pelo corto y una barba, y tiene los ojos azules. Es alto, delgado simpático y extrovertido. La señora Pirúlez tiene el pelo largo y moreno, con ojos verdes. Es delgada, fría y antipática. 7 **a** ¿Qué hora es? **b** Mi amigo y yo

[228]

Answer Key
(Units 10–13)

preferimos el café. **c** Teresa quiere vivir en Madrid. **d** Yo tengo/tú tienes el pelo largo y liso. **e** Juana está enferma. **f** A Marta le gusta jugar al tenis. **g** Quiero un billete de ida y vuelta para Alicante. **h** El salón es amplio y bonito. **j** Me duele la espalda. **8 a** Buenos días. ¿A qué hora hay vuelos a Bogotá? **b** Quisiera un billete de ida para el sábado por la mañana. **c** ¿Cuánto es? **d** Me llamo ... Estoy en el hotel Caribe, habitación 537. **e** ¿A qué hora tengo que estar en el aeropuerto?

Unit 11

Section 1 (pp 118–20)

Ex.1 Una habitación individual con baño; para el fin de semana; 78 €; habitación y desayuno. **Ex.2** En la temporada baja: dos habitaciones dobles (134 €) y cuatro desayunos (26,44 €) = 160,44 €. **Ex.3** 1 Habitación individual (no 207). **2** Habitación doble con cama doble (no quedan habitaciones). **3** Habitación doble (no 105). **Ex. 5** Hotel facilities: aire acondicionado, hilo musical, teléfono, televisión en color, cuarto de baño completo. Room facilities: No hay servicio de habitaciones. Price per night: low season – 65 €; high season 75 €.

Section 2 (pp 120–1)

Ex.1 She has to write her address (dirección), passport number (número de pasaporte), signature (firma) and her credit card (tarjeta de credito). Room 2097 is up the steps on the right (subiendo las gradas a la derecha). **Ex.4** No hay toallas; no hay papel higiénico; no hay agua caliente; no funciona la cocina; no funciona la televisión. **Ex.5 1** Total €76.090 pesos. En efectivo. **2** 852,35 €.

Section 3 (pp 122–3)

Ex.1 b un festival de teatro (play). **c** una exposición de pintura (painting exhibition). **g** un concierto. **Ex.2** Un festival de teatro clásico (Calderón and Shakespeare). Un festival de cine de películas españolas. Dos conciertos de música clásica. Un partido de fútbol entre Alcázar y Realejos. **Ex.4 a** Verdadero. **b** Falso. **c** Falso. **d** Falso. **e** Verdadero. **Ex.5** El precio de la entrada es de 20 €. Quiero dos entradas.

Práctica (pp 125–6)

A 1 ¿Tiene una habitación libre? **2** ¿Cuánto es por noche? **3** ¿Se puede comer en el restaurante? **4** ¿Hay entradas reservadas para el festival? **5** ¿Puedo alquilar un coche? **B 1** *Soy un sinvergüenza* (obra de teatro) in Sevilla. **2** Flamenco en los claustros de Santo Domingo. **3** Zarzuela in Huelva. **4** Picasso in Málaga. **5** *The Return of the Dynosaurs* in Málaga. **6** Woody Allen films. **7** *Sueños flamencos* in Sevilla. **C** Possibly *Sueños flamencos*.

Unit 12

Section 1 (pp 128–9)

Ex.2 Yes, they both like the seaside. **Ex.3 a** María suele ir al campo en Francia. **b** A Juan y Teresa les gusta ir a las islas en Grecia. **c** Gloria, Pedro y Elvira suelen ir a un lago en Irlanda. **d** A Carlos y Pedro les gusta ir a la montaña en los Alpes suizos. **Ex. 5 1** Acapulco, México. **2** Menorca. **3** Cazorla, Andalucía. **4** Galicia. **5** Brasil. **Ex. 6** María ¿dónde fuiste el año pasado? – Estuve en el campo francés. **b** Juan y Teresa ¿dónde fuisteis el año pasado? – Fuimos a las islas griegas. **c** Gloria, Pedro y Elvira ¿dónde fuisteis el año pasado? – Fuimos a un lago en Irlanda. **d** Carlos y Pedro ¿dónde fuisteis el año pasado? – Estuvimos en los Alpes suizos. **Ex.7** Acapulco, Mexico: increíble, buenísimo. Menorca: muy relajado. Galicia: muy bien, fenomenal. Brasil: estupendamente, maravilloso.

Section 2 (pp 130–1)

Ex.1 1 Two weeks. **2** Yes she had a good time. **3** She visited churches and museums and she went to many restaurants; she had lunch on El Panecillo (a hill). **4** El Cotopaxi. **5** The Galápagos. **Ex.3** His wife said he rode on a bike (anduvo de bicicleta) and he took photos (sacó fotos) which he doesn't himself mention. **Ex.4** Visitó iglesias y museos. Fue a muchos restaurantes. Comió en el Panecillo. Subió al refugio. **Ex.5 d** nadar. **e** bucear. **c** cenar. **a** bailar.

Section 3 (p 131–2)

Ex.1 Me levanté temprano, me duché, fui a la piscina, volví a casa, desayuné (tomé un zumo), leí un libro, fui al supermercado. **Ex. 2 a** Se levantó a las diez. **b** Tomó una taza de café a las diez y cuarto. **c** A las diez y media fue al supermercado. **d** A la una comió en un restaurante. **e** Luego a las dos y media fue al bar y tomó una cerveza. **f** Por último a las cuatro y

media volvió a casa, donde leyó el periódico y vio la televisión. **Ex. 5** Cenó en un restaurante italiano anteayer. Ayer fue al supermercado. La semana pasada fue al bar. Y el mes pasado fue a la ópera. **Ex.6** El martes pasado visitó la fábrica UMLO, y comió con el gerente. El miércoles preparó la conferencia. Confirmó el vuelo con Iberia. El jueves fue al aeropuerto a las siete. Se encontró con el señor Tomás. Firmó el contrato anteayer, y compró regalos para la familia. Ayer llamó un taxi y llamó por teléfono a Pedro. **Ex.7** Pareja 1: said: 'we water-skied (esquiamos), had lunch (fuimos a comer), swam (nadamos) in the afternoon and went to a bar (estuvimos en un bar)'. Pareja 2: said: 'we went swimming (fuimos a nadar), had lunch (comimos) in the hotel, and walked (fuimos a caminar) around the town. Pareja 3: 'we went to the museums (estuvimos en los museos), ate Mexican food (cenamos comida mexicana), listened to (escuchamos) a student band'.

Práctica (pp 135–6)

A Carlos estuvo en Nerja de vacaciones. Le gustó muchísimo. La primera semana nadó mucho, tomó el sol, y un día buceó con el club local. Mari Carmen y Carlos jugaron al tenis en las pistas del hotel. ¡Ella ganó siempre! La segunda semana Carlos alquiló un coche y en dos ocasiones fueron a Sierra Nevada – esquiaron en Pradollano. ¡La sierra está a sólo 80 kilómetros de la playa! La última noche cenaron en Jardines Neptuno, un restaurante que es también una sala de fiestas de Granada. Allí bailaron en la fiesta flamenca. ¡Lo pasaron fenomenal! **B** 1f. 2d. 3e. 4b. 5c. 6a.

Unit 13

Section 1 (pp 138–9)

Ex. 2 Patricia: swimming (every evening) and volleyball (Tuesdays and Thursdays) Alberto: football and basketball (at weekends between 5 and 7 p.m.). **Ex. 3 a** At three she started to play golf; when she was five she began to be coached by Barry Willardson; at eight she won her first championship. **b** She was the youngest person to have become junior world champion and she'd won it five times. **c** Concentration and relaxation. **d** She planned to go to university and to get a grant for a golf school in the USA. **Ex. 5** Nowadays she likes swimming; when she was younger she used to like judo and gymnastics.

Section 2 (pp 140–1)

Ex.1 From 8.30 to 2:00. **b** She had lunch and dinner at home. **c** Yes. **d** She used to go out with her friends to a bar or a friend's house. **Ex. 2 a** Yes, he had a hard time. He was teased and laughed at. He was small for his age and used to have to fight to defend himself. **b** He liked James Bond films and he was a fan of Sean Connery. He used to ride and he loved basketball. **Ex. 4** He was tall, fair and very handsome. He wore glasses and was always very smart. He was strict but a good teacher and Antonia liked him. **Ex. 5 a** Era bajo y calvo. Tenía un bigote largo y andaba siempre de mal humor. Daba clases de matemáticas ¡y no entendíamos nada! **b** Era rubia y con el pelo largo. Era muy atractiva y llevaba gafas. Daba clases de geografía. **c** Era alto y tenía barba. Llevaba unas gafas muy grandes. Daba clases de francés y nos gustaba mucho.

Section 3 (pp 141–2)

Ex.1 Ahora se levanta a las ocho, antes se levantaba a las nueve. Hoy no desayuna, antes tomaba un café con leche y bollos. Ahora come sobre la una, antes comía sobre las tres. **Ex. 2 1** Antes la vida era mucho más rigurosa; ahora es menos rigurosa. **2** Antes los horarios se respetaban al máximo; ahora no se respetan tanto. **3** Antes existía la hora del almuerzo; ahora no existe el tema del almuerzo, es más elástico. **4** Antes no teníamos heladeras; ahora tenemos heladeras. **5** Antes nos bañábamos en la laguna; ahora nos bañamos en la pileta. **6** Antes el campo estaba poblado; ahora el campo está despoblado. **Ex.3** The place was quieter. There was only one restaurant and not much traffic. Nowadays there are lots of shops, restaurants and bars. Together with noise and dirt. **Ex.4** Hace 100 años: **1** no había lámparas de escritorio. **2** No había ordenadores. **3** No había coca-cola. **4** No había teléfono. **5** No había televisión. No había calefacción.

Práctica (pp 145–6)

A Cada sábado iban a jugar fútbol; a veces llegaban tarde y bastante sucios a casa, y tenían que bañarse rápidamente, porque por la noche siempre salían a tomar una copa con su familia. Era una diversión bonita, pues trabajaban mucho durante la semana y esperaban con impaciencia el partido del sábado. El domingo lo dedicaban a trabajar en el jardín, y se dormían temprano porque el lunes empezaban el trabajo de nuevo. **B 1b** Ahora tienen una casa en la ciudad; antes tenían una casa en el campo. **2c** Ahora van a la

Answer Key
(Units 13–15)

universidad; antes iban a clase en la escuela. **3a** Ahora tengo cuatro hijos; antes no tenía familia. **4c** Ahora jugamos con ordenadores; antes leíamos libros. **5d** Hoy día vemos la televisión; antes escuchabamos la radio. **C** Es un hombre entre 20 y 25 años. Es alto y delgado. Tiene el pelo moreno y largo y lleva gafas.

Unit 14

Section 1 (pp 148–9)

Ex.1 She comes from the southern hemisphere. **Ex.2** They have two seasons: dry and rainy. **Ex.5** Ecuador: En el verano, hace bastante viento y (hace) sol. Spain (Almagro): (Hace) mucho calor en verano y (hace) mucho frío en invierno – un clima continental extremo. **Ex.6 a** En Río Gallegos hace frío. **b** En San Juan hace mucho calor. **c** En Buenos Aires hace calor. **d** En Ushuaia hace frío. **e** En Jujuy hace frío y hay chaparrones. **f** En Posadas hace mucho calor. **Ex.7 a** Extremadura and Madrid. **b** El País Vasco.

Section 2 (pp 150–1)

Ex. 1 a in the towns and cities near the coast. **b** in Lleida (Lérida). **c** in Girona (Gerona) or in the north of Lleida (Lérida). **d** in Lleida and the Pyrenees. **e** in Tarragona. **Ex.2 a** En San Juan hace más calor que en Buenos Aires. **b** En Río Gallegos hace más frío que en Posadas. **c** En Buenos Aires hace más calor que en Ushuaia. **d** En el sur hace más frío que en el centro. **e** En el norte hace más calor que en el centro. **Ex.4 1** likes Buenos Aires but prefers the country. **2** the country is nicer than the town. **3** prefers seaside to mountains. **Ex. 5** e.g. **a** Oxford es más antiguo que Los Angeles. **b** Londres es más pequeño que México. **c** Nueva York es más moderno que Buenos Aires. **d** Toledo es más bonito que Los Angeles. **e** Madrid es más interesante que Barcelona. **Ex.6 a** Miguel es más alto que Federico. **b** Pilar es más guapa que Miguel. **c** Juan es más delgado que Federico. **d** Pilar tiene más pelo que Federico. **e** Federico es mayor que Pilar.

Section 3 (pp 152–3)

Ex.1 1 b. **2** a. **3** e. **4** c. **5** d. **Ex.2** El río más largo del mundo: Speaker 1 Nilo; Speaker 2 Amazonas. El país más grande de habla hispana: Speaker 1 Argentina: Speaker 2 Argentina. El país más pequeño de habla hispana: Speaker 1 República Dominicana; Speaker 2 Santo Domingo. Speaker 2 is wrong about the longest river and he is also wrong about the smallest Spanish-speaking country. **Ex.4 a** About 1,500 species. **b** About 30,000. **c** The most beautiful: Catleya Digbyana; the largest: Brassia Longissima; the smallest: Platystele. **Ex.5** El más alto es Miguel. El menor es Juan. El mayor es Federico. La más guapa es Pilar.

Práctica (p 157)

A 1 calor ... sol ... 30 grados ... tormentas. **2** viento ... frío ... 15 grados. **3** hiela ... nieva ... frío. **4** suave. Llueve ... abril. **B a** El Hotel Mar es más grande que el Playa Sol. **b** El Hotel Mar tiene más habitaciones que el Playa Sol. **c** El Hotel Mar tiene más facilidades que el Playa Sol. **d** El Hotel Playa Sol es menos caro que el hotel Mar. **e** El Hotel Mar está más cerca de la playa que el Playa Sol. **C 1**c. **2**a. **3**d.**4**b.

Unit 15

Section 1 (pp 160–1)

Ex.1 Nací en Italia; pasé a América; viví cuatro años en Estados Unidos; viví algunos años en México; trabajé como experto en Guatemala; trabajé como jefe de misión en El Salvador; pasé dos años en Guatemala; pasé tres años en El Salvador. **Ex. 2 a** Antonio Poch. **b** Jordi estudió ocho años y Antonio nueve años. **c** Jordi Moliner. **d** Jordi Moliner. Jordi: Nací en Badalona el 18 de Julio de 1957. Estudié arquitectura en la Universidad de Barcelona. Empecé la carrera en 1974 y la terminé en 1982. Me casé en 1980 y tengo dos hijos. Antonio: Nací en Badalona el 14 de abril de 1955. Estudié arquitectura en la Universidad de Barcelona. Empecé la carrera en 1973 y la terminé en 1982. Me casé en 1984 y tengo un hijo. **Ex. 3** Antonio. **Ex. 4 a** Verdadero. **b** Falso. **c** Verdadero. **d** Falso. **e** Verdadero. **f** Verdadero. **g** Verdadero. **Ex. 5** Nos visita Mario Posla, un experto de la OIT. Mario Posla nació en Italia, y luego pasó a América y se naturalizó costarricense hace veintidós años. Vivió por su trabajo en muchos países. Vivió cuatro años en Estados Unidos, de profesor en un "college" en Minesota. Luego vivió en México algunos años dedicado a la pesca del camarón, con un primo suyo. Y luego vivió en Centroamérica en varias partes. Como experto trabajó en Guatemala; En El Salvador como Jefe de Misión. Luego hizo misiones en Argentina, en Uruguay. En El Salvador pasó tres años. En Guatemala pasó dos años. **Ex.6** e.g. Javier es de Madrid pero nació en México en 1950. Pasó su niñez en México pero sus padres se trasladaron a Madrid cuando Javier tenía 12 años y desde entonces ha vivido en Madrid. Estudió la carrera de derecho en la Universidad Complutense de Madrid. Empezó a trabajar el mismo año que terminó la carrera para una firma de abogados muy famosa y se casó en 1979. Tiene tres hijos. Lucía es de Mojácar en Almería y trabaja de directora en un hotel de Mojácar. Nació en Málaga en 1953 y vivió en Málaga hasta que se casó en 1980. Estudió la carrera de turismo en la Escuela de Turismo de Málaga. Empezó a trabajar muy tarde en 1985 porque primero se dedicó a sus dos hijos.

Section 2 (pp 161–2)

Ex. 1 a 1st couple: 25 years; 2nd couple, 32 years. **b** 1st couple: in México, México Distrito Federal; 2nd couple, in Costa Rica. **c** 2nd couple met when he was visiting San José. **Ex. 2 a** ¿Cuánto tiempo hace que te casaste? **b** ¿Dónde conociste a tu marido? **c** ¿Cuánto tiempo hace que dejaste Ecuador? **d** ¿Cuánto tiempo llevas enseñando en Londres? **a** Hace tres años. **b** En una universidad en el norte de Inglaterra. **c** Hace como seis años. **d** Cerca de dos años. **Ex.3 a** They met in a doctor's surgery. **b** In September 1992 they began to be seen together and rumours of their relationship began to circulate. **c** Rocío had to have her marriage anulled; a priest refused to marry them; Ortega was gravely wounded in a bullfight. **Ex. 4** Rocío Jurado y Ortega Cano se conocieron en la consulta del doctor Mariscal en junio de 1992. El 13 de agosto Ortega asistió al cumpleaños de Rocío. Apareció en su chalé en Yerbabuena. Empezaron los rumores de un posible noviazgo. Rocío y su marido se divorciaron y Rocío solicitó la nulidad de su matrimonio. Anunciaron su boda en la Macarena para fines del año. El cura de la Macarena no aceptó casarles. Anunciaron una nueva fecha de matrimonio. En enero Ortega sufrió una herida grave en una corrida. Finalmente se casaron y ofrecieron una gran recepción en la finca Yerbabuena el 17 de febrero de 1995.

Section 3 (pp 163–4)

Ex. 1 a Verdadero. **b** Verdadero. **c** Falso. **d** Verdadero. **e** Falso. **Ex. 2** She's standing in La Plaza Mayor in Trujillo, at a spot where she can see El palacio de la Conquista and La estatua de Pizarro. **Ex. 3** Bartolomé de Las Casas; Sor Juana Inés de la Cruz; Simón Bolivar; Rubén Darío; Pablo Neruda. **Ex. 4** Bartolomé de Las Casas fue un fraile que defendió a los indígenas; nació en 1470 y murió en 1566. Sor Juana Inés de la Cruz fue una poetisa mexicana; nació en 1651 y murió en 1695. Simón Bolivar fue el libertador de América; nació en 1783 y murió en 1830. José de San Martín fue el líder de la independencia de Argentina y Chile; nació en 1778 y murió en 1850. Rubén Darío fue escritor; nació en Nicaragua en 1867 y murió en 1916. Pablo Neruda fue escritor; nació en Chile en 1904 y murió en 1973.

Práctica (pp 167–8)

A (fundarse) se fundó; (volverse) se volvió; (convertirse) se convirtió; (empezarse) se empezó; (terminarse) se terminó; (registrarse) se registró; (mandarse) se mandó; (construirse) se construyó; (liberarse) se liberó. **B 1** Espera el bus desde hace dos horas. **2** Hace cuatro horas que desayunó. **3** Hace cuatro años que se casó. **4** Espera a Manuel desde hace tres días. **5** Hace nueve meses que llegó. **C a** Ayer, vi a mi madre. **b** Llamé por teléfono a mi hermano. **c** Visité a mi tía. **d** Me encontré con mi amigo. **e** Anoche, vi a mi hermano.

Puesta a punto 3 (pp 169–70)

1 a Me encanta ir al teatro. **b** ¿Cuál es el precio de la habitación? **c** La ducha no funciona y las toallas están sucias. **d** ¿Dónde puedo conseguir las entradas? **e** Quiero una habitación individual para dos noches. **f** ¿Qué hay para ver en el cine? **g** Julia es más alta que Fernando. **2** Across: 1 pumas. 3 baloncesto. 4 tenis. 7 hielo. 8 marcar. Down: 1 pelota. 2 fútbol. 3 béisbol. 5 vela. 6 gol. **3** hizo sus estudios; luchó en la batalla; perdió un brazo; fue prisionero; regresó a España; se casó con Catalina; publicó su primera obra; murió el 23 de abril de 1616. **4** bueno, mejor, el mejor; malo, peor, el peor; pequeño, más pequeño; el más pequeño (with age: pequeño, menor, el menor); caro, más caro, el más caro. **5** En el verano: hace calor; hay tormentas; hace sol. En el otoño: hay niebla; está nublado; llueve, hace viento. En el invierno: nieva; hace mucho frío, hiela mucho. En la primavera: llueve; hace sol, etc. **6 a** vi. **b** iii. **c** i. **d** ii. **e** iv. **f** v. **7 a** ¿Qué deporte practicas/practica? **b** Tus/sus padres ¿dónde suelen ir de vacaciones? **c** ¿Cómo lo pasaste/pasó en Acapulco? **d** ¿Hace cuánto tiempo os casasteis/se casaron. **e** Quién construyó el primer submarino? **f** ¿Dónde la conociste/ conoció? **8 a** nos. **b** al. **c** nada. **d** que. **e** hace. **f** se. **g** la. **h** mayor. **9** Me llamo ... Quisiera reservar una habitación doble con ducha. Es para dos

Answer Key
(Units 15–19)

semanas, desde el ocho al veintidós de julio, media pensión. ¿Cuánto es la habitación? ¿Puedo pagar con tarjeta de crédito? ¿Me puede confirmar la reserva por escrito? Mi dirección es ... y mi número de teléfono es ...

Unit 16

Section 1 (pp 172–3)
Ex. 2 De primero: gazpacho, macarrones, dos de judías verdes; de segundo: chuletas de cordero, caldereta, cochinillo asado (a la brasa), ternera; de beber: vino. **Ex. 5 a** La sopa está buenísima. **b** El pollo está rico/el pescado está rico/la ensalada está rica. **c** El vino está muy bueno. **Ex. 6** They have got today: flan de la casa, natillas caseras, helados y fruta. They order: natillas, melón, helado de fresa con caramelo, café solo (no dessert).

Section 2 (pp 174–5)
Ex. 2 2 Español: café con leche y churros y zumo de naranja. **3** Mexicano: un vaso de leche, un par de blanquillos y frijoles. **Ex. 4** Lunch can last about 6 hours (desde las dos hasta las ocho). **Ex. 5** Ion: Pues yo al mediodía como ensalada y también como carne. María: Al mediodía normalmente como primero lentejas, garbanzos, todo tipo de legumbres y luego, carne o pescado. **Ex. 6 1** perritos calientes o hamburguesas. **2** pollo asado. **3** perritos calientes o bocadillos de tortilla.

Section 3 (pp 176–7)
Ex. 2 Se pica el perejil. Se corta la cebolla. Se pican los tomates. Se machaca el ajo. Se baten los huevos. Se cuecen las patatas. Se fríe la carne. Se calienta el aceite. Se añade sal. **Ex. 3** una cebolla grande, dos tomates medianos picados, un pepino picado, cuatro dientes de ajo, un cuarto de litro de aceite, tres cuartos de litro de agua, un chorrito de vinagre, aproximadamente cien gramos de miga de pan, sal y pimienta al gusto. **Ex. 4 1** Se machacan los ajos pelados con un poquito de sal. **2** Se añade el aceite y se bate. **3** Se añade la miga de pan previamente remojada y exprimida. **4** Se mezcla todo bien hasta formar una pasta. **5** Se añade agua fría poco a poco y se remueve. **6** Se sazona con sal y pimienta. **7** Se enfría. **8** Antes de servir, se añaden los tomates y el pepino. **Ex. 5** Se pica la cebolla. Se pelan y cortan los aguacates en trocitos. Se ralla el limón y se saca el jugo. Se pone la cebolla, el ajo, el jugo, la ralladura del limón y los aguacates en la licuadora. Se añade sal. Se sirve inmediatamente.

Práctica (pp 178–9)
A 1 manzanilla. **2** ternera. **3** jamón. **4** empanada. **5** calamares. **6** trucha. **B 1** ¡Qué asco! **2** ¡Qué suerte! **3** ¡Qué rico! **4** ¡Qué guapo! **5** ¡Qué pena! **C** 1c. 2d. 3a. 6e. 5b. 4f. **D** Se cortan los melocotones en trozos y los limones en rodajas. Se añaden todos los ingredientes en una fuente de cristal y se remueven bien. Se pone la fuente en el frigorífico. Se sirve con cubitos de hielo.

Unit 17

Section 1 (pp 182–3)
Ex. 1 1c. 2a. 3b. **Ex. 2** 1f. 2e. 3c.4d.5a. 6b. **Ex. 3** Quiere ser una gran actriz, cantar y bailar al mismo tiempo. Quisiera vivir en un pueblo de México o en una montaña. Quiere trabajar en México y después en Londres y Europa. Quisiera viajar por Europa, por India, por Egipto.
Ex. 4 a Quiere ser campeona de patinaje. **b** Quiere ser médico. **c** Le gustaría ser piloto.

Section 2 (pp 183–4)
Ex. 1 1 "Quiero ser modelo. Voy a preguntar en esta agencia." **2.** "¿Qué quisiera hacer?" "Me gustaría ser modelo." **3** "Pase al estudio entonces. Tiene que hacer un ensayo." "Muchísimas gracias." **Ex. 2** 1a. 2c. 3d 4b. **Ex. 3** Levántate. Toma el desayuno. Termina tus deberes. Bebe la leche. ¡Corre al colegio! **Ex. 4** Vaya hacia el bus. Suba. Siéntese. Espere algunos minutos. Baje otra vez.

Section 3 (pp 184–5)
Ex. 2 Cuando se siente triste: ropa negra, vestido negro, zapatos negros. En casa cuando está sola: una vieja camisa de hombre, pantalones cortos. **Ex. 3** Luisa lleva un traje rojo con un sombrero negro y zapatos negros; Jorge lleva una camiseta blanca y azul con pantalones cortos azules. **Ex. 4** Speaker 1: shorts, tee-shirt. Speaker 2: jeans, old shirt, tennis-shoes. Speaker 3 naked. **Ex. 6** Un gaucho argentino.

Práctica (p189–90)
A 1 Desenchufa la televisión. **2** Riega las plantas. **3** Saca la basura. **4** Deja las llaves a la vecina. **5** Apaga las luces. **6** ¡Cierra la puerta! **B 1** Lleve una camisa de manga larga para protegerse de los mosquitos. **2** Póngase repelente de insectos en manos y cuello. **3** Lleve un sombrero. **4** Póngase zapatos cómodos. **5** Siga al guía todo el tiempo.

Unit 18

Section 1(pp 192–3)
Ex. 1 a True. **b** False. **c** False. **Ex. 3** ¿Qué vas a hacer mañana? ¿Qué vas a hacer el viernes por la noche? ¿Qué vas a hacer el próximo fin de semana? **Ex.4 a** Mañana por la mañana voy a ir a clases y por la tarde voy a ir a la biblioteca. **b** El viernes por la noche voy a ir a la fiesta de Juan. **c** El sábado no voy a hacer nada y el domingo voy a misa y después a comer en casa de Pepe. **Ex. 5** El jueves Maite va a ir a la piscina por la mañana y va a ir a clases por la tarde. El domingo va a ir a misa y después va a comer en casa de Pepe. **Ex. 7 1** a cenar en mi casa; domingo por la noche; sí, puede. **2** un paseo en el parque; mañana por la tarde; no puede. **3** a la discoteca; viernes por la noche; sí, puede. **Ex. 8 1** go shopping. **2** go out for a drink about 6. **3** go out for a coffee about 11. **4** go to a restaurant with me.

Section 2 (pp 193–5)
Ex. 2 1 Quiero el vestido rojo. **2** Quiero la camisa blanca de lunares verdes. **3** Quiero la blusa blanca de rayas amarillas. **4** Quiero los zapatos negros. **5** Quiero la camisa azul a cuadros. **6** Quiero la bufanda azul. **7** Quiero el sombrero gris. **8** Quiero los pantalones azules. **Ex. 3 a** The red sweater in the shop window. **b** Red, navy blue, and mauve. **c** Navy blue. **d** Yes, it fits very well (me queda muy bien). **Ex. 4 1** ¿Puedo probarme este vestido negro en el probador? **2** Me queda muy corto. **3** ¿Lo tiene en azul? **4** Me queda negro, me lo llevo. **¿Qué** precio tiene? **Ex. 5 1** ¿Puedo probarme este vestido rojo? ¿Lo tienen en otros colores? **2** ¿Puedo probarme esta camisa blanca de lunares verdes? ¿La tienen en otros colores? **3** ¿Puedo probarme esta blusa blanca de rayas amarillas? ¿La tienen en otros colores? **4** ¿Puedo probarme estos zapatos negros? ¿Los tienen en otros colores **5** ¿Puedo probarme esta camisa azul a cuadros? ¿La tienen en otros colores? **5** ¿Puedo probarme esta bufanda azul? ¿La tienen en otros colores? **7** ¿Puedo probarme este sombrero gris? ¿Lo tienen en otros colores? **8** ¿Puedo probarme estos pantalones azules? ¿Los tienen en otros colores? **Ex. 6 a** un anillo de oro. **b** un vestido de lino. **c** unos zapatos de gamuza. **d** un cinturón de piel. **e** una chaqueta de lino. **f** una corbata de seda. **g** unos calcetines de lana. **h** una camisa de algodón. **i** una bufanda de lana. **j** un sombrero de paja. **Ex. 7 1** zapatillas blancas, con cordones; número 39, Reebok 65 €. **2**. cinturón de cuero, color negro, medida 80; 92 pesos.

Section 3 (pp 195-6)
Ex. 1 In Cartagena: hamacas, tambores, maracas, artesanía. In San José: cerámica, collares, cajas de madera, carretas, cuadros. **Ex. 2** una hamaca de rayas azul y blanca y un par de maracas. **Ex.3** Yes, she manages to get the *zampoña* reduced from 18 to 15 (dollars).

Práctica (pp 200–1)
A 1 No puedo, el martes voy a jugar al tenis con Marta. **2** No puedo, el miércoles voy a llevar a mis padres al aeropuerto. **3** No puedo, el jueves voy a ir de compras. **4** No puedo, el viernes tengo una reunión con mi jefe. **5** No puedo, el sábado voy a lavarme el pelo. **6** No puedo, el domingo voy a visitar a la abuelita. **B 1** ¿Quiere la camisa? Sí, la quiero/Voy a comprarla. **2** ¿Va a comprar los zapatos? No, no voy a comprarlos. **3** ¿Quiere los pantalones? No, no los quiero/No voy a comprarlos. **4** ¿Va a comprar las gafas? Sí, voy a comprarlas. **5** ¿Quiere la corbata? No, no la quiero/No voy a comprarla. **6** ¿Va a comprar las sandalias? No, no voy a comprarlas.
C Quisiera comprar una chaqueta, tengo la talla 42. Quisiera comprar una camisa, tengo la talla 39 de cuello. Quisiera comprar unos pantalones, tengo la talla 42. Quisiera comprar unos zapatos, gasto el número 40.

Unit 19

Section 1 (pp 204-5)
Ex. 1 The second person (B) seems to have spent more time at home. **Ex. 2** Luis ha dado de comer al perro y al gato. No ha regado las plantas. Ha recogido el correo. Ha abierto las ventanas. No ha sacado a pasear al perro. No ha escuchado los mensajes en el contestador automático. **Ex. 4** They are planning to see "El Pianista". **Ex. 5** ¿Has visto la nueva película James Bond? La vi el mes pasado. Pero no he visto la última película de Almodóvar.

Section 2 (pp 205-7)
Ex. 1 His sweater was blue and white and it has been handed in.

Answer Key
(Units 19–20)

Ex. 2 ¿Qué ha perdido Carme? Una chaqueta. ¿Dónde la dejó? En el andén seis, en el banco en la estación. ¿Cuándo? Ayer por la tarde. ¿A qué hora? A las seis. ¿Cómo era? De color rojo, de hilo... y forma americana, con botones dorados. ¿Lo tienen en la oficina de objetos perdidos? Sí. **Ex. 4** Los dos chicos van en una motocicleta verde. Tienen el pelo largo y liso. Uno lleva vaqueros y una camiseta azul, el otro una camiseta negra. **Ex.5** The motorbike was green (not red). One man was wearing jeans and a blue tee-shirt (not a green one). They both have straight hair (one does not have curly hair). **Ex. 6 a** Me han robado unos pendientes. Eran de oro. **b** Me han robado la mochila. Era gris y azul, grande con varios bolsillos. **c** Me han robado la maleta. Era negra con ruedas. **d** Me han robado el monedero. Era negro y llevaba muchas tarjetas de crédito. **e** Me han robado un collar. Era largo y de plata.

Section 3 (pp 207–8)
Ex. 1 1c. 2b. 3d. 4a. **Ex. 2 a** His grandmother because of the things she said and the words she used. **b** That women are in charge of the world.

Práctica (p 211)
A 1 El rey ha visitado la catedral de Sevilla. **2** Esta mañana José María Aznar se ha entrevistado con el primer ministro británico. **3** Un elefante se ha escapado del zoo municipal. **4** Hoy ha comenzado la Vuelta ciclista a España. **5** Esta semana, el director Almodóvar ha estrenado una nueva película. **6** Este mes hemos tenido escasez de agua en toda Andalucía y Levante. **B** (tener) he tenido un día terrible; (levantarse) nos hemos levantado todos tarde; (desayunar) hemos desayunado corriendo; (romper) he roto varios platos; (pararse) el coche se ha parado; (llegar) he llegado tarde al trabajo; (parar) no he parado de recibir llamadas; (hacer) no he hecho mucho trabajo; (llamar) la escuela ha llamado; (telefonear) tu madre ha telefoneado. **C** 1c. 2e. 3b. 4a. 5d.

Unit 20

Section 1 (pp 214–5)
Ex. 1 1b. 2a. 3c. 4d. **Ex. 2 1** ¡Dígame! Sí, soy yo. **2** ¿Puedo hablar con ...? **3** ¿De parte de quién? ¿Quieres dejarle algún recado? **Ex. 3 a** number 4. **b** number 1. **c** number 2. **d** number 3. **Ex. 4 1** ¡Hola! Está Pedro?/Un momento, ahora se pone. **2** ¡Hola! Está Dolores?/Dolores no está./¿Quieres dejarle algún recado?/Sí, dígale que me llame. **3** ¡Hola! Está María/Carlos?/Soy yo, ¿quién habla?/Soy... **4** ¿Está Juan? No es aquí. Se ha equivocado./Lo siento, adiós. **Ex. 5** She does not get through to him because he is on another line She decides to hold on. **Ex. 6 1** La Sra Carmen Pérez (No). **2** El Sr Figueroa (Sí).

Section 2 (pp 216–7)
Ex.1 a They'll probably be going to the beach in the morning and the cinema in the afternoon. **b** But if the weather's bad, they'll spend the morning shopping in town and go to the cinema in the afternoon. **c** They agree to meet at Ana/Noeli's house at nine o'clock. **Ex. 2 1** lunch; agreed; at 2 o'clock in the café. **2** dinner; agreed; at 8:30 outside the Astoria. **3 a** walk; not agreed; to talk again the next day or on Saturday. **Ex. 3 a** No puedo. Tengo que ir a la biblioteca. **b** No puedo. Tengo que ir al dentista. **c** No puedo. Tengo que preparar la cena. **d** No puedo. Tengo que ir al aeropuerto. **Ex. 5** Speaker 1: 5/10 minutes late; not too important. Speaker 2: punctual; it is important. Speaker 3: very punctual (the first); it is essential. Speaker 4: tries to be punctual; it is important.

Section 3 (p 218)
Ex. 1 a Thursday at 11 o'clock. **b** Viasa. **c** Phone to confirm it. **Ex. 2** On Saturday, they will go and have lunch with Pepe and Susana, (iremos a comer) then go for a walk (iremos a dar un paseo) round the harbour. In the evening they'll go to the Sanchez' house (iremos a casa de los Sánchez) as it's Julia's birthday. On Sunday morning they'll rest. Then in the afternoon their aunt Bertha will be coming (vendrá nuestra tía Berta). Then in the evening they plan to go to The Barber of Seville. **Ex. 4. a** Dejaré de fumar. **b** Dejaré de comer chocolate. **c** Visitaré París. **d** Romperé con mi novio.

Práctica (p 222)
A 1 El Sr. Jiménez preparará el café a las once y media. **2** El Sr. López llevará las cartas a Correos. **3** Paco y Luís irán a buscar a los nuevos clientes y **4** comerán con ellos en el restaurante. **5** Matías escribirá el informe para Benítez. **6** Todos tendremos permiso para terminar el trabajo a las cuatro. El miércoles estaré de nuevo en la oficina. **B** (casarse) te casarás muy pronto; (tener) tendrás diez hijos; (tocar) te tocará la lotería; (necesitar) no necesitarás trabajar más; (viajar) viajarás por todo el mundo; (visitar) visitarás a tus amigos de Finlandia; (perder) perderás todo el dinero en el casino; (saber) no sabrás qué hacer; (visitar) me visitarás otra vez.

Puesta a punto 4 (pp 224–5)
1 ¿Qué va a tomar?/De primero/de segundo plato/De acuerdo/Agua mineral/algo de postre/Muy bien. **2** Paella: pimientos, arroz, azafrán, pollo, cebollas, mariscos. Tortilla: huevos, pimientos, cebollas, patatas. Sangría: vino tinto, limonada, azúcar, limones, melocotones. **3 a** El jersey, lo quiero más largo. **b** La falda, la quiero más ancha. **c** Los zapatos, los quiero más estrechos. **d** Las camisas, las quiero más pequeñas. **e** El vestido, lo quiero más moderno. **f** La chaqueta, la quiero más grande. **4 a** Esta semana hemos jugado en Barcelona **b** El Barça ha perdido el partido ¡qué bien! **c** He marcado un gol contra el Barça. **d** Hoy han venido muchos aficionados al partido. **e** El entrenador está contento con nosotros. **f** En el entrenamiento no he jugado bien. **5 a** Sí, las han traído. **b** No, todavía no los ha llevado a mi casa. **c** No, todavía no la ha recogido. **d** Sí, la han organizado. **e** Sí, ha llegado para la fiesta. **f** Sí, la hemos hecho. **6 a** Viajaremos por Europa. **b** Conduciré un Rolls Royce. **c** Mis hijos podrán disfrutar con una nueva moto. **d** Celebraremos una gran fiesta para toda la familia. **e** No pensaré en mi trabajo, sólo en el ocio. **f** Me pondré un traje elegante. **g** Tendremos un profesor de gimnasia individual. **h** Construiré una nueva casa para la familia. **7 a** ¿Está Jaime? Soy Alicia. **iv** Hola, Alicia. ¿Qué tal? **b** Muy bien. Jaime ¿qué va a hacer el sábado? **i** voy a un concierto. Quieres venir? **c** Buena idea. ¿A qué hora es? **ii** A las siete en el Teatro Real. **d** Muy bien. ¿Quedamos de seis y media a siete? **v** Vale. Pues ¿dónde quedamos? **e** En la puerta del teatro. **iii** Muy bien. Hasta el sábado. **8 a** servicio de ambulancias. **b** servicio de asistencia en carretera. **c** servicio de autobuses. **d** servicio de Correos. **e** servicio de bomberos. **f** servicio de policía. **g** servicio de RENFE. **9 1** Primero pon yerba mate en la calabaza. **2** Incorpora un poco de agua fría. **3** Calienta agua a punto de hervor. **4** Añade el agua al mate y azúcar al gusto. **5** Bebe con la bombilla. **6** Vuelve a llenar con agua.

Grammar

1. ARTICLES

Articles are words meaning 'the', 'a', 'an'.

1.1 Definite article (Units 2, 3)

The definite article ('the') changes in Spanish according to the gender and number of the noun it accompanies.

	masculine		feminine	
singular	el el hijo	the (the son)	la la familia	the (the family)
plural	los los hijos	the (the sons)	las las familias	the (the families)

a **a + el** becomes **al**; **de + el** becomes **del**
b The definite article is used with:
  i titles of people when you are talking about them (not to them): **el señor/la señora Serrano, la señorita Montes**
  ii names of some countries: **el Perú, El Salvador, la Argentina, los Estados Unidos**
  iii names of oceans, seas, rivers, mountain ranges, etc: **el Pacífico, el Nilo, los Pirineos**
  iv names of languages: **el francés, el español**
  v the time: **las tres y media de la tarde**
  vi days of the week: **el lunes, el martes**
  vii dates: **el cinco de enero**
  viii when using nouns in a general sense:
    los hombres beben más que las mujeres
    men drink more than women
  ix with nouns used with **gustar** and **doler**: **me gusta el café; me duele la cabeza**
c When a group contains both masculine and feminine nouns, the masculine article and noun is normally used: **los hermanos** – the brothers and sisters

1.2 Indefinite article (Unit 3)

The indefinite article ('a', 'an') also varies according to number and gender:

	masculine		feminine	
singular	un un libro	the (a book)	una una casa	the (a house)
plural	unos unos libros (some books)	some	unas unas casas (some houses)	some

The indefinite article is not used:
a when describing occupations: **soy profesor** – I'm a teacher

b with adjectives **otro, medio** :
  dame otro libro – give me another book; **quiero medio kilo** – I want half a kilo
c with certain interrogative and negative sentences:
  ¿Tienes hijos? – Do you have any children? **No, no tengo hijos** - No I don't have any children

2. NOUNS (Units 2, 3)

Nouns are words used for naming people, animals, places, objects and concepts.

2.1 Gender

a In Spanish, nouns are either masculine or feminine. Many nouns end in -**o** or -**a**. Nouns ending in -**o** are usually masculine; those ending in -**a** are usually feminine: **el aparcamiento, la ventana**.
  There are some exceptions:
  la mano; la radio; la foto; el día; el clima; el mapa; el programa; el sistema; el tema.
b Names referring to people (occupations, nationalities, etc.) usually (but not always) have a masculine and a feminine form: **el funcionario/la funcionaria**
c Words ending in -**or** are usually masculine, and the feminine form is normally -**ora**: **el profesor/la profesora**
d Some nouns end in -**e**, -**ista** or with a consonant. Some of these are masculine and others feminine: **el coche** (the car), **la catedral** (the cathedral), etc. When a noun ending in -**e** or -**ista** is used to describe a person, the gender of the person is shown by the use of a masculine or feminine article: **el estudiante/la estudiante; el dentista/la dentista**

2.2 Making plurals

The plural of a noun is formed by adding -**s** when the noun ends in a vowel or -**es** when it ends in a consonant. Thus:

sing.	plural	sing.	plural
el libro	los libros	la casa	las casas
el profesor	los profesores	la catedral	las catedrales

a Some nouns normally only occur in the plural:
  e.g. **las vacaciones** (holidays); **las gafas/las lentes** (spectacles)
b Some nouns have a plural meaning but are usually used in the singular: **la gente** (people)

3. ADJECTIVES

Adjectives are words used to describe people or things.

Grammar

3.1. Agreement (Units 2, 3)

Adjective endings change to agree with the gender and number of the noun they accompany.

a Adjectives ending in **-o** for masculine nouns change to **-a** for feminine nouns (and **-os/-as** in the plural)

	masculine	feminine
singular	un vestido bonito	una casa bonita
plural	los libros viejos	las mesas largas

b Adjectives ending in a consonant or in **-e** do not change except with a plural noun.

	masculine	feminine
singular	el campo verde	la ventana azul
plural	los campos verdes	las ventanas azules

c Adjectives of nationality ending in a consonant add **-a** for the feminine form: **inglés/inglesa**; **español/española**, etc.

3.2 Position of adjectives

a Adjectives usually come after the words they describe:
un barrio tranquilo   a quiet district
b Some common adjectives, such as **bueno** and **malo**, often occur before the noun. In front of a masculine singular noun, they are shortened to **buen/mal**:

feminine	una buena película	a good film
masculine	un buen chico	a good lad

Other adjectives which have a shortened form include **grande**, **primero**, **tercero**, **ninguno** and **alguno**:
algún amigo   some/one friend
el tercer piso   the third floor

c A few adjectives have different meanings when placed before or after the noun:

la pobre señora	the poor (wretched) woman
la señora pobre	the poor (penniless) woman
el gran hombre	the great man
el hombre grande	the big man

3.3 Possessive adjectives (Unit 2)

Possessive adjectives express ownership or possession. As they are adjectives, they agree with the noun they refer to in both number and gender.

singular	plural	
mi	mis	my
tu	tus	your (informal)
su	sus	your (formal), his/her/its
nuestro/a	nuestros/as	our
vuestro/a	vuestros/as	your (informal)
su	sus	your (formal), their

e.g. **mis padres** – my parents; **tu hermana** – your sister; **su perro** – his/her/your/their dog; **nuestra casa** – our house; **vuestra madre** – your mother; **sus libros** – his/her/their books

Possessive adjectives are not used with parts of the body in Spanish. You say:
Me duele la espalda   My back aches

3.4 Demonstrative adjectives (Unit 5)

These are words used to define someone/something in terms of where he/she/it is in relation to the speaker. In Spanish there are three forms: **este** (this), **ese** (that), **aquel** (that one further away). As adjectives, they agree with the noun in gender and number.

	singular (this, that)	plural (these, those)
masc.	este, ese, aquel	estos, esos, aquellos
fem.	esta, esa, aquella	estas, esas, aquellas

Este/ese hotel es el mejor de la ciudad
This/that hotel is the best in the city
Aquella mujer es mi hermana
That woman is my sister

For Demonstrative pronouns see para 4.6

3.5 Comparison of adjectives (Unit 14)

a Comparatives are normally formed by putting **más/menos** before an adjective. Superlatives are formed by putting **el/la/los/las más/menos** before the adjective. Thus:

	comparative	superlative
moderno modern	más moderno/a(s) more modern	el/la/los/las más moderno/a(s) the most modern
pequeño/a small	más pequeño/a(s) smaller	el/la/los/las más pequeño/a(s) the smallest
grande big	más grande bigger	el/la/los/las más grande(s) the biggest

i To say 'more/less'... 'than' you say **más/menos ... que**:
El hotel Sol es más moderno que el hotel Sombra
The Sol Hotel is more modern than than the Sombra Hotel
ii To say something is 'the most...' or 'the largest of all', you say:
El hotel Sol es el más moderno de todos
The Sol Hotel is the most modern
iii To say 'more/less'... 'than' referring to quantity you say **más/menos de**:
Esta camisa cuesta menos de cincuenta pesos.
This shirt costs less than 50 pesos.

Grammar

b **Bueno** and **malo** have irregular comparative and superlative forms:

bueno/a(s)	mejor	el/la/los/las mejor(es)
good	better	the best
malo/a(s)	peor(es)	el/la/los/las peor(es)
bad	worse	the worst

c **Grande** and **pequeño** have different comparative and superlative forms when they refer to differences in ages:

grande(s)	mayor	el/la/los/las mayor(es)
old	older	oldest
pequeño/a(s)	menor	el/la/los/las menor(es)
young	younger	youngest

Note: You can also express the idea that something is very good, bad, etc, by adding **-ísimo** or **-ísima**:
El clima del Caribe es buenísimo.
The Caribbean climate is very good.

4. PRONOUNS

Pronouns are words used to stand in for a noun.

4.1 Subject pronouns (Unit 1)

yo	I
tú	you (informal singular)
usted	you (formal singular)
él	he
ella	she
nosotros/as	we
vosotros/as	you (informal plural, Sp)
ustedes	you (formal plural, Sp; formal & informal, LA)
ellos, ellas	they

a Subject pronouns are often omitted in Spanish because the verb endings clearly indicate the subject of the verb. They are used only where there is need for clarification, or for emphasis.
b In writing, **usted** and **ustedes** will often be shortened to **Ud** or **Vd**, **Uds** or **Vds**.
c **Ustedes** is the usual plural form in southern Spain and Latin America, where **vosotros** is not often used.
d In parts of Latin America there is a pronoun **vos** which is another form for **tú**.

4.2 Reflexive pronouns (See reflexive verbs, para. 9.3)

4.3 Direct object pronouns (Unit 15, 18)

These replace the object of the verb and agree in gender and number.

singular		plural	
me	me	nos	us
te	you (informal)	os	you (informal)
lo/le*	you (formal)/him	los/les*	you (formal)/them (masc. people)
lo	it (masc)	los	them (masc. objects)
la	you (formal)/her	las	you (formal)/them (fem. people & objects)

* In some parts of Spain and Latin America, the forms **le** and **les** are usually used.
¿Quiere comprar las camisas? – Sí, las compro
Do you want to buy the shirts? – Yes, I'll buy them
¿Dónde está Juan? – No lo/le veo
Where is Juan? – I don't see him
Lo/le conozco muy bien. I know him very well.

4.4 Indirect object pronouns (Unit 20)

a These stand for a person who is the indirect object of a verb, often the beneficiary of an action.

me	(to) me	nos	(to) us
te	(to) you	os	(to) you
le	(to) you (formal)/(to) him/her	les	(to) you (formal)/(to) them

Me ha escrito una carta
He has written a letter to me
María le da el libro
María gives him/her the book

b Indirect object pronouns are also used with the verbs **gustar** and **doler**. See also para. 16.
Me gusta el café I like coffee
Le duele la espalda His back aches

Note: in order to avoid ambiguity, or when you want to emphasise who you are referring to, you can add **a** plus the name of the person or one of the following pronouns.

a mí	a nosotros	a tí	a vosotros
a usted	a ustedes	a él/ella	a ellos/ellas

A mí me dio un regalo, a ella no le dio nada He gave me a present, he gave her nothing
A mí me gusta el café I like coffee
A Juan le duele la espalda Juan's back is hurting him

4.5 Position of object pronouns (Unit 18)

a Object Pronouns mostly go before the verb. However, they join on to the end of the verb when it is in the imperative form:
¡Bébelo! Drink it! **¡Háblame!** Speak to me!
b When they occur with two verbs, one of which is in an infinitive, they can either come before the first

Grammar

verb, or they can be added on to the infinitive:
Puede llamarnos/Nos puede llamar You can ring us
Voy a buscarlo/Lo voy a buscar I'm going to look for it

4.6 Demonstrative pronouns

a   Demonstrative pronouns – **éste**, **ése**, **aquél**, etc. – stand in place of a noun (this one, that one, etc.). They often have an accent to distinguish them from demonstrative adjectives. (See Table in para 3.4)
¿Cuál es tu coche? Es aquél, el rojo
Which is your car. It's that one, the red one
b   The neutral form: **esto**, **eso**, **aquello** – may be used when the noun is not specified.
¿Qué es esto? What's this?
Eso no me importa That doesn't matter to me

4.7 Indefinite pronouns

| algo | something | nada | nothing |
| alguien | someone/anyone | nadie | nobody |

If **nada** or **nadie** come after the verb, **no** must come before it.
¿Quieres tomar algo? Would you like to have something?
No, gracias, no quiero tomar nada No thanks, I don't want anything
¿Hay alguien en la casa? Is there anyone at home?
No, no hay nadie No, there is nobody (in)

5. QUESTION WORDS

¿Adónde?	Where (to)?	¿Adónde vamos?
¿Cómo?	How?	¿Cómo estás?
¿Cuál?	Which?	¿Cuál es mi cama?
¿Cuándo?	When?	¿Cuándo llegamos a Cancún?
¿Cuánto?	How much?	¿Cuánto cuestan las jarapas?
¿Cuántos/as?	How many?	¿Cuántos plátanos quiere?
¿De dónde?	Where (from)?	¿De dónde eres?
¿Dónde?	Where?	¿Dónde está el banco?
¿Por qué?	Why?	¿Por qué estudias español?
¿Qué?	What?	¿Qué haces?
¿Quién?	Who?	¿Quién vive en Madrid?

Question words always have an accent even when they are quoted indirectly.
No me quiere decir quién es. He won't tell me who he is.

6. ADVERBS

Adverbs are words used to describe a verb – how you do something or how something is done. Unlike adjectives, they do not change their form.

6.1 Formation of adverbs

Adverbs are normally formed by adding **-mente** to the feminine form of the adjective:

| rápido | rápidamente | quickly |
| lento | lentamente | slowly |

6.2 Irregular adverbs

bien	well
demasiado	too much
mal	badly
bastante	quite, enough
más	more
poco	a little
menos	less
mucho	a lot, much
muy	very

Some adverbs do not end in **-mente**. These include:
a   **Muy** can be used with an adjective or another adverb.
Estamos muy cansados. We are very tired.
Pedro está muy bien. Pedro is well.
b   **Mucho** can be used with a verb, an adjective, or another adverb:
Fuma mucho He smokes a lot.
El canta mucho mejor He sings much better.
Este vestido es mucho más caro This dress is much more expensive.
c   **Poco**, **mucho**, **bastante** and **demasiado**, may also be used as adjectives to describe a noun. When this is the case, they follow the same rules as other adjectives and change their endings according to the gender and number of the noun.

7. PREPOSITIONS

Prepositions are words usually placed before a noun or its equivalent to mark some relation.

7.1 'a'

a   to (in the direction of): **a Madrid, a mi casa** to Madrid, to my house
b   at (in expressions of time): **a las cuatro** at 4 o'clock

7.2 'de'

a   from: **ella es de Madrid** ... from Madrid
b   made of: **la falda es de lana** ... made of wool
c   of (indicating possession): **es el coche de Juan** ... John's car

Grammar

7.3 'en'

a   in: **ellos están en la sala** ... in the sitting room
b   on: **el libro está en la mesa** ... on the table

7.4 'por'

a   through: **pasas por el túnel** ... through the tunnel
b   along: **sigues por esta calle** ... along this street
c   in (with expressions of time): **por la mañana** in the morning
d   per: **por noche** per night; **por ciento** per cent
e   around: **¿hay un parque por aquí?** ... around here

7.5 'para'

a   for: **este vino es para mí** ... for me
b   in order to: **como para vivir** ... in order to live
c   for (in the direction of): **el tren sale hoy para Cuzco** ... for Cuzco

8. CONJUNCTIONS

Conjunctions are words that connect two sentences or parts of a sentence together.

8.1 'y'

and: **tú y yo** you and I
Before words beginning with **i**, **y** becomes **e**:
Pilar e Isabel ... and Isabel

8.2 'o'

or: **voy a visitar Sevilla o Córdoba** ... Sevilla or Córdoba
Before a word beginning with **o**, **o** becomes **u**:
visitaré un sitio u otro ... or the other

8.3 'pero'

but: **Es de España pero vive en Londres**
... but she lives in London

VERBS

Verbs are words which denote physical or mental actions or states.

Verb groups (Conjugations)

All Spanish verbs belong to one of three verb groups (or conjugations), defined by whether the infinitive ends in -**ar**, -**er** or -**ir**. The -**ar** verbs are the largest group.

9. PRESENT TENSE (Units 1–6)

9.1 Formation

This tense is formed by removing the -**ar**/-**er**/-**ir** and adding the following endings to the stem of the verb.

	-ar	-er	-ir
	comprar	comer	vivir
	(to buy)	(to eat)	(to live)
yo	compro	como	vivo
tú	compras	comes	vives
él/ella/Vd	compra	come	vive
nosotros/as	compramos	comemos	vivimos
vosotros/as	compráis	coméis	vivís
ellos-as/Vds	compran	comen	viven

9.2 Radical-changing verbs (Units 5, 10)

In some verbs the vowel in the verb stem changes when the verb is conjugated. (See para. 17 for a fuller list.)
a   There is no vowel change in the 1st and 2nd pers. pl.
b   **Jugar** is the only example of **u** changing to **ue**.
c   The verb endings are the normal ones.

e/ie	e/i	o/ue	u/ue
empezar	seguir	dormir	jugar
(to begin)	(to follow)	(to sleep)	(to play)
empiezo	sigo	duermo	juego
empiezas	sigues	duermes	juegas
empieza	sigue	duerme	juega
empezamos	seguimos	dormimos	jugamos
empezáis	seguís	dormís	jugáis
empiezan	siguen	duermen	juegan

9.3 Reflexive verbs (Unit 6)

Reflexive verbs always have a reflexive pronoun – **levantarse**, **bañarse**, etc. They have the same endings as the group to which they belong, but the pronoun changes according to the person doing the action.

me	nos
te	os
se (for **usted**, **él**, **ella**)	se (for **ustedes**, **ellos**, **ellas**)

bañarse	ponerse	irse
(to bathe)	(to put on)	(to go away)
me baño	me pongo	me voy
te bañas	te pones	te vas
se baña	se pone	se va
nos bañamos	nos ponemos	nos vamos
os bañáis	os ponéis	os vais
se bañan	se ponen	se van

Grammar

9.4 Irregular verbs: ser and estar

Some verbs do not follow the normal pattern in some way. A list of irregular verbs is given below (para. 18), but among those in common use are two which mean 'to be':

ser	estar
soy	estoy
eres	estás
es	está
somos	estamos
sois	estáis
son	están

9.5 Uses of ser and estar (Units 7,8)

Ser is used for:
a Nationality: **Gloria Estefán es cubana**
b Occupations: **Jaime es médico**
c Description of places and objects: **El salón es espacioso**
d Description of people: **Juan es alto y simpático**
e The time: **Son las cuatro y media**
f Marital status (LA): **Soy soltero; soy casado**
g Events: **El concierto es en el Teatro Real**

Estar is used:
a To indicate location/position: **El banco está enfrente de la farmacia**
b To describe physical state and mood: **María está enferma y deprimida**
c With past participles: **La habitación está reservada**
d For marital status (Sp): **Estoy soltero; estoy casado**

9.6 Present continuous

The present continuous is formed by joining the verb **estar** and the present participle of the verb. The present participle is formed by taking the stem of the verb (infinitive minus the ending) and adding:

-ando	for -ar verbs
-iendo	for -er verbs
-iendo	for -ir verbs

Estoy preparando la cena I am getting the dinner ready
El tren está llegando The train is arriving

a Radical-changing verbs do not as a rule change their stems in this tense, with the exception of the **e/i** group:
   está diciendo he is saying; **está sonriendo** he's smiling
b **dormir** (**durmiendo**) and **morir** (**muriendo**) have irregular participles.

9.7 Uses of the present continuous

a To describe something that is happening as you speak.
   Está lloviendo it's raining
b To emphasise something that is going on over a period of time.
   Ana está trabajando en una fábrica Anne is working in a factory

10. PRETERITE TENSE (Units 12,15)

10.1 Formation

The preterite tense is formed by adding the following endings to the stem:

comprar	comer	vivir
compré	comí	viví
compraste	comiste	viviste
compró	comió	vivió
compramos	comimos	vivimos
comprasteis	comisteis	vivisteis
compraron	comieron	vivieron

10.2 Irregular Verbs

Among the common verbs that are irregular in the preterite are **ser** and **ir** which share the same form, **estar** and **hacer** (to do).

estar	hacer	ser/ir
estuve	hice	fui
estuviste	hiciste	fuiste
estuvo	hizo	fue
estuvimos	hicimos	fuimos
estuvisteis	hicisteis	fuisteis
estuvieron	hicieron	fueron

10.3 Uses of the preterite

a To talk about what someone did, or to describe an event (or sequence of events) that occurred at a specific time in the past:
   Anoche cené en el restaurante
   Last night I had dinner in the restaurant
b To talk about historical events:
   Salvador Allende fue el presidente de Chile
   Salvador Allende was President of Chile
c If you want to say how long ago something happened you say:
   Me casé hace cinco años
   I got married five years ago

Grammar

11. IMPERFECT TENSE (Unit 13)

11.1 Formation

The imperfect is formed by adding the following endings to the stem:

comprar	comer	vivir
(to buy)	(to eat)	(to live)
compraba	comía	vivía
comprabas	comías	vivías
compraba	comía	vivía
comprábamos	comíamos	vivíamos
comprábais	comíais	vivíais
compraban	comían	vivían

11.2 Irregular imperfect

Among the irregular imperfects are:

ser	ver	ir
(to be)	(to see)	(to go)
era	veía	iba
eras	veías	ibas
era	veía	iba
éramos	veíamos	íbamos
érais	veíais	íbais
eran	veían	iban

11.3 Uses of the imperfect

There are three main situations in which the imperfect tense is used:

a To describe what was going on over time, without indicating when it started or finished:
   Cuando era joven, vivía en Bilbao
   When I was young, I lived in Bilbao
b To speak about habits in the past:
   Salía de casa a las nueve cada sábado
   I used to leave the house at nine every Saturday
c To describe someone or something in the past:
   Su madre era alta y bonita
   Her mother was tall and pretty

12. PERFECT TENSE (Unit 19)

12.1 Formation

The perfect tense is formed by using part of the auxiliary verb **haber** with the past participle of the verb, which is invariable. The past participle is formed by adding the following endings to the stem of the verb:

-ado	-ar verbs
-ido	-er verbs
-ido	-ir verbs

he trabajado	hemos bebido
has comprado	habéis vivido
ha comido	han dormido

12.2 Irregular past participles

Some participles are irregular. Here are some common ones:

abrir	abierto	morir	muerto
decir	dicho	poner	puesto
escribir	escrito	romper	roto
freir	frito	ver	visto
hacer	hecho		

12.3 Uses of the perfect

The Perfect tense is used to talk about the recent past. In some areas of Latin America the Preterite is more commonly used for the same purpose.
He terminado los deberes
I have finished my homework

13. THE FUTURE (Unit 20)

13.1 Future tense

The future tense is formed by adding the following endings to the infinitive.

comprar	comer	vivir
compraré	comeré	viviré
comprarás	comerás	vivirás
comprará	comerá	vivirá
compraremos	comeremos	viviremos
compraréis	comeréis	viviréis
comprarán	comerán	vivirán

Llegaremos mañana temprano
We'll arrive early tomorrow

13.2 Irregular future tense

Some verbs are irregular in the future, but only in the stem, not in the endings. Here are some common ones:

decir	diré	querer	querré
haber (hay)	habrá	saber	sabré
hacer	haré	salir	saldré
poder	podré	tener	tendré
poner	pondré	venir	vendré

13.3 Other ways of talking obout the future

Another way of forming a future tense is to use the verb **ir** in the appropriate person + infinitive.
Vamos a llegar mañana temprano
We're going to arrive early tomorrow
El sábado va a llover
It's going to rain on Saturday

Grammar

Note: With reflexive verbs the verb is in the infinitive but the pronoun changes according to the person speaking.
Voy a levantarme a las ocho.

14. IMPERATIVE FORM
14.1 Formation (Unit 17)

The imperative is used to tell someone to do something. It has both a formal and informal form.
a The imperative for **tú** is formed by removing the **-s** from the second person singular of the present tense;
b The imperative for **usted** is formed by changing the ending of the 3rd person singular as follows:
from **-a** to **-e** (for **-ar** verbs)
from **-e** to **-a** (for **-er** and **-ir** verbs)

	tú	usted
comprar	compra	compre
beber	bebe	beba
vivir	vive	viva

14.2 Irregular imperatives

Irregular imperatives include the following:

	decir	tener	ir	venir	hacer	poner	ser
tú	di	ten	ve	ven	haz	pon	sé
usted	diga	tenga	vaya	venga	haga	ponga	sea

14.3 Reflexive verbs in the imperative

Reflexive verbs form their imperative in the same way as other verbs but the pronoun is added to the end to make a single word.

	tú	usted
levantarse	levántate	levántese
bañarse	báñate	báñese

Note that the stress changes with the additional syllable added, and that the accent must be written in.

15. USING 'SE' (Units 10, 16)

a **Se** is sometimes used where in English we use the passive or there is no specific subject:
Se habla español en México
Spanish is spoken in Mexico
Se puede fumar en el tren
You may smoke/Smoking is permitted on the train
b To relay instructions to someone, you can also use **se**:
Se pelan las patatas
You peel the potatoes

16. GUSTAR AND DOLER (Units 8 and 9)

Gustar and **doler** have only two forms: in the present tense these are **gusta/duele** for the singular and **gustan/duelen** for the plural.

Me gusta el té	I like tea
Me duele la cabeza	I have a headache
Me gustan las novelas	I like novels
Me duelen las piernas	My legs ache

a Definite articles (**el, la, los, las**) are used with nouns that occur with these verbs.
b The singular form is used when these verbs are followed by another verb:
Me gusta escuchar la radio
c Other verbs that follow this pattern include: **encantar** (to love something, to love doing something) and **apetecer** (to want something, to feel like doing something)
See also para. 4.4 for indirect object pronouns.

17. SOME COMMON RADICAL-CHANGING VERBS

(See para. 9.2 for the formation of these verbs)

o/ue

acordarse de to remember
almorzar to have lunch
cocer to cook
contar to tell (a story); to count
costar to cost
doler to hurt
dormir to sleep
encontrar to meet; to find
llover to rain
morir to die
poder to be able
recordar to remember
soler to usually do
soñar to dream
volver to return

u/ue

jugar to play

e/ie

cerrar to close
calentar to heat
despertarse to wake up
empezar to begin, start
hervir to boil
pensar to think
preferir to prefer
querer to love, to want, to wish
sentarse to sit down
sentir to feel
tener to have
venir to come

e/i

conseguir to get
convertirse to convert
decir to say
despedirse to say goodbye
freír to fry
pedir to ask for
seguir to follow; to continue
servir to serve
vestirse to dress

Grammar

18. SOME COMMON IRREGULAR VERBS

PRES	PRET	IMP	FUT	PERF	IMPER
dar					
doy	di	daba	daré	he dado	da
das	diste	etc.	etc.	etc.	dé
da	dio				
damos	dimos				
dais	disteis				
dan	dieron				
decir					
digo	dije	decía	diré	he dicho	di
dices	dijiste	etc.	dirás	etc.	diga
dice	dijo		dirá		
decimos	dijimos		diremos		
decís	dijisteis		diréis		
dicen	dijeron		dirán		
estar					
estoy	estuve	estaba	estaré	he estado	
estás	estuviste	etc.	etc.	etc.	
está	estuvo				
estamos	estuvimos				
estáis	estuvisteis				
están	estuvieron				
hacer					
hago	hice	hacía	haré	he hecho	haz
haces	hiciste	etc.	harás	etc.	haga
hace	hizo		hará		
hacemos	hicimos		haremos		
hacéis	hicisteis		haréis		
hacen	hicieron		harán		
ir					
voy	fui	iba	iré	he ido	ve(te)
vas	fuiste	ibas	etc.	etc	vaya(se)
va	fue	iba			
vamos	fuimos	íbamos			
vais	fuisteis	íbais			
van	fueron	iban			
poder					
puedo	pude	podía	podré	he podido	
puedes	pudiste	etc.	podrás	etc.	
puede	pudo		podrá		
podemos	pudimos		podremos		
podéis	pudisteis		podréis		
pueden	pudieron		podrán		

PRES	PRET	IMP	FUT	PERF	IMPER
querer					
quiero	quise	quería	querré	he querido
quieres	quisiste	etc.	querrás	etc.	
quiere	quiso		querrá		
queremos	quisimos		querremos		
queréis	quisisteis		querréis		
quieren	quisieron		querrán		
saber					
sé	supe	sabía	sabré	he sabido	
sabes	supiste	etc.	sabrás	etc.	
sabe	supo		sabrá		
sabemos	supimos		sabremos		
sabéis	supisteis		sabréis		
saben	supieron		sabrán		
ser					
soy	fui	era	seré	he sido	sé
eres	fuiste	eras	etc.	etc.	sea
es	fue	era			
somos	fuimos	éramos			
sois	fuisteis	érais			
son	fueron	eran			
tener					
tengo	tuve	tenía	tendré	he tenido	ten
tienes	tuviste	etc.	tendrás	etc.	tenga
tiene	tuvo		tendrá		
tenemos	tuvimos		tendremos		
tenéis	tuvisteis		tendréis		
tienen	tuvieron		tendrán		
volver					
vuelvo	volví	volvía	volveré	he vuelto	vuelve
vuelves	volviste	etc.	etc.	etc.	vuelva
vuelve	volvió				
volvemos	volvimos				
volvéis	volvisteis				
vuelven	volvieron				

Transcripts
(Units 0–3)

Unit 0
Section 2
4 (p. 3)
1. – Buenos días.
   – Buenos días.
2. – ¡Hola! ¿Qué tal?
   – Bien gracias. ¿Y tú?
   – Bien también.
3. – Buenas tardes, señor.
   – Buenas tardes. ¿Cómo está usted?
4. – ¡Hola! ¿Cómo estás?
   – ¡Hola! Muy bien.
5. – ¡Hola! Buenas noches.
   – Buenas noches, señora.

Unit 1
Section 1
5 (p. 7)
1. – ¿Cómo te llamas?
   – Me llamo Matilde Muro.
2. – ¿Cuál es su nombre?
   – Mi nombre es Hernán Sierra Nieto.
3. – ¿Cómo se llama?
   – Yo me llamo José Julio Toaquiza Vega.

8 (p. 7)
– ¿Cómo se llama?
– Yo me llamo Blanca Margarita Bojorquez, viuda de Ferros.
– ¿Es un nombre típico de aquí?
– Es un apellido español.
– ¿Y cómo se escribe?
– B-O-J-O-R-Q-U-E-Z – Bojorquez.

Section 2
2 (p. 8)
– Pues, se encuentra Venezuela, Costa Rica, Ecuador, Chile, eh, Panamá, Guatemala, Uruguay, Paraguay, eh, Argentina, México...

3 (p. 8)
– ¿Cómo te llamas?
– Yo soy Claudia Patiño
– Y ¿De dónde eres?
– Soy de México y vivo en México D.F.

5 (p. 9)
1. – Me llamo Adriana Larrañaga.
   – ¿De dónde eres y dónde vives actualmente?
   – Nací en la Ciudad de México y vivo aquí en la Ciudad de México.
2. – Me llamo Silvia Poll.
   – ¿Y de dónde eres?
   – Soy de San José, Costa Rica.
3. – Me llamo Alicia Carolina Tejada.
   – ¿Dónde vives?
   – Vivo en San Francisco, California, en Oakland.
   – ¿Y de dónde eres?
   – Soy del Salvador.
4. – Buenos días.
   – Eh ¿cómo te llamas?
   – Me llamo Carmen.
   – ¿Y de dónde eres?
   – Soy de Salamanca.
   – ¿Y dónde vives?
   – Vivo en Salamanca también.
5. – Buenas tardes.
   – Buenas tardes.
   – ¿Cómo se llama?
   – Carmen Rosa.
   – ¿De dónde es usted?
   – De Chile, de Viña del Mar.
   – ¿Dónde vive?
   – En Madrid.

Section 3
5 (p. 10)
1. – ¡Hola! Buenas tardes. ¿Cómo te llamas?
   – Me llamo Begoña.
   – ¿De dónde eres?
   – Soy del País Vasco.
   – Y ¿qué idiomas hablas?
   – Hablo vasco y hablo español también.
2. – ¿Cómo te llamas?
   – Me llamo Linda. Soy de Suecia. Hablo sueco, inglés y un poquito de alemán y español.
3. – ¿Cómo te llamas?
   – Me llamo Fátima.
   – Y ¿de dónde eres?
   – Soy de un pueblo de Salamanca.
   – Y ¿qué lenguas hablas?
   – Pues ... claro, hablo español, hablo portugués, francés.
4. – Me llamo Simona. Soy de Italia. Hablo español, francés e italiano.

Un paso más
3 (p. 14)
– Me llamo Ion. I latina O– N. Soy del País Vasco. Vivo en San Sebastián. Hablo el euskera y el español.

Unit 2
Section 1
6 (p. 16)
1. – ¿Cómo te llamas?
   – Me llamo Simona.
   – ¿De dónde eres?
   – Soy de Italia.
2. – ¿Cómo te llamas?
   – Me llamo Linda.
   – ¿De dónde eres?
   – Soy de Suecia.
3. – ¿Cómo te llamas?
   – Me llamo Stephen.
   – ¿De dónde eres?
   – Soy de California, en los Estados Unidos.
4. – Mi nombre es Martín... Soy argentino, de Buenos Aires.
5. – ¿Cómo te llamas?
   – Me llamo Begoña.
   – ¿De dónde eres?
   – Soy del País Vasco.

Section 2
3 (p. 17)
1. – Mi nombre es Marco Antonio Castillo Morán... Soy médico.
2. – Me llamo Cristina Pereira... soy pintora...
3. – Felipe Briceño para servirle.
   – ¿En qué trabajas?
   – Soy carpintero de obra.
4. – Mi nombre es Marisa. Secretaria, 29 años en el consulado de Brasil.
5. – Hola, me llamo Mónica Patiño. Soy mexicana. Vivo en México D.F. Soy cocinera.
6. – ¿Cómo te llamas?
   – Andrés Macis.
   – Y ¿a qué te dedicas?
   – Yo soy estudiante.

8 (p.18)
1. – ¿Cómo te llamas?
   – Me llamo Sandra Patricia Tejada.
   – Y ¿a qué te dedicas?
   – Yo trabajo y estudio a la misma vez. Trabajo en una óptica y estudio para enfermería.
2. – ¿Cómo te llamas?
   – Me llamo Yaseña González.
   – ¿A qué te dedicas?
   – Estudiante y trabajo también. Estudio administración de empresas y estudio... trabajo de recepcionista.
3. – Me llamo Alicia Carolina Tejada... Trabajo y estudio. Estudio el diseño y la decoración, y trabajo cuidando tres niños.

Section 3
5 (p. 20)
1. – ¡Hola! Te presento a Dolores...
   – Encantado.
2. – Sr. Gómez, le presento a la Sra. Ruiz.
   – Mucho gusto.
3. – Juan, éste es Manuel.
   – ¡Hola! ¿Qué tal?
4. – Amalia, le presento a Magali.
   – Encantada.

8 (p. 20)
– Mi nombre es Esperanza Andrango Flores.
– ¿Tienes familia?
– Tengo tres hijos y soy sola.
– ¿Cuántos años tienen tus hijos?
– El uno tiene doce, la otra tiene diez y el otro tiene tres años.

Un paso más
2 (p. 24)
1. – Mi nombre es Sheila. Yo soy nacida en Perú y estoy viviendo en California .... Estudio para administración.
2. – Mi nombre es Esteban Cortijo. Trabajo como profesor de Filosofía. Soy español. Nací en la provincia de Cáceres.
3. – Me llamo Carmen. Soy de Salamanca. Trabajo como secretaria. Vivo en Salamanca.

Unit 3
Section 1
4 (p. 27)
1. – ¡Hola!
   – ¡Hola! Es grande, pues que es un barrio bonito... es muy acogedor.
2. – Antiguo, bonito y muy, muy, muy aburrido.
3. – Bonito, bonito y bonito.

6 (p. 27)
1. – México en tres palabras ... es bonito, es muy divertido ... es muy cálido.
2. – ¿Cómo se llama la ciudad donde vives?
   – La ciudad donde vivo se llama San Sebastián.
   – ¿La puedes describir solamente en tres palabras?
   – Sí. Es una ciudad muy grande, muy turística, ... y muy famosa.
3 – Almagro es un pueblo turístico, también es artístico porque tiene, tiene varios monumentos... es un pueblo antiguo, artístico.

Section 2
2 (p. 28)
– ¿Cuántos edificios puedes nombrar?
– El Ayuntamiento, el hotel, la oficina de Correos, la Casa de Cultura, el juzgado, el bar, el hospital, el teatro, el cine, la residencia, la casa de ancianos.

Transcripts
(Units 3–5)

Section 3
4 (p. 31)
1. – Perdone. ¿Hay un supermercado por aquí?
   – Sí, hay uno en la calle Santa Ana.
2. – ¿Sabe si hay un restaurante cerca de aquí?
   – Sí, hay uno en la calle Chuauhtemoc.
3. – ¿Me puede decir si hay una platería por aquí?
   – Sí, hay una en la avenida John F. Kennedy.
4. – ¿Hay una farmacia por aquí?
   – Sí, hay una en la calle de Chuauhtemoc.
5. – ¿Hay un Mercado de artesanías cerca de aquí?
   – Sí, hay uno en la calle San Nicolás.

Un paso más
1 (p. 36)
– ¿Cómo se llama la ciudad donde vives?
– La ciudad donde vivo se llama San Sebastián.
– Y ¿puedes describírmela?
– Sí. Es una ciudad muy grande, muy turística que está al lado del mar. Tiene muchos edificios importantes, y desde lo alto de los montes tiene unas vistas muy bonitas.
– ¿Qué piensas de tu ciudad?
– Pienso que es muy famosa, sobre todo por unos acontecimientos como son el festival de cine, por las playas, por su parte vieja, la catedral.
– ¿Cuántos edificios diferentes puedes nombrar?
– Por ejemplo, la Casa de Cultura, el Ayuntamiento, la iglesia, el convento, la casa de los municipales, el restaurante, los bares, el hotel, la cafetería, el polideportivo, las escuelas, la facultad...

Unit 4

Section 1
4 (p. 39)
– ¿Dónde está Correos?
– Está enfrente del hotel.
– ¿Dónde está la iglesia?
– Está en la esquina, enfrente del convento.
– ¿Dónde está el estanco?
– Está al lado de la lavandería.

5 (p. 39)
– ¿Dónde está el museo?
– Cerca del hotel.
– ¿Dónde está la iglesia de San Pedro?
– Está en la Plaza de San Pedro – a dos calles de aquí.
– ¿Dónde está el teatro Cervantes?
– Está enfrente del hotel.
– ¿Dónde está la oficina de turismo?
– Está muy lejos.

Section 2
5 (p. 40)
– Y amigos, los cinco números premiados son el veintiocho, ... veintiocho, el cuarenta y cuatro, repito, el cuarenta y cuatro, el sesenta y seis, el sesenta y seis; el treinta y nueve ... treinta y nueve... y el número diecisiete, el diecisiete. Y ahora... el número mayor es el... ochenta y ocho, el ochenta y ocho. Y el premio para el ganador es un viaje para dos a la capital de España y excursiones a Toledo y otros lugares de interés cerca de Madrid.

7 (p. 41)
– ¿A qué distancia están estos lugares de Madrid? ¿Están cerca?
– Sí. El Escorial, por ejemplo, está muy cerca, a 49 kilómetros al noroeste de Madrid. Guadalajara también está muy cerca, a 56 kilómetros... Ávila ... pues está un poco más lejos, a 115 kilómetros de aquí. Navacerrada está al noroeste de Madrid, a tan sólo 50 kilómetros. Segovia, está en la misma dirección, a 81 kilómetros de aquí.
– Y Cuenca? ¿A qué distancia está?
– Pues vamos a ver, está a 167 kilómetros de Madrid.

Section 3
3 (p. 42)
1. – Perdone, ¿dónde está la catedral?
   – La segunda calle a la izquierda, todo recto y luego giras a la derecha.
2. – ¿Por dónde se va al ayuntamiento?
   – Pues, para ir al ayuntamiento, tomas la primera a la derecha, después sigues todo recto, y después a la izquierda y allí está.
3. – Oiga, por favor señor, ¿por dónde se va a la biblioteca?
   – La biblioteca, sí, vamos a ver. Mire, siga todo recto.
   – Entonces todo recto.
   – Sí, todo recto. Es la primera calle a la derecha.
   – Primera calle a la derecha.
   – Sí, después sigue recto por esa calle.
   – Recto...
   – Sí. Y es la segunda, la tercera a la izquierda.
   – Entonces, la tercera a la izquierda.
   – Allí está la biblioteca.
   – Pues muchas gracias.
   – De nada. Adiós.

Un paso más
2 (p. 47)
– Oiga, por favor, ¿para ir a la Casa de las Conchas?
– ¿A la Casa de las Conchas? La Casa de las Conchas está muy cerca de aquí.
– Coja esta calle, siga todo recto...
– Todo recto...
– Y al final de la calle gire a la derecha.
– A la derecha.
– Después, cuando llegue a la plaza, coja la segunda calle a la izquierda.
– Segunda calle a la izquierda, ¿no?
– Y allí, sí, la segunda a la izquierda, y allí está la Casa de las Conchas.
– Vale, muchas gracias.

Unit 5

Section 1
2 (p. 50) and 5 (p. 51)
1. – ¡Hola! Buenos días.
   – Buenos días.
   – ¿Me da una barra de pan?
   – ¿Qué más?
   – ¿Tiene jamón?
   – Sí, ¿de qué jamón quieres, jamón york o jamón serrano?
   – Jamón serrano.
   – ¿Qué más?
   – Eh, una botella de vino.
   – ¿Algo más?
   – No nada más.
2. – ¡Hola! Buenas tardes.
   – ¡Hola! Buenas tardes.
   – ¿A cómo están las patatas?
   – A 0,90.
   – Pues, quiero un kilo y medio.
   – ¿Tenéis queso de Burgos?
   – Sí ¿cuánto le pongo?
   – Pues ponme 500 gramos.
   – ¿Algo más?
   – Eh ... una botella de aceite.
   – ¿De qué aceite quiere?
   – Eh ... quiero aceite de girasol.
   – ¿Algo más?
   – No. Esto es todo.

9 (p. 52)
– El pan lo compro en la panadería, las verduras las compro en el mercado, la carne, la compro en la carnicería, las bebidas las compro en el mercado; los pasteles los compro en la pastelería... pescado lo compro en la pescadería.

Section 2
2 (p. 52)
– ¿Qué es lo que venden ustedes en el puesto?
– Bueno, tenemos sandías, melones, naranjas para zumo, manzanas de golden, tomate para ensalada, tomate para frito, peras de agua, melocotón, ciruela amarilla, ciruela roja, albaricoques, nectarinas, aguacates, kiwis, acelgas, coliflores, tenemos también calabacines, berenjenas, pepinos, cebollas, patatas, apio, puerros, plátanos, zanahorias para guisar.

3 (p. 53)
1. – ¿Cuántos pepinos quiere?
   – Ah, como medio kilo.
2. – ¿Tiene patatas?
   – ¿Cuántas patatas quiere?
   – Me da dos kilos.
3. – ¿Cuántos plátanos desea?
   – Quisiera un kilo, por favor.

4 (p. 53)
– Buenos días.
– Buenos días.
– Quería comprar para una ensalada... ¿tiene pimientos?
– Sí, hay pimiento verde, rojo, amarillo...
– Un pimiento rojo, uno verde y uno amarillo.
– Un kilo señorita.
– Okey gracias. Y ¿a cómo son estos tomates?
– Ése le sale a ocho el kilo.
– ¿Y las cebollas?
– A siete el kilo.
– Bien, un kilo de tomates...
– Un kilo.
– Un kilo.
– ¿Qué más señorita?
– Un kilo de cebollas por favor.
– ¿Qué otra cosita le doy?
– Pues, los pepinos.
– ¿Cuántos pepinos quiere?
– Ah como medio kilo.
– ¿Qué otra cosita?
– ¿Me dice cuánto es, por favor?
– Serían diecinueve por eso.
– De acuerdo, muchas gracias.

Section 3
1 (p. 54)
1. – Y ¿a cómo son estos tomates?
   – Ése le sale a siete el kilo.
2. – ¿Me dice a cómo es el kilo de mangos?
   – El kilo de mangos está a catorce pesos.
   – Catorce pesos. De acuerdo, gracias.
3. – ¿A cómo está la almendra ahora?
   – La tenemos a cuarenta y cinco el kilo.

Transcripts
(Units 5–7)

3 (p. 54)
1. – Ya está ¿qué más quieres?
   – ¿Cuánto es?
   – Doce euros con veinte.
   – Aquí tiene. Gracias. Adiós.
   – Adiós.
2. – ¿Cuánto es?
   – ¿Eso es todo?
   – Sí.
   – Bueno, veinte pesos.
3. – ¿Me dice cuánto es?
   – Diecisiete cincuenta.
   – De acuerdo. Tome.
4. – ¿Me dice cuánto es, por favor?
   – Son quince mil pesos, señorita.
5. – ¿Cuánto es todo?
   – Siete euros con treinta y cinco.
   – Tenga.

Un paso más
3 (p. 58)
– Los ingredientes que necesitas son: un cuarto de kilo de zanahorias, dos puerros, una coliflor pequeña, un kilo de patatas, 100 gramos de jamón serrano, dos cucharas de aceite, un litro y medio de agua, un vaso de vino blanco, una pizca de sal. ¡Qué aproveche!

Unit 6

Section 1
1 (p. 62)
– ¿Qué tareas domésticas haces tú normalmente?
– Pues, preparar la cena y lavar los platos casi todas las noches, limpiar la casa los fines de semana, ... lavar la ropa.

4 (p. 62)
– ¿Y tú Isabel? ¿Qué tareas domésticas haces normalmente? ¿Limpias la casa? ¿Lavas la ropa? ¿Planchas?
– Limpio la casa y barro el patio una vez a la semana, preparo la cena todas las noches, lavo la ropa ... dos veces a la semana, y nunca plancho.

7 (p. 63)
1. – Mira, yo leo el periódico todos los días y escribo cartas cada fin de semana. Me encantan los chocolates y los como una vez a la semana al menos. Hablo por teléfono – la verdad – varias veces al día; con mis amigas y mi familia por ejemplo. Vino – pues bebo vino cada día, en la comida normalmente.
2. – Sí, sí. Yo también bebo vino todos los días, en la comida. Hablo poco por teléfono, pero escribo cartas casi todos los días. Los chocolates no me gustan – como una vez al mes como mucho. Sólo leo el periódico los fines de semana.

Section 2
1 (p. 63)
1. – ¿Qué hora es?
   – Son las diez.
2. – ¿Qué hora es?
   – Es la una.
3. – ¿Qué hora es?
   – Son las dos en punto.

3 (p. 64)
1. – Buenos días. Son las siete de la mañana, hora de levantarse ...
2. – Y ahora música clásica cuando son las diez de la noche.
3. – Buenas tardes. Ahora es la una en punto y es la hora de escuchar ...
4. – Son las tres de la tarde y vamos a escuchar ...
5. – Y ahora las noticias internacionales cuando son las seis de la tarde.

5 (p. 64)
– Cine Omni, buenas tardes.
– Buenas tardes, ¿me puede decir a qué hora es En el Nombre del Padre?
– En el Nombre del Padre... un momento, por favor.
– Sí, es a las cuatro, a las seis y cuarenta y cinco y a las nueve la última función.
– A las cuatro... a las seis y cuarenta y cinco ... y a las nueve.
– Sí.
– De acuerdo, gracias.
– De nada.
– Adiós.

Section 3
4 (p. 66)
– ¿Cómo es tu rutina diaria? Es decir, ¿qué haces habitualmente?
– Normalmente, me levanto a las siete de la mañana; desayuno zumo de naranja y café con leche. Salgo de casa a las ocho y voy a clase. Como a las dos en la cafetería de la universidad. Termino clases hacia las seis de la tarde y vuelvo a casa. Ceno sobre las nueve o nueve y media y me acuesto alrededor de las doce.

Un paso más
2 (p. 70)
– ¿Cómo es su rutina diaria?
– Mi rutina diaria, pues muy sencilla. Me levanto a las 5:15 de la mañana para ir a trabajar. A las seis entro. Y entonces de 6 a 2, entonces, trabajando aquí en el metro... Y a las dos salgo y después, pues, voy a mi casa, como y echo un ratito la siesta. Y después por la tarde me voy a trabajar a otro sitio porque el dinero que gano aquí no me da para poder vivir...
– ¿Qué horario tiene usted por la tarde?
– Por la tarde no tengo ningún horario.
– ¿A qué hora va a casa por la noche?
– Por la noche, pues, sobre las 11 o por ahí.
– ¿A qué hora se acuesta?
– A las 12.
– Duerme muy poco.
– Poquísimo.
– ¿Qué hace los fines de semana?
– Los fines de semana, pues, me voy al pueblo.
– Y ¿qué hace en el pueblo?
– Pues, en el pueblo, pues, trabajar también, en la agricultura.

Unit 7

Section 1
2 (p. 72)
1. – ¿Vives en una casa o en un piso?
   – No, en una casa.
2. – ¿Dónde vives? ¿En una casa o en un piso?
   – Yo vivo en una casa. Mi casa es pequeña.
3. – ¿Vives en una casa o en un piso?
   – Vivo en un piso.
4. – ¿Dónde vives? ¿En una casa o en un piso?
   – En una casa. Yo vivo en una casa campesina.
5. – Y ¿vives en una casa o un piso?
   – En un piso. Vivo en un piso. Es pequeño.

4 (p. 73)
1. – Marisa, ¿cuál es tu dirección?
   – Calle Orense número 68, tercer piso, 27004 Lugo.
2. – José María, ¿me das tu dirección?
   – Plaza de Ledesma, 105, 37003 Salamanca.
3. – ¿Y cuál es tu dirección, Óscar?
   – Paseo de Zorrilla número 60, tercero D, 47007 Valladolid.
4. – ¿Y la tuya, Isabel?
   – Calle Ponzano 8, piso bajo – derecha. 50004 Zaragoza.
5. – Eulalia, quiero tu dirección.
   – Sí, Avenida San Juan de la Cadena, 18, cuarto C, 31010 Pamplona.

5 (p. 73)
– ¡Hola! Buenas tardes.
– ¡Hola! Buenas tardes.
– Estoy buscando un piso por el centro. ¿Tenéis algo?
– Depende de lo que quieras. – Eh... ¿qué quieres? ¿piso? ¿buhardilla? ¿apartamento?
– Quería un... un apartamento. Una o dos habitaciones.
– Exactamente. ¿Apartamento? ¿Con ascensor?
– Sí, con ascensor.
– ¿Calefacción? ¿Aire acondicionado?
– Con ascensor y ... y bueno, a ver qué es lo que tiene.
– Garaje no, ¿no?
– No, sin garaje.
– ¿Posibilidades económicas?
– Bueno ... ciento cincuenta mil euros aproximadamente.
– Bueno. Vamos a ver.

Section 2
1 and 2 (p. 74)
– ¿Y dónde estamos?
– Estamos en el dormitorio principal... y, bueno, es una parte muy antigua de la casa. Éste es el baño... un baño muy grande. Tiene su propria chimenea. Éste es el dormitorio de mis hijas. Son las dos mujeres que siempre traen una amiga, por eso es que hay una tercera cama – Éste es un cuarto de estar, aquí generalmente tenemos la televisión. Éste es el comedor que es lo más lindo. Tiene un estilo bien definido – es estilo inglés, provenzal, ¿no?
– ¿Y ahí a la derecha?
– A la derecha tenemos la chimenea. Esto es el 'living' que da al frente de la casa.

4 (p. 75)
1. – ¿Vives en una casa o en un piso?
   – En un piso. Vivo en un piso.
   – ¿Y cómo es el piso?
   – Es pequeño. Tiene dos habitaciones, una sala, una cocina y un cuarto de baño.
2. – ¿Vives en una casa o en un apartamento?
   – Es una casa de dos niveles.
   – ¿Y cuántas habitaciones tiene?
   – Son cuatro habitaciones ... tiene dos baños, tiene una cocina y tiene un patio ...
   – ¿Tiene jardín?
   – Tiene jardín, sí. Tiene un jardín muy bonito.
3. – ¿Cómo es tu casa?
   – Mi casa es de una sola planta, es una casa interior, y es muy amplia ...
   – ¿Cuántas habitaciones tiene?
   – Tres dormitorios, una sala, un estudio, la cocina y el comedor.
4. – ¿Cuántas habitaciones hay en tu casa?
   – Mmm ¿en mi casa? Mi casa tiene dos

[244]

Transcripts
(Units 7–9)

habitaciones, una sala, cocina, patio y ... y el baño.

Section 3
6 (p. 77)
- ¿Qué bebidas os gustan?
- A mí me gusta mucho el café, el café solo.
- A mí me gusta el chocolate.
- A mí ... pues a mí me gusta el vino.
- Y a mí me gusta la cerveza.

Un paso más
3 (p. 82)
- Bueno eh... ¿quieres que te enseñe mi casa?
- Sí claro. A ver.
- Pues mira, aquí a mano derecha, tenemos una habitación que es muy pequeñita, que es la habitación de los invitados...
- Aquí hay la cocina que es superpequeñita. Muy pequeñita.
- Más fácil de limpiar ¿no?
- Sí. Aquí tenemos un wáter suelto, que esto es muy habitual aquí, en la eixample separar esto de la ducha.
- Separar esto de la ducha y ... el lávabo. Es muy habitual aquí. Aquí, a mano izquierda, tengo una habitación que, como el piso no es muy grande, la utilizo como armario de ropa, para planchar y tengo la nevera; porque la cocina es tan pequeñita que no me cabe la nevera. Aquí tenemos el baño, que es como muy desproporcionado... que también hay un armario, como puedes ver; hay una bañera que a mí me encanta, suerte tengo esta bañera; aquí tengo la máquina de lavar y bueno, es muy cómodo. Me gusta mucho porque da a mi habitación.
- Está bien. Por aquí se va ¿no?
- Aquí está mi habitación, que es bastante bonita.
- Ah sí, está ahí.
- El comedor es donde paso también muchas horas; donde escucho música...
- Tienes la tele también.
- Pero la tele no la veo nunca.
- ¿No te gusta?
- No me gusta nada la tele.

Unit 8
Section 1
1 (p. 84)
1. Es joven, baja, morena, un poco gorda y es muy guapa.
2. Es alto, delgado y rubio, pero no es guapo.
3. Es mayor, bajo, moreno y muy delgado.
4. Es joven, alta, rubia y guapísima.

4 (p. 85)
- ¿Conoces a Pepe?
- No, no lo conozco.
- Pues, Pepe está sentado a la izquierda – es alto, moreno.
- El moreno... ¡Ah, sí! Y las chicas ¿quiénes son?
- Teresa está sentada a la derecha, la morena.
- Pues hay dos morenas.
- ¡Ah, sí! pues, Teresa tiene el pelo corto, rizado. La otra es María, la del pelo largo.
- ¿Conoces a la rubia?
- No, no la conozco.
- ¿Y quién es el chico pelirrojo?
- Es Carlos. Vamos para presentártelos.

7 (p. 85)
- ¿Y qué te parecen mis amigos?
- Pues, Teresa y María son muy simpáticas y divertidas. Pepe es un poco tímido, pero me parece que es muy inteligente. Y bueno, Carlos ... pues ... es bastante antipático. ¿No te parece?

Section 2
5 (p. 86)
- Hola, buenos días.
- Buenos días. ¿En qué le puedo ayudar?
- Me duele el estómago.
- ¿Es la primera vez que viene?
- Sí, es la primera vez que vengo.
- ¿Me dice su nombre?
- Mi nombre es Nieves Martínez Carrión.
- ¿Edad?
- 27 años.
- ¿Estado civil?
- Estoy casada.
- ¿Tiene hijos?
- Sí, tengo tres hijos.
- ¿Desde cuándo le duele el estómago?
- Desde ayer por la tarde.
- ¿Cuando le duele, le duele antes de las comidas o después de las comidas?
- Me duele después de las comidas.
- Bueno, vamos a pasar para hacerle una exploración.

Section 3
2 (p. 87)
1. - ¡Hola! Buenos días.
   - Buenos días.
   - Mire, tengo un problema; me duele desde ayer por la tarde mucho el estómago.
   - Pues para eso le puedo dar un antiácido. Se lo puedo dar en sobre, pastillas o jarabe. ¿Qué prefiere?
   - ¿Los sobres son lo mejor?
   - Es lo mejor.
   - ¿Y cómo tengo que tomarlos?
   - Después de las comidas.
2. - Buenas tardes.
   - Buenas tardes señorita.
   - Mire, me duele la garganta. ¿Puede usted mandarme algo para el dolor?
   - Mire este jarabe va bien para su dolor de garganta.
   - Eh ¿cuándo tengo que tomarlo?
   - Tómese una cucharada tres veces al día durante cinco días.
3. - Buenos días. ¿Qué tal? ¿Cómo estas?
   - Buenas. Bien, ¿y usted qué tal?
   - Ahí más o menos. Hombre, vengo a ver, para ver qué me puedes recomendar para ... una quemadura de sol que tengo fuerte.
   - Sí, generalmente acá tomamos ... un analgésico, o sea para el dolor de la quemada y una cremita hidratante.
   - Hay una preguntita que te quería hacer: ¿cuántas veces al día debo de tomar las... las pastillas y la, la... la crema, cuántas veces debo untármela?
   - O sea, la cremita aplicársela dos o tres veces al día y tomarse el analgésico cada seis horas una tableteca.

Un paso más
2 (p. 92)
- ¿Qué edad tienes, Mari?
- 31 años.
- ¿Tu estado civil?
- Casada.
- ¿A qué te dedicas?
- Trabajo como profesora en una escuela primaria.
- ¿Cómo te has sentido con tu embarazo Mari?
- Pues he tenido problemas... las náuseas, vómitos son muy frecuentes.
- ¿Alguna molestia que hayas tenido en tus ojos, en tu visión, en tus oídos?
- Los ojos sí me duelen, me molesta mucho la luz del sol.
- ¿Molestias para respirar?
- Sí cuando me acuesto boca arriba, es una dificultad mínima.
- ¿Palpitaciones de tu corazón?
- Sí, de vez en cuando, una o dos veces al día, sudoraciones, bochornos....
- ¿Dolor de espalda?
- Sí, en la parte baja de la cintura...
- ¿Dolor de cabeza?
- También, también, de vez en cuando....
- ¿Dolor de piernas?
- No, se me hinchan un poquito los pies, pero no, no hay dolor.

Unit 9
Section 1
1 (p. 94)
- ¿Qué es lo que te gusta hacer los domingos?
1. - Me gusta estar con mis amigos...
2. - Quedarme en la cama... me gusta no hacer nada... pues leer, mirar alguna película de video...
3. - ¿Qué te gusta hacer los domingos?
   - ¿Los domingos? Me gusta descansar normalmente.
4. - Pues ir al parque, ir al Retiro, ir al parque de atracciones, ir a Casa de Campo, ir al parque de abajo, que está cerca de nuestra casa, y al parque al lado de casa.

5 (p. 95)
- ¿Te gusta ir al cine?
- Sí, mucho.
- ¿Con qué frecuencia vas al cine?
- Pues una vez a la semana.
- ¿Y al teatro?
- Pues sí, también, pero no voy con frecuencia – una vez al mes quizá.
- ¿Te gusta ir de compras?
- No, no me gusta nada.
- ¿Y hacer deporte?
- Pues tampoco.

6 (p. 95)
1. - ¡Hola, Rosa! Mira, soy Pepe y tengo 23 años. ¡No soy tan viejo verdad! Me encanta el cine y el teatro, y los domingos voy a jugar fútbol con mi equipo local. Casi siempre como en casa porque mi madre cocina – pero también me gusta salir a comer. Me dicen que soy guapo.
2. - Rosita, ¿cómo estás? Soy Juan Manuel. Trabajo en una oficina, tengo 22 años. Me gusta mucho quedarme en casa los fines de semana a escuchar música y leer. Cocino muy bien y siempre preparo la cena. Me encanta ir a conciertos pero el cine no me gusta tanto.
3. - ¿Qué tal Rosita? Me llamo Ramón y tengo 20 años. Trabajo en una fábrica textil. Empiezo a las ocho pero siempre salgo a correr por la mañana. Los fines de semana

Transcripts
(Units 9–11)

me encanta ir a la discoteca los sábados y al cine el domingo. Practico la natación.

Section 2
2 (p. 96)
1. – ¿Qué fecha es hoy?
   – Es el 25 de junio.
2. – ¿A qué estamos?
   – Estamos a 10 de abril.
3. – ¿A qué estamos hoy?
   – Estamos a 18 de septiembre.
4. – ¿Qué fecha es hoy?
   – Es el 5 de febrero.

3 (p. 96)
– ¿Y fechas que sean importantes para usted?
– Pues vamos a decir que la fecha importante para mí pues puede ser la fecha de mi nacimiento que es el veinticuatro de junio.
– ¿De qué año?
– Del cuarenta y uno. Otra fecha importante pues no sé ... pues no sé ... la de la boda, el día, el día trece de noviembre, del sesenta y seis, y no sé, pues la fecha de ingreso a Correos que fue el veintiocho de febrero del sesenta y seis también, no sé, la fecha de cuando ingresé aquí, concretamente en esta oficina que fue el dieciocho de julio del sesenta y seis, y no sé puede haber otras más fechas ...

Section 3
2 (p. 98)
1. – ¡Hola! Buenos días. ¿Qué van a tomar?
   – ¿Tú qué vas a tomar, María?
   – Yo una Coca-cola.
   – Una Coca-cola y un mosto, por favor.
2. – ¡Dígame!
   – Ponme un café solo con hielo y una botella de agua mineral.
   – ¿Algo más?
   – No, gracias. ¿Cuánto le debo?
   – Tres euros.
   – Aquí tiene, gracias.
   – A usted.
3. – Buenos días.
   – ¡Hola! ¿Qué hay? ¿qué van a tomar?
   – Una Coca–cola.
   – Dos Coca–colas entonces.
   – En botella, por favor, Gracias.

5 (p. 99)
– ¡Hola! Buenas tardes.
– Buenas tardes.
– ¿Qué van a tomar?
– Eh yo voy a tomar una tónica, y ... una Coca-cola para ella.
– Muy bien.
– ¿Tenéis algo para comer?
– Tenemos bocadillos.
– ¿Y de qué son?
– Hay de jamón, de queso, de chorizo.
– Hmm... Yo quiero uno de jamón. ¿Cuánto cuesta?
– Seis euros.
– Vale. Uno de jamón.
– Muy bien, ¿usted quiere algo más?
– No, gracias.
– Gracias.

Un paso más
2 (p. 104)
1. – Soy joven y de aspecto agraciado, romántico y cariñoso. Tengo una buena posición económica soy muy serio para las cosas serias (pero me gusta divertirme), me encanta (además de los churros) viajar en metro, lustrarme los zapatos, mirar escaparates, escupir lejos y las chicas. Aborrezco la verdura, lavarme los dientes, escribir postales y oír la radio. ¿Te gustaría conocerme mejor?

2. – Ah, soy muy maniático, entonces mi tiempo libre lo dedico a arreglar cosas, a leer, no sé estar quieto. Cuando estoy quieto es cuando duermo, sólo. Cuando estoy despierto estoy haciendo siempre algo. Eh, escucho música, leo, ah, arreglo cosas, o construyo algo... Paseo, me gusta pasear, me gusta, me gusta mucho andar. Me gusta mucho, pasear por las calles, mirar las casas, fijarme en los detalles. Me gusta ir al mar, me gusta pasear por la playa. En fin, yo creo que me gusta el hacer cosas como a mucha otra gente.

Unit 10
Section 1
2 (p. 106)
1. – ¿Siempre va usted en autobús?
   – Siempre en autobús, sí exactamente...
   – ¿Y le gusta viajar en autobús?
   – Me encanta.
2. – Uso el metro por las mañanas para ir a trabajar.
   – ¿El tren lo usas?
   – Uso el tren ocasionalmente. Algunos fines de semana viajo para visitar a mi familia fuera de Madrid, y algún otro viaje de placer; normalmente, fines de semana.
3. – Ehh... ¿tú coges normalmente el tren?
   – Sí, bastante.
   – ¿Y para qué lo coges? ¿Dónde vas en tren?
   – Bueno, voy mucho a Málaga, durante los fines de semana.

Section 2
3 (p. 108)
– A Arequipa puede ir en avión, en tren o en autobús. Hay varios vuelos diarios desde Lima. El vuelo dura una hora y cuarto aproximadamente. En autobús se tarda entre dieciséis y veinte horas.
– A Cuzco puede ir en avión, en autobús, o en tren. Hay dos vuelos diarios desde Lima; el vuelo dura una hora. Si quiere ir en tren tiene que ir primero a Arequipa y de Arequipa tomar el tren a Cuzco. El viaje en tren de Arequipa a Cuzco le toma dieciséis horas aproximadamente.
– A Machu Picchu puede ir en bus o en tren desde Cuzco y le toma aproximadamente cuatro horas. También puede ir a pie tomando el camino del Inca.
– Si prefiere ir a Iquitos en el Amazonas peruano, tiene que tomar un avión. Es la única forma de llegar desde Lima. El vuelo dura noventa minutos.

4 (p. 108)
– Buenos días.
– ¡Hola!
– Quiero que me dé información sobre trenes para Barcelona.
– Tiene tres trenes por la mañana y cinco por la tarde y noche.
– ¿A qué hora salen los de la mañana?
– A las 7.00, a las 9.00 y a las 10.55.
– ¿Y a qué hora llega a Barcelona el tren de las 9.00?
– A las 16.03.
– ¿Qué servicios tiene ese tren?
– Lleva restaurante, y cafetería.
– Y ¿cuál es el precio del billete?
– El precio del billete es 44 € ida y 75 € si saca ida y vuelta.
– ¿Se puede hacer reservas?
– Se puede hacer reservas siempre, hasta con 24 horas de antelación y por Internet.

Section 3
3 (p.109)
– Buenos días.
– Buenos días. ¡Dígame!
– Quería comprar un billete para ir a Sevilla el próximo miércoles, y lo quisiera de ida y vuelta.
– Muy bien. Dígame a qué hora quiere ir y a qué hora quiere volver.
– Quisiera ir por la mañana y volver por la noche.
– Por la mañana tiene a las siete, ocho, nueve y once.
– A las ocho de la mañana.
– Bien, y la vuelta, por la noche el último a las nueve de la noche.
– A las nueve de la noche para volver el sábado.
– Muy bien. ¿Va a pagar usted con tarjeta de crédito o en efectivo?
– No, voy a pagar con dinero.

4 (p. 110)
– ¿Quiere un billete de ida solamente o de ida y vuelta?
– ¿A qué hora quiere salir?
– ¿Y a qué hora quiere volver?
– ¿Va a pagar en efectivo o con tarjeta de crédito?

Un paso más
3A (p. 114)
1. – El Talgo procedente de Granada efectúa su entrada por vía número 7.
2. – El tren AVE con destino Madrid efectúa su salida por vía número 8.
3. – El tranvía con destino Córdoba efectuará su salida por vía 10.

3B (p. 114)
1. – Salida del vuelo de Iberia 584 con destino La Palma. Señores pasajeros diríjanse a la puerta de embarque número 3.
2. – Llegada del vuelo 673 de la compañía British Airways procedente de Miami.
3. – Salida del vuelo 253 de la compañía Viva Air con destino Londres. Señores pasajeros diríjanse a la puerta de embarque 19.

Unit 11
Section 1
3 (p. 119)
1. – Buenos días. Bienvenida al Hotel Colón. ¿Le puedo ayudar en algo?
   – Sí, quiero una habitación.
   – ¿De qué tipo desea la habitación?
   – Individual.
   – De acuerdo. Un momentito, por favor. Le daremos la 207.
2. – Buenos días. Quería una habitación doble, con cama doble para dos noches.
   – Lo siento, no nos quedan habitaciones con cama doble.
   – Ah, pues vale, gracias. Hasta luego.
   – Hasta luego.
3. – Buenas tardes, ¿qué desea?
   – ¿Tiene una habitación libre para esta noche?
   – ¿Individual,o doble?
   – Doble.
   – Un momento, por favor ... Sí, nos queda

[246]

Transcripts
(Units 11–13)

una. Es la habitación 105 en el primer piso.
– De acuerdo.

5 (p. 120)
– ¿Qué servicios tiene la habitación?
– Tiene aire acondicionado, hilo musical, teléfono, televisión en color, cuarto de baño completo.
– ¿Tiene servicio de habitaciones?
– No, servicio de habitaciones no hay.
– ¿Cafetería, restaurante?
– Sí, cafetería y restaurante, sí.
– ¿Cuál es el precio de la habitación por noche?
– En esta época, setenta y cinco euros, la doble.
– Ahora estamos en temporada alta.
– Sí.
– ¿Y en temporada baja?
– Sesenta y cinco euros.

Section 2
2 (p. 121)
– ¿Cuál es su apellido, por favor?
– ¿Por favor me da el número de su identificación?
– ¿Su dirección permanente?
– ¿Por cuántos días va a permanecer aquí en el hotel?
– ¿En qué forma nos cancelaría su cuenta?
– ¿Me la permite, por favor? Su habitación es la trece cero ocho.

5 (p. 121)
– […] Sí, ¿me permite la llave?
– Sí, aquí tiene.
– Habitación 2006.
– Exacto.
– ¿La señora va a cancelar con tarjeta de crédito o en efectivo?
– No, en efectivo.
– ¿En efectivo?
– Sí.
– ¿Cancela en pesos o en dólares?
– En pesos.
– En pesos. Su cuenta total es de 676.690 pesos.
– Aquí tiene.
– Bueno, todo correcto. Que tenga buen viaje.
– […] El cargo que hay aquí es de habitación, de restaurante, de teléfono, de mini-bar y un fax. Más el seis por ciento de iva.
– ¿Me puede decir el total?
– Sí, son 852 euros con 35.
– De acuerdo, pues muchas gracias por su servicio.
– Gracias a usted, señora.
– Hasta luego.
– Adiós, buen viaje.

Section 3
2 (p. 122)
– ¿Me puede decir qué hay para ver o hacer esta semana?
– Este mes tenemos el Festival Internacional de Teatro Clásico de Almagro, que es un evento muy importante. Esta semana, por ejemplo, puede ir a ver la obra 'El Médico de su Honra' de Calderón de la Barca y la próxima semana una obra de Shakespeare. Si le interesa el cine, hay un festival de cine de películas españolas del 15 al 20 de julio. Hay también dos conciertos de música clásica y otros eventos … Y si le interesa el fútbol, pues el domingo hay un partido entre el Alcázar y el Realejos.

Un paso más
1 (p. 126)
– Sr. Gough, no podemos hacer la reserva para el día 28 pero es posible para el día 29. Podemos hacer la reserva de la habitación doble. Lo sentimos pero todas las habitaciones individuales son con ducha. El precio de la habitación doble es de 95€, y el de la individual es de 75 €, las dos son con desayuno incluido. El precio de la habitación también incluye entrada a un espectáculo. El hotel tiene piscina, restaurante, sala de televisión y vídeo.

Unit 12
Section 1
5 (p. 129)
2. – Dime dónde fuiste de vacaciones la última vez.
– La última vez fui de vacaciones a Menorca.
3. – ¿Dónde fuiste de vacaciones el año pasado?
– El año pasado estuve en Cazorla, en Andalucía.
4. – ¿Dónde fuiste de vacaciones la última vez?
– La última vez que fui de vacaciones fui a Galicia.
5. – ¿Dónde fuiste de vacaciones el año pasado?
– A Brasil.

7 (p. 129)
1. – ¿Dónde fuiste de vacaciones el año pasado?
– Fui a Acapulco.
– ¿Qué tal?
– ¡Ay! ¡Increíble, buenísimo!
2. – Dime dónde fuiste de vacaciones la última vez.
– La última vez fui de vacaciones a Menorca.
– ¿Cómo te fue en Menorca?
– Muy bien, muy relajado.
3. – ¿Dónde fuiste de vacaciones la última vez?
– La última vez que fui de vacaciones fui a Galicia.
– ¿Cómo te fue?
– Me fue muy bien. Hizo buen tiempo y lo pasamos fenomenal.
4. – ¿Dónde fuiste de vacaciones la última vez?
– A Brasil.
– ¿Y cómo te fue?
– Estupendamente. Fue un mes maravilloso.

Section 2
3 (p. 130)
– Me bañé, comí, leí, recorrí el parque, visité todos los lugares de interés de este parque. Subí a las montañas del parque, vi los ríos, animales; dediqué todo mi tiempo a estar en la naturaleza y pasarlo lo mejor posible.

5 (p. 131)
– Fuimos a bucear, nadamos.
– Cenamos.
– En la noche fuimos a … a bailar, bailamos toda la noche.

Section 3
1 (p. 131)
– Me levanté temprano y me duché. Luego fui a la piscina. Volví a casa y desayuné – tomé un zumo de naranja. Leí un libro el resto de la mañana y después fui al supermercado.

7 (p. 132)
2. – ¿Qué hicisteis ayer en Guanajuato?
– Cuando llegamos al hotel fuimos a nadar, comimos allí en el hotel, y por la tarde nos fuimos a caminar al pueblo.
– Estuvimos en los museos – hay muchos museos que conocer – y plazas. Comimos comida típica mexicana; bueno cenamos comida típica mexicana, muy rica, con mucho chile.
– Y paseamos toda la noche por ahí, y nos tocó una estudiantina. Escuchamos sus canciones, ahí mismo en la plaza, bajo el quiosco.
3. – Fuimos a bailar a 'Extravaganza'. Vinimos aquí un rato a la playa, después estuvimos en el 'Lobby' del hotel, y después salimos a bailar, a la, a la discoteca.

Un paso más
3 (p. 136)
1. – Bueno, ¿y qué es lo que han hecho hasta ahorita?
– Fuimos a Taxco. Ahí anduvimos paseando por las calles.
– Vimos la procesión en Taxco, compramos muchísimas cosas de artesanía.
– Visitamos las iglesias, regresamos a Acapulco…
– Anduvimos por el pueblo de Acapulco.
2. – ¿Qué lugares visitaron de restaurantes?
– Fuimos al 'Frox', que es un 'bar and grill', fuimos al 'Spicy' que es un restaurante de comida internacional. Anduvimos a la discoteca 'Palladium'.
– Sí, ahí fue donde bailamos toda la noche.
– ¿Y qué fue lo que cenaste?
– Cené camarones al mojo de ajo, con una copa de un buen vino blanco y una ensalada.

Unit 13
Section 1
2 (p. 138)
1. – ¿Cómo te llamas?
– Yo me llamo Patricia.
– ¿Cuántos años tienes?
– Yo tengo diez años.
– ¿Practicas algún deporte?
– Sí.
– ¿Qué deportes practicas?
– Yo practico el voleibol y la natación.
– ¿Y cuándo los practicas?
– La natación la practico los, los lunes, bueno todos los días, por las tardes, y el voleibol los martes y los jueves.
2. – ¿Cuál es tu nombre?
– Me llamo Alberto.
– ¿Qué edad tienes?
– Once años.
– ¿Qué deportes practicas?
– Fútbol y baloncesto.
– ¿Cuándo los practicas?
– Los fines de semana.
– ¿De qué hora a qué hora?
– Por la tarde. De cinco a siete.

Section 3
3 (p. 142)
– Pues, hace diez o veinte años el barrio era más tranquilo. Había solamente un restaurante y no había muchos coches. Hoy, hay mucha actividad – hay tiendas de todo tipo, hay restaurantes y bares. Hay mucho ruido y suciedad también.

Transcripts
(Units 13–15)

Un paso más
3 (p. 146)
– Vamos a ver. Te preguntamos antes en Trujillo había gente que se dedicaba a actividades distintas. ¿Había por ejemplo más ganaderos?
– Muchos, muchos más.
– ¿Dónde era la actividad de los ganaderos normalmente?
– Pues aquí en el mercado de la plaza era donde normalmente se venían reuniendo, cada jueves a ofrecer su, sus ganados y el precio, a ver quién apostaba más.
– Y tenían... Por ejemplo, en tu familia había muchos ganaderos. ¿Desde cuándo?
– En mi familia de siempre. Mi abuelo se dedicó en principio a pieles, y recorría pues las dehesas, las majadas, los chozos. Donde había una piel allí estaba él.
– Oye, y, y luego tu padre siempre, era el ganao.
– Mi padre ya luego era el ganao. Mi padre el ganao.
– ¿Y, y hacía trashumancia?
– Sí. De toda la vida, desde los años cuarenta. Hacia el cuarenta y cinco, o el cuarenta y siete en adelante.
– ¿Iban...hacia dónde?
– Ellos casi siempre subían a León. A los puertos de León, hacia la parte de Riaño. El valle ese le encantó, desde que lo vio se enamoró de él y, y siempre, siempre.

Unit 14
Section 1
1 (p. 148)
– ¿Cuándo es verano en tu país?
– En diciembre, enero y febrero.

5 (p. 149)
– ¿Y cómo son los veranos?
– En el verano hace por aquí bastante viento, y sol, así.
– En Almagro tenemos lo que se llama clima continental extremo. Es decir, mucho calor en verano y mucho frío en invierno.

Section 2
4 (p. 151)
1. – ¿Te gusta más estar en el campo o en la ciudad?
   – Buenos Aires, bueno yo estoy acá en Buenos Aires así más o menos seis años. Me gusta pero prefiero el campo más que todo.
2. – ¿Te gusta más estar en el campo o en la ciudad?
   – No, en el campo.
   – ¿Y por qué te gusta más estar en el campo?
   – Porque sí, es como mejor, se siente uno mejor. Pues que más chévere es el campo. En la ciudad hay mucha rutina, y sí, es como si... es pues como que uno se siente más apretado en la ciudad; en el campo se siente más libre... más como... sí, como más optimista para todo.
3. – ¿Te gusta la playa? ¿O te gusta más la montaña?
   – Me gustan las dos cosas pero más la playa.

Section 3
2 (p. 152)
1. – ¿Cuál es el río más largo del mundo?
   – El Nilo. El río más largo del mundo podría ser el Nilo.
   – ¿Y tú sabes cuál es el país más grande donde se habla español?
   – ¿El más grande? Pues alguno de Sudamérica. Podría ser, el más grande, pues Argentina, por ejemplo.
   – ¿Y el más pequeño?
   – Pues República Dominicana, podría ser, es muy chiquitito.
2. – Y ¿cuál es el río más largo del mundo?
   – El río más largo del mundo es el Amazonas.
   – Y, ¿cuál es el país más grande donde se habla español?
   – El país más grande donde se habla español es Argentina.
   – ¿Cuál es el país más pequeño donde se habla español?
   – Pues, el país más pequeño donde se habla español puede ser Santo Domingo.

4 (p. 152)
– ¿Cuántas especies de orquídeas hay en Costa Rica?
– En Costa Rica nosotros tenemos unas mil quinientas especies de orquídeas, de la totalidad de unas treinta mil especies que hay a nivel mundial.
– ¿Y cuál es la orquídea más bonita?
– Bueno, yo considero que la orquídea más bonita que nosotros podemos tener en Costa Rica es la 'Cattleya Digbyana', que normalmente la llaman la Guardia Turrialba.
– ¿Y cuál es la flor más grande, la orquídea más grande que hay en Costa Rica?
– Yo diría que la orquídea más grande que nosotros tenemos en Costa Rica puede ser la 'Brassia Longissima'.
– ¿Y la más pequeña?
– Bueno, hay algunas muy, muy, muy pequeñas como los 'Platysteles'.

Un paso más
3 (p. 158)
– Pronóstico del tiempo para el fin de semana. En el Norte de España, cielo cubierto con lluvia en Galicia y el País Vasco. En Cantabria, viento del Atlántico con riesgo de heladas. En el centro, despejado, mucho sol y temperaturas de hasta 35 grados. En las regiones de Cataluña y el País Valenciano, chubascos fuertes y tormentas. En el Sur, despejado y mucho calor, sobre todo en Córdoba con 40 grados. En el Este, cielo despejado cambiando a lluvia el domingo.

Unit 15
Section 1
1 (p. 160)
– Yo nací en Italia y luego pasé a América y me naturalicé costarricense hace veintidós años. Viví por mi trabajo en muchos países. Viví cuatro años en Estados Unidos, de profesor en un 'college' en Minesota. Luego viví en México algunos años dedicado a la pesca del camarón, con un primo mío. Y luego viví en Centroamérica en varias partes. Como experto trabajé en Guatemala; trabajé en El Salvador como Jefe de Misión. En El Salvador pasé tres años. En Guatemala pasé dos años.

3 (p. 160)
– Nací en Badalona en 1955. Empecé mis estudios de arquitectura en 1973 y terminé mi carrera en 1982. Me casé con mi actual mujer en 1984 y tuve mi primer hijo en 1985. Empecé a trabajar conjuntamente con mi compañero y amigo Jordi Moliner en 1982 y actualmente seguimos trabajando en nuestra propia ciudad que es Badalona.

Section 2
1 (p. 161)
1. – ¿Ustedes están casados?
   – Sí, ya, ya hace mucho.
   – ¿Cuánto tiempo hace que se casaron?
   – Veinticinco años.
   – ¿Y dónde se casaron?
   – En México, México Distrito Federal, en la Iglesia de San Agustín.
   – ¿Y cómo se conocieron?
   – Casualmente.
2. – ¿Está casado?
   – Sí, y tenemos una familia grande.
   – ¿Cuántos años lleva casado?
   – Treinta y dos el día de hoy.
   – ¿Y dónde se casó?
   – En Costa Rica, en la iglesia de la Soledad.
   – Y ¿dónde conoció a su mujer?
   – La conocí en un viaje a San José. Ella es costarricense.

2 (p. 162)
– ¿Cómo te llamas?
– Me llamo María Elena.
– ¿De dónde eres?
– Soy de Quito, Ecuador.
– ¿Y cuántos años tienes?
– Tengo treinta y tres años.
– ¿Cuánto tiempo llevas en Inglaterra?
– Bueno, en Inglaterra llevo varios años. Salí de Ecuador hace como seis años.
– ¿Estás casada?
– Sí, soy casada. Mi marido es danés.
– ¿Dónde lo conociste?
– Bueno, yo vine a estudiar en una universidad en el norte de Inglaterra y él estudiaba ahí también. Y pues, nos conocimos y después, cuando terminamos los estudios decidimos casarnos. Nos casamos hace tres años.
– ¿Y por qué vinisteis a Londres?
– Porque conseguí un trabajo como profesora de español en una universidad aquí.
– ¿Cuánto tiempo llevas en Londres?
– Cerca de dos años.
– ¿Y te gusta Londres?
– Sí, me encanta.

Section 3
2 (p. 163)
– ¿Dónde estamos ahora?
– Estamos en la Plaza Mayor de Trujillo. Como ves hay muchos edificios importantes alrededor, y estamos justo en el lugar desde el que se ve el Palacio de la Conquista, la estatua de Pizarro.
– El Palacio de la Conquista, ¿a quién perteneció?
– Era de la familia Pizarro.
– Trujillo, ¿cuándo se fundó?
– Hay noticias de la fundación de Trujillo como campamento romano ... en el siglo II a.c.

3 (p. 163)
– Esta sala está dedicada a los personajes más importantes de la cultura, se puede decir a los que hicieron cultura en América. Tenemos en primer lugar Bartolomé de las Casas que era sevillano y que fue un fraile que defendió mucho el mestizaje. Seguidamente tenemos Fray Juan de Silva que fue confesor de los Reyes Católicos; la poetisa mexicana Sor Juana Inés de la Cruz; Félix

Transcripts
(Units 15–17)

Lazara que fue el primer hombre que trajo animales tropicales a España, los loros y las cotorras, el libertador Simón Bolívar, símbolo de la liberación de, de América Latina, y por último, los literatos Rubén Darío y Pablo Neruda.

Un paso más
1 (p. 168)
– ¿Cuántas fechas históricas puedes recordar?
– De fechas históricas ¿cuántas puedo recordar?
– Sí.
– Muchas, muchísimas.
– Bueno, dime tres y qué significan.
– Bueno, por ejemplo el, el veinte de noviembre de mil novecientos setenta y cinco. Eh, la muerte de Franco. Para mí es una fecha histórica, porque representa el inicio de la reconciliación en mi país.
– Pues las fechas históricas principales que me acuerdo son mil cuatrocientos noventa y dos, el Descubrimiento de América; mil novecientos catorce el inicio de la Primera Guerra Mundial; mil novecientos treinta y seis, el inicio de la Guerra Civil Española, en mil novecientos setenta y cinco, la venida de la, de la democracia a España, y en mil novecientos noventa y dos la exposición universal de Sevilla.
– Fechas históricas exactamente no conozco muchas, así de memoria y ahora rápidamente, pero creo que hay algunas importantes. Para España, por ejemplo tenemos la invasión de los musulmanes en el setecientos once, para Europa y para el mundo en general tenemos la Revolución Francesa, uno siete ocho nueve, mil setecientos ochenta y nueve.

Unit 16
Section 1
2 (p. 172)
– ¿Querían comer, verdad?
– Sí.
– Bien, pues miren, de primero tenemos gazpacho, sopa, verdura y macarrones.
– A mí un gazpacho.
– Un gazpacho para la señora.
– Yo unos macarrones.
– ¿Y usted?
– A mí me apetecen judías.
– Judías verdes.
– Yo también unas judías verdes.
– Dos de judías verdes.
– De segundo plato para ustedes hay: caldereta de cordero, muy especial de aquí, de la tierra, chuletas de cordero lechales, muy buenas.
– ¿Son tiernas?
– Sí, sí, sí,. Ternera también, muy buena y cochinillo a la brasa, muy rico, muy rico.
– Pues yo las chuletitas que has dicho, de cordero.
– Chuletitas de cordero. Muy bien.
– Yo una caldereta.
– Caldereta. ¿Usted?
– Yo voy a probar el cochinillo asado a ver qué tal.
– Pues yo quiero un poco de ternera.
– ¿Para beber qué toman?
– Pues yo creo que un vino. ¿No os parece?
– Muy bien. Pues en seguida les atendemos ¿eh? ¡Buen provecho!
– Gracias.
– Muy bien, gracias.

6 (p. 173)
– Bien, miren, de postre tenemos: flan de la casa, muy rico; hay unas natillas también que las hacemos nosotros caseras que están muy buenas; y luego hay helados típicos, vamos variados; y hay fruta. Tenemos: manzanas, naranjas, plátanos...
– A mí me apetecen unas natillas.
– Unas natillas para la señora.
– Yo ... ¿tiene melón?
– Sí, sí, sí...
– Pues me pone una tajada de melón.
– Melón para ella. Bien, pues un momentito entonces.
– Quiero un helado de fresa con caramelo.
– Un helado de fresa con caramelo. Muy bien.
– Yo no quiero postre. Un café solo.

Section 2
2 (p. 174)
2. – Pues normalmente yo desayuno café con leche y churros y zumo de naranja.
3. – Bueno, un desayuno típico es este ... servir un vaso de leche, un ... un par de blanquillos y frijoles.

5 (p. 175)
1. – ¿Qué comes al mediodía?
– Pues yo al mediodía como ensalada y también como carne.
2. – ¿Qué comes al mediodía?
– Al mediodía normalmente como primero lentejas, garbanzos, todo tipo de legumbres y luego, carne o pescado.

6 (p. 175)
1. – ¿Qué comes como comida rápida?
– Como comida rápida como perritos calientes o hamburguesas.
2. – A veces compramos un pollo asado y lo comemos en casa o unas tapas preparadas.
3. – ¿Qué comes como comida rápida?
– Como comida rápida suelo comer perritos calientes o si no, bocadillos de tortilla...

Section 3
3 (p. 176)
– ¿Tú sabes hacer gazpacho?
– Sí, gazpacho gitano.
– ¿Me puedes dar la receta?
– Sí, por supuesto.
– ¿Qué ingredientes necesito?
– Vamos a ver . . una cebolla grande, dos tomates medianos picados..., un pepino picado, cuatro dientes de ajo..., un cuarto de litro de aceite, tres cuartos de litro de agua, un chorrito de vinagre, aproximadamente cien gramos de miga de pan. Y sal y pimienta al gusto.

4 (p. 176)
– Para empezar, se machacan los ajos pelados con un poquito de sal. Luego se añade el aceite y se bate bien. Se añade la miga de pan previamente remojada y exprimida y se mezcla todo bien hasta formar una pasta. Se añade agua fría poco a poco y se remueve. Se sazona con sal y pimienta. Se enfría. Antes de servir, se añaden los tomates y el pepino. Y queda listo ya el gazpacho gitano.

Un paso más
3 (p. 180)
– ¡Hola! Buenas noches.
– Buenas noches.
– ¿Me puede decir qué hay para cenar?
– Bueno, con mucho gusto. Estamos esta noche con el festival del Langostino.
– ¿Y qué hay?
– Perdón, una ensalada de papas y langostinos.
– Muy bien.
– Seguimos con pastas y langostinos.
– Muy bien.
– Tenemos palmitos...
– Y langostinos.
– Y langostinos y espárragos.
– Ah, muy rico.
– Y qué, ¿han estado todo el día pescando langostinos?
– Pues sí, para ustedes.
– ¿Pero hoy qué nos recomienda para tomar?
– Bueno, hoy les recomiendo el bufete de langostinos.
– ¿Pero qué plato del bufete?
– Bueno, mi recomendación es que prueben todo.
– Todo.
– Todo es bueno.

Unit 17
Section 1
3 (p. 182)
– Quiero ser una gran actriz y también quiero cantar y bailar al mismo tiempo.
– ¿Dónde quieres vivir?
– Quiero vivir en un pueblo de aquí de México o en una montaña.
– ¿Y dónde quieres trabajar?
– Primero quiero trabajar aquí en México, y después en Londres y Hollywood.
– ¿Y dónde quieres viajar?
– Quiero viajar por Europa, por India, por Egipto.
– ¿Por qué te gustaría hacer esto?
– Porque me encanta ¿no?, como nunca he ido, me encantaría conocer otra cultura y otro tipo de gente.

Section 3
4 (p. 185)
1. – ¿Cómo te sientes más cómoda los fines de semana?
– Con unos pantalones cortos y una camiseta.
2. – ¿Qué prefieres llevar el fin de semana?
– Me gusta llevar blue jeans y una camisa vieja – y zapatos de tenis.
3. – ¿Qué color prefieres llevar?
– Desde pequeño siempre he llevado mucha ropa roja, y es el color que más me gusta.
– ¿Qué prefieres llevar el fin de semana?
– Me gusta estar desnudo, y cuando puedo estar desnudo en mi casa, en invierno o en verano, estoy desnudo.

6 (p. 186)
– Usa unos pantalones, que se llaman bombachas, que son muy amplios, cómodos para andar a caballo; botas altas de cuero; un cinturón que se llama rastra; una camisa de tela fuerte; un sombrero de cuero; un pañuelo atado al cuello y un poncho.

Un paso más
3 (p. 190)
1. – ¿Y, qué es lo primero que pusiste en tu maleta para venir?
– Mi traje de baño y mi ropa. La mejor ropa, los shorts y todo.
2. – ¿Qué fue lo primero que puso en la maleta?
– Éste mi bronceador.
3. – ¿Y lo primero que puso su maleta para venir de vacaciones?
– ¿Lo primero que puse? Una botella de tequila. Lo primerito.
4. – Cuando haces las maletas ¿qué es la primera cosa que metes en ellas?

Transcripts
(Units 18–20)

Unit 18

Section 1
7 (p. 193)
1. – ¿Qué vas a hacer el domingo por la noche?
   – Nada especial. ¿Por qué?
   – ¿Quieres venir a cenar a mi casa?
   – Sí, vale. ¡Estupendo!
2. – ¿Quieres ir a dar un paseo por el parque mañana por la tarde?
   – Me gustaría, pero no puedo. Tengo clases en la universidad.
3. – ¿Qué vas a hacer el viernes por la noche?
   – Pues, no lo sé. ¿Por qué?
   – Juan y yo vamos a ir a la discoteca. Quieres venir con nosotros?
   – Sí, vale.

8B (p. 193)
– ¿Quieres ir de tiendas por la tarde?
– ¿Quieres ir a tomar una copa esta tarde, a eso de las seis?
– ¿Quieres ir a tomar un café hacia las once?
– ¿Quieres ir a cenar a un restaurante conmigo?

Section 2
7 (p. 195)
1. – Quiero comprar unas zapatillas.
   – ¿Cómo las quieres?
   – Las quiero de color blanco con cordones.
   – ¿Y qué número tienes?
   – El 39.
   – Mira, a ver si te gustan éstas. Tenemos muchas marcas, Nike por ejemplo, ¿o prefieres Reebok?
   – ¿Qué precio tienen las Nike?
   – Las Nike valen 75 € y las Reebok 65 €.
   – ¿Me las puedo probar?
   – Sí, pruébatelas.
   – ¡Huy! Las Reebok son comodísimas.
   – Es verdad. ¿Te gustan?
   – Sí, me gustan mucho. Eh ... pues me quedo con las Reebok.
   – De acuerdo.
2. – Hola. Buenas tardes. Quiero comprar un cinturón de cuero.
   – Bueno, hay diferentes tipos de cuero, hay en gamuza y hay en cuero de suela.
   – ¿Y en qué colores?
   – En color suela, en color marrón y en color negro.
   – El cinturón es para mí. ¿Qué medida tienes?
   – Como para ti un 80.
   – Me gusta éste, pero eh ... en color negro.
   – Sí, hay en color negro.
   – ¿Cuánto sale?
   – Eh, éste sale 92 pesos.
   – Muy bien. Lo llevo.

Section 3
1 (p. 196)
1. – Buenos días.
   – Buenos días.
   – Quiero comprar un regalo. ¿Qué es lo más típico de aquí?
   – Bueno, lo más típico de aquí de la costa ... tenemos las hamacas; hay sillas hamacas, hay tambores; hay maracas, que es lo más típico de aquí, de Cartagena, especial de Cartagena. Tenemos mucha artesanía en realidad.
2. – ¿Y qué otro tipo de souvenirs tiene?
   – Tenemos cerámica, collares, este ... tengo cajas de madera muy preciosas, en maderas finas, que son hechas, aquí en Costa Rica. También le ofrezco las carretas típicas, ¿verdad?, que eso es muy típico, valga la redundancia, de Costa Rica. Además tengo esos cuadros, ¿verdad?, que son con ... cuadros típicos, con figuras de caballos, carretas, ahh ... agricultores.

2 (p. 196)
– ¿Qué precio tienen las hamacas?
– Las hamacas hay de diferentes precios según el tamaño de la hamaca. Eh, así es el precio de la hamaca: la hamaca de una sola persona salen 22.000 pesos; la de un tamaño mediano en 33.000 pesos.
– Me gusta mucho ésta de rayas, azul y blanca. ¿Cuánto vale ésa?
– Ésa tiene un precio de 33.000 pesos.
– Voy a llevar ésa. Y las maracas, ¿qué precio tienen?
– Las maracas tienen un precio de 1.000 pesos el par.
– Y un par de maracas.
– OK. Está bien.
– ¿Cuánto es?
– Bueno, son 33.000 pesos más 1.000 pesos el par de maracas son 34.000 pesos.
– De acuerdo, muchas gracias.

Un paso más
3 (p. 202)
– ... Níjar es típico por las jarapas y la cerámica. Las jarapas son, eh, trapos, trapos de estos que, que ya la gente no utiliza, de vestido y eso, que lo recortan en tiras y los prensan en telares, y, y hacen como mantas, cortinas, alfombras, y todo eso. Es una tradición muy antigua en Níjar y que, junto con la cerámica pues, da vida al pueblo y hace que, que este pueblo sea muy visitado, aparte de, de por las playas y todo esto.
– ¿Qué colores es los que más le gusta?
– Bueno, normalmente la cerámica suele ir pintada en tonos azules y verdes, luego claro, hay cerámica más moderna que va en tonos marrones y, y color cobre, eh, los repintados, las flores, y todo eso. Luego está también la cerámica amarilla y verde y, pero por lo general pues, eh, tonos azules son los que predominan en toda la cerámica.

Unit 19

Section 2
2 (p. 206)
– ¡Hola! Buenos días.
– Buenos días.
– Mira, que ayer en el autobús que viene de Valencia me dejé una chaqueta aquí en la estación.
– Sí. ¿Recuerdas exactamente dónde la olvidaste?
– Pues, creo que era en el andén seis, en el banco.
– Sí, y me dices fue ayer ¿por la tarde?
– Sí, ayer por la tarde, a las seis.
– A ver, un segundo que lo consultaré... Sí, ¿me puedes describir la chaqueta, por favor?
– Sí, mira, la chaqueta es de color rojo, de hilo ...
– Sí.
– ... y forma americana, y tiene unos botones dorados.
– Perfecto. Pues sí, has tenido suerte.
– ¡Ah! ¡¡Qué bien!
– ... la hemos encontrado.
– ¡Ah! ¡Qué ilusión!
– Un viajero nos la trajo ayer.

5 (p. 206)
[camiseta verde]
– Es decir uno llevaba pantalón vaquero y camiseta negra.
– Sí.
– Y el otro ¿me ha dicho?
– Le he podido ver una camiseta verde.
– Camiseta verde. ¿Cómo eran: altos, bajos gruesos?
– Uno era alto con el pelo rizado.
– Uno alto con el pelo rizado.
– Ojos... ojos oscuros.
– Bueno. Le voy a enseñar unas fotografías para ver si usted identifica a los supuestos autores del robo, y bueno...

Section 3
1 (p. 207)
– ... como nací en un pueblo pequeñito, íbamos en un caballo mi padre, mi hermano y yo, y yo iba el primero y entonces nos caímos y ... y cayeron los dos encima de mí, que se, se, el caballo se cayó hacia adelante y entonces los dos cayeron sobre mí ...

Un paso más
3 (p. 212)
– Soy Elena, tengo cuarenta años, dos hijos, una casada con una bebé, o sea que soy abuela.
– ¿Y qué haces aquí con la cooperativa?
– Eh, empecé en el año ochenta y cuatro. Eh, como enmadejadora para exportación. Después pasé a ser hilandera y ahora sigo, sigo siendo hilandera y trabajo en la administración.
– Y, ¿tu tenías toda la educación necesaria para hacer esto antes de entrar o tenías ... ?
– No, no, para nada, yo era ama de casa, este, llegó el momento en que necesité de un, de aumentar el salario que tenía mi esposo, y entré en Manos, como única fuente de trabajo en el medio. Este, y ahí fui capacitándome para todas las tareas de, de acá dentro, de administración, de directiva, de... un montón de capacitación que te desarrolla como mujer. Eso me entusiasmó mucho, este, con el correr del tiempo, este, fue a través de la capacitación como te decía, adquiriendo un desarrollo como mujer muy importante, y, y en eso estoy.

Unit 20

Section 1
3 (p. 215)
1. – ¡Diga!
   – ¿Está Pedro?
   – Sí, un momentín, ahora se pone.
2. – ¡Dígame!
   – ¿Está Teresa?
   – Sí, pero ahora no puede ponerse; está en la ducha. ¿De parte de quién?
   – De Carmen.
   – Vale, yo le digo que has llamado, cuando salga de la ducha.
3. – ¡Diga!
   – ¿Está Julia, por favor?

Transcripts
(Unit 20)

– Sí, soy yo.
– Ah, hola Julia. No te reconocí. Soy Mari.
4. – ¿Está Don Tomás, por favor?
– No, no es aquí, se equivoca.
– Lo siento, gracias.
– Adiós.

6 (p. 216)
1. – Nueva Imagen, buenos días.
   – ¿Me puede poner con la Sra. Carmen Pérez?
   – Un momento, por favor.
   – Está comunicando.
   – Gracias. Llamaré más tarde. Adiós.
   – Adiós.
2. – Nueva Imagen, buenas tardes.
   – ¿Me puede poner con el Sr. Figueroa?
   – ¿Cómo?
   – Con el Sr. Figueroa.
   – Un momento, ahora le paso.
   – Sí, ¡Dígame!
   – Sr. Figueroa, soy Ana María Pérez, de la compañía de seguros Bella Vista...

Section 2
2 (p. 217)
1. – Oye, ¿qué vas a hacer? ¿adónde vamos a ir a comer?
   – Pues no sé, adonde quieras. Vamos a la cafetería ... Sí... a las dos.
   – ¡Ah! Perfecto, nos vemos a las dos en la cafetería.
   – Sí.
   – Vale.
2. – ¿Quieres venir esta noche a cenar con nosotras?
   – ¡Ah! pues sí, porque no tengo ningún plan.
   – Quedamos entonces enfrente del cine Astoria, en Amara.
   – ¿A qué hora quedamos?
   – ¿A las ocho y media?
   – Pues, muy bien, allí nos veremos.
   – Vale, de acuerdo, hasta luego.
   – Hasta luego.
   – Hasta luego, agur.
3. – ¡Dígame!
   – ¡Hola, Yolanda! Soy Pepe.
   – Sí, hola Pepe, ¿qué tal?
   – Pues bien, esta tarde Carlos, Juan y yo vamos a dar un paseo. ¿Quieres venir con nosotros?
   – ¿Esta tarde? Lo siento no puedo, tengo que ir a la universidad.
   – Pues, vale; hablamos mañana o el sábado.
   – Vale, adiós.
   – Adiós.

5 (p. 217)
1. – Cuando tienes una cita con alguien, ¿sueles llegar a tiempo?
   – Llego, suelo llegar tarde, cinco minutillos, diez.
   – ¿Es importante para ti la puntualidad?
   – Regular, no mucho...
2. – ¿Sueles ser puntual?
   – ¡Huy! sí muy puntual.
   – ¿Es importante la puntualidad?
   – Para mí sí.
3. – ¿Sueles llegar a tiempo?
   – Sí, me gusta llegar el primero.
   – ¿Es importante la puntualidad?
   – Para mí sí, y creo que la puntualidad es una cosa fundamental.
4. – ¿Cuando tienes una cita con alguien, sueles llegar a tiempo?
   – Procuro llegar a tiempo ...
   – ¿Es importante entonces la puntualidad?
   – Sí.

Section 3
2 (p. 218)
– ¿Y qué vamos a hacer el fin de semana?
– El sábado iremos a comer con Pepe y Susana.
– Sí.
– Después iremos a dar un paseo en el puerto y por la noche iremos a casa de los Sánchez pues es el cumpleaños de Julia.
– ¿Qué Julia?
– La hija mayor de los Sánchez.
– ¡Ah! sí.
– Tienes el domingo por la mañana para descansar. Por la tarde vendrá nuestra tía Berta para saludarte y por la noche si te apetece podemos ir al teatro; tengo dos entradas para El barbero de Sevilla.
– Ah pues, vale, muy bien.

Un paso más
2 (p. 222)
– Este es un mensaje de la Sra. Gómez, de la empresa Cofrusa de Madrid. Desgraciadamente me resulta imposible reunirme con usted a la hora que usted me sugiere. Tengo libre el martes a las once de la mañana. Si le conviene, podríamos reunirnos aquí para revisar su proyecto y después, si dispone del tiempo, podríamos comer juntos en algún restaurante del centro. Espero sus noticias. Hasta pronto. Adiós.

Translations
(Temas)

Translations of poems and songs from Temas

Unit 1

Muévete/Get going There's no bullet that can kill the truth. To end racism in South Africa – the kids sing it, and mum and dad. To save the world from so much evil – People are demanding it on every corner... Get going
Colombia, Mexico, Argentina, Cuba, Guatemala! Listen Costa Rica, Peru and Nicaragua, today it needs you! Brazil and Bolivia, Chile and Paraguay. Oh sing, Venezuela! Sing, Uruguay, Jamaica, Trinidad, Guadeloupe!
Let's go, Salvador! Come on Martinique, Dominican Republic! Go forward, Ecuador!

Unit 4

Romance del rey moro que perdió Alhama/ Ballad of the Moorish king who lost Alhama
The Moorish king was walking around the city of Granada
from the Elvira Gate to the Vivarrambla Gate
Woe is me, Alhama!
There an old Moor spoke and he said this
'Why do you call us, king, what is this call for?
Woe is me, Alhama!
I must tell you, my friends, of another tragedy.
Brave Christians have taken Granada from us.

Cante hondo/Deep song
It is deep, truly deep... much deeper than the heart that creates it and the voice that sings it, because it is almost infinite. It comes from distant peoples... It comes from the first cry and the first kiss...

Flamenco
The weeping begins
from the guitar.
It is useless to silence it.
It is impossible
to silence it.
It weeps on a single note
like the water weeps
like the wind weeps
on the snow-capped mountain.
It is impossible
to silence it.
It weeps for
distant things.

Los gitanos de hoy/The gypsies of today
'Four gypsy shacks burned in Salamanca.'
'500 inhabitants of Barcelona patrol their district and beat up drug addicts.'
'A gypsy family murdered in Bilbao.'
'People are against the gypsies because 90 per cent of them take drugs.'

¿Por qué se margina a la sociedad gitana?/Why are gypsy people marginalised?
Cristina Traver: Because they have a different culture to ours and they don't have the same morals as we do.
Alejandro Lorza: They're different and they're poor.
Ruth Alonso: Because of a lack of understanding. Nobody is interested in their customs, or in helping them to integrate.

¿Es España una sociedad racista?/Is Spain a racist country?
Alejandro: People don't accept it, but we are a racist society.
Susana Lareo: I think most people are racist, though adults are more so than young people.
Ruth Alonso: I think the vast majority of people aren't racists.
David Lopez: No, not all gypsies sell drugs. We're the ones that are really to blame.
Susana Lareo: Not all gypsies sell drugs, many of them are honest. The ones who sell drugs do it out of necessity.

Unit 5

Oda a la cebolla/Ode to the onion
the earth
made you like this,
onion,
clear as a planet
and destined
to gleam,
a constant constellation,
round rose of water
on
the table
of the poor people...

Unit 8

Síndrome/Syndrome
I've still got nearly all my teeth
almost all my hair and not many grey ones,
I can make love and unmake it,
climb a stair two at a time,
and run forty metres to catch a bus
so I shouldn't think of myself as old;
but the really serious part is that before
I never thought about such details.

POPOCHCOMITL
One of the simplest ceremonies, and one which is very beautiful in practice, is the ceremony known as ZAHUMACIÓN BLANCA. The Zahumación ceremony is a Purification Ceremony of enormous significance... The incense can purify the air and make people feel warm and friendly towards each other... .

Unit 9

Coplas/Couplets on the death of his father
Our lives are the rivers
that flow into the sea
that is death;
there the gentlemen
go straight to their end
and are consumed;
there there is equality
between those who live by their labour
and the rich.

Aztec poem...
Is it true perhaps that we live on earth ?
Forever on earth, perhaps? Only a brief instant here! Even the finest precious stones break, even gold can be destroyed, even precious feathers can be torn apart. Forever on earth, perhaps? Only a brief instant here!

La Semana Santa/Holy Week
January:
15 and 16: Festival of San Antón, the patron saint of my district. As he is also the patron saint of pets, everyone turns up with donkeys and bulls and goodness knows what. I always have a stall there.

February:
Cadiz, 5 February to 4 March: Shrovetide. Long festival which was suppressed for many years under Franco. Nowadays it's celebrated once again. I sell a lot.

April:
Holy Week: I always go to Tobarra (Albacete). The people of the town walk around the streets with drums and play them continuously for three days. Then to Seville or Granada – because the tourists buy lots of religious objects. I love the Moors and Christians – puppets which enact the ancient Moorish battles against the Christians throughout Andalucia.

May:
I go to Talavera de la Reina for the festival of San Isidro. It is a big festival for the workers and I love it.

June:
Corpus Christi: a big procession and a lot of prayers. It's good business!

Unit 10

El tren/The train
For every journey
– always on the wooden seat
of my third class carriage –
I travel light.
If it's at night, because I don't usually sleep,
or by day, because I watch
the trees go by,
I never sleep on the train,
and yet I'm content.
This pleasure in going away!
London, Madrid, Ponferrada,
such lovely places...to leave!

Unit 12

Deportes/Sports
What do I know about boxing,
I who confuse a jab with an uppercut?
And yet, at times
even since childhood,
like a great cloud from the depths of a valley,
Johnson rises up, comes to me,
the mountainous black man,
the magnetic athletic dandy

What do I know about chess?
I never moved a rook, a pawn,
I'm blind
to algebra, Greek characters
and that philosophical chessboard
where every figure is a question.
But I can remember Capablanca.

As a kid, I played baseball.
I loved Ruben Dario, that's true
with his violent roses.
But there at the highest point of my dreams
I always kept a pure green place
for Mendez, the pitcher - my other master.

Unit 13

Martin Fierro
I have known this land
Where the countryman lived

Translations
(Temas)

And he had his little farm
And his wife and kids
It was wonderful to see
How he spent his days

I found not a trace of my farm
Only a ruin was left
By God, that was enough
to sadden my heart
Then I swore
That I would be worse than a beast

I'll open up with my knife
The road that I'm to follow.

Unit 14

Paisaje tropical/Tropical landscape
The boat advances slowly through the waters of the Amazon. Now and again a house appears in the rainforest masked by impenetrable lianas, and a naked child waves to the people in the boat. On the deck, full of people, someone is reading the Bible aloud, but people prefer to laugh and sing while bottles and cigarettes are passed from mouth to mouth.

A Swiss journalist is travelling on this boat. For hours he's been watching a poor bony old man who spends all his time clutching a big cardboard box, and he doesn't let go of it even to sleep. Halfway along the route, in the middle of the forest, the old man disembarks. The Swiss helps him to get his big cardboard box down and then, opening the top slightly, he peeps inside; inside the box, wrapped in cellophane, is a plastic palm tree.

Unit 15

Tenochtítlan
Weary of beauty, the conquistadors ride along the road. Tenochtitlan looks as though it has been torn out of the pages of Amadís, with things that have never been heard of, never been seen or even dreamed of. The sun rises behind the volcanoes, it moves into the lagoon and tears the floating mist into shreds. The city, streets, gutters, temples with their tall towers, unfold and gleam.

La maldición de Malinche/Malinche's curse
They were riding beasts
Like demons
They had fire in their hands
And they were covered in metal

It was because of the bravery of a few
That there was resistance to them
And when they saw the blood flow
They were overcome by shame

That was our error, to surrender
the greatness of the past
and because of that error
we were slaves for 300 years

And we were left with the curse
of offering the foreigner
our faith our culture
our bread our money

Unit 16

Judías del tío Lucas/Tío Lucas's haricot beans
Fry the bacon in oil and add haricot beans, onions, garlic, parsley, cumin, a bay leaf, salt and paprika. Cook for at least four hours.

Hora cero/Zero hour
The Honduran peasants brought the money
in their hats
when the peasants sowed their crop
and the Hondurans were masters of their own land.
When there was money
and there were no foreign loans...
and the fruit company did not compete with
the small producer.
But the United Fruit Company came
with its subsidiaries the Tela Railroad Company
and the Trujillo Railroad Company
linked to the Cuyamel Fruit Company
the Unit ed Fruit Company
with its revolutions to gain concessions
and exemptions of millions from import and
export
taxes.....

Unit 17

Sueños y pesadillas/Dreams and nightmares
I wish I were like the wind
so that I could caress
the blonde hair of that girl,
or like the tight trousers
so close to her legs.
That's why I wouldn't want to leave the barrio
so that I can see her.
(Lumbi)

I dream of a table and chair
I dream I'm out driving in a car
I dream I'm making a film
I dream of a petrol pump
I dream I'm a luxury tourist

I dream of a bearded lady
I dream I'm going down stairs
I dream I'm winding up a pianola
I dream that my glasses are broken
I dream I am making a coffin
I dream of the solar system....
(Parra)

Unit 18

Ya todos saben para quien trabajan/Everyone knows who they're working for now
I translate an article from Esquire
on a sheet of paper made by the Kimberley Clark Corp.,
on an old Remington typewriter.
I'll correct it with an Esterbrook pen
What they pay me
will swell by a few pesos the coffers
of Carnation, General Foods, Heinz,
Colgate-Palmolive, Gillette
and the California Packing Corporation.

Nocturno de los tejedores viejos/Nocturne of the old weavers
Over are the divine days
when we danced by the sea
and siestas in the wind
smelling of pollen and salt
or siestas slept in cornfields
where the turtle dove nests.
So far away are the years
of bread made with wholemeal flour
enjoyed on pinewood tables
that we're better to deny them
and we'll say our lives were always
just as they are today

and we'll sell the whitened memory
that we left hanging in the doorway.

Las arpillerías/the patchworks
I can remember my first patchwork quite clearly... I can see myself as a young woman with my son in my arms. After that, great clouds with barbed wire which I saw my son coming out of.

Unit 19

Aprendizaje/Apprenticeship
I can't remember
what we said to each other
what happened.
My dresses were long.
I did my hair in a bun.
It happened.
That was all,
when I was innocent.
....
Sitting on my hill
I watched the sun set
The landscape was smooth
purple blue
thick blue.
It would have been hard not to love
at that time
with that landscape
and my innocence.
I began to know myself....

For days I don't meet myself
I pass before the mirror
but my image is not reflected.
I've no time to talk to myself.
I don't even miss myself at times.
I live when I am rewarded
with sunsets
and the laughter of my child.
I accept rows, sleeplessness, disappointments
I cannot bear indifference...
Life is not hope
It's more volatile
more precise
Something less than love
Something more than the daily grind

Para recordar/To remember
Do you remember the old patio
of our house in the town
where a geranium was planted
by our mother and it never died
with her tender hands
those of a Nicaraguan woman
the same hands that kneaded
the bread that we eat today.

You remember too the old man
making his wooden xylophones
and on the high sea singing
his sailor's dream
all those acrobatics
navigating against the wind
to earn the future
you have to dream it first.

And today when we travel the roads
and there's ash in our hair
our children have grown
as our memories have grown
memories to be written
in mid-journey
to remember you also
must be awake.

Word groups

In this section you will find words grouped into different areas of meaning, such as countries and nationalities, the family and occupations.

Notes:
1 The translations given here correspond to the contexts used in the book.
2 Next to some words you will find 'Sp' which stands for Spain, or 'LA', which stands for Latin America. 'Sp' indicates that the word is mostly used in Spain and 'LA' that the word is mostly used in more than one Latin American country; if there is no indication of usage, it means that the word is used in both Spain and Latin America. Occasionally you will also find other abbreviations such as 'Mex' which indicates the word is used in Mexico, or 'Arg', meaning Argentina.

1 Countries & nationalities

(a) Spanish speaking

Argentina	**argentino/a**
Bolivia	**boliviano/a**
Chile	**chileno/a**
Colombia	**colombiano/a**
Costa Rica	**costarricense**
Cuba	**cubano/a**
Ecuador	**ecuatoriano/a**
El Salvador	**salvadoreño/a**
España	**español/ola**
Las Filipinas	**filipino/a**
Guatemala	**guatemalteco/a**
Guinea Ecuatorial	*
Honduras	**hondureño/a**
México	**mexicano/a**
Nicaragua	**nicaragüense**
Panamá	**panameño/a**
Paraguay	**paraguayo/a**
Perú	**peruano/a**
Puerto Rico	**portorriqueño/a**
Rep. Dominicana	**dominicano/a**
Uruguay	**uruguayo/a**
Venezuela	**venezolano/a**

(b) Other countries

Australia	**Australia**	**australiano/a**
Belgium	**Bélgica**	**belga**
Brazil	**Brasil**	**brasileño/a**
Canada	**Canadá**	**canadiense**
China	**China**	**chino/a**
Denmark	**Dinamarca**	**danés/esa**
Egypt	**Egipto**	**egipcio/a**
England	**Inglaterra**	**inglés/esa**
France	**Francia**	**francés/esa**
Germany	**Alemania**	**alemán/ana**
Greece	**Grecia**	**griego/a**
G.B.	**Gran Bretaña**	**británico/a**
Holland	**Holanda**	**holandés/esa**
India	**La India**	**indio/a** (Sp)
Ireland	**Irlanda**	**irlandés/esa**
Israel	**Israel**	**israelí**
Italy	**Italia**	**italiano/a**
Japan	**Japón**	**japonés/esa**
Korea	**Corea**	**coreano/a**
Lebanon	**Líbano**	**libanés/esa**
Morocco	**Marruecos**	**marroquí**
N. Z.	**Nueva Zelanda**	**neozelandés/esa**
Nigeria	**Nigeria**	**nigeriano/a**
Norway	**Noruega**	**noruego/a**
Pakistan	**Pakistán**	**pakistaní**
Portugal	**Portugal**	**portugués/esa**
Russia	**Rusia**	**ruso/a**
Scotland	**Escocia**	**escocés/esa**
S. Africa	**Sudáfrica**	**sudafricano/a**
Sweden	**Suecia**	**sueco/a**
Switzerland	**Suiza**	**suizo/a**
USA	**Estados Unidos**	**norteamericano/a**
Vietnam	**Vietnam**	**vietnamita**
Wales	**Gales**	**galés/esa**

2 Occupations

actor/actress	**actor/actriz**
accountant	**contable** (Sp); **contador/ora**
architect	**arquitecto/a**
carpenter	**carpintero/a**
chef	**chef**
child minder	**niñera**
civil servant	**funcionario/a**
clerk	**oficinista**
cook	**cocinero/a**
dentist	**dentista**
doctor	**médico/a; doctor/ora**
engineer	**ingeniero/a**
footballer	**futbolista**
manager	**gerente**
nurse	**enfermero/a**
painter	**pintor/ora**
photographer	**fotógrafo/a**
receptionist	**recepcionista**
teacher	**profesor/ora**
secretary	**secretario/a**
shop assistant	**dependiente/a**
singer	**cantante**
solicitor/lawyer	**abogado/a**
student	**estudiante**
waiter/waitress	**camarero/a; mesero/a** (LA)
worker	**trabajador/ora**

3 Family

father	**padre; papá** (fam.) LA
mother	**madre; mamá** (fam.) LA
son/daughter	**hijo/a**
brother/sister	**hermano/a**
cousin	**primo/a**
uncle/aunt	**tío/a**
nephew/niece	**sobrino/a**
grandfather/-mother	**abuelo/a**
grandson/-daughter	**nieto/a**

4 Languages

Arabic	**árabe**
Basque	**vasco/euskera**
Catalan	**catalán**
Chinese	**chino**
Danish	**danés**
Dutch	**holandés**
English	**inglés**
French	**francés**
German	**alemán**
Greek	**griego**
Hebrew	**hebreo**
Hindi	**indi**
Hungarian	**húngaro**
Italian	**italiano**
Japanese	**japonés**
Persian	**persa**
Portuguese	**portugués**
Russian	**ruso**
Spanish	**español**
Welsh	**galés**

Word groups

5 Numbers

(a) Cardinal numbers

1	uno/un; una	22	veintidós
2	dos	23	veintitrés
3	tres	24	veinticuatro
4	cuatro	25	veinticinco
5	cinco	26	veintiséis
6	seis	27	veintisiete
7	siete	28	veintiocho
8	ocho	29	veintinueve
9	nueve	30	treinta
10	diez	33	treinta y tres
11	once	40	cuarenta
12	doce	42	cuarenta y dos
13	trece	50	cincuenta
14	catorce	56	cincuenta y seis
15	quince	60	sesenta
16	dieciséis	65	sesenta y cinco
17	diecisiete	70	setenta
18	dieciocho	80	ochenta
19	diecinueve	90	noventa
20	veinte		
21	veintiuno/ veintiún/ veintiuna		

100	cien
102	ciento dos
110	ciento diez
125	ciento veinticinco
200	doscientos/as
232	doscientos/as treinta y dos
300	trescientos/as
400	cuatrocientos/as
500	quinientos/as
600	seiscientos/as
700	setecientos/as
800	ochocientos/as
900	novecientos/as
1.000	mil
1.044	mil cuarenta y cuatro
2.000	dos mil
10.000	diez mil
100.000	cien mil
1.000.000	un millón

Notes:
a There is a feminine form for these numbers: 1 (**uno/a**), 200-900 (**doscientos/as**, etc.).
b The 'o' in 'uno' is dropped when followed by a masculine noun.

(b) Ordinal numbers

first	primero/a
second	segundo/a
third	tercero/a
fourth	cuarto/a
fifth	quinto/a
sixth	sexto/a
seventh	séptimo/a
eighth	octavo/a
ninth	noveno/a
tenth	décimo/a

6 Buildings, places and monuments

airport	el aeropuerto
bank	el banco
bar/pub	el bar/el pub
building	el edificio
bullring	la plaza de toros
bus station	la estación de autobuses; la terminal de buses (LA); la central camionera (LA)
castle	el castillo; el alcázar
cathedral	la catedral
church	la iglesia
cinema	el cine
café, coffee shop	la cafetería
factory	la fábrica
gallery	la galería
garden	el jardín
hospital	el hospital
hotel	el hotel
launderette	la lavandería
library	la biblioteca
monument	el monumento
museum	el museo
palace	el palacio
park	el parque
post office	(la oficina de) Correos/ el correo
restaurant	el restaurante/ el restorán
school	la escuela
square	la plaza
main square	la plaza mayor; la plaza de armas (LA)
railway station	la estación de ferrocarril
stadium	el estadio
theatre	el teatro
tourist office	la oficina de turismo
town hall	el ayuntamiento
underground station	la estación de metro
university	la universidad

7 Descriptions of places

big	grande
boring	aburrido/a
cheerful	alegre
clean	limpio/a
cold	frío/a
cosmopolitan	cosmopolita
dangerous	peligroso/a
dirty	sucio/a
enormous	enorme
famous	famoso/a
friendly; warm	acogedor/ora; cálido/a
fun	divertido/a
historic	histórico/a
hostile	hostil
hot	caluroso/a; caliente (LA)
impressive	impresionante
industrial	industrial
interesting	interesante
lively	vivo/a
modern	moderno/a
noisy	ruidoso/a
old	antiguo/a
picturesque	pintoresco/a
quiet	tranquilo/a
romantic	romántico/a
small	pequeño/a
ugly	feo/a

Word groups

8 Shops

bakery	la panadería
bookshop	la librería
butcher's	la carnicería
cake shop	la pastelería
chemist's/drugstore	la farmacia
clothes shop	la tienda de ropa
delicatessen	la charcutería
dry cleaner's	la tintorería
fishmonger's	la pescadería
food/grocery shop	la tienda de comestibles
fruit shop	la frutería
jeweler's	la joyería
market	el mercado
handicraft market	el mercado de artesanías
hardware store	la ferretería; la tlapalería (Mex)
newspaper stand	el kiosko/el quiosco; el puesto de periódicos (LA)
petrol/gas station	la gasolinera; la bomba de gasolina (LA)
shoe shop/store	la zapatería
shopping centre/mall	el centro comercial
silversmith's	la platería
stationer's	la papelería
supermarket	el supermercado
sweet/candy shop	la confitería
tobacconist's	el estanco (Sp)
travel agency	la agencia de viajes

9 Means of transport

aeroplane/airplane	el avión
boat/ship	el barco; el bote (small)
bus	el autobús; el bus (LA); el camión (Mex); el omnibús (Per); la micro (Chi); la guagua (Cuba); el colectivo (Arg & Ven)
car	el coche (Sp); el carro/auto (LA)
coach	el autocar (Sp); el autobús/bus/ pullman (LA)
ferry	el ferry
motorcycle	la moto
taxi	el taxi
train	el tren
underground/subway	el metro

10 Fruit, vegetables

apple	la manzana
apricot	el albaricoque (Sp); el damasco (LA)
avocado	el aguacate; la/el palta (LA)
banana	el plátano; la banana/ el banano (LA)
cherry	la cereza
fig	el higo
grape	la uva
grapefruit	el pomelo; la toronja (LA)
lemon	el limón
melon	el melón
orange	la naranja
paw paw	la papaya
peach	el melocotón (Sp); el durazno (LA)
pear	la pera
pineapple	la piña; el ananá(s) (Arg)
plum	la ciruela
raspberry	la frambuesa
strawberry	la fresa; la frutilla (LA)
watermelon	la sandía
asparagus	el espárrago
aubergine/egg plant	la berenjena
beans (kidney)	los frijoles/porotos
cabbage	la col; el repollo (LA)
carrot	la zanahoria
cauliflower	la coliflor
celery	el apio
chilli	el chile; el ají
corn	el maíz; el choclo (LA); el elote (Mex)
cucumber	el pepino; el pepinillo (LA)
leek	el puerro
lentil	la lenteja
lettuce	la lechuga
mushrooms	las setas (Sp); los champiñones; los hongos (LA)
onion	la cebolla
pepper	el pimiento
potato	la patata; la papa (LA)
spinach	la espinaca
spring onion	la cebolleta
tomato	el tomate; el jitomate (Mex)

11 Containers and measures

bag	una bolsa
bottle	una botella
box/case	una caja
bunch	un racimo (de uvas)
can/tin	una lata; un bote (Sp)
cup	una taza
dozen	una docena
jar	un bote
kilo	un kilo
litre	un litro
loaf	una barra
packet	un paquete; una cajetilla (de cigarillos)
pound	una libra

12 Fish, meat, poultry and seafood

anchovies	anchoas
bacon	el bacon; el tocino
beef	la carne de vaca/res
chicken	el pollo
cod	el bacalao
duck	el pato
fish	el pescado
hake	la merluza
ham	el jamón
herring	el arenque
lamb	el cordero
lobster	la langosta
meat	la carne
mussels	los mejillones
pork	el cerdo;
sucking pig	el cochinillo, lechón
prawns	las gambas (Sp); los langostinos
rabbit	el conejo
salami	el salchichón
salmon	el salmón
sardine	la sardina
sausage	la salchicha; el chorizo (spicy)
seafood	los mariscos
shellfish	las almejas
trout	la trucha
tuna	el atún; bonito (Sp)
turkey	el pavo; el guajolote (Mex)
veal	la ternera

Word groups

13 Personal habits

to brush your teeth	lavarse los dientes; lavarse la boca (LA)
to comb your hair	peinarse
to get up	levantarse
to get ready	arreglarse; alistarse (LA)
to go to bed	acostarse
to put makeup on	maquillarse; pintarse
to put on (clothes)	ponerse
to shave	afeitarse
to take a shower	ducharse; bañarse (LA)
to take a bath	bañarse
to take off clothes	sacarse; quitarse (LA)
to wake up	despertarse
to wash/wash up	lavarse
to wash your face	lavarse la cara

14 The house

(a) Rooms

attic	el ático/el desván
balcony	el balcón
basement	el sótano
bedroom	el dormitorio; la habitación; el cuarto; la recámara (Mex)
dining room	el comedor
fireplace	la chimenea
floor	la planta; el piso (LA)
first floor	la primera planta; el primer piso (LA)
garage	el garage/garaje
ground floor	la planta baja
hall	el pasillo; el corredor
kitchen	la cocina
living room	el salón (Sp); el cuarto de estar; la sala/el living (LA)
room	la habitación; el cuarto
terrace	la terraza
toilet	el cuarto de baño (Sp); el baño (LA); el servicio; el wáter (Sp)

(b) Furniture & appliances

armchair	el sillón
bath(tub)	la bañera; la tina de baño (LA)
bed	la cama
bedside table	la mesita/mesilla (de noche); el velador (LA)
bookcase	la estantería; el librero (LA)
carpet	la alfombra; la moqueta (fitted) (Sp)
chair	la silla
chest of drawers	la cómoda
cooker	la cocina
cupboard	el aparador
curtains	las cortinas
desk	el escritorio
dishwasher	el lavaplatos; la lavadora de platos (LA)
furniture	muebles
lamp	la lámpara
light	la luz
(microwave) oven	el horno (de microondas)
refrigerator	el frigorífico (el frigo); la nevera; la refrigeradora (LA)
shelf	el estante
shower	la ducha; la regadera (Mex)
sink	el fregadero
sofa	el sofá
table	la mesa
TV set	el televisor; la televisión
wardrobe	el armario; el guardarropa (LA); el clóset (LA)
wash-basin	el lávabo
washing-machine	la lavadora; el lavarropas (Arg)

15 Drinks

beer	la cerveza; la caña (draught beer)
chocolate	el chocolate
coffee	el café;
black coffee	café solo (Sp)/negro/tinto (LA)
milky coffee	café con leche
white coffee	café cortado
coke	la Coca Cola
fruit juice	el zumo (Sp); el jugo (LA)
grape juice	el mosto
herbal tea	la infusión
lemonade (fizzy)	la gaseosa (Sp); el refresco de limón (LA)
lemonade (real)	la limonada
milk shake	el batido; la malteada (LA)
rum	el ron
sherry	el jerez; el fino (dry sherry) (Sp)
soft drink	el refresco; la gaseosa (LA)
tea	el té
vermouth	el vermú/vermut
water	el agua (mineral)
wine	el vino
sparkling wine	el cava
drink served on crushed ice	el granizado

16 Descriptions of people

(a) Appearance

dark	moreno/a
fair	rubio/a
good looking	guapo/a
heavily built	corpulento/a
middle-aged	de mediana edad
old	viejo/a; mayor
pretty	bonita (women only); linda (LA)
red-haired	pelirrojo/a
short	bajo; pequeño/a
slim	delgado/a; esbelto/a
slightly built	menudo/a
tall	alto/a
ugly	feo/a
young	joven

(b) Character and personality

affectionate	cariñoso/a
boring	aburrido/a
dynamic	dinámico/a
extrovert	extrovertido/a
friendly	amigable; amistoso/a
fun	divertido/a
funny	gracioso/a; chistoso/a
intelligent	inteligente
interesting	interesante
introvert	introvertido/a
nice	simpático/a
optimistic	optimista

Word groups

pessimistic	pesimista
quiet	callado/a
selfish	egoísta
sensitive	sensible
shy	tímido/a
silly	tonto/a
stubborn	testarudo/a; terco/a (LA)
thoughtful	atento/a
unpleasant	antipático/a

17 Parts of the body

arm	el brazo
back	la espalda
chest	el pecho
chin	el mentón; la barbilla
ear	la oreja (outer); el oído (inner)
elbow	el codo
eyebrows	las cejas
eyes	los ojos
finger	el dedo
foot	el pie
forehead	la frente
hair	el pelo; el cabello
hand	la mano
head	la cabeza
knee	la rodilla
leg	la pierna
lips	los labios
mouth	la boca
nail	la uña
navel	el ombligo
neck	el cuello; la nuca (nape)
nose	la nariz
shoulder	el hombro
throat	la garganta
toes	los dedos del pie
tooth	el diente; la muela
tummy	la barriga/tripa (Sp); la guata (LA)
waist	la cintura

18 Symptoms and illnesses

allergy	la alergia
backache	el dolor de espalda
catarrh	el catarro
cold	el resfriado
cough	la tos
diarrhea	la diarrea
earache	el dolor de oído
fever/temperature	la fiebre
flu	la gripe
headache	el dolor de cabeza
infection	la infección
migraine	la jaqueca
sore throat	el dolor de garganta
stomach ache	el dolor de estómago
stress	el estrés/la tensión
sunburn	la insolación
tonsilitis	la amigdalitis; las anginas
toothache	el dolor de muela(s)
vomiting	el vómito

19 Days and months

Monday	el lunes
Tuesday	el martes
Wednesday	el miércoles
Thursday	el jueves
Friday	el viernes
Saturday	el sábado
Sunday	el domingo
January	enero
February	febrero
March	marzo
April	abril
May	mayo
June	junio
July	julio
August	agosto
September	septiembre
October	octubre
November	noviembre
December	diciembre

20 Expressions of time

in January	en enero
in winter	en invierno
at Christmas	en Navidad
on Saturday	el sábado
at the weekend	el fin de semana
this week/month	esta semana/este mes
last week	la semana pasada
next week	la semana próxima/ la semana que viene
today	hoy
now	ahora
yesterday	ayer
tomorrow	mañana
every day	todos los días
every year	todos los años
always	siempre
often	a menudo/ frecuentemente
never	nunca
almost never	casi nunca
sometimes	a veces
from time to time	de vez en cuando
once a week	una vez a la semana
twice a month	dos veces al mes
a week ago	hace una semana

21 Sports and pastimes

aerobics	los aeróbicos/el aeróbic
athletics	el atletismo
badminton	el bádminton
baseball	el béisbol
basketball	el baloncesto; el básquet
canoeing	el piragüismo
cycling	el ciclismo
D.I.Y.	el bricolaje
fishing	la pesca
football	el fútbol
gardening	la jardinería
golf	el golf
horse riding	la equitación
jogging	el footing (Sp)
judo	el judo
mountain climbing	el montañismo; el andinismo (Andean region); el alpinismo (in Europe)
sailing	la vela
skiing	el esquí
squash	el squash
trekking	el senderismo
swimming	la natación
tennis	el tenis
volleyball	el voleibol

22 Events

bullfight	la corrida de toros
carnival	el carnaval
championship	el campeonato
circus	el circo
concert	el concierto
dance (ballet, etc.)	la danza
dance (ballroom, etc.)	el baile
festival	el festival

Word groups

film	la película
(football) match	el partido (de fútbol)
parade	el desfile
play	la obra de teatro
procession	la procesión
race	la carrera
show	el espectáculo

23 Geography

bay	la bahía
beach	la playa
coast	la costa
countryside	el campo
desert	el desierto
environment	el medio ambiente
forest	el bosque
hill	la colina
island	la isla
lagoon	la laguna
lake	el lago
marsh	el pantano
mountain	la montaña
mountain range	la sierra; la cordillera
plateau	la meseta
rainforest	la selva
river	el río
sea	el mar
volcano	el volcán

24 Cooking and eating

(a) Utensils and appliances

beater	la batidora
blender	la licuadora
coffee-pot	la cafetera
food-processor	el procesador de alimentos
frying-pan	la sartén
pot	la cazuela (Sp); la olla/cacerola
saucepan	el cazo

(b) Crockery & cutlery

bowl	el tazón
cup	la taza
glass	el vaso; la copa (de vino)
plate	el plato
saucer	el platillo
cutlery	los cubiertos
fork	el tenedor
knife	el cuchillo
tablespoon	la cuchara grande
teaspoon	la cucharita

25 Clothes & accessories

belt	el cinturón
blouse	la blusa
boots	las botas
coat	el abrigo
dress (general)	la ropa
dress (for a woman)	el vestido
earrings	los pendientes; los aretes (LA)
hat	el sombrero; la gorra
jacket	la chaqueta; el saco (LA)
jeans	los vaqueros; los (blue) jeans
jogging suit	el chándal; el buzo (LA)
necklace	el collar
raincoat	el impermeable
robe	la bata (Sp); el salto de cama (LA)
sandals	las sandalias; los huaraches (Mex)
scarf	el pañuelo; la bufanda
shirt	la camisa
shoes	los zapatos
shorts	los pantalones cortos
skirt	la falda
socks	los calcetines
suit	el traje
sweater	el jersey; el suéter (LA)
swimsuit	el traje de baño; el bañador (Sp)
tie	la corbata
tights/pantyhose	las medias; pantimedias (Mex)
trainers, tennis shoes	las zapatillas (Sp); los zapatos de deporte
trousers	los pantalones; el pantalón
t-shirt	la camiseta

Spanish-English Glossary

Glossary for Sueños World Spanish.

Introductory Note: the **word order** is letter by letter according to the Spanish alphabet. All nouns are preceded by the definite article. This is bracketed in the following cases:
1. (el) inglés – where the word may be either a noun or an adjective with the same form and translation. Where these differ, the words are listed separately. 2. (la) España – names of countries with which the definite article is not normally used. Where the article before the name of a country is not bracketed, it indicates that the article is normally used.
Radical-changing **verbs** are indicated by the change within brackets. Irregular verbs are indicated by [*irr*]. **Abbreviations** used: *m.* masculine, *f.* feminine, *sing.* singular, *pl.* plural, *abb.* abbreviation. An oblique followed by 'o' or 'a' indicates the alternative ending for gender.

A

    a a; to
    abajo downstairs, down below
        de arriba abajo from top to bottom
    abarcar to take in
el **abonado** subscriber
    abonarse to subscribe to
    aborrecer to loathe
    aborrezco I loathe
    abrazarse to hug one another
    abrazos kind regards
    abrigado/a warm, sheltered
    abril April
    abrir to open (past part. **abierto**)
la **abuelita** grandma, granny
(el/la) **abuelo/a** grandfather/grandmother
    aburrido/a boring, tedious
    acabar to finish, to end
    acabar de to have just done (something)
    acabarse to come to an end
el **acantilado** cliff
    acaso perhaps
el **aceite (de oliva)** (olive) oil
la **aceituna** olive
    aceptar to accept
la **acequia** canal
    acercarse to approach, to draw nearer
    acogedor(a) friendly
    acoger to receive, to welcome
la **acomodación** accommodation
    acondicionado: aire acondicionado air conditioning
el **acontecimiento** event
    acordarse (ue) de to remember
    acostarse (ue) to lie down; to go to bed
    acostumbrarse to get used to
        así se acostumbra this is the way we do things
las **actividades** activities, events
el/la **actor/actriz** actor/actress
la **actuación** theatre performance
    actual modern; present-day, up-to-date
    actualmente now, nowadays
    actuar to act (perform on stage, etc.)
el **acueducto** aqueduct
el **acuerdo** agreement
        de acuerdo all right, O.K., agreed
    adaptado/a adapted
la **administración** administration, management
el/la **admirador(a)** admirer
    admirar to admire
    adiós goodbye
el/la **adolescente** teenager

¿adónde? where (to)?
adquirir (ie) to obtain
el **aeropuerto** airport
    afeitarse to shave
la **afición** pastime, interest
el/la **aficionado/a** fan, follower
    afirmativo/a affirmative
la **agencia** agency
la **agenda** diary
    agosto August
    agradable pleasant
    agrícola (*m./f.*) agricultural
el **agua** (*f.*) water (*pl.* **las**)
el **aguacate** avocado
el **aguilucho lagunero** pool eaglet
    ahí there
    ahora now, here, today
        y ahora tú it's your turn now
    ahorita now (this very minute)
el **aire** air (atmosphere; appearance)
        aire acondicionado air conditioning
        al aire libre in the open (air)
    ¿aja? aha? what?
el **ajedrez** chess
el **ajillo** garlic sauce
el **ajo** garlic
    al (a + el) to the, at the
la **alambrada** wire
    albergar to accommodate; to shelter
los **albores** dawn (earliest days of something)
    alcanzar to reach, to achieve
    alegre cheerful, happy
    alejarse to go away
(el/la) **alemán/alemana** German
el **alemán** German language
el **alfabeto** alphabet
el **alfil** bishop (chess)
el **alga marina** seaweed
    algo something
el **algodón** cotton
    alguien someone
    algún/uno/una a, any, some
    alguno/a(s) some; any
el **alimento** food
el **alma** (*f*) soul, spirit
la **almendra** almond
    almorzar (ue) to lunch/to have for lunch
el **almuerzo** lunch
    alquilar to hire out
    alrededor de around
los **alrededores** surroundings
la **alternativa** alternative
        tomar la alternativa to become a professional bullfighter
    alto/a tall, high
la **altura** height
    alzarse to rise up, stand
    allí there
    amarillo/a yellow
    amazónico/a Amazon (*adj.*)
el **ambiente** atmosphere
la **amenaza** threat, menace
el/la **amigo/a** friend
la **amistad** friendship
    'amo de casa' 'house-husband'
el **amor** love
    amplio/a roomy, spacious; big; full
el **analgésico** analgesic, pain-killer
la **anchoa** anchovy
    andar [*irr*] to go (walk)
        andar a pie to go on foot
el **animal** animal
el **anillo** ring
    anoche last night
    ansioso/a anxious, uneasy
    anteayer day before yesterday

antelación: con atelación in advance
antes before
la(s) **antigüedad(es)** antiques
antiguo/a ancient, old; former, previous
antipático/a disagreeable, unpleasant
anunciar to announce
el/la **anticuario/a** antiquarian; antique dealer
añadir to add
el **año** year
    los 'años viejos' (literally, 'old years') effigies burned on New Year's Eve
apagar to turn out, to switch off
el **aparcamiento** car park
la **apariencia** appearance
el **apartamento** (*abb.* **apto.**) flat
el **apellido** surname, family name
apenas hardly, scarcely
apetecer to fancy, feel like
    ¿Qué te apetece tomar? What do you fancy?
el **aportación** contribution
aportar to bring (to)
aprender to learn
apretado/a oppressive
apurarse to hurry (up); to make an effort
aquí here
    aquí está here it is
    de aquí local; home-grown
(el/la) **árabe** Arab
el **árbol** tree
el **arca** (f) coffer
el **arco** arch
(el/la) **argentino/a** Argentinian
la(s) **arma(s)** arms, weapons
el **armario** cupboard
arqueológico/a archaeological
el/la **arquitecto/a** architect
arquitectónico/a architectural
arreglar to tidy
arriba upstairs; up , above
    de arriba abajo from top to bottom
    más arriba higher up
arrojar to throw
el **arroz** rice
el **arte** (*m. sing.*) art
las **artes** (*f.pl.*) (the) arts
la **artesanía** handicraft
la **articulación** joint
articular joint (*adjective*)
el **artículo** article
artístico/a artistic
arzobispal archepiscopal
asado/a grilled; baked
ascender (ie) to ascend, to go up
asco: ¡qué asco! how horrible!
aseo: los aseos toilet, lavatory, WC
asesinado/a assassinated
así so; in this way
    así se acostumbra this is the way we do things
    así se habla/así se dice this is how we say it
    así se nos va el día this is how we spend the day
asistir to attend
la **aspirina** aspirin
atar to tie, to fasten
el **atardecer** sunset, dusk
atender (ie) to attend, to serve
el **atletismo** athletics
la **atracar** to land
la **atracción** attraction; amusement; entertainment
atrás de behind
el **atún** tuna (see also **bonito**)
aumentar to grow, to increase

Spanish-English Glossary

	aún still; yet
el	autobús bus
el/la	autor(a) author; perpetrator
los	autos de navidad Mystery Plays
	¡avanza! advance!
el	ave *(f.)* bird
la	avenida *(abb. av.)* avenue
	aventurero/a adventurous
la	aviación air force; aviation
el	avión aeroplane
la	avioneta light aeroplane
el	aviso notice
la	avutarda great bustard
	¡ay! oh!
	ayer yesterday
	ayudar to help
el	ayuntamiento city/town hall; city/town council
el	azúcar sugar
	azul blue
	azul marino navy blue

B

el	bacalao cod
	bailar to dance
	bajar to descend; to get off (a bus); to lead down to
	bajo/a short; small; low
la	bala bullet
las	(islas) Baleares Balearic Islands
el	baloncesto basketball
el	banco bank
la	banda band
el	bañador swimsuit
	bañarse to have a bath; to bathe, swim
el	bar bar (drinks)
	barato/a cheap
la	barba beard
la	barra loaf (of bread); oblique stroke/slash
la	barraca street theatre
la	barranca gully, ravine
	barrer to sweep
el	barrio district, quarter (of small town); suburb
la	basílica basilica
	bastante enough; quite
la	basura rubbish
	batir to beat
	beber to drink
la	bebida drink
la	beca grant; scholarship
	bello/a beautiful; fine
	Bellas Artes Fine Arts
	¡Bendito sea Dios! Blessed be God! God be praised!
el	besugo red bream
la	biblioteca library
la	bicicleta bicycle; cycling
	en bicicleta by bicycle
	bien well
	bien surtido well stocked
	bienvenido/a welcome
los	bienes property
	bienvenida welcome
el	bigote moustache
el	billete ticket
	billete de ida y vuelta return/round trip ticket
la	biografía biography
la	biología biology
la	biosfera biosphere
	Reserva de la Biosfera Ecological Reserve
el	bistec teak
	blanco/a white
la	blusa blouse

la	boca mouth
el	bocadillo Spanish bread sandwich
la	boda wedding
el	bolígrafo ball-point pen
(el/la)	boliviano/a Bolivian
el	bollo bread roll
la	bolsa bag
	bolsa de aseo toilet bag
	bolsa de cotillón lucky dip
el/la	bolso/a handbag
las	bombachas baggy trousers
	bonito/a pretty
el	bonito tuna (see also atún)
la	bota boot
el	bote boat
la	botella bottle
la	brasa hot coal
	a la brasa barbecued
el	brazo arm
el	bricolage/bricolaje DIY
	brindar to offer
el	broche clasp
el	bronce bronze
el	bronceador suntan lotion
	bucear to dive; to swim under water
	buenísimo/a very good
	bueno(s)/buena(s) good
	buenos días good morning
	¡Buen provecho! Enjoy your meal!
la	bufanda scarf
la	buhardilla small flat
	bullicioso noisy, rowdy
el	burlador joker
	buscar to look for
	se busca 'wanted' (announcement)
	en busca de in search of
la	butaca stall (theatre
	butaca turista reclining chair (overnight travel)

C

	cabalgar to ride
el	caballo horse;
	montar a caballo horse-riding
la	cabeza head
la	cabina telefónica telephone box/booth
	cacereño/a of/from Cáceres
	cada each, every
	a cada loco con su tema each to their own
	cada uno/a each one
la	cadena chain
	caer *[irr]* to fall
el	café coffee; *(adj.)* light brown
la	cafetería café, coffee shop
la	caja box
	caja de cartón cardboard box
el	calamar squid
el	calcetín sock
la	caldereta stew
la	calefacción heating
	calentar (ie) to heat up
	cálido/a hot (climate)
	caliente warm, hot (soup, etc) (climate, LA)
el	calor heat
	hace mucho calor it's very hot
	caluroso/a hot
	calvo/a bald
la	calzada causeway, pavement
	calzar to take/wear (size of shoes)
las	calzas breeches
la	calle street
los	callos tripe
la	cama bed
	cama de matrimonio double bed

la	camarote cabin
	cambiar to change
el	cambio change; exchange
	en cambio on the other hand/instead
la	cámara camera
	caminar to walk
la	caminata walk
la	camisa shirt
la	camiseta t-shirt
el/la	campeón/ona champion
el/la	campesino/a peasant
el	campo field; course; pitch
	casa de campo country house
el	Canadá Canada
(el/la)	canadiense Canadian
Las	Canarias Canary Islands
las	canas grey hairs
la	canastilla baby's layette
el	canasto large basket
	cancelar to pay/settle an account (LA)
la	canción song
	canoso/a grey/white-haired
	cansado/a tired
el/la	cantante professional singer
	cantar to sing
la	cantidad quantity
el	cañón cannon
el	capitán captain; commander
(el/la)	caprichoso/a capricious, wilful (person)
la	cara face
el	caracol snail
	característico/a characteristic
	¡caramba! well! good gracious!
la	carabela caravel
la	carne meat
	caro/a expensive
	carpe diem (Latin) seize the day
el	carpintero carpenter; woodworker
la	carrera course; race
la	carreta cart
la	carta letter (correspondence)
la	cartera wallet (Sp); handbag (LA)
la	casa house; home
	casa/caja de cambio bank; bureau de change
	casa de campo country house
	Casa de Campo park in Madrid
	de la casa of the house (menu)
	me voy a casa I'm going home
(el/la)	casado/a married (person)
	casado/a con ... married to ...
	casarse to get married
la	cascada waterfall
el	casete cassette
la	casete cassette player (Sp)
	casi almost
	¡casi me muero! I almost died!
el	casino casino
el	caso case, instance, situation
	castaño/a chestnut-coloured; brown
el	castillo castle
la	casualidad chance
	por casualidad by chance
el	catarro catarrh; (a) cold
el/la	catalán/catalana Catalan, Catalunian
la	catedral cathedral
	católico/a Catholic
la	cebolla onion
	celebrar to celebrate
	celebrarse to be held, celebrated
la	cena dinner/supper
	cenar to have dinner/supper
el	céntimo cent (euro currency)
el	centro centre
	centro de salud health centre
	centro de veraneo summer resort

Spanish-English Glossary

el	cepillo de dientes	toothbrush
la	cerámica	ceramics; pottery
	cerca	nearby
	cerca de	near
	cercano/a	close
el	cerdo	pork
	cerrar (ie)	to shut, to close
la	cerveza	beer
el	chalé	chalet
el	chalet	(larger) house (Sp)
el	chaparrón	cloudburst, downpour
	chapuzar	to do odd jobs (around the house)
la	chaqueta	jacket
	charlar	to chat
el	chef	chef
el	cheque de viajero	traveller's cheque
	chévere	nice, fine (LA)
el/la	chico/a	young boy/girl
(el/la)	chileno/a	Chilean
la	chimenea	fireplace
el	chocolate	chocolate
la	choza	shack
el	chubasco	shower (rain)
la	chuleta	cutlet
el	churro	fritter
la	ciática	sciatica
el	ciclismo	cycling
el	ciclomotor	motorcycle
la	ciencia	science
la	cifra	number
el	cilantro	coriander
el	cine	cinema
el	cinturón	belt
la	cita	appointment, date
	citar	to make an appointment
la	ciudad	city
	ciudad de los sueños	city of dreams/dream city
	civil	civil
	claro	of course; really (often for emphasis); clearly
la	clase	class
el	claustro	cloister
	clausurar	to close
el	clavo	clove
el/la	cliente	client, customer
el	clima	climate
la	clínica	clinic
	cocer (ue)	to cook
la	cocina	kitchen
	cocinar	to cook, do the cooking
el/la	cocinero/a	cook
el	cóctel	cocktail
el	coche	car
	coger	to take (transport/travel); to pick up
	cojo el autobús	I take the bus
la	cogida	goring, tossing (bullfight)
el	colegio	secondary school
la	coliflor	cauliflower
la	colina	hill
	colonial	colonial
el	color	colour
el	collar	necklace
	combinar	to combine
el	comedor	dining room
	comentar	to discuss; to gossip
	comenzar (ie)	to begin, to commence
	da comienzo	begins (first performance)
	comer	to eat
	¡A comer!	Let's eat!
el	cómico	comic actor; comedian
la	comida	food
	comida rápida	fast food
la	comisaría	police station
	como	as
	¿cómo?	why? how? what?
	¿cómo es?	what is it like?
	¿á cómo está?	how much is it?
	¿cómo te llamas?	what is your name?
la	cómoda	chest of drawers
la	comodidad	comfort
	cómodo/a	comfortable
la	compañía	(airline) company
	comparar	to compare
	competir (i)	to compete
	completo/a	complete, full
la	composición	composition
el/la	compositor(a)	composer
	completamente	completely
	complicado/a	complicated
	comprar	to buy
	comprarse	to buy (for oneself)
	compras: ir de compras	to go shopping
	comprensivo/a	comprehensive; tolerant, understanding
el	comprimido	pill, tablet
el	computador	computer
	comunicando	engaged (telephone)
	comunitario/a	(adj.) community
	con	with; what has been added
	coñac	brandy, cognac
	conceder	to concede
	concentrar	to concentrate
el	concierto	concert
la	condesita	little countess
la	condición	condition
la	configuración	shape
	confirmar	to confirm
	conformarse	to conform; to resign oneself
el	confort	comfort
	confundir	to confuse
el	congreso	assembly, conference
	conmigo	with me
	conocer	to know; to meet, to get to know
	la conozco	I know her
	conocerse	to meet one another; to get to know one another
	conocido/a	known
la	conquista	conquest
	conseguir (i)	to obtain, to get
el	consejo	advice
el	consomé	clear soup, consommé
	constante	constant
la	construcción	building, construction
	construir	to build
la	consulta	(doctor's) surgery, practice
	consultar	to consult; to look up
el	contacto	contact
la	contaminación	pollution
	contar	to tell
los	contenidos	content(s)
	contento/a	happy, contented
el	contestador automático	answerphone
	contestar	to reply
	no contestan	there's no reply
el	contrato	contract
(el/la)	contrario/a	contrary, opposite
	al contrario	on the contrary
el	contraste	contrast
	controlar	to control, keep a strict eye on
el	convento	convent
	convertirse (i)	to change; to convert
el/la	convocado/a	participant
la	copa	wine glass
	coproducido/a	co-produced
la	corbata	tie
el/la	cordero/a	lamb
la	cordillera	mountain range
	corregir (i)	to correct
	correr	to run
	correspondiente	(adj.) corresponding
la	corrida (de toros)	bullfight
el	cortijo	farmhouse
	corto/a	short
el	coronel	colonel
	cortar	to cut
la	cosa	thing
	otra cosa	something else
	una cosa así	something like that
el/la	cosechero/a	picker; grower
	pequeño cosechero	small farmer
la	costa	coast
(el/la)	costarricense	Costa Rican
la	costilla	chop (meat)
la	costumbre	habit
la	costurera	dress-maker
el	cotillón	New Year's Eve party
	crear	to create, to invent
la	creación	creation
el	crédito	credit
	tarjeta de crédito	credit card
	creer	to think, to believe
la	crema	cream
la	criada	maid, servant
el	cristal	glass
(el/la)	cristiano/a	Christian
el	Cristo	Christ
	crítico/a	critical
la	crónica	chronicle, account
	cruzar	to cross
el	cuaderno	notebook
la	cuadra	block (of houses, buildings)
el	cuadro	picture; square
	de/a cuadros	checked (pattern)
	cuádruple	for 4 (people)
	¿cuál?	which? what?
	cualquier	any
	cuando	when (adverb)
	¿cuándo?	when? (interrogative)
	¿cuánto/a/os/as?	(interrogative) how much?
	¿cuánto es?	how much is it?
	¿cuántos?	how many?
	¿cuántos años tiene?	how old are you?
	cuarteado	jointed
el	cuarto	room; fourth; quarter
	cuarto de baño	bathroom
	cuarto de estar	living room
(el/la)	cubano/a	Cuban
la	cubierta	deck
	cubierto/a	covered; overcast
el	cubito	cube
	cubrir	to cover
la	cucharada	spoonful
el	cuello	neck
la	cuenta	account, bill
el	cuero	leather
el	cuerpo	body
el	cuidado	care
	¡cuidado!	take care, be careful, go carefully
	cuidar	to look after, to take care of
el	cultivo	cultivation
	de cultivo	arable
la	cultura	culture
la	cumbre	summit
el	cumpleaños	birthday
la	cuna	cradle
	curar	to cure (someone)
las	curiosidades	sights, attractions
	cursar	to take a course
la	custodia	custody

Spanish-English Glossary

D
- el **dado** die, dice
  - **en dados** diced
- la **danza** dance; dancing
- **dar** [irr] to give
  - **dar de comer** to feed
  - **darse cuenta** to realise
  - **darse la vuelta** to turn around
  - **¿me da ...?** can I have?
- **de** of, from
- **de** what something is made of: **sopa de tomate** tomato soup
- **debe** should (see **deber**)
- **deber** to have to do something/must
- los **deberes** homework
- **decente** respectable
- **declarar** to declare
- **decir (i)** [irr] to say, to tell
- la **decoración** decoration
- **dedicado/a** dedicated
- **dedicarse** to take up, to go in for
- **¿a qué te dedicas?** what do you do?
- **defenderse (ie)** to defend oneself
- el/la **defensor(a)** defender; protector
- **definido/a** definite; well defined
- **dejar** to let, to allow; to leave; to give up
  - **diecisiete dejamos** we'll settle for/let it go for 17
  - **dejar de fumar** to give up smoking
  - **dejarse llevar** to let oneself go
  - **sin dejar recuerdos** without leaving a trace
  - **te voy a dejar estas** I'm going to give you these (tablets)
- **del** (de + el) of the
- **delante (de)** in front (of)
- **delgado/a** thin; slim
- la **delicia** delight
  - **delicias navideñas** Christmas sweets
- **demasiado** too much
- el/la **dentista** (m.f.) dentist
- **dentro** within
- **denuncia: quiero poner una denuncia** I want to report a crime
- el **departamento** department
- **depender de** to depend on
- el/la **dependiente/a** shop assistant
- el **deporte** sport
- **deprimido/a** depressed
- la **derecha** (abb. **dcha.**) right (direction)
  - **a la derecha** on the right
- (el/la) **desamparado/a** helpless
- **desaparecer** to disappear
- el **desarrollo** development, evolution
- el **desastre** disaster
- **desayunar** to have breakfast
- el **desayuno** breakfast
- **descalzo/a** barefoot
- **descansar** to rest; to lie down
- el **descanso** rest, break
- el **descenso** descent
- **describir** to describe
- el/la **descubridor(a)** discoverer
- el **descubrimiento** discovery
- **descubrir** to discover
- **desde** from; since; outside (beyond)
- **desenchufar** to disconnect
- el **desengaño** disappointment
- el **deseo** desire, wish
- **desértico/a** desert-like, arid
- la **desertización** desertification, process of turning land into a desert
- el **desierto** desert
- **desierto/a** deserted
- **despectivo/a** contemptuous, scornful
- **despejado/a** brightening up, clearing up

- **despierto/a** awake
  - **sueña despierto** he/she daydreams
- **desplegarse (ie)** to unfold (itself)
- **despoblado/a** depopulated
- **después** then; after
- **destacar** to highlight
- el/la **destinatario/a** potential audience
- el **destino** destination
- **detrás (de)** behind
- el/la **devoto/a** devout person/worshipper
- el **día** (m.) day
  - **el día de los difuntos/de los muertos** All Souls Day/Day of the Dead (2 November)
  - **el día de la Hispanidad** Columbus Day (12 October)
  - **el día de Navidad** Christmas Day (25th December)
  - **el día de Reyes** Epiphany (6 January)
  - **el día de los santos inocentes** Holy Innocents (28 December)
  - **el día de trabajo** Labour Day (1st May)
- **diariamente** daily
- el **diario** daily newspaper
- **diario/a** daily
- el **diccionario** dictionary
- **diciembre** December
- el **diente** tooth
  - **diente de ajo** garlic clove
- **diferente** different
- **difícil** difficult
- el/la **difunto/a** dead person
- la **difusión** distribution
- **¡Dígame!** Hello? (on telephone)
- **digo** I say (see **decir**)
- **Dinamarca** Denmark
- **dinámico/a** dynamic
- el **dinero** cash, money
- la **dirección** address
- la **dirección asistida** power steering
- el/la **director(a)** director
- la **discoteca** disco, discothéque
- **discreto/a** discreet, quiet
- **¡disculpe!** excuse me
- la **discusión** discussion
- el/la **diseñador(a)** designer
- el **diseño** design; pattern
- **disfrutar** to enjoy
- **disponer de** [irr] to have at its disposal
- la **distancia** distance
- la **distinción** distinction
- **distinto/a** distinct, separate
- el **distrito** district, region, zone
- la **diversión** pastime, relaxation
- **divertido/a** amusing
- **dividir** to divide; to split up
- las **divisas** currencies
- **divorciarse** to get divorced
- **doble** double
- el/la **doctor/a** medical doctor; Doctor (academic degree)
- **doler (ue)** to hurt; to ache
- el **dolor** pain
- **doméstico/a** household, domestic
- el **domicilio** home; address
- el **domingo** Sunday
- **donde** where (relative pronoun)
- **¿dónde?** where?
- **dorado/a** golden
- **dormir (ue)** to sleep
- el **dormitorio** bedroom
- **doy** I give (see **dar**)
- el **drama** drama
- **dramático/a** dramatic
- el/la **dramaturgo/a** dramatist, playwright
- la **ducha** shower

- **ducharse** to have a shower
- el **dueño** owner
- la **duración** period, length of time
- **durante** during
- **durar** to last; to continue
- **duro/a** hard, harsh

E
- **económico/a** economic
- **económicamente** economically
- el/la **ecoturístico/a** 'ecotourist' (interested in ecological matters)
- (el/la) **ecuatoriano/a** Ecuadorian
- **ecuestre** equestrian
- la **edad** age
- la **edición** edition
- el **edificio** building
- **educar** to educate
- **efectivo/a** effective
  - **en efectivo** with cash
- **efectuar** to bring about, to make
- el **ejemplo** example
- el **ejercicio** exercise
- **el** the (m.)
- **él** he
- **elástico/a** flexible
- la **electricidad** electricity
- el **elefante** elephant
- **elegante** elegant
- el **elemento** element
- **ella** she; her; **ellas** they (f.)
- **ello** it; **ellos** they (m.)
- el **embalse** reservoir
- el **embarazo** pregnancy
- **emborracharse** to get drunk
- el **embutido** sausage
- la **emisión** issue; broadcast
- la **empanada** meat pie
- **empeorar** to get worse
- **empezar (ie)** to start, begin
- el/la **empleado/a** employee
- el **empleo** employment, job
- la **empresa** enterprise; company; management
- el **empréstito** loan
- **en** in, into; on, upon; at
- el/la **enamorado/a** lover
- **enamorarse** to fall in love
- **encantado/a** delighted, pleased
- **encantar** to charm, to delight
- **encima de** on top of
- **encontrar (ue)** to meet
- el **encuentro** meeting
- el **enero** January
- **enfadado/a** annoyed; angry
- la **enfermería** nursing
- el/la **enfermero/a** nurse
- **enfermo/a** ill, sick
- **enfrente** opposite; facing
- **enfriar** to cool
- **enmascarado/a** masked
- la **ensalada** salad
- la **ensenada** bay, cove
- **enseñar** to teach; to show
- el **ente** official body; **ente televiso** official television
- **entender (ie)** to understand
- **entero/a** entire
- **entonces** so, then
- la **entrada** entrance ticket, admission; first course/starter
  - **de entrada** as a first course/starter
- **entrar** to enter
- **entre** between; among
- **entreabrir** to half-open
- la **entrega** delivery

Spanish-English Glossary

el	entregar to surrender	
el	entremés side dish; short sketch or farce	
los	entremeses hors d'oeuvres	
el/la	entrenador(a) trainer, coach	
el	entrenamiento training, coaching	
	episcopal episcopal	
la	época period, epoch	
la	equitación horse-riding	
	equivocado/a mistaken (telephone: wrong number)	
la	era era, period	
la	erosión erosion	
	esa (f.) that ; ésa that one	
	esas (f) those; ésas those ones	
la	escalera staircase/stairs	
el	escaparate shop window	
	escaparse to escape	
la	escarcha frost	
la	escasez scarcity, shortage	
la	escena stage	
el/la	esclavo/a slave	
(el/la)	escocés/escocesa Scot; Scottish	
	escribir to write	
el/la	escritor(a) writer	
el	escritorio writing desk	
	escuchar to listen to, hear	
la	escuela school	
	escupir to spit	
	ese (m) that ; ése that one	
	eso that one (neuter)	
	por eso therefore, because of that	
	esos (m) those; ésos those ones	
	espacioso/a spacious, roomy	
la	espalda back (anatomical)	
(la)	España Spain	
el	español Spanish (language)	
(el/la)	español/a Spanish (nationality)	
el	espárrago asparagus	
la	especia spice	
	especial special	
la	especie species	
la	especificación specification	
	espectacular spectacular	
el	espectáculo show, spectacle, performance	
el	espejo mirror	
la	esperanza hope	
	esperar to look forward to; hope for; to wait for	
	en espera de awaiting	
el	espíritu spirit	
la	esposa wife	
el	esposo husband	
el	esquí skiing	
	esquiar to ski, to go skiing	
la	esquina corner	
	esta (f.) this ; ésta this one	
	estacionario/a stationary	
el	estado civil marital status	
la	estación station; season	
los	Estados Unidos United States of America	
la	estancia farm, ranch	
el	estanco tobacconist's shop	
el	estante rack, stand; shelf	
la	estantería shelving, set of shelves	
	estar to be	
	estas (f) these; éstas these ones	
la	estatua statue	
la	estatura height, stature	
	este (m) this; éste this one	
el	estilo style	
	esto this one (neuter)	
el	estómago stomach	
	estos (m) these; éstos these ones	
	estrecho/a tight	
	estrenar to show for the first time	
el	estrés stress	
	estresado/a stressed	
	estricto/a strict	
(el/la)	estudiante student	
la	estudiantina student band/music group	
	estudiar to study	
	estupendamente excellently	
	estupendo/a stupendous, marvellous	
el	euro euro (currency)	
el	evento event	
el	examen examination	
la	excelencia excellence; quality	
	exclusivamente exclusively	
la	excursión excursion, trip	
	exiliado exiled	
	existir to exist	
el	éxito success	
	exótico/a exotic	
la	exploración exploration, examination	
la	exposición display, exhibition, showing	
	exprimido/a pressed, squeezed	
	exquisito/a delicious	
	exterior external	
(el/la)	extranjero/a foreign(er)	
	extrañar to miss	
	extremado/a extreme, excessive	
	extremo/a extreme, last	
	extrovertido/a extrovert	

F

la	fábrica factory	
el/la	fabricante maker; manufacturer	
	fabricar to make	
	fabuloso fabulous, fantastic, great	
	fácil easy	
la	factura bill, invoice	
la	facultad faculty; university	
la	falda skirt	
	falso/a false	
la	falta lack, want, need	
la	fama fame; reputation	
la	familia family	
	familia política parents-in-law	
	famoso/a famous	
la	farmacia pharmacy, chemist's shop	
el	favor favour	
	por favor please	
la	fecha date	
la	felicidad happiness: felicidades good wishes	
	feliz happy	
(el)	femenino (m.) feminine	
	fenomenal phenomenal, marvellous	
	lo pasé fenomenal I had a great time	
	feo/a ugly	
los	fieles faithful (religious)	
la	feria-concurso fair, market; meeting	
el	ferry ferry	
el	festejo feast; public celebration	
la	fiebre fever	
la	fiesta celebration; social gathering; public holiday	
	fijar to pay attention	
el	fin end	
	por fin finally, at last	
	final final;	
	al final at the end	
la	finca farm	
	finca ganadera cattle ranch	
(la)	Finlandia Finland	
la	firma signature	
	firmar to sign	
el	flamenco flamenco	
el	flan caramel custard	
el	flash de noticias news flash	
	flojo/a weak	
la	flor flower	
el	foco focus	
la	fogata bonfire	
el	folleto leaflet; brochure	
el	fondo fund	
el	'footing' jogging	
la	forma way, method	
la	formación primary education	
la	fotografía photograph	
	sacar fotografías to take photographs	
	frágil fragile	
el	fraile friar	
(el)	francés French	
el/la	francés/francesa Frenchman/Frenchwoman	
(la)	Francia France	
la	franquicia free allowance	
	franquista of the Franco period	
la	frecuencia frequency	
	fregar (ie) to wash up (Sp)	
	freír (i) to fry	
la	fresa strawberry	
	fresco fresh	
el	frigorífico refrigerator	
el	frijol kidney bean	
	frío/a cold	
	frito/a fried	
la	frontera frontier, border	
la	fruta fruit	
	fue he/she was (see ser); he/she went (see ir)	
la	fuente large dish; fountain; front (weather)	
	fuera (de) outside (of)	
	fuerte strong, intense; thick	
la	fuerza force	
	fui I was (see ser); I went (see ir)	
	fulgurar to shine	
el/la	fumador/a smoker	
	fumar to smoke	
el/la	funcionario/a civil servant	
	fundar to found (establish)	
el	fundador(a) founder	
el	fútbol football	

G

la	gaceta gazette	
las	gafas spectacles, glasses	
la	galería gallery; passage	
la	galleta biscuit	
el	gallo cock, cockerel	
	Misa del Gallo Midnight Mass	
la	gama range	
la	gamba prawn	
la	gamuza suede	
el	ganadero stockbreeder	
	ganar to win	
el	garbanzo chick pea	
la	garganta throat	
la	gárgara: hacer gárgaras to gargle	
la	gasolina petrol	
	gastar to spend; to take, to wear (a size)	
el	gato cat	
la	gaviota seagull	
	gaviota reidora black-headed gull	
el	gazpacho Andalusian cold soup	
la	generación generation	
	general general	
	por lo general generally/in general	
la	gente people	
	gente de hoy people of today	
la	geografía geography	
el/la	gerente manager	
la	gimnasia gymnastics	
	girar to turn	
	girar en torno a to revolve around	
el/la	gitano/a gypsy	
el	gobierno governor	

Spanish-English Glossary

	gordo/a fat; stout, plump		de habla hispana Spanish-speaking		el	invierno winter
la	gota drop		Hispanidad Spanish (speaking) world			invitar to invite
	gótico/a Gothic		el día de la Hispanidad Columbus Day			ir [irr] to go
la	grabación recording	la	historia history			ir de compras to go shopping
	gracias thank you		histórico/a historical		la	isla island
	gracioso/a graceful		¡hola! hello!		las	Islas Afortunadas Fortunate Isles (Canary Islands)
la	gramática grammar	el	hombre man			isleño/a island (adj.)
	gran big, large (before noun m/f sing.)	la	hora hour		(la)	Italia Italy
(la)	Gran Bretaña Great Britain	el	horario timetable		(el/la)	italiano/a Italian
	grande big, large	la	horchata drink made with almonds		el	itinerario itinerary
la	grandeza greatness	el	horno oven		el	IVA (impuesto sobre el valor añadido) VAT
el	granizado iced drink		al horno baked		la	izquierda left (direction)
	granizar to hail (weather)	el	hospital hospital			
	grave serious	la	hostelería hotel business		**J**	
el	gremio guild, union	la	hostería inn; small hotel		el	jabón soap
la	gripe influenza, 'flu'		hostil unfriendly; hostile		el	jalapeño (kind of) chilli
	gris grey	el	hotel hotel		(el/la)	jalisciense from Jalisco, Mexico
el	grupo group		hoy today; now, nowadays		el	jamón ham
	guapo/a good-looking, handsome		huesudo emaciated, bony		el	jarabe syrup
	guardar to keep	el	huevo egg		la	jardinería gardening
	guarnición de served with	la	huida escape		el/la	jefe chief, head, boss
la	guerra war	la	humanidad humanity		el	jersey jersey, sweater
el/la	guía guide	la	humedad humidity		la	jornada day's work; conference
	gustar to like		húmedo/a humid			joven young; youthful
	me gusta el té I like tea				el/la	joven young man/woman;
	me gustaría I would like	**I**				los jóvenes young people
el	gusto pleasure	la	ida departure; single (ticket)		la	joya jewel
	mucho gusto pleased to meet you		de ida y vuelta return ticket		la	judía green/French bean
		el	idioma (m.) language		el	judo judo
H		la	iglesia church		el	juego game; play (acting)
	haber [irr] to have		igual equal		el	jueves Thursday
la	habitación bedroom		ilimitado/a unlimited		el/la	juez(a) judge
	habitación de matrimonio double room	la	ilusión illusion, wishful thinking, dream			jugar (ue) to play (a game)
el/la	habitante inhabitant		ilustre illustrious, famous			jugar al tenis play tennis
	habitualmente usually	la	impaciencia impatience		el	jugo juice (LA)
el	habla (f) speech	el	impuesto tax		el	juguete toy
	de habla hispana Spanish-speaking	la	inauguración inauguration			julio July
	hablar to speak		incitar to incite			junio June
	así se habla this is how we speak		incluir to include			junto a next to
	hacer [irr] to do, to make, to build	la	inconstancia inconstancy, fickleness			juntos/as together
	hace 26 años 26 years ago		increíble fantastic, incredible, unbelievable		la	juventud youth
	hace sol/viento/calor/frío it's sunny/windy/hot/cold	la	independencia independence		el	juzgado court-house
	hacer caso to pay attention		indicar to indicate			
	hacia about; towards	el	indicativo code		**K**	
	hago I do, make (see hacer)	el/la	indígeno/a native inhabitant		el	Kas de limón brand name of lemon drink
el	hall hall		individual single		el	kilo kilo
la	hamaca hammock	la	infancia infancy; childhood			un medio kilo half a kilo
la	harina flour		infantil children's; junior			un cuarto de kilo quarter of a kilo
	harina candeal wheatmeal flour		campeona infantil (f.) junior champion		el	kilometraje distance in kilometres, mileage
	hasta until		infeliz unhappy		el	kilómetro kilometre
	hay there is; there are	la	información information			
	¿hay? is there? are there? (see haber)	el	influjo influence		**L**	
	no hay... there isn't/ there aren't...	la	infusión infusion (herbal tea)			la the (f. sing.); her; it (f)
	hecho past part of hacer	el/la	ingeniero/a engineer		el	lado side
la	hectárea hectare	(el/la)	inglés/inglesa Englishman/woman; English			al lado de beside, next to
la	helada frost	el	ingreso entry; joining, admission		el	lago lake
el	helado ice-cream	la	inicial initial (letter of alphabet)		la	laguna pond
la	heladera refrigerator	el	inicio start, beginning		la	lámpara lamp
	helar (ie) to freeze	la	inscripción registration		la	lana wool
la	herida wound	el	insecto insect		el	langostino prawn
la	hermana sister		insistir to insist			lanzar to launch
la	hermandad brotherhood	el	instituto secondary school			largo/a long, large
el	hermanito little (baby) brother	el	instrumento instrument			las the (f. pl.); them (f.pl)
el	hermano brother		interesante interesting		el	latifundio large farm/estate
la	hermosura beauty		interior interior; inland		la	lavandería launderette
	hervir (ie, i) to boil		intermedio/a intermediate			lavar to wash (something)
el	hervor boiling		internacionalmente internationally			lavarse to wash (oneself)
	hidratante moisturizing		interprovincial long-distance (transport)			le him; to him; you; to you
el	hielo ice-cube; ice, frost	la	insolación sunstroke			le presento a ... can I introduce you to ...
la	hija daughter		instalar to install		la	leche milk
los	hijos children (m & f)		inteligente intelligent		la	lechuga lettuce
el	hijo son		intranquilo/a restless; anxious			leer to read
el	hilo musical piped music		intrigante intriguing; fascinating		la	legumbre vegetable
el	himno hymn		inútil useless			lejos far
	hispana Hispanic	la	invasión invasion			
			invertir (i) to invest			

[265]

Spanish-English Glossary

	lejos de far from
la	lengua language; tongue
el	lente lens
	lento/a slow, gradual
	lentamente slowly
la	leña firewood
	les them; to them; you (pl).; to you (pl)
la	letra letter (of alphabet)
las	Letras Arts
	levantar to lift up
	levantarse to get up, to lift oneself up
la	liberación liberation
el/la	libertador(a) liberator
	libre free
el	libro book
el/la	licenciado/a Bachelor (academic degree)
la	licuadora liquidizer
el/la	líder leader
la	liebre hare
el	limón lemon
la	limonada lemonade
	limpiar to clean
	limpiar el polvo to dust
la	limpieza general spring-cleaning
	limpio/a clean
	lindo/a pretty; fine; nice
la	línea line
el	lino linen
	liso/a straight
la	lista list
	literario/a literary
	llamar to call
	llamar por teléfono to telephone
la	llave (door) key
	llegar to arrive, to get to
	llevar to carry; to wear
	lleva horas for hours he's been
	lleva dos meses en Madrid he's been in Madrid for two months
	llevamos una vida decente we lead a respectable life
	llover (ue) to rain
la	llovizna drizzle
la	lluvia rain
	lluvioso/a rainy
	lo it (neuter)
el	local premises
	locamente madly, wildly
el	locutorio operator-controlled telephone booth
	luego then; soon
	hasta luego see you later/soon
el	lugar place
el	lujo luxury
	me puedo dar el lujo I can afford it
el	lunar spot
	de lunares spotted (pattern)
el	lunes Monday
	lustrar to polish
la	luz light; las luces lights

M

los	macarrones macaroni
la	macedonia de frutas fruit salad
	machacar to crush
la	madera wood
la	madre mother
la	madrugada dawn
	maduro/a ripe
el	maestro master; expert
la	maldad evil
el	maleficio curse
la	maleta suitcase
	malísimo very bad/evil
	malo/a bad
	hace mal (tiempo) it's bad weather

	malva mauve
	malversar to misappropriate
	mamá mum, mummy
	manchego/a of/from La Mancha
la	manera way, manner
la	manipulación manipulation
la	mano (f.) hand
la	mantequilla butter
la	manzana apple
la	manzanilla camomile; a type of sherry
la	mañana morning; tomorrow
	mañana por la mañana tomorrow morning
el	mapa (m.) map
	maquillarse to make up (cosmetic)
la	máquina machine (typewriter)
el	mar sea
la	maraña tangle
	maravilloso/a marvellous, wonderful
	marcar to dial
la	marejada heavy sea, swell
el	marido husband
el	marisco shellfish
	marítimo/a maritime
	marrón chestnut, brown
el	martes Tuesday
	marzo March
	más more; el más the most
	¿qué más?/¿algo más? anything else/more?
	nada más nothing else/more
	más o menos more or less, approximately
el	masaje massage
	masculino masculine
	masticar to chew
el	matador matador
	matar to kill
las	matemáticas mathematics
el	matrimonio marriage
	cama de matrimonio double bed
el	máximo utmost; maximum
	mayo May
	mayor older, elder
el/la	mayor main, principal; eldest, oldest; biggest; most
la	mayoría majority
	me me, to me, myself
la	medalla medal
	mediano/a medium-sized
la	medicina medicine
la	medianoche midnight
el/la	médico (medical) doctor
	médico cabecera family doctor
	médico/a medical
la	medida size
	medida de cuello collar size
	medio/a half
	media pensión half board
	medio kilo half a kilo
el	medio means, way, method
la	mediodía midday
el	Mediterráneo Mediterranean
	mejor better
el/la	mejor best
el	melocotón peach
el	melón melon
la	menestra lentil/bean stew
	menor younger
el/la	menor youngest
	menos less
	las cuatro menos veinte 3.40 pm
la	menta peppermint
el	menú menu
	menudo/a small; slightly built
el	mercader merchant
el	mercado market

la	merluza hake
la	mermelada jam
el	mes month
la	mesa table
la	meseta plateau
la	mesita small table
el	metro underground, subway
(el/la)	mexicano/a, mejicano/a Mexican
la	mezcla mixture
	mezclar to mix
	mi my
	mí me; a mí sí I do (like it); para mí for me
el	miedo fear; tiene miedo he/she is afraid
el	miércoles Wednesday
la	miga de pan breadcrumb
	migratorio/a migratory
(el)	mil thousand
	mil y uno thousand and one
la	'mili' military service
la	milla mile
un	millón million
el/la	millonario/a millionaire
la	minería mining
el	minifundio tiny farm/plot of land
el	mínimo/a minimum
la	misa mass; Misa del Gallo Midnight Mass (literally 'of the cockerel')
la	misión mission
el/la	mismo/a same
el	misterio mystery
	misterioso/a mysterious
	mixto/a mixed
	moda fashion; de moda fashionable
la	modalidad form
el/la	modelo model
	moderno/a modern
el	moisés Moses basket, cradle
	molestar to tease; to annoy
el	momento moment
	un momentín just a moment
el	monasterio monastery
la	montaña mountain
el	montañismo mountaineering
	montar to ride
	montar a caballo to go horse-riding
el	montón heap, pile
el	monumento monument; memorial
	morado/a purple
	moreno/a dark, dark-haired
	morir (ue) to die
la	mosca fly
el	mosquito mosquito
el	mosto grape-juice drink
	mostrar (ue) to show
	móvil active
	muchísimo very much
	mucho (adv) much, a lot
	no me gusta mucho I don't like it much
	mucho/a/os/as (adj.) much, many, a lot of
	hace mucho calor it's very hot
	mudo dumb
el	muelle pier, wharf
la	muerte death
los	muertos (the) dead
	¡muévete! get going! move!
la	mujer woman
	multifocal multifocal (bifocal)
	mundial world-wide, world (adj.)
el	mundo world
	municipal municipal
la	muralla city wall, rampart
el	museo museum
la	música music
e/la	músico musician
(el/la)	musulmán Muslim
	muy very

Spanish-English Glossary

N

- nacer to be born
- el nacimiento birth
- la nación nation
- la nacionalidad nationality
- nada nothing
  - de nada not at all, don't mention it
- nadar to swim
- nadie no one
- el naipe playing card
  - juego de naipe card game
- la nariz nose
- la nata cream
- la natación swimming
- natal native
- las natillas custard
- náutico/a nautical
- navegar to sail
- la Navidad Christmas
- el navío ship
- la neblina mist
- necesitar to need, to want
- negar (ie) to deny
- la negativa refusal
- los negocios business
- negro/a black
- nervioso/a nervous
- nevar (ie) to snow
- la nevera refrigerator
- ni ... ni neither ... nor
- (el/la) nicaragüense Nicaraguan
- el nidal nest
- la niebla fog
- la nieta granddaughter
- el nieto grandson; los nietos grandchildren
- ningún/ninguno/a no; not . . . any
- el nivel level
- la niñez childhood
- el niño small boy, child; los niños the boys, the children
- la niña small girl
- no not
- la noche night; evening
  - Noche Vieja New Year's Eve
  - Nochebuena Christmas Eve
  - por noche per night
  - todas las noches every night
- nocturno/a night (adj.)
- el nombre name
  - a nombre de in the name of
  - su nombre y apellido your full name
- el noreste north-east
- normalmente normally, usually
- el noroeste north-west
- el norte north; guide
- (el/la) norteamericano North American
- nos us, ourselves
- nosotros/as we; us; ourselves
- notable notable, remarkable
- notar to notice; to see (perceive)
  - se nota one can see
- la noticia piece of news
- la novela novel
- la novia girlfriend; fiancée; bride
- el noviazgo engagement
- noviembre November
- el novio boyfriend; fiancé; bridegroom
- nub./clar. (weather symbol) cloudy/brightening up
- nuevo new; fresh
  - de nuevo again
  - veamos de nuevo let's look at it again
- el Nuevo Mundo New World
- la nulidad annulment
- el número number
- nunca never, not ... ever

O

- o or
  - o sea that is
- el obispo bishop
- el objeto object
- la obra work; (theatre) play
- observar to observe
- obsesionar to obsess
- obtener [irr] to obtain, to achieve
- la ocasión occasion
- el occidente west
- el ocio leisure
- octubre October
- ocular ocular, eye (adjective)
- el/la oculista oculist
- la ocupación occupation
- ocupado/a occupied
- odiar to hate
- el oeste west
- la oficina de Correos post office
- la oficina de turismo tourist office
- ofrecer to offer
- el oído (internal) ear; (sense of) hearing
- ¡oiga! listen!
- oír [irr] to hear; to listen to
- el ojo eye
- olímpico Olympic
- la olla pan
- el/la operador(a) operator
- la oportunidades opportunity, bargain
- la óptica optician's (business/shop)
- la oreja ear
- organizar to organize
- oriental eastern
- el origen origin; source
- el oro gold
- la orquídea orchid
- osteopático/a osteopathic
- oscuro/a dark
- el otoño autumn
- otro/a another
- el/la otro/a (the) other
- ¡oye! listen!

P

- el/la paciente patient
- el padre father
  - los padres parents
- la paella paella, famous rice dish
- pagar to pay
- el pago payment
- el país country; land, region, area
- el paisaje landscape, scenery
- la paja straw
- el pájaro bird
- la palabra word; power of speech
- el palacio palace; mansion
- la paleontología paleontology
- la palmera palm tree
- el palmito palm heart
- la paloma dove
  - paloma torcuaz turtle dove
- palustre marshy
- la pampa prairie, pampas
- el pan bread
- el panecillo bread roll
- el pantalón, los pantalones trousers
  - pantalones cortos shorts
- el pañuelo scarf, kerchief
- la papa potato (LA)
- papá dad, daddy
- el papel paper
  - papel higiénico toilet paper
- el par couple
- para for, in order to
  - estudiar para chef to study to be a chef
  - para ir al trabajo to go to work (in order to)
  - el café es para mí the coffee is for me
- la parada (de autobuses) stopping place; bus stop
- el paraíso paradise
- parar to stop
- pararse to stop, to come to a halt
- parecer to seem; to appear
  - me parece que it seems to me, it seems that
- paralelo/a parallel
- la pared wall
- la pareja pair; couple
- el parque park
  - parque de atracciones amusement park
- la parrilla grill
  - a la parrilla grilled
- la parte part, section
  - ¿de parte de quién? who's calling? (telephone)
- participar to participate
- la parroquia parish
- el partido de fútbol football match
- partir to depart/to start
  - a partir de starting from
- pasado/a past; last
  - pasada la medianoche past midnight
  - la semana pasada last week
- el pasado past
- el/la pasajero/a passenger, traveller
- pasar to pass, to spend time; to happen
  - ¿qué pasa? what's happening?
  - ¿qué te pasa? what's the matter?
  - huevos pasados por agua boiled eggs
- el pasatiempo pastime
- pasear to walk around
- el paseo stroll, walk
  - dar un paseo to go for a stroll/walk
- el paseo (abb. Po.) promenade, avenue
- la pasión passion
- el paso step (walking); interlude, sketch (theatre)
- el pastel cake; los pasteles pastries
- la pastilla tablet
- la patata potato
- el patinaje skating
- el patio patio, courtyard
- el patriarca patriarch, 'father'
- el patrón, la patrona patron
- el pavo turkey
- el/la pediatra paediatrician
- pedir (i) to ask for
- pegar to beat up, to knock about
  - pegar el tirón to snatch
- peinar to comb
  - me peinaba de moño I did my hair in a bun
- pelar to peel
- la pelea fight
- la película film (cinema/video)
- pelirrojo/a red-haired
- el pelo hair
- la peluquería hairdresser
- la pena shame; ¡qué pena! what a pity!
- la peña bar where folk music is played (Andes region)
- la pensión boarding house; board and lodging
  - pensión completa full board;
  - media pensión half board
- el peón pawn (chess)
- peor worse
- el/la peor worst
- el pepino cucumber
- pequeño/a small, young;

Spanish-English Glossary

el/la más pequeño/a youngest, smallest
la **pera** pear
perder (ie) to lose
perdone excuse me
el **perejil** parsley
el **periódico** newspaper
el/la **periodista** journalist
el **permiso de conducir** driving licence
permitir to permit, allow, let
pero but
el **perro** dog
el **personaje** character (in play, novel)
personal personal
el **Perú** Peru
(el/la) **peruano/a** Peruvian
la **persona** person
la **pesadilla** nightmare
la **pesca** fishing
el **pescado** fish
pescar to fish; fishing
la **petición** petition, request
el/la **pianista** pianist
picado/a chopped
picar to nibble, have a snack; to chop
el **pie** foot; **a pie** on foot
la **piel** skin; leather
la **pierna** leg
la **pieza** (museum) piece
la **pileta** swimming pool
el/la **piloto/a** pilot
la **pimienta** pepper
el **pincho** snack; portion
pintoresco/a picturesque
el/la **pintor/a** painter
la **pintura** picture, painting
la **piragua** canoe
el **piragüismo** canoeing
el **pirata** pirate
los **Pirineos** Pyrenees
la **piscina** swimming pool
el **piso** larger flat, apartment
la **pista de tenis** tennis court
la **pizca** pinch (quantity)
la **plancha** grill
a la plancha grilled
planchar to iron
el **plano** street map, plan
el planito small street-plan
la **planta** storey, floor;
de una sola planta on one floor only
la **plata** silver
el **plátano** banana
plátano verde asado grilled green banana
la **platería** silversmith
el **plato** dish (food); plate
la **playa** beach
la **plaza** *(abb.* **Pza***)* public square; city/town centre
el **pleito** quarrel
el **pluriempleo** several jobs at once
poblado/a populated
poblar (ue) to populate
pobre poor
el **pobretón** poor man
poco little (quantity), few
un poquito a very little
poquísimos/as very few
poder (ue) *[irr]* to be able; can
el/la **poeta** poet
la **poetisa** poet (female)
el **polvo** dust; **limpiar el polvo** to dust
la **pomada** ointment
el **poncho** poncho, blanket
poner (ue) *[irr]* to put
ponerse (ue) *[irr]* to become; to wear (to put on clothes)
pongo I put ; **me pongo** I put on (clothes)
por along; through ; per
por aquí near/round here
por favor please
por la selva through the rain forest
por noche per night
portátil portable
portuario/a port, harbour
porque because
¿por qué? why?
poseer to possess
la **posibilidad** possibility
la **posición** position
posterior subsequent, later
el **postre** dessert
el **pozo** well (water)
el pozo de los deseos wishing-well
la **práctica** practice
practicar to practise; to go in for; to play
práctico/a practical
el **precio** price, cost
precioso/a beautiful
la **precipitación pluvial** rainfall
preferir (ie) to prefer
el **prefijo** prefix; code
preguntar to enquire, ask
premiar to reward
el **premio** prize
preocupado/a worried, anxious
preparar to prepare
el **presentación** introduction
presentar to introduce, to present
la **presión** pressure
previamente previously
previo/a previous, prior
la **prevista** forecast
la **primavera** spring
el/la **primero/a** first; primer *(before m. sing. noun)*
de primero as/for a starter/first course...
primitivo/a early, original
el/la **primo/a** cousin
(el/la) **principal** principal, chief; main
el **principio** beginning
el **probador** fitting room
probar (ue) to try, to sample
el **problema** problem
procedente de coming from
procesar to put on trial
producir to produce
el **producto** product
la **profesión** profession
(el/la) **profesional** professional
el/la **profesor/a** teacher
pronosticado/a predicted, forecast
pronosticar to predict
pronto/a quick
propio/a own, of one's own
protegerse to protect oneself
protegido protected
la **provincia** province
provocar to tempt, provoke
próximo/a next
el **proyecto** plan
el **público** public
el **pueblo** town
puede he/she can, is able (see **poder**)
se puede one can, it's allowed
el **puerro** leek
la **puerta** door; gate (flight)
el **puerto** port
pues then, well
la **puesta del sol** sunset
el **puesto** stall, stand
el **punto** point, dot; knitting
en punto on the dot, sharp, punctually, exactly
punto de hervor boiling point
punto de vista point of view
puntual punctual
la **puntualidad** punctuality
la **puñada** handful
puro/a pure

Q

que *(relative pronoun)* who, whom, that; than
¿qué? what?
¡Qué asco! How horrible!
¡Qué bien! Great!
¡Qué guapo/a! How handsome/pretty!
¡Qué maravilla! How wonderful!
¡Qué pena! What a shame!
¡Qué rico! How wonderful!
¡Qué sabroso! How tasty!
¡Qué suerte! What luck!
quedar to stay; to fit/to suit (clothes)
quedar en to agree to (an arrangement)
quedarse to stay; remain
quedarse con to keep
quejarse to complain
la **quemadura** de sol sunburn
la **quena** Indian flute
querer (ie) to want, to wish for, to like
querido/a dear, darling
el **queso** cheese
quien who *(relative pronoun)*
¿quién? who? whom?
¿quién es quién? who's who?
el/la **quinto/a** fifth
quisiera I'd like (from **querer**)
quitar to remove
quizá, quizás perhaps

R

la **ración** portion
el **racismo** racism
la **radio** radio
la **ralladura** grated rind of fruit
rallar to grate
la **rapidez** speed
rápido/a rapid, fast
raro/a rare
rara vez rarely, seldom
la **rastra** thick leather belt (**gaucho**)
el **rato** short time, a while
la **raya** stripe
de/a rayas striped
la **razón** reason
la **realidad** reality
realizar to achieve, to attain
rebozado/a fried in batter
el **recado** message
el/la **recepcionista** receptionist
la **receta** recipe
recibir to receive
recientemente recently
recoger to pick up
la **recogida** collection
reconocer to recognize
el **reconocimiento** examination, check-up
reconquistar to reconquer
recordar (ue) to remember, to recall
recorrer to explore, to travel
el **recorrido** tour; route, trail
recto straight
todo recto straight on/ahead
el **recuerdo** souvenir
¡reflauta! Gosh! Good heavens!
el **refugio** shelter
el **regalo** gift, present

Spanish-English Glossary

	regar (ie) to water		**S**				Nuestra Señora Our Lady (Virgin Mary)	
el	regateo bargaining		el	sábado Saturday			señorial lordly, aristocratic	
el	régimen regime; diet		la	sábana sheet			sensible sensitive	
	regresar to go back, to return			saber [irr] to know		el	sentido sense (meaning)	
la	reina queen		el	sabor flavour			septiembre September	
el	reinado reign			sacar to put/take out		la	sequía drought	
	reírse de [irr] to laugh at			sacar a pasear el perro to take the dog for a walk			ser [irr] to be	
la	relación account (description)			sacar fotografías take photographs		el	servicio service, facility	
la	relajación relaxation			sacar la basura to put out the rubbish			servir (i) to serve	
	relajado/a relaxed			sagrado/a holy, sacred		la	sesión cinema performance	
el/la	religioso/a member of religious order		la	sal salt			sí yes	
el	reloj clock		la	sala de fiesta dance hall			si if, whether	
	remojado/a soaked		el	saladito savoury nibble/snack		la	sidra cider	
	remontarse a to go back (in time) to			salgo I leave (see salir)			siempre always	
	remover (ue) to stir		la	salida way out, outlet		la	sierra mountain range/region	
la	renta income			salir [irr] to leave, go out		el	siglo century	
el/la	rentista person of independent means		el	salón sitting-room, drawing-room		el	signo symbol	
la	reparación repair		el	salón social room for social events		la	silla chair	
	reparar to repair		la	salsa salsa music; sauce		el	sillón armchair	
	repelente repellent		el/la	salsero/a salsa singer			simpático/a likeable, nice	
el	repertorio repertoire		la	salud health			sin without	
la	representación performance (of a play)			la salud hace al hombre health makes the person/'a healthy mind in a healthy body'		la	síntoma symptom	
la	república republic			saludar to greet		la	sirvienta servant	
la	reserva booking; reserve, reservation			le saluda atentamente yours faithfully		el	sisón little bustard	
	reservado/a reserved, booked			salvar to save, rescue		el	sistema system	
	reservar to book, to reserve		la	sandalia sandal		el	sitio place, location	
el	resfriado/a cold		el	sandwich toasted sandwich			situado/a situated	
la	residencia residence		la	sangre blood			sobre on, over; about, approximately	
	respetable respectable		la	sangría wine cup drink			sobre las ocho about eight o'clock	
	respetar to respect		la	sanidad public health			información sobre trenes information on/ about trains	
la	respuesta reply		la	sanidad privada private health		el	sobre sachet	
el	restaurante restaurant		el/la	santo/a saint			sobrevivir to survive	
	restituir [irr] to restore			santo/a saintly, holy		el/la	sobrino/a nephew/niece	
	resultar to turn out, to prove to be		el	santuario sanctuary, shrine		el	socorro help, aid, assistance	
el	retablo altar-piece; votive offering			sazonar to season, to flavour with		el	sofá sofa, settee	
la	reunión meeting, gathering			se (reflexive) himself, herself, itself, yourself; one, you (impersonal)			sofisticado/a sophisticated	
	reunir to reunite, gather (together)			¿cómo se llama? what is your name?		el	sol sun	
	reunirse to meet			secar to dry			solamente only	
la	revista review		la	sección section, branch			soleado/a sunny	
la	revolución revolution			seco/a dry			soler (ue) to usually (do something), to be in the habit of	
	revuelto/a mixed; scrambled		el/la	secretario/a secretary			solicitar to petition for	
el	rey king		el	sector sector, area			solo/a alone; single, one	
la	ribera shore			secundario/a of lesser importance, secondary			una sola just one	
	rico/a wonderful; rich		la	seda silk			café solo black coffee	
	riquísimo extremely good, delicious			seguir (i) to follow; to continue, to carry on			sólo only	
el	riesgo risk			¡siga! ¡sigue! follow		la	soltera single woman	
	riguroso/a harsh, tough			según according to		el	sombrero hat	
el	rincón corner			segundo/a second			sonar (ue) to blow; to play; to sound	
la	riqueza wealth			de segundo for the main course...			¿cómo suena la zampoña? how do the pan pipes sound?	
el	río river		la	seguridad safety, security			soñar (ue) to dream	
el	ritmo rhythm		el	seguro insurance			soñar con to dream about	
el	ritual ritual			seguro/a sure			sueña despierto he/she daydreams	
	rizado/a curly		el	sello stamp (postal)			sonreír [irr] to smile	
	robar to steal		la	selva (rain) forest		la	sopa soup; sopa de letras word search	
la	rodaja slice		la	semana week			sordo/a deaf	
	rodear to surround			una vez a la semana once a week			soy I am (see ser)	
	rojo/a red			el fin de semana weekend		el	squash squash	
el/la	romano/a Roman			semanal weekly			su his, her, its, your	
	romántico/a romantic			sembrar to sow			suave mild, soft	
	romper to break			sencillo/a single; simple			subir to climb	
	romper con su novio/a to break up with your boyfriend/girlfriend		el	senderismo trekking		el	subterráneo underground, subway	
el	ron rum			sentarse(ie) to sit down			suceder to happen	
la	ropa clothes			¡siéntese! ¡siéntate! sit down!			sucio/a dirty	
	rosa/rosado/a pink			sentado/a sitting		(la)	Suecia Sweden	
el	rosario rosary (beads)			sentirse (ie) to feel; to regret, to be sorry for		el/la	sueco/a Swede, Swedish	
	rubio/a fair; fair-haired, blond(e)			lo siento I'm sorry		el	suelo soil; floor	
el	ruido sound		el	señor gentleman; sir (polite form of address)			suelto/a loose, free	
	ruidoso noisy			Muy sres. (señores) míos Dear Sirs		el	sueño dream	
el	rumbo course, direction		la	señora lady; madam (polite form of address)		la	suerte luck, chance; fate	
el	rumor rumour						¡qué mala suerte! what bad luck!	
	rural rural						sufrir to suffer	
el/la	ruso/a Russian						sujeto/a a subject to	
la	ruta route					el	supermercado supermarket	
la	rutina routine							

Spanish-English Glossary

	suponer	to involve, to entail
	suprimido/a	banned, forbidden
	supuesto: ¡por supuesto!	of course!
(la)	Suráfrica	South Africa
	surtido/a	assorted, varied
	bien surtido	well stocked

T

el	tablao	flamenco club
el	tablero	board (games)
la	tableta	tablet
los	tacos	rolled tortilla, tacos
la	tajada	slice, slab
	tal	such
	¿qué tal?	how are you?
	tal vez	perhaps
el	Talgo	inter-city high-speed train
la	talla	size, fitting
el	taller	garage (repair workshop)
el	tamaño	size
	también	also, as well, besides
el	tambor	drum
	tampoco	neither
	tan	so
el	tango	tango (dance)
la	tanguería	tango bar
	tanto	so much
	tanto/a as much; tantos/as as many	
la	tapa	lid
las	tapas	snack (with drinks at bar counter)
las	tapices	tapestry
la	taquilla	booking/ticket office
la	tarde	afternoon
	las cinco de la tarde	5 o'clock in the afternoon
	tarde	late
las	tareas domésticas	household tasks
la	tarifa	fares, charges; price list
la	tarjeta de crédito	credit card
la	tarta	cake, tart
el	taxi	taxi
la	taza	cup
	te	you (informal)
el	té	tea
	teatral	drama (adjective)
el	teatro	theatre
el/la	tejedor/a	weaver
	tejido a mano	hand-woven
la	tela	cloth, fabric
el	teléfono	telephone
	por teléfono	by telephone
la	telenovela	television soap opera
la	televisión	television
el	tema	theme; subject, topic
la	temperatura	temperature
	templeado	warm
la	temporada	season, time
	fruta de la temporada	fruits in season
	temporada alta/baja	high/low season
	temprano	early
	más temprano	earlier
	tender (ie)	to hang
	tener (ie) [irr]	to have; to hold, possess
	tener que [irr]	to have to (do something)
	tengo	I have/hold (see tener)
	¿cuántos años tienes?	how old are you?
	tengo diecinueve años	I am nineteen
	tener miedo	to be afraid
el	tenis	tennis
el/la	tercer/o/a	third
	terminar	to finish
la	ternera	veal
el	ternero	calf
	terso/a	smooth and shining

el	testigo	witness
el	textil	textile
la	terapia	therapy
	ti you (informal); a ti to you	
el	tiempo	time; weather
	¿qué tiempo hace?	what's the weather like?
la	tienda	shop
la	tierra	land, country
	tímido/a	timid, shy
el/la	tío/a	uncle/aunt
	típico/a	typical
	típico de aquí	typical of this area
el	tipo	type
	tirar	to throw; to throw away; to play
el	tirón	snatch, sudden pull
el	títere	puppet, marionette
la	toalla	towel
	tocar	to touch; to play musical instruments
	toca temas	it touches on themes
	tocar la lotería	to win the lottery
el	tocino	bacon
	todavía	still; yet
	todo	all, everything
	todo/a every; todos/as all, every	
	todo el mundo	everyone/everybody
	tomar	to take; to eat
	tomar la alternativa	to become a professional bullfighter
el	tomate	tomato
la	tónica	tonic water
	tonto/a	silly, foolish
	torear	to fight (bulls)
	torcer (ue)	to turn, twist
	tuerces a la derecha	turn right
el	torero	bullfighter
la	tormenta	storm
el	torno	turn
	en torno	around
el	toro	bull
la	tortilla	omelette; maize-flour pancake (LA)
la	tos	cough
la	tostada	toast
	total	total
	en total	altogether
el/la	trabajador(a)	worker
	trabajar	to work
	trabajar de enfermera	to work as a nurse
	trabajar de voluntario/a	to do voluntary work
el	trabajo	work
	traer [irr]	to bring/fetch/carry/take
	traigo	I fetch
el	traje	suit
	el traje de baño	swimsuit
	tranquilo/a	peaceful
el	transporte	transport
la	trapería	old clothes; junk shop
la	trascendencia	importance
la	trashumancia	movement of cattle from south to north of Spain
	trasladar	to move, transfer
	tratarse	to deal with/behave towards others
el	trato	treatment (personal relationships); formality of speech
el	tratamiento	treatment (medical)
la	travesía	crossing, voyage
el	tren	train
	trepar	to climb
el	trigo	corn(field)
	triple	triple, three-bedded
	triste	sad
el	trocito	small piece
el	trozo	a piece

la	trucha	trout
	tú	you (familiar)
	tu, tus	your (familiar)
el	turismo	tourism
	turístico/a	tourist (adjective)
(la)	Turquía	Turkey
	tus	your (familiar plural)
	tuyo	yours (informal)

U

	ubicar	to stand, be situated
(la)	Ucrania	Ukraine
	último/a	final, last
	por último	finally
el	umbral	doorway
	un, uno(s), una(s)	a, an, some
	es la una	one o'clock
	unos cuantos	a few
	unos cuatro millones	some four million
el	ungüento	ointment
	únicamente	only, solely
	único/a	only
	soy hijo único	I am an only child
la	unidad	unit; unity
	unido/a	united
la	universidad	university
el/la	universitario/a	academic; (professor/student)
	universitario/a	university (adj.)
	urbana	urban
	usar	to use; to wear
	uso el tren	I use/take the train
	usted	you (formal singular, abb. Vd.)
	ustedes	you (formal plural, abb. Vds.)
	útil	useful
la	uva	grape
	uvas de la suerte	lucky grapes

V

las	vacaciones	holiday(s)
la	vainilla	vanilla
	vale	O.K./all right; fine
el	valor	value
los	vaqueros	jeans
	variado/a	assorted
	varios/as	various; several
(el/la)	vasco/a	Basque
el	vaso	drinking glass, tumbler
las	veces	times, occasions (plural of vez)
	a veces	sometimes
el/la	vecino/a	neighbour
la	vegetación	vegetation
el	vegetal	vegetable
el	vehículo	vehicle
la	vela	sailing
	vender	to sell
la	venida	coming, arrival
	venir [irr]	to come
	vengo	I come, am coming
la	ventana	window
el	ventilador	ventilator; fan
	veo	I see (see ver)
	ver [irr]	to see
	a ver	let's see
el	veraneo	summer holiday
	centro de veraneo	summer resort
el	verano	summer
la	verdad	truth
	¿verdad?	isn't it? don't you? etc
	verdadero/a	true
	verde	green
	verde oliva	olive green
las	verduras	green vegetables
la	vereda	pavement, sidewalk
la	vergüenza	shame (disgrace)
el	vestido	dress; suit

Spanish-English Glossary

la	**vez**	time; instance; occasion
	otra vez	again
	rara vez	rarely
	tal vez	perhaps
	viajar	to travel
el	**viaje**	journey
	viaje de placer	pleasure trip
el/la	**viajero/a**	traveller
la	**vida**	life
	viejo/a	old
	viento	windy
el	**viernes**	Friday
el	**villancico**	Christmas carol
la	**vinagreta**	vinaigrette sauce
el	**vino**	wine
la	**Virgen**	Virgin Mary
la	**viuda**	widow
	viva/o	lively
	vivir	to live
las	**voces**	voices
	volcánico/a	volcanic
el	**voleibol**	volleyball
el/la	**voluntario/a**	volunteer
	volver (ue)	to return
	volverse (ue) a casar	to remarry
	vosotros/as	you *(familiar plural)*
	voy	I go (see **ir**); I'm going to (do something)
	te voy a dejar estas	I'm going to give you these
la	**voz**	voice
el	**vuelo**	flight (number)
la	**vuelta**	turn; return
	de ida y vuelta	return (ticket)
	estar de vuelta	to be back
	vuelvo	I return (see **volver**)

Y

	y	and
	ya	now; soon; already
	ya te contaré	I'll tell you about it (now/soon)
	yo	I

Z

la	**zampoña**	pan pipes
la	**zanahoria**	carrot
la	**zapatilla**	slipper
el	**zapato**	shoe
	zapatos de deporte	trainers
la	**zarzuela**	light opera; Spanish-style musical comedy
la	**zona**	zone, area
el	**zumo**	juice

ACKNOWLEDGMENTS

The authors and publisher would like to acknowledge the use of the following texts. Every effort has been made to trace all copyright holders, but the publishers will be pleased to make the necessary arrangements at the earliest opportunity if there are any omissions.

article from Cambio 16 magazine (p. 12); lyrics of 'Muévete' from *Escenas* by Ruben Blades and Juan Fornell (p. 12); extract from *Mafalda* (©) Quino/Quipos published by Ediciones de la Flor (p. 19, 63); extract from *Condorito* published by Editora Carrousel (p. 22); 'La Misión' by Francisco Alarcón from *Cuerpo en Llamas* published by Chronicle Books (p. 33); lyrics of 'Calle Melancolía' by Joaquin Sabina from Mucho Sabina, published by CBS Castellana (p. 33); 'Oda a la cebolla' by Pablo Neruda from *Odas elementales* (p. 56) and 'Deportes' by Nicolas Guillén from *La paloma del vuelo popular* (p. 134) published by Editorial Losada; 'Llanto por Ignacio Sánchez Mejias' by Federico García Lorca from *Obras completas* (©) Herederos de Federico García Lorca published by Aguilar SA de Ediciones (p. 68); 'La casa nueva' by Tito Fernández from *El Temuaco* published by Siglo 20, Lima (p. 78); 'Síndrome' by Mario Benedetti from *Antología poética* Alianza Editorial (p. 90); 'El Tren' by Antonio Machado from *Poesías completas* published by Espasa Calpe (p. 111); extracts from *Actual* Jan.1995 (p. 139, p. 161); extracts from *Woman* Oct. 25 1994 (p. 140 and p. 211); extracts from *El País* (p. 146, 154, 156, 190); illustration of Snow White by Martin Aitchison from *Snow White and the Seven Dwarfs* published by Ladybird (p. 152); extracts from *Memorias del Fuego III* (p. 154) and I (p. 165) by Eduardo Galeano; and 'Hora Cero' by Ernesto Cardenal from *Nueva antología poética* (p. 178) published by Siglo XXI; article from *Tiempo* Feb. 27 1995 (p. 161); 'Maldición de Malinche' by Gabino Palomares from *April in Managua*, and poem by Alex D. Lumbi from *Poems of Love and Revolution* (p. 193) published by Nicaragua Solidarity Campaign, London; poem by Nicanor Parra from *Antipoemas* published by Seix Barral (p. 186); 'Para recordar' by Luis Enrique Mejia Godoy from *Yo soy de un pueblo sencillo*, published by KKLA-Enigrac; 'Ya todos saben para quien trabajan' by José Emilio Pacheco from *Tarde o temprano* (p. 197); and 'Third world theme' and 'Chicanita flor del campo' by Angela Hoyos from *Chicanos – Antología histórica y literaria* (p. 220), published by Fondo de Cultura Económica; 'Nocturno de los tejedores viejos' from *Antología de Gabriela Mistral Costa-Amic* (p. 198); 'Aprendizaje' by Claribel Alegria from *Aprendizaje* published by Editorial Universitaria de la Universidad de El Salvador for (p. 210); 'Cuento' by Carlos Cumpian from *Fiesta in Aztlan* published by Capra Press (p. 219)

Picture Credits

BBC Books would like to thank the following for providing photographs and for permission to reproduce copyright material. While every effort has been made to trace and acknowledge all copyright holders, we would like to apologise should there have been any errors or omissions.
Special thanks go to Terry Doyle for the many photographs taken during the filming of the TV series.

Photographs © BBC pages 6, 87 Simon Bell; 7(l) Carmen Cobos; 47, 128 Martin Moore; 72(b), 86, 89(l&r), 96 Luz Kettle; 172, 173 James Murphy; 208(b) Gene Ferber; All remaining photographs by Terry Doyle except:

Andalucia Slide Library 14(t) Antonio Serrano; 21(t) Tele Cinco; 21(m) TVE1; 28(m), 37(l), 43(b), 45(b) 101(t), 105(l), 106(tl&r), 187(t&m), 202(b), 213(l), 216 Michelle Chaplow; 25(l) Francisco Goma; 27(bl) Gontscharoff; 36 Bernat; 40-41 Ferran Targa; 67(t) I Rodriguez; 106(tm), 133, 203(l) JD Dallet; 190; **Andes Press Agency** 16(t), 27(t), 35, 106(bm), 195(r), 198 Carlos Reyes-Manzo; 208(t); **Associated Press** 56(b); **Neil Beer** 32(b); **R Burri** 144; **Camera Press** 16(m) Tom Wargacki; *Edizioni Lancio* 22(t); *El País* 34 Ricardo Gutierrez; 45(t) Miguel Gener; **© EMPICS Sports Photo Agency** 134(m) Tony Marshall; **Express Newspapers plc** 187(b); **Foto Mas** 44(t); **Geoffrey Goode** 197(b); **Robert Harding Picture Library** 31, 43(t) Duncan Maxwell; 44(b) Adam Woolfitt; 48; 71(l) Phil Robinson; 72(t) James Strachan; 108; 195(l), 195(b) Jennifer Fry; **Getty Images** 124(m&b); 130 Jeremy Horner; 134(b) Clive Brunskill; 151 David Hiser; **Hutchison Picture Library** 95 Edward Parker; **Jorge's Estudio** 178; **Marcia Lieberman** 161(l); **Network Photographers** 61(l), 220(m) Barry Lewis; 188(t) Gerard Sioen/Rapho; 209 Gideon Mendel; **NHPA** 152(br) Stephen Krasemann; **Oxford Scientific Films Ltd** 152(bl) Geoff Kidd; **Popperfoto** 134(t); **Retna** 14(m) Patrick Quigly; **Rex Features** 16(b) Nils Jorgensen; 32(t) Mansell; 140; **Royal Botanic Gardens Kew** 152(bm); **Alison Seabrook** 128(bl); **Spectrum Colour Library** 42; **South American Pictures** 155, 161(r), 166 Tony Morrison; 164(t&bl); 164(br), 165 Kimball Morrison; 196(t) Jevan Berrange; **Travel Ink** 53 Trevor Smith; **Warner Communications** 12(m)

Many thanks also to: Barbara Ayling, Marilyn Cameron, Carmen Cobos, Tim Connell, Terry Doyle, Linda Ellery, Marisol Gower, Juan Kattan, Lucy Rodriguez, Lucila Sanz, Sue Skinner, Maria Strange

Pinnell tube